Same
Sex,
Different
Politics

Chicago Studies in

American Politics

A series edited by

Benjamin I. Page

Susan Herbst

Lawrence R. Jacobs

James Druckman

Same Sex,

Different Politics

SUCCESS AND
FAILURE IN
THE STRUGGLES
OVER GAY
RIGHTS

GARY MUCCIARONI

THE UNIVERSITY

OF CHICAGO PRESS

CHICAGO & LONDON

Gary Mucciaroni is a professor and chair of the Department of Political Science at Temple University, Philadelphia. He is the author of *The Political Failure of Employment Policy, 1945–1982* and *Reversals of Fortune: Public Policy and Private Interests*, and coauthor (with Paul J. Quirk) of *Deliberate Choices: Debating Public Policy in Congress*, also published by the University of Chicago Press.

The University of Chicago Press, Chicago 60637
The University of Chicago Press, Ltd., London
© 2008 by The University of Chicago
All rights reserved. Published 2008
Printed in the United States of America

17 16 15 14 13 12 11 10 09 08   1 2 3 4 5

ISBN-13: 978-0-226-54408-3 (cloth)
ISBN-13: 978-0-226-54409-0 (paper)
ISBN-10: 0-226-54408-7 (cloth)
ISBN-10: 0-226-54409-5 (paper)

Library of Congress Cataloging-in-Publication Data

Mucciaroni, Gary.
  Same sex, different politics : success and failure in the struggles over gay rights / Gary Mucciaroni.
       p. cm.
  Includes bibliographical references and index.
  ISBN-13: 978-0-226-54408-3 (cloth : alk. paper)
  ISBN-13: 978-0-226-54409-0 (pbk. : alk. paper)
  ISBN-10: 0-226-54408-7 (cloth : alk. paper)
  ISBN-10: 0-226-54409-5 (pbk. : alk. paper) 1. Gay rights. 2. Gays—
Social conditions. 3. Homosexuality. 4. Gays—Services for. I. Title.
  HQ76.5 .M83 2008
  323.3′264—dc22

                                                    2008015419

♾ The paper used in this publication meets the minimum requirements of the American National Standard for Information Sciences—Permanence of Paper for Printed Library Materials, ANSI Z39.48-1992.

FOR DAVID

Contents

Preface

My interest in the politics of gay rights began in earnest in the late 1990s. At the time, political scientists had just started to explore the topic seriously. For years, many individuals who were most likely to write on the subject, like me, were in the closet and worried that they would "out" themselves by undertaking such research. But in the past fifteen years we have witnessed a profusion of important works on lesbian, gay, bisexual, and transgender rights politics. We now have several studies that explain why states and localities adopt or fail to adopt gay rights measures. Other works examine the emergence, goals, strategies, and tactics of the gay rights movement. What the literature lacks is a broad exploration of why the movement has succeeded in reaching some of its public policy goals more than others. My initial acquaintance with the evolution of gay rights politics suggested a number of public policy puzzles. For example, why do Americans make it easier for gay couples to adopt children than to marry? Why do we continue to exclude gays from serving openly in the military, even though almost all other democratic nations have lifted their bans and Americans have outlawed employment discrimination where most of us live? How did gays and lesbians repeal laws in all fifty states that criminalized homosexual conduct despite the public's lingering discomfort with gay sexual conduct and a fair amount of opposition to decriminalization?

This study breaks new ground by treating differences among gay rights issues as important in understanding the movement's successes and failures. I argue that *what* gay rights supporters seek to achieve greatly determines their chances for political success. The gay rights movement has been more successful in some areas than others because of the very different politics that exist from one issue arena to the next. This book is the first to use a general model to compare and contrast gay rights struggles across several issue areas. Drawing upon data from public opinion polls, legislative debates, media coverage, and other sources, the study focuses on six key policy issues—military service, discrimination in the marketplace, adoption, hate crimes, marriage and partner recognition, and the repeal of sodomy laws. The title, *Different Politics*, refers to the distinct kinds of political conflict and levels of success that characterize each issue as the gay rights agenda has grown more diverse. "Different" also draws attention to

Fig. 1.1 The Timing of Policy Adoptions on Gay Rights in the States, 1971–2008

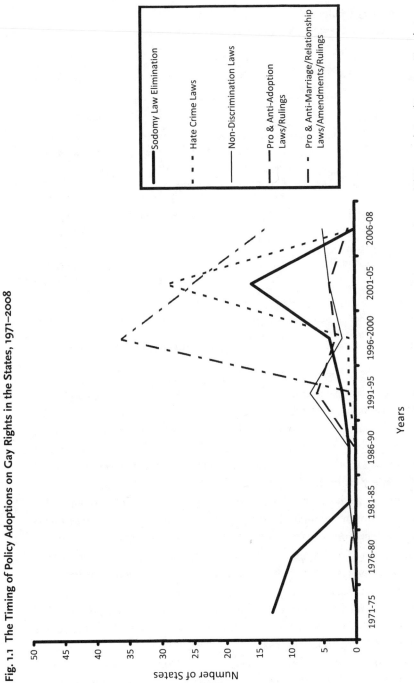

Number of States

Years

Legend:
— Sodomy Law Elimination
- - - Hate Crime Laws
— Non-Discrimination Laws
– – Pro & Anti-Adoption Laws/Rulings
–·– Pro & Anti-Marriage/Relationship Laws/Amendments/Rulings

Sources: For sodomy law elimination, see table 4.1. For other issues, see issue maps pertaining to marriage prohibitions, relationship recognition, hate crimes laws, adoption, and employment laws and policies from the Human Rights Campaign, www. hrc.org/state_laws.

Table 1.3 Policy priorities of gay, lesbian, bisexual, and transgendered persons, by age group

	Age Group			
Ranking	18–25	26–44	45–64	65 and over
1	workplace discrimination	workplace discrimination	workplace discrimination	workplace discrimination
2	hate crimes	hate crimes	hate crimes	AIDS funding
3	marriage	parenting/ adoption	securing federal benefits	hate crimes
4	parenting/ adoption	marriage	AIDS funding	securing federal benefits
5	AIDS funding	securing federal benefits	parenting/ adoption	securing state benefits

Note: Rankings derived from average amount of personal importance placed on each issue by respondents in each age group ($N = 748$).
Sources: Harris Interactive poll (December 2003) as reported in Egan and Sherrill (2005a).

struck down the remaining state sodomy laws as unconstitutional). The chart in figure 1.1 understates the level of activity that has occurred because it omits instances when issues reached the agenda but failed to culminate in a new policy and the many nondiscrimination ordinances and court decisions on adoption rights that have appeared at the local level.

This study examines the dramatically different levels of success that gay rights advocates have experienced on six key issues: the legalization of homosexual conduct, military service, adoption, marriage and partner recognition, hate crimes, and civil rights.[16] Although it does not cover every issue of concern to LGBT rights advocates, it includes most of the movement's major goals, goals that also receive the lion's share of media coverage, the movement's resources, and policymakers' attention.

The six issues also provide maximum variation on the dependent and independent variables used in this study.[17] Table 1.4 lists the issues in descending order of policy success for the gay rights movement. For example, the movement has been most successful in legalizing homosexual conduct; sodomy laws in all fifty states have been abolished. Thirty-two states, covering very disproportionately on marriage and military service, the largest LGBT organizations focus on civil rights (e.g., workplace discrimination) much more and on hate crimes and adoption somewhat more. They pay attention to marriage less, especially in the case of the NGLTF.

The priorities reflected in NGLTF press releases are similar to, but not totally consistent with, a survey of gays and lesbians that it conducted in 2006 of more than 1,400 participants at seven "LGBT pride" events in six U.S. cities. The survey asked respondents to choose which among ten "policy priorities for the LGBT community" were the most pressing (NGLTF 2006).[13] Eight hundred respondents ranked "marriage equality/partner recognition" first, 526 chose "anti-LGBT discrimination" as second, and 434 chose "hate violence/harassment" as the third most important priority to them. NGLTF press releases are consistent with a 2003 Harris Interactive poll, which found that a sample of 748 gay and lesbian respondents ranked workplace discrimination (i.e., civil rights) first and hate crimes second in order of importance.[14] Taken together, these disparate data suggest that the media's focus on marriage and military issues is somewhat unrepresentative of the movement's priorities, which continue to rank basic civil rights and hate crimes protections high.

The Harris poll also showed some important differences among LGBT age cohorts in policy priorities (see table 1.3). While all age groups rank workplace discrimination at the top and rank hate crimes as second or third, the younger age cohorts, 18–25 and 26–44, rank marriage and parenting/adoption much closer to the top than the older age cohorts. Younger cohorts are at an age when finding a life partner and parenting are top priorities. They may also have different value preferences than older generations of gays who came of age in the decades just before and after the Stonewall Rebellion in 1969.[15]

Another way to see the gay rights agenda's growth and change is to look at the timing of policy adoption. Figure 1.1 shows the number of states whose policies have changed on five gay rights issues. The chart reveals a dramatic increase in policy actions starting in the 1990s. Few, if any, states addressed hate crimes protection for gays, marriage, and adoption rights prior to the 1990s, but the number of laws, amendments and court rulings in those areas rose sharply afterward. The sharpest rise has been from the mid-1990s to the mid-2000s in marriage (mostly antimarriage state laws and amendments), hate crimes laws, and sodomy law elimination (principally because of the Supreme Court's *Lawrence v. Texas* decision, which of the movement's aims.[10] An examination of their Web sites reveals a common set of public policy goals: civil rights protection in the marketplace (e.g., employment and housing nondiscrimination); lifting the ban on gays openly serving in the military; penalties for crimes motivated by antigay bias; securing partnership rights (including marriage and civil unions) and parenting rights (custody, visitation, and adoption); and repealing sodomy laws.[11]

LGBT rights organizations have a somewhat different view of LGBT priorities than that reflected by the media's attention to LGBT issues. Table 1.2 shows the number of press releases under each issue area that the NGLTF and the HRC issued from 1995 to 2005.[12] Whereas media attention focuses

Table 1.2 **Attention to issues by major LGBT organizations, 1995–2005**

	National Gay and Lesbian Task Force		Human Rights Campaign	
	Total press releases in each issue area (N = 310)[a]	As % of total press releases	Total press releases in each issue area (N = 1,973)	As % of of total press releases
Marriage[b]	74	24	698	35
Civil rights[c]	116	37	391	20
Hate crimes	80	26	242	12
Adoption	16	5	299	15
Military	13	4	183	9
Legalization of homosexual conduct	11	4	160	8
Total		100		99

Sources: National Gay and Lesbian Task Force Web site, www.thetaskforce.org, November 2006, and Human Rights Campaign Web site, www.hrc.org, November 2006. For HRC, data include all archived documents (press releases, reports, studies, and articles) from 1995 to 2005 issued by the HRC under the rubric "News Releases."

[a]Excludes "other" gay-related press releases, including on the topics of AIDS, schools/ youth, aging, abortion, women's rights, and others (n = 76). Excludes press releases unrelated to public policy issues (n = 386).

[b]Includes civil unions and public policy issues related to domestic partner benefits. Excludes domestic partner policies of privately owned firms.

[c]Nondiscrimination in employment, housing, public accommodations, and other areas of the market.

Issues, Institutions, and Threats

Efforts to secure legal rights and protections for gays, lesbians, and bisexuals have met with mixed results.[1] The U.S. Supreme Court has swept aside sodomy statutes, and most states have hate crimes laws that protect gays and lesbians. In other areas, gays have achieved more moderate success. Roughly half of the population lives in jurisdictions that prohibit discrimination against gays in employment, housing, and public accommodations and permit them to adopt children. In still other areas, the movement's efforts have largely failed. The military bars gays and lesbians from serving openly, most states and the federal government ban gay marriage, and only a few states permit marriage, civil unions, or access to an equivalent set of benefits.

Why have gay rights supporters made greater progress in fulfilling some parts of their agenda than in others? Why does the United States prohibit gays from serving openly in the military even though a growing number of states and communities prohibits discrimination against them? Why do Americans make it much easier for gay and lesbian couples to adopt children than to get married? In short, what forces and conditions facilitate or impede political progress for gays and lesbians? And what implications do answers to these questions have for the future of the lesbian, gay, bisexual, and transgender (LGBT) movement and for our understanding of social movements generally?

The mixed record of public policy accomplishments stands in contrast to the greater visibility, tolerance, and acceptance that gays and lesbians have attained in society more generally. By almost every social indicator, gays and lesbians have made enormous gains over the past few decades: unprecedented numbers of them have "come out of the closet" at younger ages and are involved openly in same-sex relationships;[2] more Americans know gay relatives, co-workers, and friends, accept their sexual orientation, and support particular gay rights measures;[3] medical and psychological experts no longer consider homosexuality to be a mental disorder, and a long list of health and welfare professional associations support expanding gay rights; businesses market their products to gay consumers in order to attract "lavender dollars";[4] employers increasingly grant their gay employees partner benefits and pledge nondiscrimination in hiring and promotion;[5] and portrayals of gays in popular culture and the mass media are more numerous, positive, and varied.[6]

These changes are striking and have improved the political climate for gay rights, but they are no substitute for the recognition, rights, and benefits that the gay rights movement can secure only through the public policy process. Only the state can decriminalize same-sex behavior, levy penalties for crimes motivated by hate, permit gays to marry, adopt, enjoy custody and visitation of children, serve openly in the military, and provide many other more specific rights and benefits. Furthermore, laws and public policies convey important cultural meanings (Hull 2006). Every form of legal protection and inclusion of gays and lesbians promotes the cultural legitimacy of gays and lesbians and their relationships.

To address the questions posed earlier about the LGBT movement's[7] successes and failures, this study focuses on political struggles over a set of distinct issues. Policymakers consider policies related to gays and lesbians in the context of specific questions, such as whether to permit gays to marry, allow them to serve openly in the military, or include them under hate crime statutes; they do not usually debate "gay rights" in the abstract. Each issue reflects a different challenge for gays and lesbians, presents different possibilities for framing the issue, and provides varying institutional contexts in which advocates press their claims.

Casual observers may be forgiven for thinking that same-sex marriage is all there is to the politics of gay rights given the controversy over that issue and the media's extensive coverage of it. Gays and lesbians will never be fully equal until they can marry their same-sex partners, but gay rights include much more than marriage. LGBT rights advocates have sought the repeal of sodomy laws in order to decriminalize same-sex conduct and protect privacy, sought the enactment of hate crimes statutes to achieve justice and educate the public about antigay violence, sought nondiscrimination measures to promote equality of opportunity, and sought parental rights to gain custody of children. Within each area, advocates also seek more specific and concrete goals, like avoiding inheritance taxes and gaining health care coverage for a partner or a child.

As a group, these issues share little more in common than the broad aim of improving society's treatment of gays and lesbians. Each demand for LGBT rights signifies a different level of acceptance of gays and lesbians in society. Some of the movement's goals aim for greater tolerance, while others more ambitiously aim for the acceptance of gays and lesbians as fully equal citizens. For example, lifting the military ban incorporates gays into the nation's most honored patriotic institution. Granting marriage licenses to same-sex couples and allowing them to adopt children confer the same status and recognition on those families that heterosexuals enjoy. More than rights, benefits, and equality for gays and lesbians are at stake, however. Some advocates argue that gay marriage will strengthen and stabilize family relationships and that ending the military ban will attract and retain talented men and women, for example.

The number and variety of gay rights issues have expanded greatly in recent years. They encompass an array of partner recognition and family issues alongside historical concerns about privacy and civil rights protections.[8] According to Chauncey (2004b, chapter 4), marriage became a goal of the gay rights movement after gays and lesbians attained greater acceptance and visibility in many parts of the country, gay partners realized their lack of relationship rights during the AIDS crisis, and the emergence of the "lesbian baby boom" impelled many couples to seek legal protection for their children.

To see how the gay rights agenda has changed, we can look at patterns of media coverage of gay rights issues.[9] Table 1.1 shows the relative shares of newspaper coverage devoted to six gay rights issues from 1985 to 2004. The media in recent years has paid much greater attention to family-related issues, especially marriage. Military and marketplace discrimination, which dominated the agenda in earlier periods, have declined in prominence since the early to mid-1990s. Marriage and adoption accounted for a small fraction of the total coverage of gay rights issues until the late 1990s, when coverage of marriage started to rise sharply. During 2000 to 2004, the majority of articles written about gay rights issues covered marriage and adoption (overwhelmingly the former). The issues that receive the most attention today are less similar to one another than those in the past: The top two issues on the agenda in earlier periods—the military ban and civil rights—shared a concern with building tolerance and protecting

Table 1.1 Coverage of six gay rights issues in U.S. newspapers, 1985–2004 (articles about each issue as a percentage of all articles)[a]

	1985–89	1990–94	1995–99	2000–4
Civil rights[b]	19	13	13	7
Military service	54	63	42	25
Marriage	2	3	14	44
Adoption	8	7	9	8
Legalization of homosexual conduct	12	6	5	5
Hate crimes	5	9	17	10
Total	100	101	100	99
N	2,415	21,226	40,877	78,506

Coverage of six gay rights issues in the *New York Times*, 1985–2004 (articles about each issue as a percentage of all articles)[a]

	1985–89	1990–94	1995–99	2000–4
Civil rights[b]	28	13	12	7
Military service	43	62	49	38
Marriage	3	3	12	35
Adoption	7	6	9	7
Legalization of homosexual conduct	13	5	5	5
Hate crimes	7	11	13	8
Total	101	100	100	100
N	711	1,822	1,740	2,814

[a]Source: Lexis-Nexis search (May 5, 2005).
[b]Nondiscrimination in employment, housing, public accommodations, and other areas of the market.

employment opportunities for gays. The issue atop the agenda today—marriage—involves an entirely different set of claims about gay partners and families than the second most salient issue—the military ban.

We might also look at the LGBT rights agenda from the movement's own perspective. The agendas of the three largest gay rights organizations—the National Gay and Lesbian Task Force (NGLTF), the Human Rights Campaign (HRC), and Lambda Legal—provide a reasonably accurate barometer how patterns of political progress are distinct from the advances that gays and lesbians have made in attaining greater social acceptance and visibility. The political strides that gay and lesbian Americans have made are the result of distinctly political and governmental forces and conditions that are partially independent of the influence of the public's increased acquaintance with gays and lesbians and their greater tolerance of homosexuality.

Understandably, a tremendous amount of the attention to gay rights in the mass media and in political science focuses on gay marriage. Our growing preoccupation with this single issue, however, risks losing sight of the many other important goals of the gay rights movement that deserve our attention. Most gays and lesbians support efforts to gain the social recognition and material benefits that come with marriage and civil unions, but they also care about several other issues that critically affect their lives and children. Furthermore, we learn a great deal about the politics of gay marriage and partner recognition by comparing it to other issues.

I owe a great debt of gratitude to a number of individuals who helped me throughout various phases of this project. Temple University awarded me a research and study leave during 2003–4 that afforded the opportunity to collect data and begin writing several chapters. Many librarians and archivists working in state legislatures and municipal councils helped me to secure debate transcripts. Nick Catsis, Greg Graham, Mary Lou Killian, Yphtach Lelkes, Vinod Menon, and Karen Owens served as excellent research assistants. For their careful reading and helpful comments on the manuscript, I thank the two anonymous reviewers for the University of Chicago Press. The entire editorial staff at the press was extremely helpful in all phases of bringing this volume to fruition. I want to thank especially John Tryneski for taking an interest in the manuscript and helping me through the review process. Kate Frentzel and Joyce Dunne provided efficient and valuable assistance in copyediting. Finally, I want to acknowledge my partner, David Silverman, for his constant support, encouragement, and useful advice. I dedicate this work to him.

Gary Mucciaroni
Philadelphia
January 4, 2008

more than 80 percent of the U.S. population, have hate crimes laws. Twenty states and approximately 100 local jurisdictions outside of those states, representing more than half the U.S. population, have nondiscrimination laws or ordinances that cover sexual orientation. Next, ten states and the District of Columbia (covering 35 percent of the population) and some local jurisdictions in fifteen others (covering an additional 21 percent) permit same-sex couples to adopt children. Marriage and partner recognition, however, reflect less success. Only Massachusetts and California permit gays and lesbians to marry. (Californians will vote on a constitutional ban on marriage in 2008.) Another five states grant same-sex couples civil unions or a package of partnership benefits that approximate civil unions, bringing the total population covered to about 20 percent. While civil unions and comprehensive partner benefits are significant achievements, they do not give same-sex couples the social status of marriage; such unions and benefits are not portable from state to state, and the laws exclude the many benefits that the federal government offers to married couples. Furthermore, forty-four states ban same-sex marriage in their laws or constitutions, including seventeen that ban civil unions and domestic partnership in addition to marriage. Finally, the movement has been least successful in lifting the ban on gays and lesbians serving openly in the military. Although the military no longer flatly bans gays from serving, it has discharged almost ten thousand service members under the "don't ask, don't tell" policy since 1994, and its policy continues to be based on the assumption that homosexual conduct is incompatible with military service.[18] Even if advocates make progress in advancing the gay rights agenda in areas like hate crimes, nondiscrimination, and military service when a new president and Congress take over in 2009, we seek to determine why it has taken considerably longer to achieve some of these goals than others.

The book's central argument is that two basic conditions shape the level of political success that gay rights advocates encounter: *whether Americans perceive their demands as threatening* and *how political institutions mediate the resistance that arises from those perceptions.* Opposition to gay rights is rooted in the perception that they threaten society or an important segment of it. Individuals may view the threat as directed against their own or others' physical and psychological well-being, important institutions, the status of heterosexuality in the culture, the moral standards of the community, or their personal religious beliefs. Americans find some of the goals of the gay rights movement more threatening than others. As the level of perceived threat rises, citizens and advocacy groups mount efforts to resist gay rights.

Table 1.4 Levels of political success on six issues related to gay rights

Issue	Level of success	Jurisdictions covered	% of U.S. population covered[a]
Legalization of homosexual conduct	Total	All 50 states	100
Hate crimes	Very high	32 states	81.2
Civil rights (nondiscrimination in employment, housing, etc.)	Moderate to high	20 states (plus approx. 100 local jurisdictions outside of those states)[b]	52
Adoption rights	Moderate to high	10 states (plus some jurisdictions of 15 other states; 7 states ban adoption)[c]	56
Marriage/civil union (or equivalent spousal benefits through domestic partnership laws)	Low	7 states (44 states ban marriage; 17 ban marriage plus civil unions/partnership laws)[d]	20.4
Military service	Very low	none	0

Sources: U.S. Census Bureau (2000); NGLTF (2007b, 2007c, 2007d, 2007e, 2008); Human Rights Campaign (2008).

[a]Population figures calculated from U.S. Census Bureau (2006a, 2006b).

[b]For the states, see NGLTF (2007c); for the local jurisdictions, see NGLTF (2005) and Lambda Legal (2006)

[c]Ten states permit gay couples to adopt statewide. In another 15 states, at least one jurisdiction permits gay couples to adopt and usually makes it possible for couples from other areas of the state to petition for adoption.

[d]As of June 2008, six states afford same-sex partners marriage (Massachusetts and California) or civil unions (Vermont, Connecticut, New Jersey, and New Hampshire). Oregon has a comprehensive partnership law that include most of the spousal benefits afforded under civil unions, according to the Human Rights Campaign (www.hrc.org/state_laws; see also http://www.thetaskforce.org/downloads/reports/issue_maps/relationship_recognition _1_08_color.pdf, accessed June 16, 2008). Hawaii, Maine, Washington, and the District of Columbia have much more limited benefits and are not included in the percentage calculation in the table. Of the 44 states that ban gay marriage,18 states do so through laws and 26 states do so through their constitutions. Seventeen states ban civil unions and other forms of partner recognition in addition to marriage (Human Rights Campaign 2008). The National Gay and Lesbian Task Force reports that 40 states ban gay marriage and that 21 states ban civil unions and other forms of partner recognition (www.thetaskforce.org/downloads/ reports/issue_maps/anti-gaymarriagemeasures/), June 16, 2008.

Policymakers resolve gay rights issues within institutional arrangements that vary from issue to issue and that have profound influence on the momentum and effectiveness of efforts to block gay rights.

Three of the cases—adoption, military service, and the legalization of homosexual conduct—receive special attention in this book because they present the most intriguing puzzles. In this group, Americans' level of support for gay rights fails to match the level of policy success that the gay rights movement has achieved; or conversely, the public's support exceeds the level of political success. The American public favors allowing gays to serve openly in the military, yet the ban remains in place; the public is split over legalizing homosexual relations, yet legal prohibitions against consensual same-sex conduct no longer exist; it is divided over whether to allow gays to adopt, yet gays have been reasonably successful in gaining adoption rights in much of the country (and have not confronted widespread bans, as with marriage). Civil unions and partner benefits also increasingly fit the pattern of a mismatch between public opinion and public policy—between the level of perceived threat and policy success. Public support has grown for granting civil unions or an equivalent package of partner benefits, which now exceeds 50 percent in some polls. Still, only seven states permit marriage, civil unions, or comprehensive partner benefits for gays and lesbians, and seventeen states ban them from participating in *all* forms of partner recognition. All of these cases elucidate vividly the decisive impact of institutions on the relationship between public opinion and public policy.

In the three remaining cases, the high (or low) levels of threat that Americans perceive from gay rights provide a parsimonious explanation for the widely different levels of policy success that LGBT advocates have achieved. It is not surprising that marriage has been among the least successful issues for gay rights advocates and hate crimes and antidiscrimination among the most successful. The public strongly opposes marriage for gays and lesbians and strongly supports hate crimes and antidiscrimination protection. Nevertheless, institutions play a critical role in these cases as well by facilitating, amplifying, or muting the impact of public opinion on policy.

In sum, the term "different politics" in the book's title has several meanings. First, the politics of "gay rights" is really a politics of separate and substantively dissimilar issues. A distinct type of political conflict and level of policy success characterizes each gay rights issue. Second, while many of the goals of the movement in the years before and just after Stonewall remain relevant, what gays and lesbians seek from government has developed in very different directions in recent times. One could hardly imagine a few decades ago some of the contemporary movement's most important goals as its agenda has grown and become more ambitious.[19] Third, Americans confront these issues in a significantly different political landscape from what earlier civil rights movements encountered. Finally, the movement's partial successes and continued failures in public policy underscore politics as different from social integration, visibility, and acceptance.

SITUATING THE STUDY

This book focuses on one measure of a social movement's success: how well it achieves its public policy goals.[20] The gay rights movement succeeds when the state pursues policies consistent with its goals; it fails when the state refuses to pursue the movement's aims or pursues others that the movement opposes.[21] This approach excludes looking at other important goals of the gay rights movement, such as increasing collective identity, political efficacy, and participation and educating the public.[22] It leaves out the movement's efforts to improve the lives of gays and lesbians by changing civil society and the culture.[23] It stops short of evaluating the impacts of policies on gays and lesbians and society as a whole. Measuring impacts is less tractable for research and would be a considerable undertaking for all six issues.[24] Moreover, since the instrumental value of civil rights laws is arguably less important than their symbolism, assessing the laws' impacts is also less relevant than it would be in other policy areas. What civil rights laws say about society's values and how society views a group of individuals probably matter more than whether the law leads to the group's material betterment. This point is particularly apt for the gay rights movement. Gays and lesbians have not been as economically disadvantaged as other minorities because they are distributed randomly throughout the class structure and can conceal their identity. The gay rights movement achieves its paramount goal of gaining social respect and legitimacy to the extent that government adopts its preferred policies.

What Has Been Done So Far
CROSS-SECTIONAL STUDIES

Most studies of gay and lesbian politics look at only one or two issues at a time and take a cross-sectional approach, comparing states and localities that have adopted gay rights laws with those that have not.[25] We have learned that cities with larger and more educated populations are more likely to adopt gay rights legislation. Localities that have more highly organized gay communities, have gay rights organizations that build coalitions with other groups, and have fewer evangelical Protestants and other religious conservatives are also more fertile ground for gay rights measures (Button, Rienzo, and Wald 1997; Haider-Markel 1997; Haider-Markel and Meier 1996; Haider-Markel 2000). Bipartisanship, Democratic composition of legislatures, the presence of bureaucratic agents who hold favorable opinions toward gays, and a state's history of tolerance toward minorities are other correlates of gay rights success (Haider-Markel 2000). Some studies suggest that policy success increases on certain issues when the public's support grows.[26]

All of these studies treat public policy as a variable to explain, rather than as one with explanatory power. The approach taken in this book is different—*what* the supporters of gay and lesbian rights seek to achieve greatly determines their chances for political success. Different policies produce different politics (Lowi 1972, 299). Each issue area is marked by a distinct struggle and by political and institutional differences that are critical for determining success.

MORALITY POLITICS

This study also diverges from viewing gay rights through the perspective of "morality politics" (Studlar 2001, 43; Haider-Markel 2001). Central to morality politics is debate over "first principles" in which "at least one advocacy coalition . . . portray[s] the issue as one of morality or sin and use[s] moral arguments in its policy advocacy" (Studlar 2001, 43). In morality politics, "proposals or existing practices are viewed as an affront to religious belief or a violation of a fundamental moral code" (Haider-Markel and Meier 1996, 333; see also Mooney 2001a, 3; Sharp 1999, 3; Meier 1994; Mooney and Lee 1995). The morality politics perspective assumes that moral arguments are of paramount importance in gay rights debates without undertaking a systematic examination of the arguments that advocates actually put forward to justify their positions. Advocates can define issues in terms of deontological principles (whether homosexuality and discrimination are intrinsically wrong), social consequences (whether gay rights will have desirable effects on groups and institutions in society), and procedures (whether particular institutions or levels of government ought to decide issues). Opponents choose how to define issues as part of their political strategy, depending upon their estimates of which definitions are most likely to heighten the perception that gay rights pose a threat. They may perceive morality definitions as less effective politically than consequence-based or procedural definitions. Chapter 2 examines this topic in depth.

Second, empirical support for the morality politics perspective in the case of gay rights is mixed. According to Haider-Markel (2001), morality politics is characterized by high levels of partisan and ideological division, the importance of religion and affiliation with Protestant fundamentalism, and the importance of public opinion on gays and gay rights issues. Haider-Markel and Meier's (1996) fifty-state study found that the politics of gay rights most often resembled conventional "interest group politics" rather than morality politics. The conflict over gay rights resembled morality politics only when the issue became highly salient, such as when gay rights opponents were able to put measures on the ballot. States that adopted nondiscrimination policies covering sexual orientation in areas like employment, housing, and public accommodations were those in which gay rights organizations had greater resources and those with political elites sympathetic toward gays and lesbians, fewer Protestant fundamentalists, lower levels of education, greater party competition, and less support for Republicans. On the other hand, Haider-Markel's (2001) study of gay rights votes in Congress on several issues found support for morality politics. Again, morality politics became more apparent as the salience of the issue increased.[27]

If issue salience is indeed as important as Haider-Markel and Meier suggest, then it is important to identify the conditions that help to increase or decrease salience. We shall see that salience varies greatly according to issue area. Some issues evoke much greater public interest and media attention than others because some demands for gay rights evoke greater perceptions of threat and because institutional arrangements help to reduce salience on some issues and increase it on others.

SEQUENTIAL EVOLUTION

Some observers argue that governments expand gay rights incrementally and sequentially along a predictable trajectory, beginning with the legalization of same-sex consensual conduct; followed by protection against workplace discrimination and conferring of adoption and partnership rights;

and culminating in the legalization of gay marriage (Waaldijk 2001; Eskridge 2002, ch. 3). While a fair amount of evidence for this pattern exists, larger and more decentralized political systems like the United States may deviate from it. Several American states permitted gay couples to adopt before the U.S. Supreme Court struck down state sodomy laws, for example. Some states have adopted partnership rights, civil unions, and marriage, while the ban on gays serving openly in the military (workplace discrimination) remains in place.

Second, not all political systems may eventually allow gays to marry or grant them a similar status. Many of the same states that repealed their sodomy laws have enacted prohibitions on gay marriage (and in some cases, all forms of partner recognition) (Barclay and Fisher 2004). As a causal theory, the idea of a trajectory that ends up with same-sex partner recognition sounds much like the "slippery slope" argument that gay rights opponents put forward—"if we prohibit discrimination against gays in the workplace, nothing will stop them from getting the right to marry." The theory consists of a post hoc fallacy: because governments enact adoption and partner recognition rights after they eliminate sodomy laws and outlaw workplace discrimination, the repeal of sodomy laws and enactment of nondiscrimination policies must have caused the policies that came later. However, the fact that the same states react very differently to calls for the repeal of sodomy laws and allowing gays to marry, for example, suggests that different social and political forces govern the two issues. Some goals take longer for gay rights supporters to achieve because they pose greater political and institutional obstacles. We need to explore fully the forces and conditions that propel political systems along particular trajectories—*why* some issues lead in the expansion of gay rights and others lag behind.

SOCIAL MOVEMENT THEORY

Much of this study's emphasis on the importance of the institutional context in which policy is made is consistent with social movement theory. The overall configuration of the American state; how institutions aggregate preferences, distribute authority, restrict or permit access to social movements and interest groups; and the ability of movements to build coalitions with other social groups are also found in much of the literature on resource mobilization and political process theories of social movements. Resource mobilization theory focuses on whether social movements have sufficient resources at their disposal to emerge and attain their goals (McCarthy and Zald 1973, 1977; Jenkins 1983; McAdam, McCarthy, and Zald 1988; Gamson 1968, 1975).[28] Much of the work in this tradition assumes that social movements are too weak to succeed on their own (Oberschall 1973; Tilly 1978; McCarthy and Zald 1973, 1977; Jenkins 1983). Movements prevail when they can augment their resources by attracting support from outside their organizations, such as from other groups and "political entrepreneurs," and when the costs of mobilization decline (Oberschall 1973; Jenkins and Perrow 1977; Lipsky 1968, 1970; McCarthy and Zald 1973, 1977).[29] Political process theory stresses how the "political opportunity structure"—for example, the openness of formal decision-making processes, divisions among political elites, the ideological and partisan composition of the government, and the presence of influential allies—helps or hinders movements' efforts to challenge the status quo (Eisinger 1973; Kitschelt 1986; Kriesi 1995; Tarrow 1994; 1998a; Amenta 2005).[30] One study that applies social movement theories to examine which local communities are more likely to adopt nondiscrimination ordinances and educational instruction about sexual orientation found support for both resource mobilization and political process theories for understanding the pattern of adoption (Button, Rienzo, and Wald 1997).

Like other interesting social science concepts, resource mobilization and political opportunity structure lack precision about what they include and exclude. Because they each subsume conceivably a variety of phenomena, the strength of each theory may rest upon conceptual and measurement differences. For example, in some cases, a resource that movements might mobilize may also be viewed as a component of the opportunity structure. Because social movements represent a diverse array of groups and claims that emerge in a variety of historical, cultural, and political contexts, the specific kinds of opportunity structures and resources that lead to success vary widely. This is probably why, for example, scholars differ sharply on whether they think the fragmentation and decentralization of governmental authority in the United States helps or hinders social movements (see Amenta 2005; Kriesi 1995; Tarrow 1998b). Similarly, Kitschelt (1986, 79) found that antinuclear movements were most influential in political opportunity structures that were "more conducive to popular participation," and Banaszak (1998) reports that the women's suffrage movement fared better in states with the ballot initiative. Eisinger (1973), on the other hand, found that urban protest movements were influential in systems that provided a mix of opportunities and constraints, not those that were either very open or very closed to popular participation.[31] For highly unpopular groups that face a formidable grassroots opposition, like gays and lesbians, more open opportunity structures may reduce influence, at least for some issues. The same difficulty in building valid generalizations applies to the kinds of outside groups from which social movements seek to augment their resources. Studies of farm workers and other social movements that emerged in the 1960s found that their success depended upon the support they received from liberal, middle-class "conscience constituents" (McCarthy and Zald 1973; Jenkins and Perrow 1977). It would seem unlikely that liberals would play a similarly pivotal role in the success that gays and lesbians have achieved, as fewer liberals are in politics and their access to power has declined since the 1970s.

Finally, studies of "new" social movements are relevant to this work for the attention they give to "framing" (or "defining") issues (Cohen 1985; Melucci 1985; Touraine 1985; Morris and Mueller 1992).[32] These movements organize around a group identity in order to challenge culture and politics. Those who mount these challenges frequently have no public policy outcome in mind, but rather they seek to "recast the language and cultural codes that organize information" (Melucci 1996, 102; see also Darnovsky, Epstein, and Flacks 1995, xiii–xiv). Framing or defining issues involves giving a particular interpretation or meaning to a set of facts about a condition in society (Snow 1992; Stone 1988). If a movement frames grievances so that they resonate with widely shared values and symbols in society, it may reduce the level of perceived threat, win allies, and neutralize opponents (Tarrow 1994, 123; Snow et al. 1986; Klandermans 1989; Haider-Markel 1999, 245). Because people's perceptions of gay rights issues are closely linked to what they think of gays and lesbians (Wilcox and Wolpert 2000), the means that political actors use to construct the gay and lesbian population is as important as framing issues. Schneider and Ingram (1993) argue that how society constructs a group influences the group's status and power and whether it incurs greater benefits or burdens through public policy.

Social movement theories offer a useful framework for guiding research on gay rights, but they fail to treat *differences among issues* as a key variable for explaining the LGBT movement's successes and failures. Whether the political environment affords the movement opportunities or constraints partly depends on the issue under consideration. Issues vary widely in their political and institutional characteristics. Some issues arise out of social movement demands that foster higher levels of perceived threat than others. Some issues are resolved in institutional venues that are more receptive to the demands of social movements through how they aggregate preferences, make decisions, and grant access to different groups of elites and citizens. And some issues have essential and socially constructed features that permit political actors to frame them in politically compelling ways that embrace widely shared values, while others do not. Hence, issue differences provide a critical midlevel link between broad social movement theories and specific cases that contribute to building empirical generalizations.

Next, we examine the levels of support Americans give to different gay rights issues as a measure of their perceived threat. Following that, the chapter presents hypotheses related to the impacts of institutions on gay rights struggles.

PUBLIC OPINION AND PERCEIVED THREAT

Most studies of public opinion and public policy report that the two are consistent in a majority of instances (Page and Shapiro 1983; Mishler and Sheehan 1993, 1996; Stimson, Mackuen, and Erikson 1995; Bartels 1991), although a more recent study shows a decline in the congruence between the public's views and government policies (Jacobs and Shapiro 2001). Public opinion has affected legislative action on several social movement issues, including abortion, the Vietnam War, and equal employment opportunity for blacks and women (Burstein 1985, 85–87; Burstein and Freudenburg 1978; Costain 1992; O'Connor and Berkman 1995). The link between public opinion and public policy appears especially strong on morality politics issues (Mooney 2001a). Studies have found evidence for such a link, for example, on abortion and the death penalty (Norrander and Wilcox 1999; Norrander 2000; Mooney and Lee 1995, 2000). Morality policy issues tend to be highly salient and "easy" for citizens to understand because they require no technical knowledge (Carmines and Stimson 1980). Meanwhile, bureaucratic actors have less influence when issues are salient and barriers to information are low (Gray and Williams 1980; Meier 1994). However, most studies have not found a strong link between public opinion on gay rights and policies at the state level (Haider-Markel and Meier 1996; Barclay and Fisher 2003; Lewis 1999), although opinion appears to have a significant impact on the passage of legislative bans on same-sex marriage (Lewis and Oh 2006).

This section focuses on public opinion on gay rights at the national level. The level of support among the public for gay rights reveals the degree to which it perceives gay rights advocates' demands as threatening. Hence, higher levels of support reflect lower degrees of perceived threat. All gay rights issues provoke some level of threat, but Americans find some issues more threatening than others. A variety of polling organizations have tapped public attitudes and opinions about homosexuality and gay rights since the 1970s. A few sources have conveniently collated the data. Comparing the data across issues reveals a clear pattern: *issues related to sexual conduct and family life threaten Americans more than issues related to marketplace discrimination, the military, and hate crimes.* The public strongly supports laws to protect gays against hate crimes and discrimination in employment, housing, and public accommodations and also strongly supports lifting the ban on gays serving openly in the military. It opposes allowing gay couples to marry and is divided sharply over civil unions, adoption rights, and making homosexual relations legal. We shall call the latter group "relationship issues."

A majority of Americans has supported employment rights for gays for decades, and their support has grown over time. The number who think that homosexuals "should have equal rights in job opportunities" rose from 56 percent in 1977 to 89 percent in 2006 (AEI 2006, 11). Americans also support government action to make discrimination illegal. The percentage of the public that "favor[s] laws to protect gays against discrimination" rose from 52 percent in 1983 to more than 70 percent in 2004 (AEI 2004) (see figure 1.2).[33] Public support for laws to prohibit discrimination against gays in housing parallels the support for employment, with 74 percent agreeing that there "should be" such laws (Henry J. Kaiser 2001, 10).

A similar long-term pattern is evident for allowing gays to serve in the military. When asked in 1977 if "homosexuals should be hired for the Armed Forces," a bare majority (51 percent) agreed that they should (AEI 2004, 11). Support for allowing gays in the military rose to 79 percent by 2007 (AEI 2004; Roper Center 2008d) (see figure 1.2). Two caveats ought to be kept in mind, however. First, support for having gays serve has fluctuated. It hovered around 60 percent from the late 1980s until 1992, when Bill Clinton attempted to lift the ban after his election as president. It fell under 50 percent when Congress debated the issue in 1993 and then rebounded to above 70 percent in the years that followed (AEI 2004, 13; Wilcox and Wolpert 1996, 130). Second, support is lower on the specific policy

Fig. 1.2 Public support for employment nondiscrimination, hate crimes protection, and lifting the ban on gays in the military

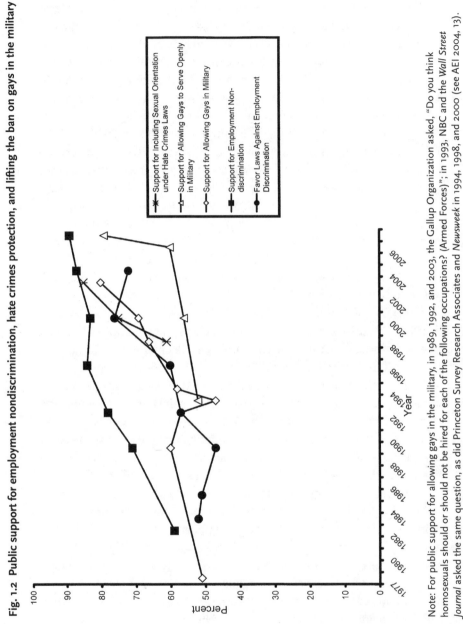

Note: For public support for allowing gays in the military, in 1989, 1992, and 2003, the Gallup Organization asked, "Do you think homosexuals should or should not be hired for each of the following occupations? (Armed Forces)"; in 1993, NBC and the *Wall Street Journal* asked the same question, as did Princeton Survey Research Associates and *Newsweek* in 1994, 1998, and 2000 (see AEI 2004, 13). For the questions corresponding to the other lines in figure 1.2, see notes 33, 34, and 35.

question of allowing gays to serve "openly." Still, support on that question has risen from 52 percent in 1993 to 60 percent in 2006 (Henry J. Kaiser 2001; *USA Today* 2007; AEI 2006, 13).[34]

The public is also behind imposing extra penalties for crimes against gays that are motivated by bias. Large majorities of Americans—more than 80 percent in recent polls—support covering gays and lesbians under hate crimes statutes (see figure 1.2; Gallup 1999; Kaiser Family Foundation 2000).[35]

Responses to questions about legalizing homosexual conduct, marriage, and adoption paint a different picture. The public has been badly split over whether to decriminalize consensual homosexual conduct. Except for the period between the late 1990s and the Supreme Court's *Lawrence v. Texas* (539 U.S. 558, 2003) decision in 2003 and very recently, support for legalizing such conduct failed to gain the support of a majority of Americans. Just after *Lawrence* was decided, the proportion in support of legalization dipped back below 50 percent; it then rose to 59 percent in 2007. Thus, only well after the Court resolved the issue have we seen evidence of a growing majority of citizens in support of legalization (see figure 1.3; AEI 2004, 4; AEI 2006, 5; Roper Center 2008f).[36]

The most threatening issue that gays and lesbians have pressed is marriage. No issue prompts such widespread perceptions of an institution under siege by a sinister force. No other provokes calls for laws and constitutional amendments to "defend" it from "attack." Only about one-third of Americans feel that same-sex marriages should be legally recognized (see figure 1.3), with support falling between about a quarter and almost 40 percent, depending upon how the questions are worded (Wilcox et al. 2007). Support has risen moderately since the question was asked first in the late 1980s (see figure 1.3). Support for civil unions is higher than for marriage, although support fluctuates markedly depending upon the wording of poll questions and when polls are conducted.[37] Between 40 and 49 percent of Americans supported civil unions in most polls taken between 2000 and 2004, but *some* more recent polls show support for civil unions rising above 50 percent, most often when the poll question omits the words "civil unions"[38] (AEI 2006, 33). Support for civil unions rises when respondents are given a choice of marriage, no legal recognition, or civil unions (Brewer and Wilcox 2005).

Americans are divided more evenly over adoption rights for gay couples than over marriage. The proportion of the public that agrees that "there should be adoption rights for gay spouses" rose from 29 percent in 1994

Fig. 1.3 Public support for legalizing homosexual relations, gay marriage, and gay adoption

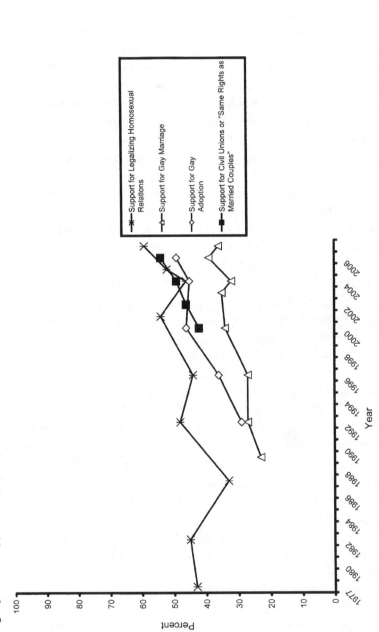

Note: For public support for allowing gays to marry, in 1989 and 1992, a Yankelovich/CNN/*Time* poll asked, "Do you think marriages between homosexual men or homosexual women should be recognized as legal by the law, or not?" (AEI 2004, 21); in 1996, 2000, and 2004, Gallup asked, "Do you think marriages between homosexuals should or should not be recognized by the law as valid, with the same rights as traditional marriages?" (AEI 2004, 21). In 2007, the Pew Forum on Religion and Public Life Survey asked, "Do you strongly favor, favor, oppose, or strongly oppose allowing gays and lesbians to marry legally?" (Roper Center 2008g).

For all years except 1992, Princeton Survey Research Associates/*Newsweek* asked, "Do you think that homosexual couples should be legally permitted to adopt children, or don't you think so?" In 1992, Yankelovich/CNN/*Time* asked: "Do you think there should or should not be . . . adoption rights for gay spouses?" (AEI 2004, 43, 42). For the questions corrresponding to the other lines in figure 1.3, see notes 36 and 37.

to 49 percent in 2006, but the same number of Americans (48 percent) believe that gays should not be allowed to adopt (see figure 1.3). Another recent poll puts the figure in favor of adoption rights at only 42 percent.[39] When respondents are asked if they approve, disapprove, or "don't feel strongly about" gay couples adopting children, only 33 percent approve and 45 percent disapprove of adoption by male couples; 36 percent approve and 43 percent disapprove of adoption by female couples.

In sum, opinion polls show significant variation across issues in the public's support for gay rights. Americans find relationship issues—involving lovers, partners, and parents—more threatening than issues related to the treatment of gay and lesbian individuals in the marketplace and the military. Large proportions of the public remain convinced that gay marriage, adoption, and sexual conduct pose threats to themselves or to society. Many fewer Americans seem threatened by efforts to protect gays and lesbians under hate crimes laws and from discrimination in the marketplace and the military. Rather than favor or oppose gay rights issues across the board, many people apparently take into account the specific demands of gay rights advocates, the levels of acceptance and equality that they seek, and the different consequences for society of expanding rights in each area.

Issue Characteristics and Threat

Why do some gay rights issues evoke much higher levels of perceived threat than others? What common characteristics do issues that induce higher levels of threat have that set them apart from the "low threat" issues? Although explaining why Americans find some issues more threatening is not our central focus, it is an important question. Three basic differences between relationship issues and the others suggest why Americans find relationship issues more threatening.[40] First, issues like gay marriage, adoption, and the repeal of sodomy laws call attention to the physical and emotional *intimacy* of same-sex relationships and increase the risk that gays will expose heterosexuals and children to "the gay lifestyle." Many people find displays of physical intimacy between two men or two women repellant (Thomas 2003). Even straight people sympathetic to the gay cause sometimes confess incomprehension about how someone could desire having sex with a person of the same gender.[41] The "ick factor" reflects the taboo of gay sex, much of it fed by centuries of religious injunctions against sexual conduct between same-sex partners (Thomas 2003, 38). Further normalizing gay relationships by legalizing their marriages, adoptions, and sexual behaviors may encourage gay couples to "flaunt" their sexuality by engaging in public displays of affection (Eskridge 1996).

Debates over whether the state should allow gays to marry, adopt, and engage in homosexual conduct remind people that gays and lesbians are physically and emotionally intimate. Adoption, for example, involves emotional intimacy and physical contact between parents and children. Some people fear that gays will harm children under their control by molesting them, "recruiting" them to become gay, or depriving them of male and female role models or fear that children raised by same-sex couples will carry a social stigma and experience greater social and psychological problems.[42]

In contrast, policies that address discrimination in employment, housing, and public accommodations protect *individuals* whose *status* is gay or lesbian, without regard to any conduct they may engage in. Employment discrimination, military, and hate crimes issues are about how we treat individuals in impersonal social spaces. Most gays and lesbians can conceal their sexual orientation in most situations when they are in public and at work. (Even when co-workers learn about an individual's personal life, social norms teach that sexual matters are irrelevant to job performance and should remain private.)[43] Concealment of sexual orientation is essentially impossible when gay couples apply for a marriage license, petition to adopt jointly, or adopt their partner's children. Such actions amount to admissions of homosexual conduct.

The second basic difference between relationship issues and other issues is that relationship issues have the potential to bring about much greater *social equality* between gays and straights than other gay rights issues. Gay marriage and adoption go far beyond tolerating and sanctioning homosexuality, elevating same-sex relationships to full legal and social equality with heterosexual couples. Many people assume that heterosexual relationships are superior and that heterosexuals make the best parents. Restricting marriage and adoption rights to heterosexual couples serves to maintain heterosexuality as culturally superior and more valuable than homosexuality.

Compared with what gays have demanded in the past, claims for equality with heterosexuals in marriage and child rearing are seen as radical breaks with tradition whose repercussions go far beyond gays and lesbians. Same-sex marriage is the culmination of the long march toward gender and sexual equality rooted in the feminist movement. When gay marriage opponents speak of a "threat to family values," they mean the threat of people failing to follow the assigned gender roles of a traditional patriarchal society (Chauncey 2004b, 148).

Until Hawaii and Vermont took up the gay marriage debate in the 1990s, the idea of a marriage between two men or two women, or that a child could have two fathers and no mother (or two mothers and no father), defied most people's understanding of how human societies work. Few people thought that there could be different, but equally valid, *types* of marriage. People had so taken for granted that only opposite-sex couples were eligible for marriage and coparenting that most state and federal statutes never clearly defined marriage as between a man and a woman. Not long ago it was about as unlikely that gay couples would adopt children together as it was that they would get married. By contrast, those who object to laws protecting gays from discrimination do not believe that it is bizarre for gays and lesbians to have jobs, own or rent houses, or serve as soldiers and sailors. That laws exist to protect women and minority groups from hate crimes and discrimination in the marketplace is commonplace. When gays demand laws against hate crimes and discrimination and for serving openly in the military, they are asking for familiar policies that other groups have been asking for (and receiving) for a long time.

The third basic difference is that gay marriage and adoption threaten heterosexual *identity*. To most people's understanding, marriage is intrinsically a heterosexual union. Marriage and coparenting have been exclusively heterosexual privileges and have constituted part of what it means for many heterosexuals to be complete. For many people, marriage is the epitome of heterosexual love and traditional family relationships. Heterosexuality is so intrinsic to marriage and family that, for the opponents of gay marriage, allowing homosexuals and bisexuals to partake in those institutions radically transforms them. (By contrast, no one argues that nondiscrimination policies in employment and housing would change the structure of labor and housing markets.) Parenting is another key aspect of heterosexual identity, which people undertake within permanent heterosexual marriages or as single-parent heterosexuals who conceived children in marriage. Even though marriage, procreation, and parenting are mutually exclusive, people often think about and experience them as closely linked. By undermining parenthood as a uniquely heterosexual project and a major rationale for keeping marriage exclusively heterosexual, gay adoption raises the specter of legal recognition and legitimization of gay relationships through the back door.

If gays can adopt and successfully parent, it weakens the case for reserving marriage as a heterosexual privilege. Likewise, the marriage of same-sex couples presumes that the two people qualify for parenthood.[44]

Each relationship issue has certain unique characteristics that heighten perceptions of threat. Marriage is a religious sacrament for many people, not only a civil status. Because clergy commonly sanctify marriages in religious ceremonies and all of the major religions reserve matrimony for heterosexuals, permitting gays to marry is tantamount to stating that gay and straight relationships are morally equal in the eyes of God. Because of the close connection between marriage and religion, some people find it much harder to set aside moral reservations about homosexuality on this issue than on others. If marriage rights carry the presumption that gay and straight marriages are morally equivalent, then individuals cannot bracket the question of homosexuality's moral status. The nexus of marriage and religion in the mind of many people helps to explain the lower levels of public opposition to civil unions and specific domestic partnership rights.

Marriage carries such profound cultural significance that it is sui generis as a gay rights issue. Gay marriage is deeply threatening to the cultural superiority of heterosexuality because marriage is an *exclusive* heterosexual privilege. Marriage confers upon gay relationships material benefits and social status that heretofore have been exclusively available only to heterosexuals. When opponents of gay marriage complain that allowing gays to marry would "redefine" marriage, they mean that marriage would lose its exclusivity. If heterosexuals share ownership of marriage with "inferior" homosexual couples, then the institution's value as a signifier of status declines. Even when opponents of gay marriage refrain from denigrating gay relationships as inferior and label them simply as "different," they maintain that society should reserve marriage for heterosexuals, because a committed, loving relationship between a man and a woman is special and distinct from all other relationships in society.[45] The public's lower level of opposition to civil unions and to giving gays specific partner benefits reveals the importance of the symbolic aspects of marriage.

Virtually nobody thinks of having a job, getting a promotion, renting an apartment, or serving in the military as exclusively heterosexual endeavors. And gays and lesbians have these opportunities available to them without legal protections against discrimination (although they often need to remain closeted in order to participate in those opportunities). Unlike getting married, most heterosexuals do not aspire to adopt children and see adoption as a second-best alternative to producing their own offspring. The state does not reserve adoption exclusively for heterosexual couples. Single individuals adopt and gain custody of children, including divorced and widowed parents, grandparents, siblings and other relatives, and strangers. Unlike the married-unmarried dichotomy, the variety and fluidity of real-world parental relationships is large.[46]

Finally, gays and lesbians can more easily portray themselves as victims with most nonrelationship issues. Because physical safety and income are basic requirements for survival, it is easy to see how hate crimes and workplace discrimination victimize people subjected to them. Marriage and children, by contrast, are not vital for survival.

Threat of Gay Rights, or Support for Gay Rights?

Does characterizing the public as threatened by gay rights skew our perspective on public opinion about gay rights issues? From the standpoint of measuring where the public stands on the issues, whether one thinks that opinion surveys reflect the public's perceived threat from gay rights or its support of them is a distinction without a difference. "Threat from" and "support for" are opposite sides of the same coin. Because levels of threat/support vary significantly across issues, it is incorrect to say that Americans are threatened by gay rights in general. Americans are badly split over some gay rights issues but not others, so both sides in the debate over whether a culture war exists among ordinary Americans can find support for their views in the politics of LGBT rights (see Fiorina 2005; Brewer and Stonecash 2007; Baker 2005; Layman and Green 2006; Hunter 1991, 1994; Frank 2004).

As a way of characterizing the level of support and opposition to the LGBT movement's demands, framing the discussion in terms of the level of perceived threat is appropriate because the struggle for gay rights is not a "consensus movement" like other social movements. The LGBT movement faces formidable opposition that reflects the genuine concerns of many Americans about the decline of a traditional social order (Wald, Button, and Rienzo 1996, 1170).[47] Because the burden of proof is upon those who propose to change public policy and people often prefer the devil they know to the devil they do not know, the focus of most policy debates is on the risk of policy change. Furthermore, gay rights opponents have a structural advantage over gay rights advocates: Unlike gay rights supporters, who appear as defenders of the rights of a small minority of the population in most estimates, gay rights opponents present themselves as spokespersons for the heterosexual majority. Gay rights supporters can never be other than spokespersons for minority interests even if they match or exceed the resources mobilized by the other side.

Of course, gay rights advocates may be more successful in dampening or deflecting perceptions of threat than their opponents are in arousing them. Gay rights advocates may effectively rebut their opponents' arguments or offer alternative arguments in favor of extending rights that those in power find more compelling. But it is differences among the issues, above all, that influence people's perceptions of threat.

Issue Definition

We have seen that a distinct set of factual conditions and socially constructed meanings characterize each issue. These essential and constructed properties constrain as well as open up possibilities for advocates to define issues in ways that either arouse or dampen the perception of threat. Issue definition, or framing, is the struggle over interpreting the meaning of a condition in society—whether it is "about" one thing or another (Stone 1987; Rochefort and Cobb 1994; Nelson and Kinder 1996; Nelson, Clawson, and Oxley 1997). For example, people may view the ban on gays openly serving in the military as about "ending discrimination," "expanding employment opportunities," "condoning an 'immoral' lifestyle," or maintaining "military effectiveness." The bare facts are the same in each instance—gays are demanding permission to serve openly in an institution from which society has barred them. Which of these definitions persuade and resonate with listeners reflects how much an issue threatens them. We will examine how each side defines the issues in chapters 2 and 3.

INSTITUTIONS AND THE EFFECTIVENESS OF RESISTANCE TO GAY RIGHTS

The more that people perceive gay rights as threatening, the more likely they are to try to resist efforts to expand them. Groups and individuals who feel threatened may contact public officials about their opposition to gay rights; work, contribute to, and vote for candidates who share their views; and engage in other forms of resistance. Public officials may share their perceptions or simply yield to their pressure. But the relationship between levels of threat, resistance, and public policy outcomes is not simple and

direct. Issues that induce greater perception of threat make it harder to expand gay rights, but they do not preclude them; issues that are less threatening make it easier to expand gay rights, but they do not guarantee them.
Institutions mediate the relationship between perceived threat and policy
outcomes.[48] Policymakers address each gay rights issue within a distinct
institutional environment that influences the level and effectiveness of the
resistance to gay rights, dampening and deflecting resistance in some instances and encouraging and accommodating it in others.

Institutions consist of the enduring structural features of the policymaking process and the purposeful behavior of officials who operate within
them.[49] Institutional rules and norms distribute authority and prescribe
how policymakers make decisions. Institutional venues expand or contract
the scope and visibility conflict, helping or hindering attempts by advocacy groups and the public to gain access to, and influence, policymakers
(Schattschneider 1960; Baumgartner and Jones 1993). For example, rules
and norms that promote openness and inclusive participation increase
people's awareness of issues and facilitate their access to decision making.
Organizational structures that decentralize authority may reduce issue salience and aggregate policymakers' preferences differently from those that
centralize authority.

Public officials' professional training, their role expectations, and the
missions of their institutions shape how they think about problems and
policy solutions. The methods by which policymakers are selected, their
terms of office, and the size and composition of their constituencies create
incentives that influence their behavior. Besides having formal authority to
make decisions, policymakers have disproportionate influence over defining issues and deciding which kinds of claims are legitimate. Which issue
definition gains the most traction is often not clear until policymakers give
an issue serious attention. Legislators, judges, and bureaucrats define issues differently from one another and from how advocacy groups define
them. They sometimes cast issues in terms of procedural and institutional
norms and principles that transcend the substantive issue under consideration—such as "judicial restraint," respect for federalism, and using states as
"laboratories of experimentation." These strategies reflect their institutional
perspectives, defuse controversy, and make decisions more opaque to out-
siders. Finally, policymakers' affiliations with political coalitions also shape
their behavior. An institution's propensity to help or impede resistance to

gay rights is partly contingent upon the coalitions that control it at a particular time. The party or ideological faction in power and its primary constituencies, supporters, and donors influence policymakers' preferences.

Three institutional variables are among the most important for understanding the political success or failure of gay rights advocates: (1) the
level of government in the federal system in which policy is made, (2) the
policy preferences of third-party stakeholders in an issue area, and (3)
whether judicial or legislative institutions are the main venue for making
policy.

Federalism and Decentralized Policymaking

Which level of government serves as the primary venue for policymaking—federal, state, local, or some combination of them—varies across gay
rights issues. Law, tradition, and political realities dictate the institutional
venue for resolving issues most of the time, but social movements sometimes have a choice in the matter, particularly in the United States, where
the state is highly fragmented (Tarrow 1998a, 81; 1998b). The following
section discusses the advantages and disadvantages of each level of government for pursuing gay rights. Gay rights advocates usually have more to
gain by operating at the subnational levels for four reasons: the salience
of national political debates and Washington's conservative and partisan
political climate; the distribution of political attitudes across states and local communities; opportunities for "retail politics" in smaller jurisdictions;
and diffusion effects.

OBSTACLES AT THE FEDERAL LEVEL

It was widely thought during the first few decades after World War II
that the federal government protected minority rights better than the states
(see Ely 1980; Peltason 1971). President Harry Truman ordered the armed
services to desegregate; the Supreme Court, led by Chief Justice Earl Warren, issued landmark civil rights and civil liberties decisions; and Congress
passed the Civil Rights Act of 1964 and the Equal Rights Amendment for
women in the 1970s. Two of President Dwight Eisenhower's Supreme
Court appointees, Chief Justice Warren and Justice William Brennan,
turned out to be liberals. Democrats controlled Congress during the entire
postwar period and the presidency for most of the 1960s and 1970s. The
Democratic Party's liberal wing had unprecedented influence in making
judicial appointments and fashioning policies friendly to minority rights.

At the same time, many states were bastions of racial and ethnic discrimination. Minority rights advocates realized that setting policy at the national level was much less costly and more efficient than fighting fifty separate battles in the states.

But the political world changed. The federal government increasingly came under control of the Republican Party, and Republicans became increasingly conservative. The GOP gained influence in the 1978 congressional elections and ascended to power with the election to president of Ronald Reagan in 1980 and congressional majorities in 1994. Building consensus on gay rights in Washington today is made more difficult because of partisan polarization and a greater distrust of a powerful federal government. Debates over "culture war" issues are directed more often at provoking emotional responses than reasoned deliberation. In this atmosphere, building a consensus is easier when policymaking is decentralized among the fifty states and thousands of local communities, each of which is more homogeneous than the entire nation, and the stakes are geographically limited.

Conflict at the state and local levels generally is less salient than at the national level because the national media gives more coverage to controversial issues in Washington than in state capitols and municipalities. Increased salience broadens the scope of conflict (Schattschneider 1960). For policy debates about unpopular minorities like gays and lesbians, greater salience has been linked with defeat for gay rights proposals (Haider-Markel and Meier 1996). Because gay rights opponents have superior political resources nationally, the greater salience of issues makes it easier to mobilize their vast network of religious and social conservatives.

GEOGRAPHIC DISTRIBUTION OF POLITICAL ATTITUDES

Religiosity, religious affiliation, place of residence, level of education, and political ideology are important predictors of support on many gay rights issues at the mass and elite levels. Gay rights supporters attend church less often, belong to nonfundamentalist religious denominations, live in big cities in the Northeast and Pacific Coast, have more education, and identify as liberals. Those who oppose them attend church more often, belong to fundamentalist denominations, live outside of cities and in the South and Midwest, have less education, and identify as conservatives (Schroedel 1999; Haeberle 1999; Gentry 1987; Herek 1988; Ellison and Musick 1993; Herek and Capitanio 1995, 1996; Seltzer 1993; Button, Rienzo, and Wald

1997; Lewis and Rogers 1999; Wilcox and Wolpert 2000).[50] As a result, support for gay rights is strong in some state and local jurisdictions even when a national majority opposes them (or when antigay elites control the national government despite a progay rights majority of the public). Gay voters are often part of winning electoral coalitions in states and cities where Democrats are in control and where gay rights activists are found in larger numbers (Haider-Markel 2000, 300). The Christian Right has a strong grip over the Republican Party in states where their activists are more numerous (Green, Guth, and Wilcox 1998). Gay rights first gained traction and expanded in college towns and large cities. Many gays and lesbians migrate to states and communities that have sizable gay popula- tions and more tolerant attitudes, which further strengthens gay rights or- ganizations. These states and communities are often racially and ethnically diverse in other ways and have legacies of tolerance toward other minorities (Dorris 1999, 48).

POSSIBILITIES FOR RETAIL POLITICS

Individuals who know gays and lesbians are more likely to feel more positively toward them (Lance 1987; Herek 1988; Ellis and Vasseur 1993; Haddock, Zanna, and Esses 2003; Herek and Glunt 1993; Herek and Capi- tanio 1996) and, in turn, are more likely to support gay rights (Wilcox and Wolpert 2000, 423). Having gay friends, family members, and co-workers reduces homophobia and fosters a view of gays as ordinary people with ordinary lives rather than as impersonal threats to the community. When gays and lesbians come out of the closet, their increased contact with the straight world induces more positive affect toward gays and lesbians as a group. Gay rights advocates use personal contact as a strategy during grass- roots campaigns to build support for legislative proposals. Retail politics is most feasible and effective in local communities and smaller states, where gay and lesbian activists can meet face-to-face with larger numbers of fel- low citizens and policymakers, share their experiences, and build trust and understanding about their issues (Killian 2006).

POLICY DIFFUSION EFFECTS

State and local governments do not make decisions as isolated jurisdic- tions. Once one or more states adopt an innovation, it often spreads to other states (Walker 1969; Gray 1973). States tend to imitate neighboring states or states located in the same region (Berry and Berry 1999; Hays and Glick 1997; Mintrom 2000; Mooney 2001b; Mooney and Lee 1995). Even if threat levels are unusually high, the diffusion of policies is possible.[51] Diffusion occurs partly because states serve as laboratories. If a few states adopt a policy and bad things do not happen, other states are more likely to follow their example. Having a few states adopt a gay rights policy makes it easier for others to follow, as they are not taking unprecedented risks.

H1a: *Advocates for gay rights are more likely to succeed
if policy is made at the state and local levels.*

At the same time, the positive impact of diffusion on gay rights effects could be limited because diffusion increases the salience of policy issues. Individuals' support for gay rights declines when the scope of conflict expands and issues become more salient (Haider-Markel and Meier 1996). We might expect diffusion to have more mixed or adverse effects for gay rights when an issue is threatening to the public. The adoption of gay marriage and civil unions by some states, for example, may induce others to ban them.

H1b: *For issues that the public finds highly threatening, diffusion
effects will dampen or reverse the spread of gay rights measures.*

Institutional contexts vary among states and localities as much as across levels of government. Public opinion may have a greater impact on public policy in jurisdictions that have processes of direct democracy, such as the ballot initiative. Evidence for this appears in the case of abortion policy, for example (Arceneaux 2002). A majority that is hostile to minority rights may have greater influence in states that permit voters to have such a direct role in policymaking. Because the majority of states put most civil rights initiatives and referenda on the ballot, including those related to sexual orientation (Gamble 1997; Witt and McCorkle 1997), states that allow direct democracy may afford gay rights opponents more leverage over policymaking. The ballot initiative process generally lacks the external and internal checks that proponents of policy change confront when they work through legislatures (Eule 1990; Gillette 1988). Anecdotal evidence suggests that opponents use the initiative process to tap into, and perhaps heighten, anti-gay sentiment, appealing to voters with low information by using rhetorical devices and dramatic visual images designed to portray gays as deviant and threatening (Witt and McCorkle 1997).

Whether ballot initiatives are as problematic for gay rights as some have assumed is not clear. Gamble (1997) found that voters approved 79 percent of the forty-three gay rights initiatives that reached the ballot between 1977 and 1993 at the state and local levels. Other researchers found that gays won more ballot initiatives than they lost at the state level from 1972 to 1996, that voters were less likely to pass antigay rights measures than other initiatives, and that antigay effects are mediated by the size of jurisdiction. Larger (and presumably more diverse) jurisdictions, with higher-educated populations, produce successful initiative campaigns sympathetic to gay rights (Donovan and Bowler 1998).[52]

H2a: *Gay rights advocates will make less progress in states that use the ballot initiative than in states that do not.*
H2b: *The availability of the ballot initiative will have no effect on the success of gay rights advocates.*

Third-Party Stakeholders

Social movement organizations and policymakers are part of policy networks that frequently include experts, professionals, and constituency groups who share a special interest in the resolution of a policy debate. Third-party stakeholders change from one institutional venue to another and are active only on a single issue. For these actors, victory or defeat for gay rights is not an end in itself but is instrumental to achieving some material, professional, organizational, or purposive goal. Although gays and lesbians are not as disadvantaged economically as groups represented by other social movements, they are a small, geographically dispersed, unpopular minority fighting for their rights at a time when their liberal allies are much weaker than they once were. Estimates of the number of gays and lesbians generally run between 5 and 10 percent of the population, and 4 percent of voters identified themselves as gay, lesbian, or bisexual in the 2004 presidential election (Herzog 1996, 1–2, 245; Sherrill 2005, 40). Although the public has become warmer toward gays over the past few decades, they remain among those groups that register among the "coldest" feelings in opinion surveys for many Americans (Yang 2003, 71; Egan and Sherrill 2005b). Third-party stakeholders, therefore, may provide critical help (or hindrance) to the cause of gay rights.

Stakeholders' disproportionate influence stems from their intense interest, involvement, and expertise in an issue area. Perhaps the most important resource they bring to bear upon a policy debate is their ability to redefine issues and disseminate arguments that policymakers can use to justify or block reform (Grattet 2005, 180). For policymakers seeking to avoid controversy, third-party stakeholders may play a critical role in transforming divisive debates over gay rights into issues about widely shared values and the need to strengthen important institutions. Because of their expertise and deep involvement, stakeholders usually speak as credible authorities about the expected consequences of expanding and limiting gay rights.

H3: *Advocates for gay rights are more likely to succeed if the policy preferences of third-party stakeholders coincide with those of the advocates.*

Judicial Involvement

Finally, institutional venues vary according to which branch of government dominates policymaking. Courts play the key role on some issues, while legislatures, bureaucracies, or a combination are at the center of resolving others. Many scholars and political activists believe that courts are more willing to support the rights of unpopular minorities than the other branches of government.[53] In the post–World War II era, the U.S. Supreme Court handed down landmark decisions in racial desegregation, women's reproductive and employment rights, and freedom of expression for groups with unpopular political viewpoints.[54] Other observers argue that this period was an aberration or that the courts were not uniquely predisposed to defend minority rights even in that period.

DYNAMIC OR CONSTRAINED?

According to the "dynamic court" perspective, courts are an independent branch of government and thus institutionally well suited to champion the interests of the less powerful, which the other branches have ignored or rejected (Rosenberg 1991). A nonelected judiciary, appointed for life, would appear as the kind of check on majority tyranny that Madisonian democracy envisioned. Judges are more at liberty to bring their own personal judgments and other criteria to bear upon controversial causes than legislators, who must heed the wishes of the public or of powerful interests (CPIL 1976; Lindblom 1980). Legislators are likely to champion social movements only when voters support their demands (Burstein 1985, 1998; Costain and Majstorovic 1994).

Courts offer a more level playing field between two sides in conflict, as resource-poor litigants do not have the burden of mobilizing citizens, donating to campaigns, and hiring lobbyists (McCann 1986; Sax 1971; Neely 1981). The adversarial process directs judges to confront arguments from all sides, collect and rigorously assess information, and buttress their decisions with legal reasoning. Judges interpret constitutions that include provisions to protect individual freedom and grant equal protection of the laws. The popularity of a policy with a majority of citizens is not sufficient reason for a judge to rule in favor of the majority. Even if courts do not create large-scale changes in policy or society on their own, they draw attention to issues and place them on the agenda. Court decisions against discrimination can legitimate a cause, educate the public, mobilize groups, and give elected officials "cover" to address gay rights claims (Bickel 1962; Scheingold 1974; McCann 1986; Salokar 2001).[55]

A more skeptical view is that the courts are too constrained to advance the interests of the less powerful (Rosenberg 1991; Pacelle 1996). Courts are politically dependent on other branches of government and citizens. Presidents appoint and the Senate confirms federal judges and expect them to reflect their philosophies. Most state judges must run for reelection. The elected branches may override the courts' statutory interpretations and change their jurisdiction. Judges do not want to be seen as usurping the role of democratically elected officials. For these reasons, courts are fairly responsive to majority opinion (Dahl 1957; Funston 1975; Mishler and Sheehan 1993, 1996; Stimson, Mackuen, and Erikson 1995).[56]

Other critics view the independence of the courts as a source of conservatism because it enables judges to preserve the status quo (Spann 1993). Judges may not believe that petitioners are entitled to benefits just because they claim that they are. Since the U.S. Constitution does not explicitly state many of the rights that gay rights advocates claim, judges have considerable discretion to decide whether they should create new rights or extend those that exist (Rosenberg 1991, 11; Harvard Law Review 1977; Gordon 1984). The normal respect that judges accord precedent (stare decisis) makes courts inherently conservative institutions. Litigants must frame their arguments in the form of technical legal principles that lessen their political force and appeal (Rosenberg 1991, 12; Handler 1978). Judges' training as generalists and their incremental, case-bound approach to broad, complex issues hamper their ability to gather information and apply it intelligently to decisions (Horowitz 1977). Finally, judges lack budgetary and police powers to ensure that other officials will carry out their orders (Rosenberg 1991, 16–21).

Assessments of the judiciary's responsiveness to gay and lesbian claims have been largely negative. According to Wald (2000, 24), "the confidence in the judicial arena as a relatively neutral forum where gays and lesbians have a level playing field may be misplaced." Brewer, Kaib, and O'Connor (2000, 378) conclude that "the Supreme Court . . . has been notoriously reluctant to enter the legal fray by repeatedly refusing to hear appeals involving important [gay] legal issues." Gerstmann (1999) argues that the dominance of a class-based, three-tiered framework of equal-protection jurisprudence has turned gays into a "constitutional underclass." Even more positive assessments identify a number of obstacles, some of which are unique, that gay rights litigants face, and they caution against assuming that gays can be as successful as earlier civil rights movements were in the courts (Cain 2000; Salokar 2001).[57]

H4: *Advocates for gay rights will be no more successful in reaching their political goals when courts are the primary institutional venue for resolving conflict than when they are not.*

Advocates of a more dynamic view of the Court argue that the other branches of government also need political support and lack sufficient authority and resources to implement decisions (Pacelle 2002, 115; Smith 1997, 12–13, 311). What appear as disabilities (e.g., the generalist training of judges) may actually be advantages. Although some critics, particularly Gerald Rosenberg (1991), have mustered considerable empirical evidence against the dynamic court view, they have chosen unduly high standards for measuring the impact of courts.[58] According to Smith (1993, 149), "[v]iewed from that [Rosenberg's] perspective, courts may very well be lesser spokes in the larger wheel of social forces that moves and changes society. This does not mean, however, that courts have no important impact."[59] For courts to matter, we do not need to find that they have single-handedly brought about sweeping change in favor of gay rights or that they consistently defend gay rights. Instead, we want to know if, despite the constraints, gay rights advocates fare better when the courts are involved in an issue area than when they are not and if advocates fare better in the courts than in other institutional venues.

Furthermore, short of directly changing policy, courts sometimes act as catalysts for change or bring changes that are underway to a conclusion. Even when they need the cooperation of the elected branches of government and the public, courts can provoke public interest in an issue and spur elected officials to act when they would not do so otherwise (Flemming, Bohte, and Wood 1997).[60] Finally, the notion that courts have little independent ability to promote minority rights does not square with the large investments that conservative groups and politicians have made in trying to get rid of "activist judges" and appoint those who share their views.

> H5: *Advocates for gay rights will be more successful in reaching*
> *their political goals when courts are the primary institutional venue*
> *for resolving conflict.*

A third approach rejects both the dynamic and constrained court perspectives as oversimplifications and argues that the impact of courts is *contingent* (Pacelle 2002). Courts may help advance minority rights when the constraints are not as stringent or when they are balanced by more favorable conditions (Rosenberg 1991). Courts may make and implement countermajoritarian rulings when public opinion is closely split on an issue, but not when the public is decidedly against a course of action; when court rulings are essentially self-executing, but not when other organizations must cooperate to implement rulings;[61] and when courts implement their own rulings. Of particular relevance to this study, courts' capacity to make decisions stand and implement them may vary from issue to issue (Pinello 2003). Some court decisions may be virtually self-executing. Because much of the political struggle over gay rights is symbolic, judicial decisions are tantamount to victory or defeat, regardless of any changes in material conditions that the decisions bring about. In some cases, judges act as "street-level bureaucrats," both deciding and implementing policy.

> *Advocates for gay rights will be more successful in reaching their*
> *political goals when courts are the primary institutional venue*
> *for resolving conflict* and:
> H6a: *public opinion is divided closely over an issue*
> H6b: *the courts can implement their rulings or their rulings are*
> *self-executing*
> H6c: *the court's ruling prompts others to act who support the*
> *court's position but who could have remained inactive in the*
> *absence of the ruling.*

STATE COURTS

The debate over courts as protectors of minority rights focuses on the federal courts, and the U.S. Supreme Court in particular. Despite a long-standing argument that state courts were institutionally inferior to federal courts in defending minority rights (Neuborne 1977; Amar 1991; Yackle 1994), a more recent study finds that state courts are more friendly toward gay rights petitioners than those at the federal level (Pinello 2003, 105–17). According to Rubenstein (1999, 618), "for a small and relatively new social movement, securing outlying but affirmative rulings may be more productive than attempting to secure an unattainable national consensus. A single court ruling can make the previously unthinkable suddenly real." State-level litigation takes advantage of policy diffusion and bandwagon effects favoring reform. "Successful challenges in one state encourage activists in other states to seek similar changes, and may create the necessary awareness nationwide to further sway public opinion in favor of reform" (Brantner 1992, 514).

At the federal level, the partisan and ideological coloration of presidential administrations appears to have a major impact on whether judges will rule favorably toward gay and lesbian petitioners. Federal judges' greater support for minority rights during the 1950s and 1960s was apparently the product of Democratic and moderate Republican administrations rather than institutional advantages of the federal judiciary for minorities (Chemerinsky 1991). Federal judges appointed by Democratic administrations are much more likely to support claims brought by gays and lesbians than Republican appointees (Pinello 2003, 114). The support of federal judges for minority rights declined beginning in the 1970s, when the federal courts became part of a conservative coalition that dominated Washington thereafter. "By 1993," Rubenstein (1999, 600) notes, "Republican presidents had appointed 75 percent of the sitting federal judges."

Courts in states with more liberal attitudes, less religiosity, fewer Christian fundamentalists, a larger LGBT population, and stronger LGBT organizations may rule favorably on issues for which no national progay rights majority exists. As Paula Brantner (1992, 513) observed at the end of the Reagan and George H. W. Bush years, "judges in the various state courts reflect a wide range of political and philosophical values based on the values of the states' citizens. The federal judiciary, however, primarily reflects the conservative values of the last two presidential administrations."

Although the requirement that most state judges stand for election would appear disadvantageous for unpopular minorities, it may also induce judges to court gay voters and local chapters of the gay bar association. This strategy may not be politically risky because some issues that are salient to gay constituents are not salient to voters generally. Judges may also enjoy a large degree of decision-making autonomy on most issues, given their generally high rates of reelection.

State courts have a number of advantages over federal courts for gay and lesbian petitioners. Their decentralized policymaking offers gay rights litigants multiple points of access (Salokar 2001) and reduces the salience of gay rights issues. States also can extend rights beyond the "floor" provided in the U.S. Constitution (see Leveno 1993–94, 1035; Cicchino, Deming, and Nicholson 1991). State constitutions are more detailed than the federal constitution and usually guarantee rights affirmatively and explicitly. The U.S. Constitution states rights as negative prohibitions against governmental authority and requires justices to "read" specific rights "into" the document (Brantner 1992, 511; *Harvard Law Review* 1982, 1324, 1355). "As a result, state courts can more readily implement unique, state-specific protections that guarantee more rights to the state's citizens than are found in the federal constitution" (Brantner 1992, 511).

State judges may be less hesitant than their federal colleagues to break new ground for gays, knowing that their rulings are geographically bounded. Federal judges who are sensitive to state sovereignty must traverse the jurisdictional hurdle of overturning *state* legislation (Rubenstein 1999, 618; Brantner 1992, 512). As the federal courts grew more conservative under the William Rehnquist Court, they helped to inspire a "new judicial federalism" that encouraged plaintiffs to turn to the state courts "as the most promising means of promoting libertarian progress and innovation" (Friedelbaum 1991–92, 1054). Justice William Brennan, one of the Court's most liberal members, encouraged civil rights and civil liberties advocates to turn to state courts in the 1980s (Brennan 1986).

Gays bring a vast majority of their lawsuits before state family, probate, and criminal courts. State judges have greater expertise in those areas of the law and a richer appreciation for how the system discriminates against gays. State judges come in much greater contact with gays and lesbians in fact-bound situations than do federal judges. They develop an understanding of the lives of gays in professional contexts. Because they do not have lifetime tenure, state court judges have greater turnover and are younger,

on average, than federal judges. Younger cohorts are generally more tolerant toward gays and supportive of gay rights.

H7: *Advocates for gay rights will be more successful in reaching*
their political goals in policy arenas in which state courts are the
primary institutional venue for resolving conflict.

State court systems are not uniform. Methods of judicial selection and
retention and length of terms of office vary substantially from state to state.
Judges who must run for election and have shorter terms are more influenced by public opinion, presumably, than are those who are appointed or
enjoy longer terms. State judges who enjoy longer terms of office are more
likely to render decisions in support of gay rights, but whether judges run
for election or are appointed has little impact on their decisions (Pinello
2003, 92).

H8: *States whose judges serve longer terms of office will be more*
supportive of gay rights than those with shorter terms, particularly
on issues that the public finds threatening.

In sum, gay rights advocates are more likely to make progress in reaching their goals when the courts, especially at the state level, take a leading
role in resolving issues; policy is made at state and local levels of government; and the interests of third-party stakeholders coincide with those of
gay rights advocates. They are less likely to make progress when legislators
and voters decide policy issues, policymaking takes place at the national
level of government, and the interests of institutional stakeholders and gay
rights advocates diverge.

MORE PARSIMONIOUS EXPLANATIONS?

Can we explain the pattern of political successes and failures that LGBT
rights movement has experienced more easily? For example, does a higher
level of success simply reflect the longer time that LGBT rights advocates
have pushed for certain goals? Gays have been pressuring for nondiscrimination laws for much longer than they have been demanding marriage
and other forms of partner recognition, for example. Advocates have had
more chances to make their case, build coalitions, and "soften up" citizens
and government officials, making nondiscrimination measures no longer
seem as novel and radical. This argument is plausible. However, many issues do not fit the pattern. LGBT activists have been pressing in earnest for

adoption and marriage for about the same length of time, yet with different levels of success. They have lobbied for protection against discrimination in the workplace longer than they have asked for protection against hate crimes, but they have been more successful in the latter. More importantly, issues like marriage and adoption have not just been on the agenda for a shorter period. They are substantively very different demands that are addressed in different political and institutional contexts that shape prospects for success.

Perhaps the variable fortunes of the gay rights movement simply reflect the difference between "gendered" and "non-gendered" issues. Gays and lesbians have done worse on the military and marriage issues because they involve institutions rooted in traditional gender roles and statuses. The legalization of homosexual conduct and the extension of adoption rights, however, do not fit this explanation. What activity in our culture could be more based upon gender distinctions than sexual conduct? Parenting has also been a highly gendered activity, yet gays and lesbians have been reasonably successful in gaining adoption rights. Other nations' militaries were as highly masculine as the American, yet they lifted their bans. Excluding women from the military was also a highly gendered issue, yet most restrictions on women have ended. Undoubtedly, the fact that homosexuality calls into question traditional gender roles is an important reason many people find gay rights threatening. Yet, as we will see, how much people perceive gay rights as threatening only partially explains the policy outcomes that we observe in these cases.

Another possibility is that LGBT patterns of success simply reflect which side in the debate—the pro- or antigay rights movement—brings to bear greater resources in the policymaking process. The explanation explored in this book synthesizes political process, resource mobilization, and framing approaches to the study of social movements. Perhaps resource mobilization theory alone provides a more parsimonious explanation for LGBT policy outcomes. Initially developed to account for the emergence of social movements, resource mobilization theory focuses on the resources that the pro- and anti-LGBT rights movements devote to reaching their political goals. According to this theory, LGBT success is most likely on issues for which gay rights organizations spend more resources than their opponents spend.

Exploring this explanation poses challenges. It is difficult to ascertain how many resources social movement organizations devote to advancing their goals on particular issues, because they generally budget resources according to organizational activities and functions that cut across issues. Comparing resource mobilization across issues is also tricky because organizational resources are often incommensurate. We have no common yardstick to compare, for example, legislative lobbying for civil rights protection with litigation on behalf of same-sex couples who seek the right to adopt children. Making correct inferences about the relationship between resources and outcomes is also fraught with difficulty. For example, the legal costs of a failed lawsuit might be a fraction of those incurred in a successful campaign to get a legislature to pass or defeat a bill. Does this mean that the expenditure of greater resources led to success, or just that campaigns to get legislatures to enact laws on controversial subjects are more expensive than lawsuits?[62] Without being able to measure the resources devoted by each side to each issue, we have no way of knowing which side mobilized greater resources in our six cases.

As an alternative to gauging the resources that movements devote to different issues, we might examine the *attention* that they pay to them as a proxy. If pro- and antigay rights organizations pay greater attention to particular issues, it is likely they will devote more of their available resources to them. We can gauge organizations' attention to different issues by examining the topics that they address in their public communications, such as press releases and reports.

Let us first examine gay rights organizations. The data in table 1.2 on the number of press releases issued by the NGLTF and the HRC for more than a decade provide very little support for the hypothesis that gay rights organizations experience greater success when they devote more attention to issues. The NGLTF and the HRC have paid greatest attention to same-sex marriage and civil rights. Marriage has been largely a failure for the movement, and civil rights a moderate success. Of the two issues that these organizations have given the least attention—the military ban and legalization of homosexual conduct—one is a clear failure and the other a clear success. Hate crimes legislation, the most successful issue after the repeal of sodomy laws, ranks third for the NGLTF and fourth for the HRC. For the NGLTF, adoption, military service, and the legalization of homosexual conduct follow distantly behind marriage, civil rights, and hate crimes, garnering only about 3 to 4 percent of the total number of its press releases that dealt with policy issues. Adoption is a moderate success, serving in the military is a clear failure, and the repeal of sodomy laws is a clear success.

Table 1.5 Attention to gay rights issues by conservative, "profamily" organizations

	Traditional Values Coalition		Family Research Council	
	Total items (N = 298)	As % of total	Total items (N = 418)	As % of total
Gay marriage, civil unions, partner recognition	96	32	164	39
Civil rights	26	9	19	5
Adoption/ parenting	14	5	24	6
Hate crimes	23	8	20	5
Legalization of homosexual conduct	5	2	9	2
Military	2	1	6	1
Other gay-related issues	132	44	176	42
Total		100		100

Note: "Other gay-related issues" includes general criticisms or warnings about homosexuality, homosexuals, and gay rights activists, or responses to them; criticisms of political leaders who generally support gay rights; "discrimination" against religious persons who speak out against homosexuality; the role of homosexuals in the clergy; gays as carriers of AIDS and AIDS prevention programs; media presentations of gays and gay rights issues; presentation/ discussion of homosexuality in schools; gays as alleged pedophiles; whether homosexuality is a choice; and various other topics.
Sources: Traditional Values Coalition, www.traditionalvalues.org/. Includes available press releases, special reports, action alerts, and editorials published from 2002 to November 10, 2006. Family Research Council, http://www.frc.org. Includes available policy papers, fact papers, commentaries, legislative alerts, press/current event announcements, and "miscellaneous" published from 2001 to November 12, 2006.

What about the groups opposed to gay rights? Table 1.5 shows the attention paid to gay rights issues by the Traditional Values Coalition (TVC) and the Family Research Council (FRC), two leading national organizations of social conservatives in the United States (Button, Rienzo, and Wald 1997, 192; John Green 2000; Herman 2000). These organizations clearly place overwhelming emphasis on banning same-sex marriage and partner recognition. The number of press releases issued by these organizations devoted to the marriage issue exceeds the frequency for all of the other issues combined. One-third of the TVC and more than one-third of the FRC releases concern marriage. The next most frequent issues, civil rights for the TVC and adoption for the FRC, trail far behind marriage. Given the disproportionate attention (and presumably resources) that these organizations devote to banning marriage and partner recognition, it appears highly likely that their opposition is an important element in the spread of bans on same-sex marriage and partner recognition across the United States.

On the other five issues, however, it is difficult to see a clear pattern between resource mobilization among antigay groups and policy outcomes. The TVC and the FRC pay meager attention to the other five issues. Part of the reason a clear link between attention and policy success and failure is difficult to discern may be the breadth and diffusion of these groups' agendas. Social conservative organizations spend a portion of their resources educating the public about non-public-policy aspects of homosexuality such as the visibility and portrayal of gays in the mass media and "ex-gay" conversion programs. And many of them, like the FRC, have policy agendas that encompass abortion, school prayer, sex education, bioethics, euthanasia, pornography, and a host of other issues unrelated to gay rights. The FRC issued 171 press releases on abortion and 124 on stem cell research, for example, several times more than the number they issued for each of the non-marriage-related gay rights issues (FRC 2006).

Even when the priorities of social movement organizations correlate with their levels of policy success, the organizations do not make decisions about where to devote their attention and resources in a vacuum. The same factors that we have hypothesized influence social movement success presumably shape their decisions about where to allocate their resources: how much the public perceives demands for gay rights as threatening and whether the institutional context facilitates or impedes effective resistance against the demands.

Social movement organizations undoubtedly take account of which issues are of greatest concern to their constituents and the public, and on which the public's preferences are most clearly in agreement with their own. For gay rights opponents, issues that the public perceives as more threatening have the greatest potential to mobilize supporters and bring about success in the policymaking process. Gay rights opponents have spent much more of their resources trying to defeat gay marriage than other LGBT goals because of the salience of the issue, which is rooted in the real or "essential" differences between marriage and other issues and the symbolic power of marriage for many heterosexuals. Moreover, the antigay rights movement realizes that a majority of the public has remained steadily opposed to same-sex marriage. These organizations' estimates of a high likelihood of success, therefore, encourage them to invest resources in seeking to defeat same-sex marriage. Their investment in efforts to ban marriage enhances prospects for success, and success encourages additional investments in campaigns to enact such bans.

On marriage and other issues, whether institutional venues include stakeholders who support their cause, provide access to sympathetic elites, and increase (or decrease) issue salience and opportunities to bring popular pressures directly to bear on the process shapes social movements' decisions about investing resources. For example, gay rights opponents can place marriage bans on legislative agendas and on the ballot in many states, which increases the salience of the issue and permits them to make policy directly. Hence, the more complex causal process of the kind described in this study influences social movement organizations' decisions about how to allocate their resources.

PLAN OF THE BOOK

The chapters that follow explore how the nexus between perceived threat and institutional context spell victory or defeat for the gay rights movement across several issues. Chapters 2 and 3 present data on how advocates for each side define gay rights issues in debates, revealing what they think is threatening about gay rights and what definitions they estimate will have the greatest chance of triggering perceptions of threat among citizens and policymakers. Advocates face a choice in defining issues in terms of principles, procedures, or consequences. Chapter 2 examines whether, as the literature on morality politics leads us to expect, gay rights opponents define gay rights in terms of moral principles about personal conduct. Chapter 3 explores the strategies that gay rights supporters pursue, specifically whether they address their opponents' definitions and try to dampen Americans' perceptions of threat, or ignore what they say and define issues in wholly different terms.

Chapters 4 (legalizing homosexual conduct), 5 (adoption), and 6 (military service) examine three issues in which public policy outcomes are inconsistent with what one would predict from knowing the level at which Americans perceive a threat from gay rights. Americans have been divided over whether to legalize homosexual relations and to allow gay couples to adopt children, yet sodomy laws no longer exist, and gays can adopt in a growing number of jurisdictions, particularly in many large communities. At the same time, growing majorities have supported lifting the ban on gays serving openly in the military, yet the ban remains in place. These cases illustrate most clearly the crucial impact of political institutions on the prospects for success of gay rights advocates. Chapter 7 looks more briefly at the three remaining cases—marriage, hate crimes, and civil rights—in which policy outcomes are consistent with what one would expect from the level of threat perceived by the public. Even in these cases, however, institutions have important impacts.

Chapter 8 returns to the central research question—why have gays and lesbians succeeded in reaching some of their goals more than others? After summarizing the book's main findings and integrating them into a typology of social movement success and failure, we proceed to assess their broader implications. First, we consider the findings on the role of the courts in gay rights in light of recent skepticism about the judiciary's contribution to protecting minority rights. Second, we see that the issue-based perspective on social movement success helps us to build empirical generalizations across social movements. Finally, chapter 8 speculates about the gay rights movement's future prospects, suggests changes in the movement's strategies that might help gay rights advocates improve their chances for success, and assesses the feasibility and effectiveness of several options.

Advocates who debate gay rights issues fashion their appeals to arouse or dampen the perception that gay rights pose a threat. They must convince people to see an issue as "about" one thing rather than another because social conditions are inherently ambiguous. Ambiguity gives rise to conflict over which facts are the most relevant and what they mean. Because politics is "a struggle over alternative realities," how advocates define or frame issues is a crucial part of their strategy to win public policy battles (Rochefort and Cobb 1994, 9; see also Nelson and Kinder 1996).[1] If gay rights supporters convince policymakers and citizens that an issue is about "ending invidious discrimination," for example, they are likely to succeed; if their opponents convince them that the issue boils down to "condoning an immoral lifestyle," gay rights advocates are almost certain to lose. A fair amount of evidence of "framing effects" indicates that how an issue is framed, usually through the mass media, can change people's understanding of, and opinions on, issues (Kinder and Sanders 1996; Nelson, Clawson, and Oxley 1997), including gay rights issues (Brewer 2002, 2003; Tadlock, Gordon, and Popp 2007).

This chapter and the next examine how opponents and proponents define gay rights issues. How opponents define the issues reveals what they find most threatening about gay rights and what they believe the public will find most threatening. In deciding how to frame issues in their effort to arouse perceptions of threat, gay rights opponents can argue that homosexuality violates moral and religious principles, that gay rights will produce undesirable consequences for society, or that the adoption of such measures violates important procedural norms and harms institutions. The first part of this chapter discusses the advantages and disadvantages of defining issues in moral terms versus consequences or procedures. The next section presents data about how opponents define the issues and looks for patterns across issues. Opponents define issues in ways that are consistent with changes in public opinion and the constraints they face in building coalitions. Contrary to theories of "morality politics," opponents usually do not place primary emphasis on moral and religious arguments in debate but emphasize consequences and the procedural aspects of issues. The conclusion addresses the implications of these findings.

STRATEGIES OF ISSUE DEFINITION

Advocates face a range of choices in defining issues in order to induce (or dampen) perceptions of threat. Broadly, they can choose definitions based upon *principles, procedures,* or *consequences.* Principled or "deontological" definitions frame policies in terms of their intrinsic rightness or wrongness, without regard to whether the consequences they produce are desirable. When gay rights opponents define issues in principled terms, they usually invoke religious teachings and natural law doctrines that deem homosexuality immoral and unnatural. According to this perspective, gay rights laws sanction and encourage homosexual behavior, which is contrary to nature and God's intentions. For example, opponents of allowing gays into the military might argue that the issue is about legitimating an immoral lifestyle and may invoke Biblical injunctions against homosexuality. Definitions that are rooted in consequences consider whether the effects of policies are desirable, and perhaps whether benefits exceed costs. Opponents of lifting the military ban might argue, for example, that we need to protect the privacy of heterosexual service members in order to maintain morale, trust, and cohesion among service members. Procedural definitions ignore the substantive merits of policies, directing attention to how policymakers should make decisions, who should make them, and whose views should be accorded the most weight. Supporters of the military ban might define the issue as paying appropriate deference to the judgments of military leaders, for instance.

Because advocates need to mobilize support from organized constituencies committed to their cause, opponents might be expected to gravitate toward morality-based issue definitions—that homosexual behavior is immoral and incompatible with their own or others' religious beliefs. If the appeals work as intended, they will activate religious and social conservatives to put pressure on policymakers to block gay rights. The importance of religion in individuals' lives is one of the strongest predictors of hostility toward gay rights. The most well-organized opponents of gay rights are religious conservatives who believe that homosexuality is immoral and violates religious proscriptions (Button, Rienzo, and Wald 1997, 173–97; Nyberg and Alston 1976; Levitt and Klassen 1974; Gentry 1987; Herek 1988; Herek and Capitanio 1995, 1996; Seltzer 1993; Lewis and Rogers 1999, 133). They see homosexuality as one of the most important moral issues of our time, along with abortion and school prayer. Definitions directed at religious and social conservatives affirm that the opponents are fighting the "good fight" against the misguided and dangerous aims of the other side. Appeals to members of the Family Research Council or Christian Coalition, for example, stress "holding the line against militant homosexuals who want us to sanction an unacceptable lifestyle."

Perhaps owing to the visibility of these groups, some political scientists depict the politics of gay rights as morality politics. According to Studlar (2001, 43), "the question of public policy regarding homosexuals is possibly the moral issue that currently most divides the U.S. population." Debates over gay rights center around "first principles," in which advocates frame the issue in terms of what is morally right or sinful (Mooney 2001a, 3; Meier 1994, 4; Mooney and Lee 1995). According to Sharp (1999, 3), gay rights and other "culture war controversies . . . are distinctive because they are rooted in deep-seated moral values . . . at least one party to the conflict is mobilized largely because proposals or existing practices are viewed as an affront to religious belief or a violation of a fundamental moral code."

Empirical evidence to support claims that gay rights battles reflect morality politics is limited and mixed. In their examination of workplace nondiscrimination policies at the state and local levels, Haider-Markel and Meier (1996) found that the politics of gay rights reflected the kind of "interest group politics" typical of many other political conflicts and resembled morality politics only when the salience of the issue expanded the scope of conflict. Haider-Markel (2001, 115) found that his analysis "of voting on lesbian and gay issues in the U.S. House of Representatives strongly suggests that the morality politics framework is useful . . . for explaining legislative behavior on issues for which at least one coalition argues its point in terms of morality." These studies did not examine other issues or the actual arguments presented by each side.

The next section suggests why we should not expect morality politics to dominate discussions of gay rights issues and then examines how opponents actually define the issues.

Reasons for Skepticism about Morality Politics

If Americans' opposition to gay rights rests upon their judgment that homosexuality is immoral, we would expect a consistent level of opposition across gay rights issues. Moral injunctions against homosexuality apply to most, if not all, policies that recognize and benefit gays and lesbians. Yet we have observed a good deal of variation in the public's support for gay rights, which should make us skeptical of the morality politics perspective. Variation in its support suggests that the public's opinions rest upon different expectations about the consequences of expanding gay rights in very different issue contexts. A public that is concerned with how gay marriage and adoption will affect families and children, for example, may not see gays serving in the military and protecting gays from job discrimination as problematic.

Opponents, in fact, have a number of reasons to deemphasize morality-based issue definitions and to stress the social consequences and procedural aspects of gay rights issues instead. First, they may not garner sufficient political support if they define gay rights issues mainly in moral terms (Button, Rienzo, and Wald 1997, 194). Definitions directed toward mobilization are unlikely to be effective for persuading those who are undecided, ambivalent, or not firmly opposed to gay rights. Appeals made to "fire up the troops" may not suffice for persuading the median voter, building coalitions among legislators, and providing judges with sound legal rationales. If their paramount concern is winning the public policy battle, advocates committed to one side or the other may need to move beyond or downplay mobilization appeals in order to persuade moderate and undecided policymakers and constituents.

The public includes liberals, conservatives, and moderates, with no group comprising a majority. Moderates comprise the largest or second largest group (depending upon the opinion poll) and occupy the vital center of the political spectrum. The degree of support for gay rights issues among moderates is a fairly accurate guide to the degree of support for gay rights among Americans generally (see table 2.1). The position that most moderates take may spell the difference between whether a majority of Americans supports gay rights or is opposed to them. For hard-core social conservatives, the argument that "laws that protect gay rights sanction an immoral lifestyle" is sufficient to justify opposition to gay rights across issues. In trying to

Table 2.1 Political ideology and support for gay rights

Percent of Americans who identify as[a]		Opposed to gay marriage[b]	In favor of employment rights for gays[c]	In favor of gays in military[c]
	All Americans	66	64	69
Liberal	24	47	84	91
Moderate	37	63	67	70
Conservative	35	79	49	57
Don't know/refused	4			
Total	100			

Sources: [a]Henry J. Kaiser Family Foundation (2001, 33).
[b]CBS/*New York Times* poll, reported in AEI (2004, 23).
[c]American National Election Studies data, reported in Haeberle (1999, 153–55).

attract moderates, however, opponents cannot rely exclusively upon general ideological arguments that appeal to their core supporters. Moderates lack ideological consistency across issues and are not as constrained in their thinking as those who have an ideological predisposition against gay rights. Morality-based ideological arguments may not persuade moderate legislators, whose constituencies may be ambivalent or divided. In forming their positions on issues, moderates are likely to take into account the effects on society of expanding gay rights in specific areas.

The second reason to deemphasize morality-based issue definitions and to stress the social consequences and procedural aspects of gay rights issues is that policymakers find it more difficult to reach consensus when they define issues in terms of the morality of personal conduct. Moral principles are categorical imperatives that people cannot compromise about easily. Compromise represents defeat. In the debate over marriage, for example, it is difficult for the two sides to settle upon civil unions or domestic partner benefits as a compromise if people view any sort of partnership recognition as legitimization of a morally deviant lifestyle.

Third, gay rights opponents must move beyond morality-based definitions because the number of Americans who believe that homosexual conduct is immoral has declined steadily over the past thirty years. The percentage of respondents who believe that "sexual relations between two adults of the same sex" is "always wrong" fell from 73 percent in 1973 to between 50 and 58 percent in 2006, depending upon the survey (AEI

2006, 2; Roper Center 2008a) (see figure 2.1). This shift in attitudes is not part of a general liberalization in the public's views toward people who deviate from traditional modes of sexual conduct.[2] Many members of the public apparently have changed their attitudes about the acceptability of homosexuality specifically rather than taken an "anything goes" approach to public morals.

Fourth, citizens who continue to have moral objections to homosexuality may "bracket" their moral judgment, sidestepping the issue of whether homosexual conduct is moral. Moral bracketing insists on "the strict separation of moral, philosophical and religious views (or what philosophers call questions of the good) from considerations of justice (or what philosophers call questions of the right)" (Ball 2003, 1). Bracketing makes it possible for people to support gay rights without feeling they are compromising their personal standards of morality. Although polling data directly measuring bracketing is difficult to obtain over time, the public has been asked if they find homosexuality "acceptable for other people but not for yourself, acceptable for other people and yourself, or not acceptable at all." Between 1978 and 2004, the proportions saying "acceptable for both" and "acceptable for others but not for yourself" rose from 6 to 11 percent and from 35 to 49 percent, respectively, and those who said "not acceptable at all" fell from 59 to 38 percent (see figure 2.2). A Princeton Survey Research Associates (PSRA)/Pew Research Center poll in 2006 asked people whether "homosexual behavior" was "morally acceptable, morally wrong, or is it not a moral issue?" Thirty-three percent said it was "not a moral issue" and 12 percent said that it was "acceptable," comprising almost half of the respondents in the poll when the responses are combined (AEI 2006, 4). In 2006, the CBS/*New York Times* poll asked adults, "Do you think homosexual relations between adults are morally wrong, or are they okay, or don't you care much either way?" Only 37 percent answered "morally wrong" and 18 percent "okay," but a plurality of 43 percent took the neutral stand of "don't care much either way" (Roper Center 2008b).

Elected officials, in particular, may seek to suspend moral judgment. First, like people generally, legislators prefer to avoid discussing and judging other people's private sexual conduct in public: "most lawmakers, by their own admission, are uncomfortable with the subject as a topic of personal or legislative debate" (Campbell and Davidson 2000, 370). Second, the subject is politically risky. In the heated political climate of gay rights, politicians face the risk of having others perceive them as either condoning

Fig. 2.2 Acceptability of homosexual behavior

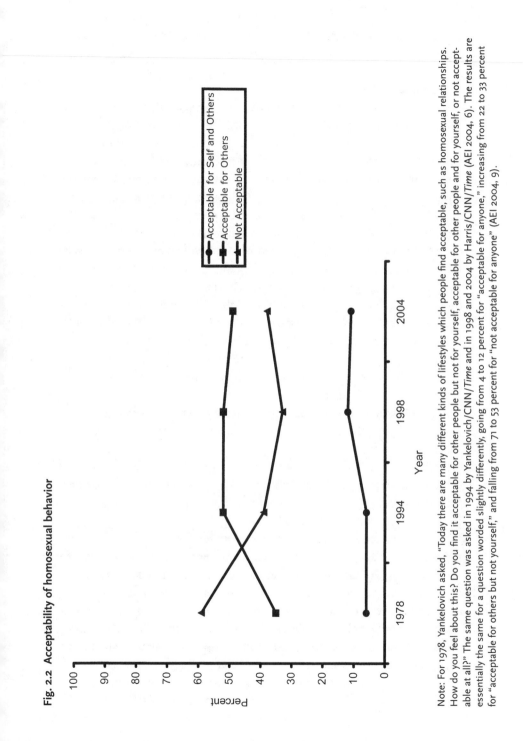

Note: For 1978, Yankelovich asked, "Today there are many different kinds of lifestyles which people find acceptable, such as homosexual relationships. How do you feel about this? Do you find it acceptable for other people but not for yourself, acceptable for other people and for yourself, or not acceptable at all?" The same question was asked in 1994 by Yankelovich/CNN/*Time* and in 1998 and 2004 by Harris/CNN/*Time* (AEI 2004, 6). The results are essentially the same for a question worded slightly differently, going from 4 to 12 percent for "acceptable for anyone," increasing from 22 to 33 percent for "acceptable for others but not yourself," and falling from 71 to 53 percent for "not acceptable for anyone" (AEI 2004, 9).

a "dangerous and aberrant lifestyle" or engaging in "bigotry and intolerance." Gay rights opponents must mobilize their backers and encourage the perception that gay rights pose a real and substantial threat without appearing bigoted.

Bracketing transforms gay rights from personal conduct issues into issues about procedures, consequences, or principles that are morally neutral with regard to personal conduct. Because definitions based on procedures and consequences are rooted in widely shared values and understandings, they are much less politically divisive and risky and offer a better chance for building support and consensus. Those who define an issue in procedural terms identify cherished constitutional principles, like federalism and the separation of powers, and norms, like deference to the views of experts or to those who will be most affected by a policy. Opponents of gay marriage, for example, might argue that the federal government must protect states that do not want gay marriage from having it imposed by other states through the full faith and credit clause of the U.S. Constitution or, in deference to the separation of powers, that "activist judges" should defer to legislative bodies and not "invent new rights."[3] Similarly, those opposed to President Bill Clinton's proposal to lift the ban on gays in the military may argue that Congress needs to pass legislation to fulfill "its responsibilities as a co-equal branch of government."

Gay rights do not always raise important procedural questions, however.[4] Nor are procedural definitions especially compelling for controversial issues, which seem to cry out for judgments on the merits. Colleagues, voters, and constituency groups may consider procedural definitions evasive or unpersuasive and insist that policymakers give substantive reasons for their decisions.[5] Many observers will see procedural arguments as transparent attempts to "pass the buck" or grab power.

A more promising strategy of issue redefinition is to link anti- (or pro-) gay rights positions to the welfare of a group or institution in society that people view positively. For example, when advocates argue against allowing gay couples to adopt children, they may deny that the issue is about gay rights and contend, instead, that it is about "what is best for kids" and, further, that same-sex couples are "unable to provide children with male and female role models." Similarly, those in favor of keeping the ban on gays in the military might argue that the issue is preserving "unit cohesion" and "military effectiveness."

Consequence-based definitions offer advocates an opportunity to persuade moderates and those on the other side of the ideological spectrum, without jeopardizing the support of their core supporters. They also give policymakers greater opportunity to find common ground and reach consensus. Linking issues to positively constructed groups and institutions transforms them into valence issues that reduce political divisiveness and the risks of taking a position, and increases the appeal of the advocates' position.[6] Politicians do not want people to think that they oppose an effective military, protecting marriage and families, and doing what is best for children. The claim that we should not allow gay couples to adopt children because it is "in children's best interest," for example, is a rationale for limiting gay rights without seeming to discriminate. Those who embrace the definition can argue that they were protecting children, not endorsing discrimination and limiting civil rights. For opponents of lifting the military ban, likewise, invoking military effectiveness is a way to exploit heterosexual anxieties about homosexuals without clearly seeming to share the homophobic attitudes of many in the military.

Hence, the next section explores the following hypothesis:

Opponents will prefer to define gay rights issues most often in terms of negative consequences for society and procedural aspects of issues rather than "sanctioning the immorality of homosexuality." Only when they have no opportunity to link their position to the welfare of positively constructed groups or institutions will opponents turn to morality-based definitions.

What kinds of strategies do opponents actually pursue in defining issues? Do they mainly define issues in terms of morality and the violation of religious precepts? Or do they favor considerations about social consequences and the procedural aspects of different issues? Before we address these questions, we turn to a brief discussion of data sources and measurement.

Data

We can observe how advocates define issues by listening to what they say in legislative debates and testimony, news accounts, and other sources of public record. The definitions that advocates use in legislative debate are especially useful because they indicate what those who are about to decide policy issues think are the most important ways to define them. We would not expect the kinds of arguments that advocates use in other public forums, such as in news conferences or editorials, to deviate significantly from what they say in legislative venues like committee hearings and floor debate. An advocate cannot assert one thing in a committee hearing or news interview and admit the opposite in floor debate.

Much of the data reported in this chapter and the next are from twenty-two legislative proceedings, mostly floor debates as well as several public hearings.[7] The debates and testimony took place in eleven different legislative bodies from 1984 to 2003 and covered proposals to outlaw discrimination against gays in employment, housing, and credit; ban or permit gay marriage and adoption; enact hate crimes legislation covering sexual orientation; and codify the ban on gays serving in the military. An analysis of the content of the debates reveals the frequency with which advocates for each side, and across different levels of government, put forward specific definitions of the issues.

The legislative record available for analysis varies widely from issue to issue depending upon which level of government has jurisdiction over it. The record of debate for the U.S. Congress is much more complete and accessible than for legislative bodies at the state and local levels. Most state legislatures and local legislative bodies do not keep verbatim accounts of their debates. If they do, debates over gay rights issues are often so brief (perhaps driven by a desire to avoid controversy) that they are useless. In addition, debate in Congress seems likely to be more representative of debate among Americans generally than debates that occur in particular states and localities. Five key debates in Congress over gay rights were analyzed: the 1993 debate over lifting the ban on gays serving in the military; the 1996 debate over the Defense of Marriage Act (DOMA); the 1996 debate over the Employment Non-Discrimination Act (ENDA), which only the Senate debated; the Local Law Enforcement Act of 2000; and the Local Law Enforcement and Hate Crimes Prevention Act of 2004. An extensive set of hearings held in the state of Connecticut from 2001 to 2003 over gay marriage and civil unions supplement the federal DOMA debate. An analysis of 329 newspaper articles published between 1985 and 2000 supplement the congressional debates over the proposed federal hate crimes act. Data are relatively plentiful for debates over employment and housing discrimination because many states and localities have considered including sexual orientation in their civil rights laws and ordinances. The data reported here are from debates and public hearings held by two municipal councils (Ithaca, New York and Palm Beach County, Florida) and four state legislatures (Massachusetts, Rhode Island, Maryland, and Minnesota).[8]

Legislative debate over gay adoption and the legalization of homosexual conduct issues is difficult to obtain. Few state legislatures have debated gay adoption. Only a single recorded state legislative debate (from Connecticut) was located. The Connecticut adoption debate is analyzed along with a much larger number (532) of observations from an analysis of newspaper articles on gay adoption, published between 1994 and 2004. All news reports, editorials, and letters to the editor located through LexisNexis under "gay" or "homosexual adoption" during that period were analyzed. The articles were coded using the same criteria as the legislative debates. State legislative debates on the repeal of sodomy laws took place mainly in the 1970s and are similarly difficult to locate. Data for the debate over the repeal of sodomy laws are from a LexisNexis search of newspaper articles from 2003 to 2006, which yielded 310 articles that contained gay rights opponents' issue definitions.

Tables 2.2 through 2.12 present data on all of the issue definitions that advocates put forward in the debates, hearings, and news articles. The relative importance of each definition is measured in two ways: (1) the number of speeches or articles that include a particular definition of an issue as a percentage of the total number of speeches given by opponents and (2) the number of assertions of a particular definition as a percentage of the total number of assertions of all definitions.

LEGALIZATION OF HOMOSEXUAL CONDUCT

We begin by looking at how opponents define the legalization of homosexual conduct, specifically the repeal of sodomy laws. Table 2.2 presents the principal issue definitions that opponents put forward from 2003 to 2006, before and after the Supreme Court announced its decision in *Lawrence v. Texas* that declared such laws unconstitutional. No single definition dominates, but opponents emphasize most often the idea that the repeal of sodomy laws is a "slippery slope" that will lead to gay marriage (39 percent of speeches), followed by the argument that repeal is about "activist judges" usurping the role of elected representatives and citizens (35 percent of speeches). For example, according to a writer for the Manchester, New Hampshire, *Union Leader,* "Gay marriage stands an excellent chance of becoming the law of the land now that the Supreme Court has ruled that states can't 'discriminate' against sexual behavior between consenting adults" (Malone 2003). According to a writer for the *Portland* (ME) *Press Herald,* "If the court holds there is an absolute privacy interest in adult

Table 2.2 Definitions of the legalization of homosexual conduct by opponents of the repeal of sodomy laws, 2003–6

	Frequency of definition as % of all definitions asserted ($N = 643$)	% of articles that include definition ($N = 310$)
Slippery slope (repeal will lead to gay marriage, partner recognition, etc.)	21 (135)	39 (122)
Judicial activism (courts usurp role of legislatures and popular majorities; courts "taking sides in culture war")	21 (134)	35 (108)
Slippery slope (repeal will lead to legalization of prostitution, bigamy, bestiality, incest, etc.)	15 (96)	30 (92)
Immorality (homosexuality immoral, violates religious proscriptions, legitimates homosexuality)	17 (108)	30 (92)
Government role (regulation of personal conduct appropriate; repeal would "end morals legislation")	13 (85)	23 (72)
Health (sodomy/homosexuality carries health risks)	8 (49)	13 (40)
Other[a]	6 (36)	12 (36)
Total	101	

Notes: Numbers in parentheses are frequencies. When summed, the frequencies for the "percent of articles that include definition" exceed the total N because many articles include more than one definition.

[a]Definitions found in less than 10% of articles: Supreme Court decision condones criminality; sodomy laws protect children; homosexuality damages family/society; sodomy laws protect traditional values; gays want special rights.

sexual activity, society will be unable to prohibit gay marriage, incest, big-amy and marriages between multiple partners. In fact we will destroy the institution of marriage as the West has known it for thousands of years" (Harmon 2003). According to John Lainhart (2003), in an editorial to the *Houston Chronicle*, "I do not want the Supreme Court to legislate morality for the sate of Texas. The people of Texas should decide these issues, not the Supreme Court. Sodomy laws may be stupid, but that is for us to decide.". And for Jim Clymer, quoted in Lancaster, Pennsylvania, *Intelligencer Journal,* "This court . . . deliberately chose to take upon itself the role of an activist court, meddle in the affairs of an individual state, and consequently, crush the powers of the people of Texas who elected the representatives who passed this law to begin with" (see Quinn 2003).

Opponents define the issue in moral or religious terms about as much as they define it as a slippery slope that will lead to legalizing prostitution, bestiality, and other illegal activities (30 percent of speeches). For example, according to the Reverend Rob Schenk, quoted in the *New York Daily News,* "The Court has said today that morality, matters of right and wrong, do not matter in the law" (Kennedy 2003). According to the Reverend Dan Allen, quoted in the *Lancaster* (PA) *New Era,* "How do we live in a society where blatant sin against God is the standard? How do we react to a court that tells us that obviously what God has said doesn't matter anymore?" (Spidaliere 2003).[9]

In sum, a little over one-third of all definitions that opponents put forward have to do with the likely consequences of repeal—slippery slopes to marriage and the legalization of all forms of sexual conduct. Another third cast the debate in procedural terms, as judicial activism and the appropriateness of governmental regulation of consensual sexual conduct. Combined, these proportions are twice as high as the number of times that opponents define the issue in moral or religious terms.[10]

MARRIAGE AND CIVIL UNIONS

We turn next to how opponents of gay marriage defined the issue during congressional debate over the 1996 federal Defense of Marriage Act (DOMA) and in three hearings before the Connecticut legislature from 2001 to 2003 (see tables 2.3 and 2.4). Opponents expressed very similar concerns at the debates and hearings. Above all, they defined gay marriage as a grave threat to marriage and the family.[11] Half of the speeches in the U.S. House of Representatives and Senate included this definition, and thirty-two percent of the definitions in the two chambers referred to the adverse consequences for marriage and families if society allowed same-sex couples to marry.[12] The threat of gay marriage to vital social institutions was also the leading definition in the Connecticut legislative hearings. Opponents frequently described gay marriage as a major "assault" and "attack" that would entirely change and "redefine" marriage. The titles of federal

Table 2.3 Definitions of gay marriage by proponents of the Defense of Marriage Act in congressional debate, 1996

	House		Senate		Total	
	Frequency of definition as % of all assertions of definitions (N = 108)	% of speeches that include definition (N = 46)	Frequency of definition as % of all assertions of definitions (N = 49)	% of speeches that include definition (N = 16)	Frequency of definition as % of all assertions of definitions (N = 157)	% of speeches that include definition (N = 62)
Gay marriage threatens/will weaken traditional marriage and family	21 (23)	50 (23)	16 (8)	50 (8)	20 (31)	50 (31)
Marriage across time/cultures limited to men and women	19 (21)	46 (21)	20 (10)	63 (10)	20 (31)	50 (31)
States need federal protection or will have gay marriage imposed	14 (15)	33 (15)	29 (14)	88 (14)	18 (29)	47 (29)
Homosexuality/gay marriage immoral/ sanctions homosexuality; violates religious precepts	17 (18)	39 (18)	8 (4)	25 (4)	14 (22)	35 (22)

Gay relationships not equivalent to heterosexual in status/importance to society; gay marriage ends special status of heterosexual marriage; heterosexual relationship of superior quality	6 (7)	15 (7)	10 (5)	31 (5)	8 (12)	19 (12)
High cost to federal budget	5 (5)	11 (5)	10 (5)	31 (5)	6 (10)	16 (10)
Public/bipartisan opposition to gay marriage	8 (9)	20 (9)	0 (0)	0 (0)	6 (9)	15 (9)
Other[a]	10 (10)	19 (8)	6 (3)	19 (8)	8 (13)	21 (13)
Totals	100		99	99	101	

Notes: Numbers in parentheses are frequencies. When summed, the frequencies for the "percent of speeches that include definition" exceed the total N because many speeches include more than one definition.

[a]Definitions found in less than 15% of speeches: dictionary definition/plain meaning of "marriage" is between man and woman; slippery slope, will lead to more radical forms of marriage.

Table 2.4 Opponents' definitions of gay marriage issue in hearings before the Connecticut legislature, 2001–3

	Frequency of definition as % of all definitions asserted ($N = 165$)	% of speeches that include definition ($N = 58$)
Gay marriage threatens/will weaken traditional marriage and family	19 (32)	55
Marriage uniquely heterosexual because of "procreative" and "unitive" capabilities; procreation is key purpose of marriage	16 (26)	45
Homosexuality/gay marriage immoral/ sanctions homosexuality; violates religious precepts	12 (20)	34
Marriage across time/cultures limited to men and women	10 (16)	28
Slippery slope; will lead to more radical forms of marriage	10 (16)	28
Gay relationships not equivalent to heterosexual in status/importance to society; gay marriage ends special status of heterosexual marriage; heterosexual relationships of superior quality	7 (11)	19
Children need a mother and father/male and female role models	5 (9)	16
Other[a]	21 (44)	36
Total	100	

Notes: Numbers in parentheses are frequencies. When summed, the frequencies for the "percent of speeches that include definition" exceed the total N because many speeches include more than one definition.

[a]Definitions found in less than 15% of speeches: gay relationships defective, diseased, selfish, hedonistic, promiscuous; sexual orientation chosen; practical need for gay marriage exaggerated/gays already can get legal protection; studies of gays as good parents are flawed; gay marriage unpopular; not long enough to know effects in Vermont; heterosexuals will want civil unions too; gay marriage will trample on religious freedom; claims on benefits high for government; minorities are subjugating the majority; dictionary definition of "marriage" is between man and woman.

and state *"defense* of marriage" acts convey the sense of an institution under siege. The debate transcripts are replete with warnings that gay marriage will set off an apocalyptic chain of events ending in the destruction of marriage, the family, and "our civilization." Examples include the following:[13]

> If traditional marriage is thrown by the wayside, brought down by your manipulation of the definition that has been accepted since the beginning of civilized society, children will suffer because family will lose its very essence. Instead of trying to ruin families we should be preserving them for future generations. (U.S. Congress, House 1996, H7488)

> I am convinced that our country can survive many things, but one thing it cannot survive is the destruction of the family unit which forms the foundation of our society. Those among us who truly desire a strong and thriving America for our children and grandchildren will defend traditional heterosexual marriage and will vote for final passage of this [DOMA] bill. (U.S. Congress, House 1996, H7442)

Opponents frequently place gay marriage in a broader historical context of the social changes ignited by the sexual revolution and feminist movement of the 1960s. Gay marriage, they argue, would further weaken institutions beleaguered by high rates of divorce, out-of-wedlock births, cohabitation, and single parenthood: "The institution of marriage is already reeling because of the effects of the sexual revolution, no-fault divorce, and out-of-wedlock births. We have reaped the consequences of its devaluation. It is exceedingly imprudent to conduct a radical, untested and inherently flawed social experimentation on an institution that is the keystone and the arch of civilization" (U.S. Congress, House 1996, H7276).

In the federal DOMA debate, almost half of the speeches also defined the issue procedurally—as the need for the federal government to protect states that did not want to recognize gay marriages. Forty-four percent of the assertions spoke to a variety of procedural (e.g., federalism), political (public disapproval), and nonmoral (e.g., "tradition") principles. Senate supporters of DOMA sidestepped the substantive merits of the issue most often, arguing that the federal government was obligated to protect states from being forced to recognize same-sex marriages by "activist" judges in other states and to guard the federal Treasury against gay and lesbian claims for benefits. According to Senator Don Nickles:

It has become clear that advocates of same-sex unions intend to win the lawsuit in Hawaii and then invoke the full faith and credit clause to force the other 49 states to accept same-sex unions. Many states are justifiably concerned that Hawaii's recognition of same-sex unions will compromise their own laws prohibiting such marriages. . . . This bill would address this issue head-on, and it would allow each State to make the final determination for itself. . . . I cannot envision a more appropriate time for invoking our constitutional authority to define the nature of the States' obligation to one another. (U.S. Congress, Senate 1996b, S10103)

Morality and religion were less important than other definitions. About one-third of the speeches in the House and Senate debates defined the issue in terms of morally sanctioning homosexuality or violating religious principles. House members were more likely to assert the definition (39 percent) than senators (25 percent). The moral/religious definition ranked third in importance in the House debate, sixth in the Senate, and fourth in the two chambers combined. It constituted only 14 percent of all definitions asserted for the debates in the two chambers. In the Connecticut marriage debate, speakers put forward the moral definition in about one-third of the speeches, ranking it a fairly distant third.

A Threat to Heterosexual Status

What do opponents find so threatening about gay marriage? How do they think same-sex marriage will harm marriage and the family? Supporters of same-sex unions often seem baffled by the argument that gay marriage will damage society.[14] They point out that heterosexuals would remain entitled to all of the rights and benefits that they currently enjoy whether or not society allows same-sex couples to marry. Opponents are not distressed by the prospect of losing anything tangible, however. Their anxiety stems from a conviction that sharing their exclusive privileges with a class of citizens whose relationships are inferior will jeopardize the superior status of heterosexuality in the culture:[15]

Destroying the *exclusive* territory of marriage to achieve a political end . . . may eventually be the final blow to the American family. (U.S. Congress, House 1996, H7276, emphasis added)

To insist that male-male or female-female relationships must have the *same status* as the marriage relationship is more than unwise, it is patently absurd. (U.S. Congress, Senate 1996b, S10109, emphasis added)

The family is the basic unit of society. Treating other relationships as being equal to traditional marriage will significantly harm marriage, family and society. . . . Homosexuals do not have . . . a right to have their relationships recognized in law as having *a status in any way similar to the union of a heterosexual married couple.* (Connecticut General Assembly 2001, emphasis added)[16]

Rationales for Heterosexual Privilege

What reasons do gay marriage opponents give for reserving marriage exclusively for heterosexuals and defining it as a heterosexual institution? Opponents argue on a variety of grounds for privileging heterosexuality. One of the most important is *tradition*—that society has always reserved marriage for heterosexuals. Half of the opponents' speeches in the House and Senate and more than a quarter in the Connecticut hearings included the argument that marriage over time and across cultures was limited to men and women. For many speakers, the mere fact that few, if any, societies have allowed same-sex marriages was proof that it could not possibly be a good idea: "for thousands of years and across many, many different cultures, a definition of marriage that transcends time has always been one man and one woman united for the purposes of forming a family" (Rep. Steve Largent, R-OK, U.S. Congress, House 1996, H7443).

The question of who society should allow to marry is beyond political contestation: "the institution [of marriage] is not a creation of the State. It is older than the government, older than the Constitution and the laws, older than the Union, older than the Western tradition of political democracy from which our Republic springs, and I think it is deeply rooted in the basic precepts of our civilization" (Rep. James Talent, R-MO, U.S. Congress, House 1996, H7446).

A second important justification for reserving marriage for heterosexual couples is that they are superior to homosexual relationships. Gay rights opponents designate the traditional family of a heterosexual couple with children as the "ideal" and "standard" against which all other relationships must be judged. Homosexual relationships lack "equivalence" to those of heterosexuals and cannot possibly attain the standard set by heterosexual unions:[17]

> Marriage is a social, legal and spiritual union between a man and a woman. Other relationships may be loving, but have not been accorded the *same status* as marriage because they do not contribute in the same way to the social good. (Connecticut General Assembly 2001, emphasis added)[18]

> My district says it is time to say that homosexuality should not be sanctioned on an *equal level* with heterosexuality, and there are lots of reasons to back that up. (Rep. Largent, U.S. Congress, House 1996, H7444, emphasis added)

> Every government must set certain standards as sign posts. It must create expectations for responsible behavior. Not every lifestyle is equal for the purpose of the common good. This does not mean the persecution of those who fall short of *the standard*, but it does mean giving legal preference to that standard. . . . A government that values freedom can permit some things that it would not encourage or condone. But a government must also promote things that are worthy examples and *social ideals*. (U.S. Congress, Senate 1996b, S4947–48, emphasis added)

What do opponents of same-sex marriage argue is the source of the superiority of heterosexual unions? First, they point out that only hetero-sexual couples can procreate:[19]

> We have set up our society on the basis of children who come into the world, and we honor the institution that brings children into the world and gives them values, by according special standing to marriage. (Sen. John Ashcroft, R-MO, U.S. Congress, Senate 1996b, S10121)

> [S]aying to me that homosexual persons have a great relationship, that they make great parents doesn't, in and of itself, mean that their relationship is the same as marriage. It doesn't mean it's the same as a man and a wife begetting and raising children. (Connecticut General Assembly 2002)[20]

Some opponents also argue that homosexual relationships provide a poor foundation for raising children because they are "unstable," cannot provide children with male and female role models, and will affect children adversely in a variety of ways.

Finally, opponents justify the privileged position of heterosexuality on moral grounds:

> [Gay marriage] is an attempt to evade the basic question of whether the law of this country should treat homosexual relationships as morally equivalent to heterosexual relationships. This is what is at stake here: should the law express its neutrality between homosexual and heterosexual relationships? (Rep. Charles Canady, R-FL, U.S. Congress, House 1996, H7447)

> Our law should not treat homosexual relationships as the *moral equivalent* of the heterosexual relationships on which the family is based. (U.S. Congress, House 1996, H7441)

Civil Unions

Many opponents of gay marriage also view civil unions or any status that approximates marriage as a threat.[21] They worry that civil unions will create a new institution that would compete with marriage or that people may view as an acceptable alternative to it. According to an opponent of a bill to establish civil unions in Connecticut, "What the proponents [of civil unions] forget . . . is that the law does something other than just cure inequities. It teaches. And what it teaches when you allow civil unions . . . is that we don't have in our society one institution, one social institution that is preeminently the institution that creates and nourishes the family, but we say that it is only one of several ideals" (Connecticut General Assembly 2001, 67).

In sum, opponents most prefer to define gay marriage as a serious threat to the institutions of marriage and the family, the tradition and "ideal" of exclusively heterosexual marriage, and, at the federal level, the need to protect the states from having same-sex marriage imposed on them. Morality definitions rank third and fourth in importance, well behind these others.

ADOPTION

Opponents of allowing gays to adopt children stress the negative effects of such a policy on children, marriage, and families. They define the issue in terms of moral disapproval of homosexuality much less often. Tables 2.5 and 2.6 report the definitions that opponents of gay adoption used in news

Table 2.5 Opponents' definitions of gay adoption, news articles, January 1994–July 2004[a]

	Frequency of definition as % of all definitions published ($N = 588$)	% of articles that include definition ($N = 532$)
Families headed by heterosexual couples better for children; homosexual relationships unstable, inferior	21 (124)	23 (122)
Homosexuality immoral, unnatural, violates religious precepts, will harm children morally	14 (82)	15 (80)
Children need both male and female role models for their social and psychological development	10 (61)	11 (59)
Gay parents endanger health, welfare, and development of children	10 (61)	11 (59)
Children of gay parents more likely to experiment with homosexuality, become gay, or struggle with sexual identity	8 (48)	9 (48)
Activist judges should show restraint; defer to legislatures in adoption policy	7 (44)	8 (43)
Studies showing positive results of gay parenting inconclusive, poorly designed or biased	5 (29)	6 (32)
Gay adoption threatens traditional marriage, family, or society	5 (27)	5 (27)
Slippery slope, gay marriage will redefine marriage, may lead to marriage; effort to advance other parts of gay agenda	4 (25)	5 (27)
Law does not permit second-parent adoption	4 (24)	5 (27)
Other[b]	9 (41)	9 (48)
Total	100	

Notes: Numbers in parentheses are frequencies. When summed, the frequencies for the "percent of speeches that include definition" exceed the total N because many speeches include more than one definition.

[a]LexisNexis search of news reports, editorials, and letters to the editor under "gay adoption" and "homosexual adoption" for years specified.

[b]Definitions found in less than 5% of articles: children will be stigmatized, harassed; gay adoption is unconstitutional; gay adoption could lead to multiple parents, bizarre family structures; studies show heterosexual families superior, more stable, gays are unstable; states should decide issue; sexual orientation chosen; only married people should be allowed to adopt.

Table 2.6 Opponents' definitions of gay adoption, Connecticut legislature, 2000

	Frequency of definition as % of all assertions of definitions (N = 23)	% of speeches that include definition (N = 15)
Slippery slope; gay adoption may lead to gay marriage; "real" aim is gay marriage	26 (6)	40 (6)
Heterosexual parents "best" for children; children need male and female role models to prevent gender/sexual identity confusion, homosexuality	17 (4)	27 (4)
May allow heterosexuals to parent outside of marriage if gays allowed to adopt	13 (3)	20 (3)
Threatens traditional marriage and family; will lead to family disintegration	9 (2)	13 (2)
May lead to gays as legally protected class; give gays "special rights"	9 (2)	13 (2)
Homosexuality immoral, goes against religious teaching; children may be morally harmed	9 (2)	13 (2)
Other[a]	17 (4)	27 (4)
Total	100	

Notes: Numbers in parentheses are frequencies. When summed, the frequencies for the "percent of speeches that include definition" exceed the total N because many speeches include more than one definition.

[a]Children may reject parents; become stigmatized (1); may lead to adoption by more than two adults (1); judges should investigate/take into account sexual orientation of prospective parents (1); standards for adoption are too vague (1).

reports and editorials from 1994 to 2004 and the debate in the Connecticut legislature in 2000.[22] The survey of newspaper articles provides a much larger number of observations and a more representative sample of opponents' definitions.

Opponents define the issue most frequently in terms of parental qualifications—the kinds of parents that are "best" for children. The *Tampa Tribune* quoted Mathew Staver, president of the Liberty Counsel, a conservative public interest law firm in Florida, as follows: "The real basis for the law in the [adoption] case is not morality, it is the best interests of the children." Having children raised by heterosexual parents is an "undisputed fact" (Silvestrini 2003). The *Deseret News* in Salt Lake City, Utah, quoted the Reverend Louis P. Sheldon, chairman of the Traditional Values Coalition, as stating that "a child is best brought up in a two-parent family consisting of a man and a woman" (Farrington 2001b). According to the *Pittsburgh Post-Gazette*, Kay Eisenhour, director of adoptions at Catholic Charities of the Diocese of Harrisburg, Pennsylvania, "while these [same-sex] living arrangements exist in our society, they are not considered to be optimal for the well-being of children" (Bull 2001).

Why do opponents think that straights make better parents than gays? First, they argue that gay relationships are unstable and problematic. According to Dr. William Brown (2002), a pediatrician quoted in the *Rocky Mountain News*, "Many of us believe that the sexual practices of homosexuals do not provide a healthy environment for children. The homosexual coupling is much more fragile and short-lasting than heterosexual marriages." Fred K. Schwartz, in a letter to the editor of the *Pasadena Star-News*, wrote, "The International Journal of Epidemiology has reported that among homosexuals there is an increased incidence of suicide, depression, multiple sexual partners and domestic violence compared to the heterosexual population. Surely, children deserve a more stable environment!"[23]

Most importantly, opponents allege that gay parenting harms children in a variety of specific ways. The harms that gay parents inflict upon children constitute a majority of the definitions put forward by opponents. Same-sex parenting deprives children of male and female role models that they need to appreciate each gender's "unique" nature and avoid confusion about their sexual orientation and gender identity. According to Tom Prichard, president of the Minnesota Family Council, who was quoted in the Minneapolis *Star Tribune*, "Clearly, foster care is not the ideal, but do we want to open up the door to other problems in the child's life? Children look at how their parents interact as a mom and a dad. With gay or lesbian parents there would be gender confusion issues in the mind of a small child" (Francis 2004). The Associated Press quoted Kenneth Connor, president of the Family Research Council, who argued that "We oppose adoption by homosexuals because it trivializes the contribution that each gender, male and female alike, make[s] to the physical, emotional and psychosocial development of their children" (Viega 2002).[24] Many opponents quote from a denunciation of gay marriage and adoption that the Vatican issued in 2003, which describes allowing gays to adopt children as "doing violence to these children, in the sense that their condition of dependency would be used to place them in an environment that is not conducive to their full human development" (quoted in Fusco 2003).

In sum, well over half of the definitions asserted in the news reports and editorials dealt with the superior quality of heterosexual relationships and parenting and the negative impacts on children, marriage, and the family that one might expect if society allowed gays to adopt.

Table 2.6 reports data from the Connecticut legislative debates. It shows opponents expressing a greater concern than shown in the news articles that allowing gays to adopt will lead to gay marriage. The "slippery slope" definition ranked at the top of the list in the Connecticut debate but showed up much less often in the newspaper articles:

> You know what's going on in this place. . . . The passage of this [bill] will only lead to the goal of its promoters which is the recognition of same sex marriage. (Connecticut General Assembly 2000c, 201, 203)[25]

> This is another step along the way where we are denigrating and taking away from the public policy standard that we ought to have with respect to marriage. (quoted in Gorlick 2000)

The argument that adoption would pave the way to marriage was plausible given the virtual certainty that the legislature would approve gay adoption, and opponents were looking to the next gay rights battle.

Issue definitions rooted in moral and religious disapproval of homosexuality show up more prominently in the newspaper articles than in the legislative debate. Perhaps this is because the newspaper sample includes letters to the editor written by spokespersons for socially conservative groups and members of the public committed to fighting gay rights, rather than legislators. The articles also include newspapers from the South, where fundamentalist Christians are much more numerous than they are in a New England legislature. Still, only 15 percent of the articles defined the issue in terms of the immorality of homosexuality, the violation of religious injunctions against homosexuality, or same-sex couples harming children's moral development if the state allowed gays to adopt. Morality definitions constituted a similarly modest proportion of total definitions asserted in the articles. And when opponents expressed moral reservations, they often did so in the context of fear about children's development rather than their disapproval of homosexuality as intrinsically immoral.

In sum, although morality is not a trivial consideration in how opponents define same-sex marriage and adoption, opponents prefer to frame these issues mainly in terms of negative consequences for marriage, family, and children.

MILITARY, HATE CRIMES, AND CIVIL RIGHTS ISSUES

We saw in chapter 1 that hate crimes, military, and civil rights (marketplace discrimination) issues threaten the public much less than relationship issues. Nondiscrimination in employment, housing, and military service are not directly relevant to the legitimacy of homosexual relationships and do not confer a status that has been exclusively reserved for heterosexuals. Yet how gay rights opponents define these issues still matters. The military ban remains in place, and many states and localities still do not have hate crimes and antidiscrimination laws covering sexual orientation. The way that opponents define issues may reduce the public's support for gay rights at critical times, such as when an issue is up for a decision. Although a majority of the public has favored lifting the ban on gays in the military, their level of support dropped when the issue was on the agenda in 1993. Most polls showed that between 57 and 60 percent of the public favored lifting the ban between 1989 and 1992, but support dropped to between 37 and 47 percent in 1993.[26] Even when support for gay rights remains consistently high, as with some efforts to enact laws against discrimination in employment and housing, how opponents define issues helps to mobilize their supporters, which in turn may spell defeat for antidiscrimination measures in states and localities where antirights forces are more numerous.

The Military Ban

Table 2.7 reports opponents' issue definitions in congressional debate on whether to lift the ban on gays serving in the military or codify it under the "don't ask, don't tell" policy. About one-third of the opposition's assertions and more than half of their speeches addressed the consequences that lifting the ban would have on military effectiveness; how the loss of privacy would reduce effectiveness; and, more vaguely, how lifting the ban was incompatible with the "unique" nature of military service.

Members of Congress argued most often that the issue was about pre-serving morale, trust, and cohesion within military units and their impor-tance for the effectiveness of the armed services:[27]

> This is a matter of winning on the battlefield. Second place does not count on the battlefield. Unit cohesion is uppermost. (U.S. Congress, House 1993, H7078)[28]

> Cohesion is the single most important factor in military success. Open homosexuality destroys it. In units with such problems, a breakdown in morale and effectiveness is sure to follow. A commander is faced with practical problems of dissent and resentment that can undermine everything he has carefully built. (U.S. Congress, Senate 1993, S7607)[29]

Procedural definitions also accounted for more than one-third of all the definitions that members of Congress asserted. Legislators insisted that the issue was about deferring to the views of the military's rank and file[30] and leaders on the Joint Chiefs of Staff, who had the most familiarity with military life and whom lifting the ban would directly affect:[31]

> Those Members [of Congress] that support the total lifting of the ban on homosexuals, that have never fired a shot in anger, that have never been in combat, I would ask them to stick to the areas that they are knowledgeable about. Because both Colin Powell, the Joint Chiefs, and the rest of them, have stated that homosexuals are not compatible in the service. Ninety-seven percent of those people that have to serve with them say it is not compatible with what they do. . . . When 97 percent of the military do not support it, it is wrong. (U.S. Congress, House 1993, H6070)[32]

> It was General [Norman] Schwarzkopf who commented—and General Schwarzkopf . . . was commander of personnel during the eighties before he advanced to his assignment as commander of our forces in the Persian Gulf, and so he had some very direct experience with personnel policies—and commenting on that he said: In every case—not most cases—in every case where homosexuality became known in the unit, it resulted in a breakdown in morale, cohesion, effectiveness—with resulting dissent, resentment and even violence. (U.S. Congress, Senate 1993, S7604)[33]

Table 2.7 Definitions offered by opponents to congressional lifting of ban on gays in the military, 1993

	House		Senate		Total	
	Frequency of definition as % of all assertions of definitions (N = 52)	% of speeches that include definition (N = 22)	Frequency of definition as % of all assertions of definitions (N = 39)	% of speeches that include definition (N = 13)	Frequency of definition as % of all assertions of definition (N = 91)	% of speeches that include definition (N = 35)
Lifting ban threatens morale, trust, cohesion of military units	23 (12)	55 (12)	18 (7)	54 (7)	21 (19)	54 (19)
Service members and veterans favor ban; predict negative consequences	17 (9)	41 (9)	8 (3)	23 (3)	13 (12)	32 (11)
Congress obliged to codify/clarify policy; codification necessary	6 (3)	14 (3)	16 (6)	46 (6)	10 (9)	26 (9)
Military unique job; U.S. military unique	10 (5)	23 (5)	8 (3)	23 (3)	9 (8)	23 (8)
Powell,[a] other military leaders support ban	10 (5)	23 (5)	5 (2)	15 (2)	8 (7)	20 (7)

Definition						
Homosexuality immoral/violates religious precepts/constituents feel that way	17 (6)	7 (6)	8 (1)	3 (1)	23 (5)	10 (5)
President Clinton supports "don't ask, don't tell"	17 (6)	7 (6)	23 (3)	8 (3)	14 (3)	6 (3)
Privacy of heterosexual personnel	14 (5)	6 (5)	31 (4)	10 (4)	5 (1)	2 (1)
Serving in military not a constitutional right	11 (4)	4 (4)	8 (1)	3 (1)	14 (3)	6 (3)
Courts upheld ban; courts defer to military and Congress	11 (4)	4 (4)	23 (3)	8 (3)	5 (1)	2 (1)
Other[b]	16 (6)	11 (11)	25 (3)	16 (6)	23 (5)	10 (5)
Totals		100		101		101

Notes: Numbers in parentheses are frequencies. When summed, the frequencies for the "percent of speeches that include definition" exceed the total N because many speeches include more than one definition.

[a] Refers to Gen. Colin Powell, then chairman of the Joint Chiefs of Staff.

[b] Definitions found in less than 10% of speeches: the military is "no place for social experiments"; RAND (1993) study includes faulty inferences; analogies to race/gender are inappropriate; homosexual status is for all purposes the same as conduct; public opinion against lifting ban; lifting ban will worsen AIDS crisis.

Other procedural arguments were that Congress was institutionally obliged to codify the ban, that the courts had ruled that there was no constitutional right to serve in the military, and that President Clinton supported the "don't ask, don't tell" compromise:

> The Constitution . . . makes it very clear that Congress has the responsibility to deal with matters of this nature affecting the Armed Forces of the United States. . . . The question of whether homosexuals should serve in the military is an issue on which Congress and the President share constitutional authority. (U.S. Congress, Senate 1993, S755)[34]

> [T]his approach will make the ban law, avoiding the lawsuits that would have resulted under the President's ambiguous policy, and effectively concluding this painful and divisive debate by removing it from the realm of administrative policy. (U.S. Congress, Senate 1993, S11227)[35]

Less than 10 percent of all assertions made during this congressional debate were about the immorality of homosexuality, and the morality definition appeared in less than 20 percent of the speeches.

Hate Crimes

Next, we look at how opponents define the issue of covering gays and lesbians under hate crimes laws at the federal and state levels. Tables 2.8 and 2.9 present the definitions put forward in news articles and congressional debate on the issue. First, once again, opponents do not make the morality of homosexuality and religious injunctions against it a central part of their effort to define the issue of including gays in hate crimes laws. The morality definition ranks fourth in importance among eight definitions as only 7 percent of all definitions put forward; further, only 12 percent of articles included the morality definition. Second, turning to the congressional debates over the issue, the morality/religious definition does not register at all. Not a single speech could be found in the 106th and 108th Congresses, the time frame in which the issue was on the agenda and debated, in which members of the House or Senate argued that gays should not be included in the hate crimes law because of the morality of homosexuality or its inconsistency with religious precepts.

In congressional debate, opponents frame the issue most often in procedural terms. They argue that federal hate crimes laws are unnecessary

Table 2.8 Opponents' definitions of including sexual orientation under hate crimes laws, news articles, 1985–2000

	Frequency of definition as % of all definitions published ($N = 526$)	% of articles that include definition ($N = 316$)
Confers "special rights"; treats citizens unequally; divides/differentiates among Americans	29 (152)	45 (142)
Tramples on free speech/expression; government control of thought	24 (128)	36 (114)
Hate crimes laws unnecessary; violent crimes already illegal; better enforcement of existing laws needed	13 (70)	22 (70)
Condones homosexuality; homosexuality immoral, against God, religious teachings	7 (40)	12 (38)
Cannot "legislate morality"; will not deter hate crimes	7 (35)	11 (35)
Federal government interference with states; federal intervention unnecessary	7 (35)	10 (32)
Hate crimes too difficult to prosecute; cannot determine motives; burdensome for police	5 (27)	8 (25)
Places gays on par with other protected classes; slippery slope will lead to additional gay rights	5 (28)	9 (28)
Other	2 (11)	3 (9)
Total	99	

Note: Numbers in parentheses are frequencies. When summed, the frequencies for the "percent of speeches that include definition" exceed the total *N* because many speeches include more than one definition.

because murder, assault, and other violent acts are already crimes; federal hate crimes laws further "federalize" criminal law and place greater burdens on federal prosecutors; and hate crimes legislation is an unconstitutional expansion of Congress's regulatory powers and violate the equal protection clause of the Fourteenth Amendment. Senator Orrin Hatch (R-UT), the leading opponent of expanding the federal hate crimes law,

Table 2.9 Opponents' definitions of including sexual orientation under hate crimes laws, debates in the 106th U.S. Congress (1999–2000) and 108th Congress (2003–4)

	Frequency of definition as % of total assertions of definitions ($N = 74$)	% of speeches that include definition ($N = 33$)
Federal government interference with states; federal intervention unnecessary	35 (26)	79 (26)
Confers "special rights"; treats citizens unequally; divides/differentiates among Americans	19 (14)	42 (14)
Hate crimes laws unnecessary; violent crimes already illegal; better enforcement of existing laws needed	12 (9)	27 (9)
Tramples on free speech/expression; government control of thought	9 (7)	21 (7)
Hate crimes too difficult to prosecute; cannot determine motives; burdensome for police	8 (6)	18 (6)
Condones homosexuality; homosexuality immoral, against God, religious teachings	0 (0)	0 (0)
Other	16 (12)	36 (12)
Total	99	

Note: Numbers in parentheses are frequencies. When summed, the frequencies for the "percent of speeches that include definition" exceed the total N because many speeches include more than one definition.

put it this way in his characterization of Senator Edward M. Kennedy's (D-MA) proposed measure to include gays under the hate crimes law (U.S. Congress, Senate 2000a, S5339):

> For supporters of the Kennedy amendment, Federal leadership necessitates Federal control. I do not subscribe to this view, especially when it comes to this problem. . . . It proposes that to combat hate crimes Congress should enact a new tier of far-reaching Federal criminal legislation. That approach strays from the foundations

of our constitutional structure—namely, the first principles of federalism that for more than two centuries have vested States with primary responsibility for prosecuting crimes committed within their boundaries. As important as this issue is, there is little evidence that a broad federalization of hate crimes is warranted. . . . In addition, serious constitutional questions exist regarding the Kennedy hate crimes amendment.

Setting aside Congressional opponents' focus on procedural definitions, the debates and news articles show that opponents most often define the issue as unequal treatment before the law ("special rights" for gays and other hate crimes victims) and as an infringement upon freedom of expression and thought. Those two definitions appear in 45 percent and 36 percent of articles, respectively.[36] According to William Raspberry (2000) in the Albany, New York, *Times Union*:

I have two problems with that line of thinking [hate crimes laws]. First is the division of American citizens into various categories more or less worthy of whatever protection the law can give them. If we want to provide special status for blacks and Jews, for instance, what about homeless bums who may find themselves subject to attack for what they are? What about special protection for abortionists, or drug dealers, or prostitutes? . . . And the other problem: Hate-crime legislation finally turns out to be an attempt at thought control. It says we'll punish you for what you did, yes, but also for what you were thinking when you did it. It says we'll punish you not merely for your racist or antigay behavior but also for your bigoted beliefs. How can so many thoughtful people believe that punishing thought is a good idea?

An editorial published in *The Record* of Bergen County, New Jersey (1999), states, "hate crimes legislation would create a special class of victim, in essence, saying crimes against some people are worse than crimes against others." Jeff Jacoby (2000), in the *Milwaukee Journal Sentinel*, wrote, "there is no way around it: A law that cracks down harder on criminals who harm members of certain groups by definition goes easier on those who target victims from other groups." And the *South Bend* (IN) *Tribune* (2000) asked, "How would a prosecutor prove bigoted thought? By citing its expression in bigoted speech, of course, at the expense of the First Amendment. There is no other way." Representatives of conservative religious and "profamily" groups often argue on freedom of expression grounds that their antigay views will be used to muzzle their opposition to hate crimes legislation. Such laws, according to Steven Schwalm, a spokesperson for the Family Research Council, "have nothing to do with perpetrators of violent crime and everything to do with silencing political opposition. It would criminalize pro-family beliefs. This basically sends a message that you can't disagree with the political message of homosexual activists" (quoted in Brooke 1998).[37]

In sum, like the other issues we have looked at, opponents of including gays and lesbians under hate crimes laws do not usually define the issue in terms of morality and religious principles. Opponents to the issue speaking in the congressional chambers focus most often on procedural issues concerned with the law, federalism, and constitutionality. Citizens, columnists, and state and local political actors most often define the issue in terms of equal treatment under the law and freedom of thought and expression.

Antidiscrimination in the Marketplace

Finally, we turn to how opponents define the issue of antidiscrimination in employment, housing, and public accommodations. Table 2.10 reports the results for the U.S. Senate debate over the Employment Non-Discrimination Act, which would guarantee civil rights protection in employment for gays and lesbians throughout the United States. First, opponents defined the issue in terms of increased regulatory burdens, litigation, and government power over business. This definition appeared in 94 percent of all the opponents' speeches. For example:

> Mr. President, while the proponents of this bill have tried to minimize the potential impact of the bill, the fact is that, if it passes, the public and private employers of America subject to title VII [of the Civil Rights Act] will face the juggernaut of the Federal enforcement machinery. Anyone who contends that this bill will not result in a litigation boom is not paying attention to the caseloads at the [Equal Employment Opportunity Commission] and Department of Justice. (U.S. Congress, Senate 1996a, S100003)[38]

> I believe that the act sets the stage for an enormous expansion of Federal power over employers. The bill virtually guarantees an avalanche of costly litigation which could hurt small businesses most of all. (U.S. Congress, Senate 1996a, S10004)[39]

Table 2.10 Opponents' issue definitions in the debate over the Employment Non-Discrimination Act, U.S. Senate, 1996

	Frequency of definition as % of total assertions of definitions ($N = 65$)	% of speeches that include definition ($N = 18$)
Increasing regulatory burdens/ "big" government	26 (17)	94 (17)
Curtailing freedom of religion/ religious association	17 (11)	61 (11)
Homosexuality/homosexual conduct immoral/violates religious teaching; law would legitimate	15 (10)	56 (10)
Threatening the welfare of children	12 (8)	44 (8)
Giving gays "special rights"	8 (5)	28 (5)
Gay orientation chosen	6 (4)	22 (4)
Other[a]	15 (10)	55 (10)
Total	99	

Notes: Numbers in parentheses are frequencies. When summed, the frequencies for the "percent of speeches that include definition" exceed the total N because many speeches include more than one definition.

[a]Definitions found in less than 15% of speeches: discrimination is not a problem; slippery slope, will lead to gay marriage, etc.; will lead to divisions in the workplace; public does not support; exemptions too limited; sodomy laws still in existence; states' rights; gays have more money and opportunity than other Americans and do not need protection; gays are powerful and militant.

Second, opponents defined the issue in terms of protecting religious freedom and freedom of association (61 percent of speeches). For example, "ENDA would mean that ethical and religious objections to homosexual or bisexual conduct would have to be pushed aside or closeted. Those objections could no longer touch the workplace" (U.S. Congress, Senate 1996a, 10135).[40]

The debates at the state and local levels paint a different picture. Opponents most often define the issue in moral terms and much less often as a regulatory burden imposed by government (see table 2.11). Moral or religious objections as grounds for opposing nondiscrimination laws made up

Table 2.11 Opponents' issue definitions in debates over employment and housing nondiscrimination legislation, state and local levels

	Frequency of definition as % of total assertions of definitions			% of speeches that include definition		
	1984–90 (N = 150)	1991–2001 (N = 115)	Total (N = 265)	1984–90 (N = 70)	1991–2001 (N = 80)	Total (N = 150)
Homosexuality/homosexual conduct immoral/violates religious teaching; law would legitimate	26 (39)	21 (24)	24 (63)	56 (39)	30 (24)	42 (63)
Discrimination not a problem	17 (25)	13 (15)	15 (40)	36 (25)	19 (15)	27 (41)
Curtailing freedom of religion/religious association	13 (20)	16 (18)	14 (38)	29 (20)	23 (18)	25 (38)
Threatening the welfare of children	9 (14)	16 (18)	12 (32)	20 (14)	23 (18)	21 (32)
Slippery slope/will lead to gay marriage, etc.	14 (21)	5 (6)	10 (27)	30 (21)	8 (10)	18 (27)
Increasing regulatory burdens/"big" government	7 (10)	12 (14)	9 (24)	14 (10)	18 (14)	16 (24)
Giving gays "special rights"	7 (10)	10 (11)	8 (21)	14 (10)	14 (11)	14 (21)
Gay orientation chosen	7 (11)	8 (9)	8 (20)	16 (11)	11 (9)	13 (20)
Total	100	101	100			

Note: Numbers in parentheses are frequencies. When summed, the frequencies for the "percent of speeches that include definition" exceed the total N because many speeches include more than one definition.

about a quarter of all the assertions and appeared in more than 40 percent of speeches. For example:

> I think that we're heading down [sic] the wrong direction and I
> think our very Judeo-Christian principles, ethics and morals are going
> to be questioned and we are going to be fighting for our very lives
> philosophically, religiously and spiritually. (Maryland Senate 2001, 23)[41]

> There are matters on which we are morally obliged to discriminate.
> What we do here today flies in the face of nearly four thousand years of
> recorded history. (Rhode Island House 1990, 1)[42]

Typically, opponents' condemnations of homosexuality are somewhat ambiguous and implicit. Instead of explicitly condemning homosexuality as immoral and invoking religion and God, they argue that the issue is about the state condoning and legitimating a particular lifestyle.[43] For example:

> The issue is that the primary purpose of this bill . . . [is] to put the stamp
> of approval on a particular lifestyle. I don't think we should get into that
> kind of business. (Massachusetts House 1989, 25)[44]

> In Minnesota, the Human Rights Commission will be directed to enact
> policies to educate the public. I don't know how you can educate the
> public without endorsing the lifestyle. That is a concern for me and
> others. (Minnesota Senate 1993)[45]

As prevalent as the morality definition is in this case, opponents have been using it less than in the past. Table 2.11 divides the sample into two periods, before and after 1991, which was about the time when opinion polls began to report a decline in the public's moral disapproval of homosexuality (see figure 2.1). The table shows a sharp decrease from 56 to 30 percent in the proportion of speeches in which the morality definition appears. Second, aggregating the separate definitions related to the social consequences of antidiscrimination laws reveals that opponents assert definitions concerning social consequences more often than moral aspects of the issue. Thirty-one percent of the definitions that speakers asserted were about the impacts of such laws on children, marriage, and regulatory burdens combined. Finally, when opponents define the issue in moral terms, they favor the implicit moral definition rather than the stronger explicit condemnation (see table 2.12). The implicit definition appears in one-third

Table 2.12 Frequency of implicit and explicit morality definitions of employment and housing discrimination issue

	Frequency of definition as % of total assertions of definitions			% of speeches that include definition		
	1984–90	1991–2001	Total	1984–90	1991–2001	Total
Legitimating homosexuality/ homosexual conduct	18 (30)	16 (19)	17 (49)	43	24	33
Homosexuality/homosexual conduct immoral/violates religious teaching	16 (26)	8 (10)	13 (36)	37	13	24

Note: Numbers in parentheses are frequencies. Frequencies total more than for combined morality definition calculated in table 2.11 because some of the explicit and implicit definitions appeared in the same speeches and were counted separately for the purpose of illustrating relative frequencies of the two kinds of morality definitions.

of the speeches, and the explicit definition shows up in less than a quarter of them. The explicit condemnation also fell more sharply than the implicit definition over the two periods, going from 37 percent to 13 percent compared with dropping from 43 percent to 24 percent for the implicit definition.

In sum, moral definitions were of secondary importance when the U.S. Senate debated whether to add sexual orientation to the nation's basic federal civil rights law. News reports indicated that the recent U.S. House of Representatives debate on the same legislation followed the same pattern (Neuman 2007). Opponents frame the issue most frequently in moral terms in debates at the state and local levels. Even in those venues, the proportion of speakers who assert moral definitions has declined and speakers prefer implicit moral judgments.

CONCLUSION

How opponents define the issues reveals what they find most threatening about gay rights and what they believe the public will find most threatening. In debates over gay marriage, adoption, legalization of homosexual conduct, and openly serving in the military, opponents most often define gay rights issues in terms of adverse consequences for key institutions and groups in society, such as marriage, the family, children, the military, and business. In debates over hate crimes, they define the issue most often in terms of liberal principles like freedom of thought and expression and equal treatment before the law. They also frame most of these issues in procedural terms by arguing that the federal government must protect states that do not want gay marriage, the views of the military should be controlling on the issue of banning gays, Congress is responsible for codifying the ban on gay service members, hate crimes laws should not be federalized and the states are prosecuting them effectively, and the repeal of sodomy laws is about judicial activism.

Gay rights opponents also define these issues as moral judgments about homosexuality, but those definitions were usually of secondary importance.[46] This finding suggests that opponents have strong incentives to downplay moral discourse in favor of talk about social consequences and procedures, despite the prevalence of religious fundamentalists and social conservatives among the opposition. Defining gay rights in moral terms is less politically advantageous than linking those rights to adverse impacts on a positively constructed group or institution and signals that opponents do not have a more compelling reason to oppose them. The number of Americans who object to homosexuality on moral grounds has declined, and the number willing to bracket whether homosexuality is immoral has increased. If the opponents' argument rests upon moral considerations alone, then those who bracket the moral question and who think the state should remain neutral lack a compelling reason to reject gay rights. Opponents may also find that they need to attract support from a pivotal group of moderates for whom ideological and religious objections to homosexuality may not resonate. Finally, framing issues in terms of consequences and procedures is less risky than harsh moral condemnations.

Opponents stress moral objections to homosexuality only at the state and local levels in debates over whether to pass laws against discrimination in employment and housing markets. Even in that context, they have lessened their use of morality-based definitions over time and have softened their tone by implying that homosexuality is immoral rather than explicitly condemning it. The fact that gay rights opponents at the state and local levels continue to rely upon framing the employment and housing discrimination issue in moral terms suggests that opponents recognize that they lack compelling arguments that expanding gay rights in this area will produce negative social consequences. Thus, they may view the old morality-based arguments as their only viable option. The propensity to frame gay rights issues in moral terms may also vary according to the institutional venue in which political actors debate issues. Congressional opponents, for example, apparently believe that arguments about social consequences (regulatory burdens imposed by "big government") are more persuasive than moral condemnations.

We can begin to see the relationship between issue definitions, perceptions of threat, and policy outcomes. Part of the argument of this book has been that whether gay rights advocates succeed in getting their policies adopted depends partly upon whether Americans view their demands as threatening. Hate crimes and nondiscrimination in employment and housing provide the clearest support for this thesis. We would not have expected that gay rights advocates would be relatively successful on these issues simply knowing the institutional context in which such measures are considered. Proposals to include sexual orientation in hate crimes and civil rights laws and ordinances are considered by elected legislative bodies and (in some jurisdictions) by voters through ballot referenda. These processes are highly vulnerable to campaigns by antigay rights forces and popular prejudices against gays that still exist.

The lack of threat that Americans perceive from protecting gays and lesbians against hate crimes and discrimination in employment and housing is critical for understanding the gay rights movement's relative success on these issues. The public overwhelmingly supports the principles that individuals should be judged solely on their performance on the job and that they should be secure from physical harm. The impersonal nature of marketplace and public safety issues raises none of the concerns that some heterosexuals have about homosexual conduct and relationship issues. These issues are the easiest for people to bracket the question of the morality of homosexuality. Hate crimes, in particular, are simple to frame as a public safety/criminal justice issue rather than gay rights.

Furthermore, opponents have a difficult time pointing out plausible adverse social consequences from instituting laws that protect individuals from hate crimes and discrimination in the marketplace. Although the argument against including gays under employment nondiscrimination, that it will add to regulatory burdens, has had currency in debate at the federal level, the economic costs argument is not as prevalent when the issue is debated at the state and local levels. Opponents, instead, resort to defining these issues either in terms of freedom of speech and equal treatment (in the case of hate crimes) or in moral terms (in the case of marketplace discrimination). But the morality definition is increasingly unpersuasive and irrelevant because fewer Americans today believe that homosexuality is immoral, and more of them are inclined to engage in moral bracketing.

The chapter's findings on same-sex marriage are also consistent with the thesis that threat perceptions shape the political fortunes of gay rights advocates. Most Americans find gay marriage highly threatening, and gays have been least successful on that issue. Marriage opponents frame the issue as a social calamity in which same-sex marriage will destroy marriage and the family. This definition exploits people's perceptions of gay marriage as a radical break with tradition that will make gay relationships more visible, jeopardize the cultural superiority of heterosexuality, and threaten heterosexual identity.

The findings from the military case are inconsistent with our expectation that gays will make more progress on issues that the public perceives as less threatening. The ban on gays in the military remains in place, even though a large number of Americans supports lifting it. Nevertheless, higher levels of perceived threat may remain latent until brought to the surface when the issue reaches the agenda. Once it became apparent that the ban on gays in the military might actually occur, and once antigay forces depicted such a possibility as jeopardizing military effectiveness, Americans became more anxious about lifting the ban, and President Clinton abandoned his plan to allow gays to serve in the military. This does not mean, however, that public opinion caused Clinton's failure and begs the question of who or what exploited the public's ambivalence.

The adoption and regulation of sexual conduct cases provide the least support for a link between perceptions of threat and relative success or failure of the gay rights movement. Americans are deeply split over permitting gay couples to adopt, yet a growing number of states and counties have been granting such adoptions. Americans are also divided over whether homosexual conduct should be legalized. Yet sodomy laws are a thing of the past. Gays have made more progress in adoption and legalizing homosexual conduct than in the military, even though the level of public support in these cases would have led us to expect the opposite outcome. They have also made much more progress in adoption and legalizing homosexual conduct than in marriage, even though Americans are generally uncomfortable with expanding gay rights in all three areas.

Why did gay rights opponents fail to translate the threat that Americans perceive from legalizing homosexual conduct and permitting gays to adopt children into effective resistance, as they have done with marriage? How have they succeeded in blocking efforts to lift the ban on gays in the military despite public support (or at least acquiescence) for the change? We explore these outcomes in chapters 4, 5, and 6, but first we turn to an examination of the definitions that those who support gay rights put forward.

Advocating Gay Rights

3

Gay rights advocates inside and outside of government are visible participants in the policymaking process. What advocates have to say about issues indicates what definitions they believe might help their cause, even though it is not clear how much their efforts contribute to political attitudes and policy decisions. The media disseminates what advocates say about their goals and the likely effects of the policies they support. What they say may help to mobilize their supporters (and perhaps their opponents) and persuade those who are ambivalent to adopt a firm position on an issue. Some citizens and policymakers may be persuaded by what advocates tell them (or what they hear from others) in public discourse, even though what advocates say is only one possible source of attitudes toward gays rights issues.

This chapter starts by examining how gay rights supporters define the three issues that the public perceives as least threatening, followed by the issues that it perceives as more threatening. We look to see if the kinds of issue definitions change across issues, according to their substantive properties or the level of threat that citizens perceive, or if they remain consistent. Next, we compare and contrast supporters' and opponents' strategies for defining issues and suggest reasons for the similarities and differences. Do gay rights supporters frame debates in terms of consequences and procedures, as their opponents do, or do they emphasize principles? Finally, we consider the implications of these findings for the gay rights movement's successes and failures.

HATE CRIMES

We begin with whether hate crimes laws should cover gays and lesbians, one of the issues that Americans find among the least threatening. Table 3.1 shows how proponents of hate crimes legislation define the issue in congressional debate and print journalism. Supporters put forward a mix of definitions based upon procedures, principles, and consequences. Members of Congress most often argue that the federal government has an important role in hate crimes prosecution that needs to be strengthened and broadened. Sixty percent of congressional speeches include this procedural definition about intergovernmental relations, although it appears in only a tiny minority of print articles. According to the Senate's sponsor of federal hate crimes legislation, Edward M. Kennedy (D-MA):

> The federal government has a special role in protecting civil rights and preventing discrimination. . . . We . . . need to add gender, sexual orientation, and disability to the types of hate crimes where federal prosecution is available. Our goal is to make the Justice Department a full partner with state and local governments in investigating and prosecuting these vicious crimes. . . . The silence of Congress on this basic issue has been deafening, and it is unacceptable. We must stop acting like we don't care—that somehow this fundamental issue is just a state problem. It isn't. It's a national problem, and it is an outrage that Congress continues to be AWOL [absent without leave] in the national battle against hate crimes. (U.S. Congress, Senate 2000b, S5301)[1]

Advocates in Congress and the print media focus on three substantive definitions. First, they stress that the issue is about justice. Hate crimes laws achieve justice because hate crimes warrant harsher penalties than ordinary crimes. According to Jack Reed (2000), writing in the *Providence* (RI) *Journal-Bulletin*, "Hate-crime laws recognize that a violent act committed against someone just because of who they are is intended to intimidate and frighten people other than the immediate victim. While a hate crime might be targeted at one person, it is really directed at an entire community. . . . Hate-crime laws express society's judgment that a violent act motivated by bigotry deserves greater punishment than a random crime committed under the same circumstances."[2]

Second, supporters stress the principle that laws play a crucial role in expressing society's values and educating the public. Hate crime laws express society's condemnation of hate, violence, and bigotry. As Senator Joseph Lieberman (D-CT) declared, "One of the things we try to do in this Chamber, as lawmakers, is to adopt laws that express and encode our values as a

Table 3.1 Proponents of including sexual orientation in hate crimes laws, debates in the 106th (1999–2000) and 108th (2003–4) U.S. Congress and in news articles, 1985–2000

	Congressional Speeches		News Articles	
	Frequency of definition as % of total assertions of definitions (N = 252)	% of speeches that include definition (N = 120)	Frequency of definition as % of total assertions of definitions (N = 567)	% of articles that include definition (N = 329)
Stronger federal role necessary; states need federal support	29 (72)	60 (72)	4 (21)	6 (21)
Serving justice; making punishment fit crime; hate different from other crime	25 (62)	52 (62)	26 (146)	40 (132)
Stating moral condemnation against/teaching against, hate, violence, bigotry	17 (43)	36 (43)	30 (169)	47 (155)
Public safety/protection; deterrence	17 (42)	35 (42)	25 (143)	39 (129)
Motive is legitimate consideration for penalty enhancement; does not infringe on freedom of speech/thought	5 (13)	11 (13)	7 (42)	13 (42)
Other	8 (20)	17 (20)	8 (46)	13 (46)
Total	101		100	

Note: Numbers in parentheses are frequencies. When summed, the frequencies for the "percent of articles that include definition" exceed the total N because many articles include more than one definition. The same applies to the frequencies for the "percent of speeches that include definition."

society, to, in some sense, put into law our aspirations for the kind of people we want to be. . . . Tolerance has been a hallmark of American society. . . . In other words, this is another way for our society to express our disdain, to put it mildly, at acts of violence committed based on a person's race, religion, nationality, gender, disability or sexual orientation" (U.S. Congress, Senate 2000b, S5303).[3]

Third, hate crime law supporters define the issue in terms of desired consequences: protecting potential victims and deterring would-be perpetrators. As one Seattle activist pointed out, "Many opponents of the legislation believed it extended special protection to homosexuals. That's clearly not the case, [unless] you consider walking safely down the street or being safe in your home a special protection" (*Oregonian* 1991).[4]

In sum, while congressional advocates of expanding hate crime laws to include gays and lesbians define the issue most often in procedural terms, other supporters stress principles—justice and condemnations of hate, violence, and bigotry—and, secondarily, consequences (protection and deterrence).

EMPLOYMENT AND HOUSING DISCRIMINATION

Supporters define nondiscrimination in employment and housing in principled terms as well. Table 3.2 reports on the issue definitions put forward by gay rights advocates in eleven legislative debates and hearings that took place in nine legislative bodies from 1984 to 2001. Of overriding importance to supporters is upholding civil rights principles—nondiscrimination and fair treatment. Sixty-one percent of all speeches include this definition, and it constitutes almost half of all the definitions asserted. Speaker after speaker argued that gays and lesbians were denied basic rights and fair treatment:[5]

> The type of discrimination we are talking about today happens to be about homosexuals, but we are really dealing with a far broader issue. We all believe in equal justice under law. . . . We are really not standing up for equal justice under law when we support that principle only for groups that we identify with or sympathize with. . . . Are we going to prove that we really believe that discrimination against our fellow citizens is wrong, and prove it when that discrimination is focused on a group that many of us disagree with, that have a different lifestyle than the great majority of us, simply because they are citizens of our society

Table 3.2 Proponents' issue definitions in debates over employment and housing nondiscrimination legislation, 1984–2001

	% of speeches that include definition (N = 207)	Frequency of definition as % of total assertions of definitions (N = 280)
Discrimination against gays and lesbians wrong, unfair; struggle for equality; need to protect minority rights	61 (126)	45 (127)
Discrimination, intolerance toward gays a real problem; lack of protection exists	32 (66)	24 (66)
Legislation protects status, not conduct; does not legitimate conduct; employers can still punish employers for bad conduct	14 (29)	10 (28)
Sexual orientation not chosen	13 (27)	10 (27) .
Jurisdictions with similar laws have positive experience; no problems/unintended consequences encountered	9 (19)	6 (18)
Other[a]	7 (14)	5 (14)
Total		100

Notes: Numbers in parentheses are frequencies. When summed, the frequencies for the "percent of speeches that include definition" exceed the total N because many speeches include more than one definition.

[a]Definitions less than 5% of speeches: God, Bible supports gays, requires treating them with equality/respect; nondiscrimination good for economy.

and it is wrong to discriminate against them? That is the heart of the issue. (Rhode Island Senate 1995)

As I have wrestled with this issue, I would say to . . . members of the gay and lesbian community, as a Norwegian Lutheran, I do not understand your lifestyle. . . . But at the same time, I am reminded of the oath I took . . . that said that I would uphold the Constitution of the United States as well as the State of Minnesota. . . . If we pass this legislation it's because it is the right thing to do. Not because we totally understand, but because we want to be a state that does not discriminate against its people. (Minnesota Senate 1993)

Proponents frequently situated the struggle for gay civil rights in the nation's long tradition of fighting against discrimination. According to Senator Kennedy, the chief sponsor of the Employment Non-Discrimination Act in the U.S. Senate:

> This act will eliminate job discrimination against gays and lesbians, and it represents the next major chapter in the American struggle to secure civil rights for all of our citizens. . . . Our country has a respected tradition of enacting anti-discrimination legislation to deal with discrimination against recognized groups of people. Time and again Congress has chosen justice over injustice and fairness over bigotry. After decades of discrimination against gays and lesbians, the Senate can send a strong signal that merit and hard work—not bias and stereotypes—are what counts in . . . the workplace in America in 1996. (U.S. Congress, Senate 1996a, S9986)

Some speakers argued that the government needed to protect civil rights, regardless of whether people choose their sexual orientation. For these legislators, the notion that civil rights protections were afforded, or should only be afforded, to classes of people with immutable characteristics was utterly incorrect. As a sponsor of the legislation in the Rhode Island House (1990) put it, "we have found it necessary throughout history to protect not just people based upon an immutable characteristic of birth—race or sex—but to protect people from discrimination because of their beliefs. Roger Williams founded this state because of the discrimination against him based upon his beliefs."

In sum, supporters have a simple, dominant strategy when they advocate for nondiscrimination policies in employment and housing: they embrace widely shared values like equality and fairness and the civil rights struggles of the past. This strategy also conveys the notion that extending civil rights protections to gays and lesbians is an incremental extension of civil rights to another oppressed minority rather than a radical break with tradition.

THE MILITARY BAN

Proponents of lifting the ban on gays in the military see it as a civil rights struggle as well. Table 3.3 reports on the definitions used by supporters of lifting the ban on gays in the military when Congress debated the issue in 1993. They most frequently framed the issue in terms of the wrongness of discrimination and the violation of gays and lesbians' civil rights.[6] About

Table 3.3 Definitions of congressional proponents of lifting ban on gays in the military, 1993

	House		Senate		Total	
	Frequency of definition as % of all assertions of definitions (N = 90)	% of speeches that include definition (N = 29)	Frequency of definition as % of all assertions of definitions (N = 64)	% of speeches that include definition (N = 17)	Frequency of definition as % of all assertions of definitions (N = 153)	% of speeches that include definition (N = 46)
Ban discriminates, is unfair; civil rights	20 (18)	62	21 (13)	76	20 (31)	67
Codification unnecessary, unwise	14 (12)	41	16 (10)	60	14 (22)	48
Gays serve honorably, with valor, sacrificed	14 (12)	41	10 (6)	35	12 (18)	39
Conduct, not status, should be grounds for dismissal	10 (9)	31	13 (8)	47	11 (17)	37
Studies/experience of other nations, police and fire orgs., women and minorities support lifting ban	11 (10)	34	19 (12)	71	14 (22)	48
Ban is rooted in prejudice and bigotry	9 (8)	28	0 (0)	0	5 (8)	17
Ban imposes high costs on retraining, investigating, litigating	4 (4)	14	5 (3)	18	5 (7)	15
Ban encourages lying, deception	4 (4)	14	6 (4)	24	5 (8)	17
Other[a]	14 (13)	36	11 (7)	24	13 (20)	27
Total	100		101		99	

Notes: Numbers in parentheses are frequencies. When summed, the frequencies for the "percent of speeches that include definition" exceed the total N because many speeches include more than one definition.

[a]Definitions that appeared in less than 15% of speeches: Sexual orientation irrelevant; ban is rooted in unfounded, exaggerated fears; military will adjust; leadership can reduce problem; ban unconstitutional; church and state should remain separate; social role of military is important; public opinion supports lifting ban; literal interpretations of Bible faulty; adulterers not banned from military; military leaders, Senator Barry Goldwater support lifting ban; sexual orientation not a choice; military's "unique" needs do not require ban.

two-thirds of congressional speeches asserted that the ban was unfair and discriminatory. For example:

> An individual's sexual orientation, just like hair color, religion, just like their ethnicity, and just like their gender is no measure of their qualifications. The Senate should not codify a policy that is just plain un-American. But that is what this policy is. (U.S. Congress, Senate 1993, S11170)[7]

> A policy that treats gay or lesbian service members unequally . . . violates the equal protection clause [of the U.S. Constitution]. Equal protection under the law requires that each individual be judged according to their ability, and not the group to which they belong. (U.S. Congress, Senate 1993, S11204)[8]

Again, speakers often drew parallels between gays and lesbians and other historically discriminated groups and invoked the legacy of other civil rights struggles:

> Why do we have an armed forces? It is not, surely simply to defend the piece of geography known as the United States of America. It is to defend and preserve and protect a document known as the Constitution, which enshrines the rights and liberties of all of our people. History teaches us that the promises of that Constitution have taken a very long time to fulfill. It was written 206 years ago by white men, many of whom owned slaves. President [Abraham] Lincoln signed the Emancipation Proclamation 130 years ago. President [Harry] Truman signed the Executive order ending racial discrimination in the armed Forces 45 years ago. President [Lyndon] Johnson signed the Civil Rights Act of 1964 29 years ago. And less than 1 year ago, this country elected the first President of the United States committed to helping us write the last chapter in the long history of civil rights, which is the history of this country. . . . What is most troubling about the [Armed Services] committee's rationale is that it is an accommodation of prejudice. It is precisely this readiness to defer to the prejudices of the majority that makes this a civil rights issue. (U.S. Congress, House 1993, H7076)[9]

> During the Second World War, when the United States Government decided that all Japanese-Americans were a categorical threat to the

security of the United States, my family and I, along with 120,000 other Americans of Japanese ancestry, were forced from our homes and into internment camps. The fact that I was an American citizen made no difference. Our loyalty to this country made no difference, our contributions to our communities made no difference, our rights under the Constitution made no difference—simply because by accident of birth we were of Japanese ancestry. More than 50 years after that decision, this House is considering a bill that would send a similar message to gay and lesbian Americans. That message says this: We do not care how qualified you are. We do not care how dedicated you are. We don't care how loyal you are to this Nation. Those things don't matter—because we don't want your kind here. (U.S. Congress, House 1993, H7083)[10]

The antidiscrimination argument in this debate, while most important, was not as dominant as it was in debates over employment and housing discrimination. Because the opposition argued that military needs trumped civil rights considerations, which was the position taken by most courts on the issue, supporters of lifting the ban often resorted to other arguments. One argument was that Congress did not need to codify what had been an administrative regulation up until this point and that it would be wiser to let the executive branch have flexibility in the matter. Another was that studies and experience suggested that opponents' fears about how rank-and-file military personnel would react if gays were allowed to serve openly were unfounded. About half of all speeches included these definitions: "If you vote for my amendment. . . . the Secretary of Defense will continue to have the authority to implement his directive. That is the same way this issue was handled under George Bush, Ronald Reagan, and every other President since the founding of the Republic, and I do not think the Congress should begin intervening in these matters now" (U.S. Congress, House 1993, H7068).[11]

About 40 percent of speeches also included the corollary argument that the military should judge gays and lesbians exclusively according to their conduct and how well they perform in their jobs: "a proper approach to this vexing issue is the implementation of a policy which emphasizes actual conduct, not behavior presumed because of sexual orientation, and holds all service members to the same standard of professional conduct" (U.S. Congress, Senate 1993, S11227).[12]

Finally, about the same proportion also defined the issue in terms of the competent and honorable service of gays and lesbians in the military: "The issue is not whether gays and lesbians serve in the military. They have. They do. They will. They have done so honorably and with distinction. Many have served as heroes" (U.S. Congress, House 1993, H7083).[13]

Thus far, we have seen that on the three issues on which Americans are least threatened, gay rights supporters frame their arguments mainly in terms of principles like equality and justice. Now we turn to the three issues that the public sees as more threatening: legalizing homosexual conduct, marriage, and adoption.

LEGALIZING HOMOSEXUAL CONDUCT

Proponents of the repeal of sodomy laws define the issue most often in terms of personal freedom and equality. Laws proscribing consensual sexual conduct, they argue, infringe on the privacy and freedom to which individuals are entitled. Definitions that emphasize privacy and personal autonomy appeared in two-thirds of the newspaper articles and editorials and constituted more than one-third of all definitions put forward (see table 3.4). According to the *Chicago Daily Herald* (2003), "What two consenting adults do sexually in the privacy of their bedroom is their business, not the government's. Some may not agree with or understand gay people, but we all should agree on our country's commitment to a right of privacy for everyone, no matter their sexual orientation." Dennis Bergren (2003), in the *Capital Times* of Madison, Wisconsin, put it more bluntly: "If you have problems with 'homosexual acts,' don't do them. . . . At the same time, mind your own business, get out of other people's bedrooms and stop trying to control other people's lives and loves."[14]

Because some states' sodomy laws applied only to homosexuals and others were enforced only against them, proponents of repeal said that the issue was also about equality under the law. Almost half of all articles included the equality/discrimination/fairness definition (table 3.4). For example, the director of the American Civil Liberties Unions' Lesbian and Gay Rights Project argued that in the wake of the *Lawrence v. Texas* decision, "States can no longer get away with that kind of unequal treatment" (Reinert and Villafranca 2003).[15]

Definitions based upon procedures and consequences for society were of secondary importance. Still, about a third of articles viewed sodomy laws as unconstitutional regulation of consensual adult conduct, a quarter viewed

Table 3.4 Definitions of the legalization of homosexual conduct by proponents of the repeal of sodomy laws, 2003–6

	Frequency of definition as % of all definitions asserted (N = 834)	% of articles that include definition[a] (N = 337)
Privacy/personal liberty	35 (297)	66 (223)
Equality/equal protection/ discrimination/fairness	23 (193)	45 (153)
Regulation of consensual adult conduct unconstitutional without compelling interest (moral disapproval insufficient)	16 (131)	33 (111)
Sodomy laws' harmful consequences (harassment of gays, discrimination, denial of civil rights, etc.)	12 (105)	27 (91)
Repeal paves the way to gay marriage and other rights	10 (87)	23 (79)
Other	3 (21)	6 (20)
Total	99	

Notes: Numbers in parentheses are frequencies. When summed, the frequencies for the "percent of articles that include definition" exceed the total N because many articles include more than one definition. The same applies to the frequencies for the "percent of speeches that include definition."

[a]Definitions found in less than 10% of articles: issue not about marriage; sexual orientation not a choice; dignity/respect for diversity; role of courts to protect minority rights; capricious enforcement of laws.

them as an impediment to gaining civil rights and a source of harassment, and a quarter viewed them as the potential for repeal to pave the way for marriage and other rights.

MARRIAGE

Supporters of gay rights are normally not supporters of same-sex marriage. They are more likely to champion a status short of marriage, such as civil unions or partner benefits. Most debates over gay marriage are about whether the government should ban it. Hence, gay rights advocates are squarely on the defensive. Gay rights supporters in Congress have pursued a different strategy than those at the state level. The federal structure of government affords them a noncontroversial and plausible procedural argument in favor of voting against federal prohibitions on same-sex marriage. More than 90 percent of Senate speeches and 59 percent of speeches in both chambers over the Defense of Marriage Act (DOMA) invoked some sort of "states rights" argument (see table 3.5). According to Senator Carol Moseley Braun, "I ask everyone listening to this debate to note that the Federal Government has yet to issue a marriage license. That is not within our purview. It is not something the Federal Government does. Yet, in this instance, the so-called Defense of Marriage Act, we are moving into the marriage business unilaterally in order to prohibit the approval by one State of another State's decision to recognize a particular marital or domestic arrangement" (U.S. Congress, Senate 1996b, S10104).[16]

The high level of partisanship and ideological combat in Congress over cultural issues also leads gay rights supporters to frame gay marriage in highly charged political terms by pointing out that the Republican leadership in Congress uses gay marriage as a "wedge issue" to mobilize their supporters. A majority of speeches in both chambers included this accusation by gay rights supporters (table 3.5). Representative Carolyn Maloney, herself a Republican from New York, called DOMA "a publicity stunt," and Representative Steven Gunderson, a gay Republican from Wisconsin, described it as "a mean, political-wedge issue at the expense of the gay and lesbian community in this country" (U.S. Congress, House 1996, H7277, H7492).[17]

Outside of Congress, proponents use familiar civil rights principles to define gay marriage (this definition is also the leading substantive definition inside Congress). In the congressional DOMA debate and the legislative hearings in Connecticut, egalitarian definitions surpassed the next most frequent substantive definition by more than double (see tables 3.5 and 3.6):

> Our experience makes us acutely aware of the fact that we are second-class citizens. Despite the fact that we work, pay taxes, and contribute to the general welfare of this state, gay men and lesbians are denied the right of a legally sanctioned family and all the protections that go with it. (Connecticut General Assembly 2002, 42)

> We're asking for equality, equal rights, the same rights as anybody else. . . . We're not asking for anything special. We are like everyone else here. We pay taxes. We go to work. And we pay our bills. . . . It's

not about sex. It's about what's fair. It's about love. My love for my partner was no different than the love for a wife. I know, I've been married twice. (Connecticut General Assembly 2003, 29)[18]

Advocates view the struggle for gay marriage, as with other issues, in the historical perspective of the struggle for racial equality: "We believe that withholding rights from persons because of their sexual orientation is as arbitrary and repulsive as drawing those same lines as on the basis of race. . . . My father's previous wife is Caucasian and they lived in Virginia where you couldn't . . . there were laws . . . against interracial marriage in many states, including Virginia until very, very recently. . . . And you know, we really ought to shake our heads that it was not that long ago that these were the kinds of challenges and hurdles that we were confronting on the basis of race and frankly, the barriers to same sex marriage in this state make us shake our heads in the same way" (remarks of Carolyn Ikari; Connecticut General Assembly 2003, 55).

After the civil rights definition, advocates in Congress emphasize how gay marriage promotes traditional values. Representative Maxine Waters (D-CA) put it this way: "Loving, long-term relationships between men and women or between same-sex couples do not threaten our children, our families, our communities. On the contrary, stable relationships enhance society's ability to raise healthy, engaged, and productive citizens. There is no problem" (U.S. Congress, House 1996, H7531).[19]

And in the Connecticut hearings and other settings where gay couples and family members get an opportunity to participate, advocates use personal stories rather than aggregate data to frame the issue in terms of practical needs and material benefits:

[M]y partner and I have been together for 18 years. We have spent thousands of dollars, literally over those 18 years having documents drafted and re-drafted and having gone to, I think who is the best attorney in the State on this issue, we still have only four documents. (Connecticut General Assembly 2002, 131)

I'm a Westport resident and I have been for eleven years. My partner was Nancy Prince. We were together for fifteen years. Before moving to Connecticut, we lived in New York where we became domestic partners. In January of 2000, Nancy was diagnosed with Leukemia and died the following August. And while losing Nancy was the

Table 3.5 Definitions of gay marriage issue by opponents of Defense of Marriage Act (DOMA) in congressional debate, 1996

	House		Senate		Total	
	Frequency of definition as % of all assertions of definitions (N = 151)	% of speeches that include definition (N = 50)	Frequency of definition as % of all assertions of definitions (N = 38)	% of speeches that include definition (N = 11)	Frequency of definition as % of all assertions of definitions (N = 189)	% of speeches that include definition (N = 61)
DOMA divisive, inspires bigotry	19 (28)	56	16 (6)	55	18 (34)	56
Federalism/ unconstitutional	17 (26)	52	26 (10)	91	19 (36)	59
Gay marriage not a threat	12 (18)	36	11 (4)	36	12 (22)	36
Equal rights; fairness; nondiscrimination; civil rights	12 (18)	36	8 (3)	27	11 (21)	34

Protects children; stabilizes relationships beneficial to families/ society	11	(16)	32	5	(2)	18	10	(18)	30
Practical needs (e.g., inheritance, taxes, hospital visitation)	9	(13)	26	3	(1)	9	7	(14)	23
DOMA politically motivated	7	(11)	22	11	(4)	36	8	(15)	25
More important issues	5	(8)	16	8	(3)	27	6	(11)	18
Other[a]	9	(13)	20	13	(5)	21	10	(18)	20
Total			101			101			101

Notes: Numbers in parentheses are frequencies. When summed, the frequencies for the "percent of speeches that include definition" exceed the total N because many speeches include more than one definition.

[a] Definitions that appear in less than 15% of speeches: need to respect gays' privacy; need to keep church-state separate; marriage is not a slippery slope; Bible is not antigay; marriage not about sanctioning homosexuality; sexual orientation immutable; cost to budget of marriage minimal.

Table 3.6 Proponents' definitions of gay marriage issue, hearings before the Connecticut legislature, 2001–3

	Frequency of definition as % of all definitions asserted ($N = 173$)	% of speeches that include definition ($N = 75$)
Equal rights; fairness; nondiscrimination; civil rights	27 (47)	63 (47)
Practical needs (e.g., inheritance, taxes, hospital visitation, etc.)	13 (23)	31 (23)
Protects children, stabilizes relationships; beneficial to families and society	13 (23)	31 (23)
Gay relationships essentially the same as heterosexual (loving, committed, etc.)	11 (19)	25 (19)
Separation of church and state; civil marriage different from religious sacrament; religions can refuse to marry gays and lesbians	8 (13)	17 (13)
Other[a]	27 (48)	45 (34)
Total	99	

Notes: Numbers in parentheses are frequencies. When summed, the frequencies for the "percent of speeches that include definition" exceed the total N because many speeches include more than one definition.

[a]Definitions that appear in less than 15% of speeches: existing legal protections, procedures for gay couples inadequate or costly; marriage as an evolving institution has become more inclusive and equitable; changes have made marriage stronger; God/religion supports gay rights; other nations/Vermont have gay marriage or civil unions; marriage will not lead to slippery slope; sexual orientation immutable; sexual orientation irrelevant to parenting; younger generation supports gay marriage; gay marriage not a threat to marriage; tradition can be stupid; gay marriage a logical next step in evolution of gay rights in Connecticut; fear of gays an irrational taboo; not all heterosexuals procreate; everyone should have freedom to love whomever they wish; cost of gay marriage would be low; social diversity is good; experts support gay marriage; gay marriage better than civil unions; Defense of marriage Act inspired by bigotry.

worst thing that's ever happened to me, one of the other things that I came to understand during that process was how hard it was to come to understand that we were being treated differently than other couples strictly because we were gay. . . . [I]n the intensive care unit, the hospital policy was that I couldn't . . . that I wasn't part of her immediate family and I was denied admittance. When Nancy died, I made her funeral arrangements and yet when it came to the end of it, as horrified as the funeral director was, he couldn't let me sign. . . . I was denied the rights of inheritance that protect family members. I paid thousands of dollars in inheritance taxes that no couple, no married spouse has to do. (Connecticut General Assembly 2003, 84–85)[20]

In sum, gay marriage advocates and opponents of bans on gay marriage present a mix of definitions, but their major definition, other than respect for federalism (in Congress), is equality and nondiscrimination.

ADOPTION
Gay rights supporters frame debate over adoption very differently. They hardly ever define it using abstract principles like equality and nondiscrimi-nation. The data from news articles and legislative debate in table 3.7 reveal that only 18 percent of articles and 11 percent of speeches in the Connecticut legislature included those definitions, or only 6 percent of all definitions. Advocates for gays to adopt children avoid overtly portraying their struggle in terms of "gay rights" and gays and lesbians suffering discrimination. Instead, they focus on the suitability of gays and lesbians as parents, doing what is best for children, and the irrelevance of sexual orientation for deter-mining the quality of parenting. Same-sex couples are portrayed as *parents* foremost, rather than as advocates for gay rights. For example:[21]

I don't see it so much as a gay rights issue. I see it as a "what's best for the children" issue. (quoted in Associated Press 1998a)

Parenting requires love and affection. It doesn't require heterosexuality. (quoted in O'Toole 1999)

Same sex adoption is not about what anyone believes about sexual orientation. It is about what is best for children. . . . All of our grandchildren are being taught ethics, values and responsibility to others. They all feel secure in the love they receive from their

Table 3.7 Proponents' definitions of gay adoption, Connecticut legislature (2000)[a] and news articles (1994–2004)[b]

	Frequency of definition as % of all assertions of definitions published (N = 63)	% of speeches that include definition (N = 35)	Frequency of definition as % of all definitions (N = 772)	% of articles that include definition (N = 532)
Best interests of children	24 (15)	43 (15)	17 (131)	25 (134)
Not about gay rights/gay marriage/will not lead to/affect marriage	18 (11)	31 (11)	0 (0)	0 (0)
Gays capable, loving parents/as good at parenting as heteros; sexual orientation irrelevant to parenting	14 (9)	26 (9)	25 (193)	36 (190)
Many children in need of good parents; hetero parents in short supply; foster care inferior	13 (8)	23 (8)	13 (100)	18 (98)
Equality for gays; nondiscrimination; denies gays equal protection	6 (4)	11 (4)	12 (93)	18 (95)

Children deserve/need adoption for legal protection/material benefits	15 (82)	11 (85)	0 (0)	0 (0)
Opposition motivated by bigotry, fear, hate, etc.	13 (68)	9 (69)	0 (0)	0 (0)
Adoption experts support gay adoption	11 (60)	8 (62)	6 (2)	3 (2)
Other[c]	9 (45)	6 (46)	42 (15)	22 (14)
Total		101		100

Notes: Numbers in parentheses are frequencies. When summed, the frequencies for the "percent of articles that include definition" exceed the total N because many articles include more than one definition. The same applies to the frequencies for the "percent of speeches that include definition."

[a] Data coded from transcript of the public hearing held by the Connecticut General Assembly's House of Representatives on March 13, 2000 (http://search.cga.state.ct.us; hard copy in possession of the author), the House floor debate held on April 28, 2000, and the Senate floor debate held on May 3, 2000, on HB5830, An Act Concerning the Best Interests of Children in Adoption Matters (http://www.cga.state.cut.us/2000/).

[b] LexisNexis search of news reports, editorials, and letters to the editor under "gay adoption" and "homosexual adoption" for years specified.

[c] Debate is not about morality of homosexuality; approval process for adoptive parents unchanged by allowing gay adoption; change in law is merely technical; existing law permits same-sex couples to adopt or should be interpreted that way; gay adoption protects/supports families; gays can already adopt as individuals; many children parented well in other nontraditional families; need for separation of church and state; adoption not "special rights"; other states allow it/few prohibit it; professionals should decide issue; bans on gay adoption cost taxpayers money; sexual orientation not a choice; gays and lesbians need to be shown respect.

parents, grandparents, extended families and friends. (*Intelligencer Journal* 2002a)

An editorial in the *Denver Post* (2003) about legislation to facilitate adoption by same-sex couples drew a distinction between the couples and the children: "Madden's bill, quite properly, doesn't give gay couples any rights they don't now have. It gives the children of such unions the same rights that the children of heterosexual unions now have. Whatever your views of same-sex relationships, HB1235 clearly is in the best interests of children who through no fault of their own, are being raised in such relationships."[22]

Another part of advocates' strategy is to counter fears that gay adoption is a Trojan horse for introducing gay marriage. The argument that gay adoption will not affect marriage laws or lead to gay marriage was the second most frequently made argument in the Connecticut debate, second only to the children's best interest:

> This is not about my relationship with [my partner] Gloria. . . . We are committed to each other, but we're also first and foremost committed to Samantha [the child]. Whether we're together or apart, Samantha is our daughter and it's not about our relationship or legalizing our relationship, but legalizing the relationship with Samantha. (Connecticut General Assembly 2000c, 188)

> There are a lot of people out there with negative feelings about gay relations. I think this requires a cool head to step back and say, "wait a minute. Why are we punishing the children because of our political views about the parents' relations?" That's very immoral. (quoted in Espenshade 2002b)

To show that sexual orientation is irrelevant, advocates try to portray gay parents as "normal" and like their heterosexual counterparts in every way.[23] In telling their stories to policymakers, gay and lesbian parents aim to convey the sense that "we are like you": responsible, loving, struggling to overcome the typical challenges that parents face, and embracing mainstream values of home and hearth, God and country. Take, for example, the testimony of gay parents before the Connecticut legislature when that state considered changing its adoption laws:

> I'd like to say that we are residents of West Hartford. We are law-abiding, God-believing, tax-paying citizens and I'd like to say that

in terms of our relationship with Samantha, we are two very, very involved parents. . . . I wake up in the morning with Sam. We have the morning routine breakfast. Mom [the other partner] heads out to work first. I drop off Sam at school. Mom picks up Sam. . . . And we take turns with the cooking and the bathing and the putting to bed and we do have our particular rituals. Mom is the story teller. I play dominoes and I do art work with Sam. . . . We do concerts together. We encourage our daughter. We instill strong moral beliefs and we want her to be a successful and law-abiding citizen, as well. When you ask me do I love Samantha—I'm not the biological mother. I'm the other parent. I am very much a parent and actually at home I'm "Mema." To the world, I'm Graciella. To Sam, I'm Mema. And when Sammy asks me how much do I love her, I tell her I love her to infinity and back 200 times, and that's a lot. (remarks of Graciella Quinnones; Connecticut General Assembly 2000c, 187)

For those of you who are parents, I don't have to tell you what it's like to be sleep-deprived. Multiply that by three. Our triplets arrived nearly three months early and my partner and I made daily visits to Yale New Haven Hospital for the eight weeks that they were in intensive care. Yet the law says that she is not their mother. My partner's employer granted her family leave and she stayed home with the triplets for six months, yet Robin has no legal relationship with our children . . . The other night our son Ian was up all night with an ear infection. We both stayed up with him to console him. That's what mothers do. (remarks of Laura Gould; Connecticut General Assembly 2000c, 55)

[M]y own daughter, Emma, was born almost a year ago today to me and my partner of fifteen years. I was there when she slipped softly into this world. I held her in the neo-natal unit as they worked to stabilize her breathing. . . . I have held her during each and every one of her immunizations, painfully aware of how her screams turn loud, very loud. I wake to soothe her each and every time she wakes in the wee hours of the morning and just last night, I confess, I was the mother closest to the toy box when the lid fell against her head and have her first bruise and my heart broke. I love my daughter more than I can ever explain. What a blessing she is to me, to my partner, to both of our families. I am one of Emma's moms. I know it. My partner knows it. Emma's grandparents, aunts, uncles, cousins know it. My colleagues know it. My church knows it. (remarks of Jodi Rowell; Connecticut General Assembly 2000c, 186)

CONCLUSION

Gay rights supporters generally put forward much different *kinds* of issue definitions than their opponents. Opponents frame issues mostly in terms of consequences. Supporters usually emphasize widely shared "American" principles like freedom, justice, and, most often, equality and nondiscrimination. They identify gay rights with African American and women's civil rights struggles. Such a strategy not only links gay rights to principles upon which there is broad support but it also frames it as another incremental step down the road to equality rather than a radical break with the culture. Adoption is the exception to this pattern. When advocates argue for gay couples to adopt, they hardly ever invoke demands for equality, justice, and freedom. They deny that adoption is really about gay rights, preferring instead to frame it as society's obligation to do "what is best for kids" and the suitability of gays and lesbians to undertake parental responsibilities.

Advocates for gay rights share one similarity with their opponents—they rely heavily on procedural definitions for some issues. They argue that the federal government has an important role in prosecuting hate crimes, but not in influencing states' marriage laws, and that Congress should leave defense policy matters to the executive branch. Those who make these arguments may genuinely feel that they are important, but procedural definitions also supply plausible and seemingly apolitical rationales for their positions that allow both sides in debate to sidestep difficult and controversial substantive policy questions.

Because advocates on both sides undoubtedly are more ideologically oriented than ordinary citizens are, gay rights opponents realize that their principles—based upon religion and traditional morality—have limited appeal among the public. Therefore, they deemphasize principles in debate. In contrast, gay rights proponents persist in defining most gay rights issues in terms of liberal principles like freedom and nondiscrimination because they are compatible with bracketing moral judgments about adult consensual conduct and thus afford citizens the opportunity to support gay rights without endorsing homosexuality.

Defining issues in terms of principles seems to work for some issues more than others, however. To the extent that strategies of political discourse matter for policy decisions, gay rights advocates must align their definitions with particular issues and institutional contexts. Reliance on liberty and equality principles makes most sense for issues related to the treatment of gays and lesbians in the marketplace and other impersonal social spaces. Despite Americans' continued support for these principles in the abstract, they may not find them sufficiently compelling and relevant when advocates ask them to legitimate intimate sexual and family relationships. Advocates have been much more effective in gaining adoption rights than marriage, in part perhaps because they have eschewed the language of "equal rights" and "freedom" and talked about how adoption affects one of society's most positively constructed groups—children—and how gay couples can make good parents. Because advocates have a certain degree of discretion in how they define many issues, depending upon what facts they wish to focus on and the meaning they impart to those facts, they can choose which definitions are a better fit with particular issues. We return to this point when discussing strategies and tactics for lesbian, gay, bisexual, and transgender rights advocates in chapter 8.

At the same time, issue definitions are not fully malleable. Issues have real, essential properties that limit the plausibility and persuasiveness of particular definitions that might be applied to them. Advocates for marriage and adoption, for example, cannot make those issues about "privacy" and "freedom," as what they are demanding is equality between gays and straights. They cannot expect a "what is best for children" definition to be as persuasive in the marriage debate as it appears to be in the debate over adoption because children are necessary for adoption while they are not for marriage.

Institutions present another set of opportunities and constraints for advocates' choice of issue definitions. Some institutional contexts are more hospitable to definitions based upon principles, even for issues that the public finds threatening. We will see that the legal experts and judicial elites who contributed to the legalization of homosexual conduct were very receptive to the libertarian principle that individuals are entitled to a zone of personal autonomy and that government should not punish "victimless crimes," despite a lack of majority support among the public. Conversely, civil rights principles that seem to suffice for some issues are insufficient in the case of the military ban because of the hostility of key institutional actors to lifting the ban, in spite of the public's relatively low perception of threat. We now turn to an examination of these cases and others.

4

On May 18, 1970, James McConnell and Jack Baker applied for a marriage license in Minneapolis. After the two men announced publicly that they were gay, the board of regents of the University of Minnesota voted unanimously to withdraw its offer of a librarian's job to McConnell. The board argued that McConnell's "personal conduct . . . [was] not consistent with the best interest of the University" because his sexual orientation and application for a license to marry another man implied that he intended to engage in sodomy, a crime under state law (*New York Times* 1970). Since the university would condone law breaking by one of its employees if it hired McConnell, the board judged him unfit for the position. A federal court declared the university's action unconstitutional, but an appeals court later reversed that ruling (Barnett 1973, 9). If McConnell had lived in Illinois, another major midwestern state, which did not have such a law in 1970, he almost certainly would have kept his job.

On the night of September 17, 1998, someone called the Harris County, Texas, police to report that "a black male was going crazy" and "was armed with a gun" in an apartment located in a lower-middle-class neighborhood of Houston.[1] When the police arrived at the apartment, they found the door slightly ajar and entered the premises. They found no sign of anyone using a gun, an accusation that turned out to be false.[2] They peered inside a bedroom, where they allegedly found John Lawrence and Tyrone Garner having anal sex.[3] Lawrence was a white, fifty-five-year-old medical technologist at a clinic. Garner was black, thirty-one years old, and unemployed. Neither man had ever been involved in gay rights activism. The authorities jailed the men and charged them with violating the Texas Homosexual Conduct law by engaging in "deviate sexual intercourse, namely anal sex, with a member of the same sex (man)" (quoted in opinion of U.S. Supreme Court Justice Anthony Kennedy for its decision in *Lawrence v. Texas*). Lawrence and Garner entered pleas of no contest. The magistrate fined each of them $200 and ordered them to pay court costs. The night after the arrests, a local gay rights activist, Lane Lewis, received word of the incident. Lewis procured lawyers for the men and persuaded Lawrence and Garner that a legal challenge to the Texas law could have a far-reaching impact for gay rights (Carpenter 2004). A Harris County Criminal Court convicted Lawrence and Garner, and a Texas court of appeals upheld their convictions. Next, the U.S. Supreme Court agreed to hear the case, *Lawrence v. Texas,* and in 2003, it decided in favor of the two men. The Court ruled that the state's law ran afoul of the due process rights guaranteed in the Fourteenth Amendment and it overturned the Court's 1986 precedent, *Bowers v. Hardwick,* which had found such laws constitutional.

As these stories illustrate, sodomy laws had profound impacts on the lives of some gay men. Their elimination could have a similarly profound impact on the gay rights movement. The immediate problem that sodomy laws posed was their threat to privacy.[4] Police and prosecutors often used the laws to harass homosexuals and enforced them selectively against gays even when they applied to heterosexuals as well. Individuals accused of violating them often received unwanted attention from the media, which could ruin their personal and professional lives (Brantner 1992, 498). During the twentieth century, the number of men arrested for sodomy and lesser offenses, like disorderly conduct and lewd and lascivious conduct, rose dramatically (Eskridge 1999, 43). Denied social acceptance of their relationships, gays often led "double lives" and resorted to casual sexual encounters in semipublic places that made them vulnerable to police surveillance and arrest. But other victims, like Michael Hardwick, the petitioner in *Bowers v. Hardwick,* were engaged in consensual, noncommercial sexual conduct in the most private of all places, their homes.

The impact of sodomy laws went far beyond their infringement on privacy rights. The state prosecuted relatively few people who engaged in anal or oral sex because of the practical difficulties in enforcing the laws. Rather, as potent symbols of society's disapproval of homosexuality, the laws played a significant role in the social construction of gays as deviants. In branding gays and lesbians social outcasts and denigrating their sexual activity, "the primary importance of sodomy laws . . . [was] the government's message to diminish the societal status of gay men and lesbians" (Leslie 2000, 114). Because law reflects the moral sentiment of the community, laws that criminalize the behavior of a group also legitimate and encourage discrimination against them. As a result, sodomy laws helped to perpetuate homophobia, discrimination, and violence against gays and lesbians (Leveno 1993–94, 1035; Tharpes 1987; Fradella 2002, 293; Barnett 1973, 9).

Sodomy laws also made it harder for gays and lesbians to attain other rights (Barnett 1973). Criminalization of the sexual practices between gays provided their opponents with a powerful public policy rationale for blocking gay rights across the board. Like the treatment accorded substance abusers and gamblers, courts used sodomy laws to deny gays and lesbians custody and visitation rights, security clearances, employment opportunities, and recognition of lesbian, gay, bisexual, and transgender (LGBT) student organizations. Such laws signified a view of gays as "criminals yet to be convicted" and therefore disqualified them from many of the privileges that law-abiding adults enjoy (Brantner 1992, 500; Fradella 2002, 289–93; Barnett 1973).

Lawrence closed an important chapter in LGBT history. Legalization of private homosexual conduct is the only issue for which the gay rights movement has achieved total success. None of the sodomy laws that existed in all fifty states in 1960 remain in effect today. This achievement might be easier to understand if the public were solidly behind the laws' elimination, but the issue split the public deeply for decades. During most of the period from 1980 to the *Lawrence* decision in 2003, a majority of the public opposed making same-sex behavior legal (AEI 2004, 4). The bare majority of Americans who favored repeal on the eve of *Lawrence* quickly evaporated soon after the Court announced its decision.

What explains the decline and fall of sodomy laws? Why did the Supreme Court reverse its earlier decision to uphold their constitutionality? How did most states eliminate their laws before the Supreme Court finally invalidated the thirteen that remained in force in 2003? What forces and conditions led to repeal by popularly elected bodies in so many states?

This chapter recounts the long and varied history of sodomy laws. The state used these laws to target same-sex consensual activity only relatively recently as part of an unprecedented repression of sexual and gender deviance that reached its apex in the middle of the twentieth century. History is of more than academic interest because the courts have looked to the historical record to support and reject claims about the constitutionality of sodomy laws.[5] Next, we look at the disappearance of sodomy laws in the United States over four decades, starting in 1960. Repeal took place during two distinct periods. Mostly legislatures repealed the first group of laws in the 1960s and 1970s, and mostly courts repealed the second group after 1980. Although different institutional conditions operated in these periods, the findings are mostly consistent with the hypotheses presented in chapter 1.

THE DEVELOPMENT OF LEGAL PROHIBITIONS
AGAINST SEXUAL CONDUCT

Society approved intimate sexual relationships between members of the same sex during long periods of the Greek and Roman civilizations (Boswell 1980; Dover 1978; Foucault 1985). In the early Middle Ages and among elite men in eighteenth-century France, church and state tolerated male same-sex behavior (Delon 1985). And in some non-Western cultures, same-sex relationships were part of the social fabric or were ignored.

American sodomy statutes had their roots in England. Henry VIII broke with the Catholic Church in 1533 and secularized what until then had been religious injunctions against nonprocreative sex. These prohibitions first appeared in the Bible ("men lying with men") and later on in natural law doctrine ("crimes against nature"). Although the law in England and America did not prohibit oral sex until almost the twentieth century, only sex undertaken as a procreative activity within marriage was approved (Eskridge 1997, 1015). English and early American law used the terms "sodomy" and "buggery," although their definitions varied across political jurisdictions and historical periods. Buggery generally included anal intercourse ("sodomy") between two men and between a man and a woman and any sexual contact between humans and animals ("bestiality"). Later statutes used even more ambiguous language like "crimes against nature" and, still later, "sexual misconduct."

In the colonial period, prohibitions against sodomy, the aim of which was to encourage population growth in the American colonies, were part of the panoply of restrictions against nonprocreative sexual behavior, including masturbation, adultery, and fornication. At the founding of the United States, only three states targeted sex between men for special punishment. Most states forbade sodomy or buggery, whether it was a man with another man, a man with a woman, or either with an animal. By the time the United States ratified the Fourteenth Amendment, not much had changed.

Instead of sodomy and buggery, many statutes referred to "infamous [or abominable] crimes against nature," but most did not single out same-sex behavior for special condemnation (Goldstein 1988, 1082–85). A survey of the enforcement of sodomy laws in the nineteenth century reveals that a sizable minority of prosecutions did not specify the gender of the accused or their alleged victims, and most of the crimes committed were apparently nonconsensual. They usually involved rape or the seduction of men with boys, men with men, men with women, and men or women with animals (Eskridge 1997, 1014). Thus, throughout most of American history, sodomy laws did not focus on same-sex intimacy (Eskridge 1997, 1012; Chauncey 2004a). Until 1880, it appears that no prosecutions for *consensual* sex took place between two men or two women (Eskridge 1997, 1015).

From the 1880s to World War I, the number of arrests for a variety of sex crimes rose sharply. Arrests for prostitution far outnumbered those for sodomy, but more significant was the way in which state and local governments expanded the enforcement of ambiguous "crimes against nature" provisions. Enforcement now included consensual sex between adults as well as oral sex (Eskridge 1997, 1026–27). Two developments in the late nineteenth century paved the way for heightened regulation of sexual activity in general and a focus on repressing same-sex behavior in particular.

The first was urbanization. As America's economy shifted from agriculture to manufacturing and industry, the population increasingly concentrated in cities near ports, like New York, Philadelphia, Chicago, Baltimore, St. Louis, and San Francisco. Urbanization concentrated large numbers of people with diverse sexual desires and tastes and made it more difficult to monitor behavior than it had been in rural areas and small towns (Chauncey 1994).[6] Individuals who had similar unconventional sexual inclinations sought out each other and developed subcultures, which encouraged others with similar orientations to migrate to the cities. Urban-industrial society also freed sex from its purely procreative function, and so it increasingly became an expressive and recreational activity; family farms no longer needed as many children to provide labor power, and larger families cost more to house in cities.

The increased regulation of sexual expression during this period reflected "a heightened state of concern for citizens who threatened not only traditional views about marriage and sex but, increasingly, entrenched gender roles as well" (Eskridge 1997, 1017). Anxious middle-class reformers ("antivice societies") were alarmed that the visibility of gay and gender-bending subcultures signaled a relaxation of social controls. They pressed for more stringent prohibitions that covered behavior that the state had not yet criminalized (like oral sex) and greater enforcement of laws against individuals who failed to adhere to traditional gender roles and sex within heterosexual marriage.

The emergence of psychiatry as a medical field in the latter part of the nineteenth century was the other major development that increased the state's regulation of sex. Psychiatrists (or "sexologists") did not view same-sex desire as a sin or a crime, but as a medical disorder that they labeled "inversion" or "homosexuality" because it deviated from what they understood as normal, healthy sex—vaginal intercourse between a masculine male and a feminine female. For the first time, society viewed those who engaged in same-sex behavior as a separate class of human beings and defined their identity solely by their sexuality. Before this time, people viewed same-sex behavior as a moral or criminal transgression that *anyone* could commit. Now, however, it became an essential part of the makeup of a perverted being—the homosexual or invert. As Foucault (1979, 43) put it, "the nineteenth century homosexual became a personage, a past, a case history, and a childhood, in addition to being a type of life, a life form and a morphology. . . . The sodomite had been a temporary aberration; the homosexual was now a species."

Psychiatrist Richard von Krafft-Ebing viewed inversion—feminine-acting men and masculine-acting women—as a congenital defect that represented a "degeneration" or retrogression to a more primitive stage of development when gender identities and roles were less clearly defined (Eskridge 1997, 1022–24). Sigmund Freud rejected the congenital explanation for sexual deviance and argued that homosexuality was the product of an arrested development. He maintained that "normal," heterosexual orientation occurs when the Oedipus complex is successfully resolved—boys learn to rid themselves of sexual feelings for their mothers and identify with their fathers, and girls do the same, only in the opposite manner (Eskridge 1997, 1054). Freud's theory and its interpretation in the United States not only made a person's sexuality a crucial aspect of their identity but it also presented a view of homosexuality that was more threatening to society. If homosexuality was shaped during one's personal development, then sexual orientation was more malleable than previously thought and almost anyone (especially impressionistic youth) could acquire the trait under the right conditions. As these ideas became popular, American sexologists ascribed a variety of negative moral, physical, and intellectual traits to the inverts, which stoked the anxieties of reformers and citizens who believed that the cities were spawning dangerous degenerates. They portrayed homosexuals as sexual psychopaths and aggressive predators with uncontrolled libidos (Eskridge 1997, 1058–59). By medicalizing sexual orientation, psychiatrists further stigmatized same-sex desire, even though they argued that homosexuals should not be punished because their disorder could not be controlled without treatment (Goldstein 1988, 1089).

"Scientific" authorities thus joined with religious and state authorities to legitimate the antigay fervor that escalated in the twentieth century. Individuals whom the police arrested under sodomy laws often lost their jobs, received jail time, were court-martialed or separated from the military, and suffered tarnished reputations in their families and communities. Those suspected or discovered to be gay were subjected to a variety of "treatments," many that we recognize today as inhumane—mandatory psychiatric counseling and institutional confinement, frontal lobotomies, electric shock therapy, hormone injections, and other aversion therapies (Eskridge 1997, 1066). Even with the liberalization of sexual expression and decriminalization of "victimless crimes" in the 1960s and 1970s, states that retained their sodomy laws enforced them disproportionately against homosexuals, and other states rewrote their laws to prohibit only sodomy between homosexuals.[7]

Sodomy laws were only one weapon that the state used to harass, punish, and intimidate gays and other "degenerates" who did not subscribe to mainstream sexual and gender norms. Anxiety over gender and sexual deviance also led to a host of other laws and police practices used against gays, such as vaguely worded vagrancy, public indecency, disorderly conduct, and indecent exposure laws (Eskridge 1997, 1037).[8] Many more individuals were caught in the net of these laws than were arrested for violating sodomy prohibitions.[9] Authorities used liquor licensing laws to prevent bars and other establishments that catered to gay and cross-dressing patrons from operating, conducted raids and arrests, and extorted bribes from owners. Immigration laws before and after World War II barred "the degenerate in sexual morality" from entering the country, and the military excluded those suspected or known to be "sodomites" and "sexual inverts" from service (Eskridge 1997, 1046, 1052). Homosexuals were also a favorite target of anti-Communist witch hunts that swept the United States in the 1950s, which branded them as emotionally unstable security risks and a danger to their younger colleagues especially. The Federal Bureau of Investigation, the U.S. Congress (most infamously under Senator Joseph McCarthy, R-WI) and other legislatures and municipal police forces conducted widespread surveillance and investigations of numerous suspected homosexuals (Chauncey 2004a, 523–25). The actions of this vast state apparatus caused many individuals to lose jobs and employment opportunities in the public and private sectors.

FEDERALISM, LEGISLATURES, AND COURTS IN THE LONG STRUGGLE TO REPEAL SODOMY STATUTES

All fifty states had sodomy laws until Illinois repealed its statute in 1961 and Connecticut followed in 1969. The pace of repeal quickened in the 1970s when twenty-two more states eliminated their laws. Repeal slowed again in the 1980s before it resumed in the 1990s and early in the twenty-first century (see table 4.1). On the eve of the *Lawrence* decision in 2003, only thirteen states retained sodomy laws, of which six criminalized oral and anal sex only between same-sex partners.[10]

Federalism played an important role in repeal. Almost three-quarters of the states repealed their own laws. Several of the largest states (California, Illinois, New Jersey, New York, and Pennsylvania) repealed their laws well before the elimination of the laws in the remaining states, by about twenty years in some cases. Although the states that repealed their sodomy statutes during the 1960s and 1970s were no more liberal than those that repealed theirs after 1980, the thirteen states that failed to abolish their laws were among the most conservative in the country (see table 4.2). It took the U.S. Supreme Court's ruling in *Lawrence* to eliminate their laws decades after the first group of states had repealed theirs. Gregory Lewis's (1999, 19–20) study in the 1990s of public opinion and sodomy law repeal shows that most of the twenty-five states in which the public was the most supportive of legalizing same-sex conduct had repealed their sodomy laws, while most of the twenty-five states in which the public was least supportive of legalization had not. Survey respondents in southern states and those in the upper Midwest were significantly less approving of homosexuality and supportive of legalizing homosexual relations (Lewis 1999, 11). These states disproportionately lagged in the repeal movement. Earlier studies showed similarly that southern states and those with larger numbers of Protestant fundamentalists were more likely to retain their sodomy laws (Nice 1988; Young 1991).

Courts repealed more state sodomy laws in total than legislatures, although not by a large margin. When states repealed their laws on their own
(i.e., pre-*Lawrence* repeals) they were more likely to follow the legislative
route (see table 4.1). The dominant political ideologies within states apparently played some role in shaping whether repeal took place under judicial or legislative auspices. States that had their laws repealed through the
courts were, on average, more conservative than those that used legislative
means (see table 4.2). The greater conservatism of judicial repeal states,
however, is due to the U.S. Supreme Court's invalidation of laws in the
thirteen states that still had them when it handed down *Lawrence* in 2003.
All of the *Lawrence* states are conservative, and most of them fall into the
"most conservative" category in table 4.2. Among the states that repealed
their laws on their own, before *Lawrence,* ideology does not seem to have
played a role in the institutional route of repeal. States that chose the judicial route were about as liberal or conservative as those that chose the
legislative route. These findings are consistent with the different methods
for selecting Supreme Court justices and most state judges. Because the
vast majority of state judges, like state legislators, must run for reelection,
we would not expect judges to enjoy greater autonomy than legislators from
public opinion in the more conservative states. It is not surprising that it
took the U.S. Supreme Court, an unelected court with lifetime appointments, to overturn the laws of the strongly conservative states that still held
onto them in 2003.

Table 4.1 also shows a distinct institutional pattern of repeal between the
earlier period (the 1960s and 1970s) and the later one (the 1980s, 1990s,
and 2000s). Almost all of the repeals before the 1980s occurred through
legislative action; almost all of those that came afterward occurred through
the courts. Again, if we exclude the states whose laws the Supreme Court
invalidated in *Lawrence,* this pattern is unrelated to ideology. The states
that repealed their laws through legislative means in the earlier period and
those that did so through the courts in the later period have virtually identical ideology scores (see table 4.2).

It is striking that almost half of the states repealed their sodomy laws
before 1980, through legislative action, when the gay rights movement was
not as large, experienced, or resourceful and there was much less public
acceptance of gays than exists today. It is hard to think that the gay rights
movement could muster enough political resources and public acceptance
to pass favorable legislation in any state during those years, much less in

Table 4.1 Date and method of repeal of state sodomy laws, 1960–79, 1980–2003

	1960–79		1980–2003	Repealed under *Lawrence*	
Illinois	1961	Pennsylvania	1980	Alabama	2003
Connecticut	1969	Wisconsin	1983	Florida	2003
Colorado	1971	Michigan	1990	Idaho	2003
Oregon	1971	Kentucky	1992	Kansas	2003
Hawaii	1972	Nevada	1993	Louisiana	2003
Ohio	1972	Montana	1996–97	Mississippi	2003
Delaware	1973	Tennessee	1996	Missouri	2003
New Hampshire	1973	Georgia	1998	North Carolina	2003
Arizona	1975	Rhode Island	1998	Oklahoma	2003
California	1975	Maryland	1999	South Carolina	2003
Maine	1975	Minnesota	2001	Texas	2003
New Jersey	1975	Arkansas	2002	Utah	2003
New Mexico	1975	Massachusetts	2002	Virginia	2003
New York	1975				
Washington	1975				
Indiana	1976				
Iowa	1976				
South Dakota	1976				
West Virginia	1976				
Nebraska	1977				
North Dakota	1977				
Vermont	1977				
Wyoming	1977				
Alaska	1978				

	Total		Legislative repeal states		Judicial repeal states	
	%	(N)	%	(N)	%	(N)
Total	100	(50)	46	(23)	54	(27)
1960–1979	48	(24)	83	(20)	17	(4)
1980–2003	52	(26)	12	(3)	88	(23)
Pre-*Lawrence*	74	(37)	62	(23)	38	(14)
Lawrence	26	(13)	0	(0)	100	(13)

Source: Donald P. Haider - Markel, "Media coverage of *Lawrence V. Texas*: An Analysis of Content, Tone and Frames in National News Reporting," New York: GLAAD Center for the Study of Media and Society, 2003, Appendix A, http://www.glaad.org/documents.

Table 4.2 States' ideology and method of repeal of sodomy laws

	Ideology Score[a]	(N)	Category Rating	Ideology Score[b]	(N)
1960–79 all repeal states	−12.3	(22)	somewhat liberal	52	(24)
1980–2003 all repeal states (excluding *Lawrence*)	−10.6	(12)	somewhat liberal	51.6	(13)
All legislative repeal states	−12.3	(23)	somewhat liberal	52.3	(23)
All judicial repeal states	−16.2	(27)	somewhat conservative	42.1	(27)
Repeal under *Lawrence v. Texas* (2003)	−22	(13)	most conservative	36.3	(13)
Judicial repeal states (excluding *Lawrence*)	−10.9	(14)	somewhat liberal	47.4	(14)
1960–1979 legislative repeal	−13	(18)	somewhat liberal	51.7	(20)
1980–2003 judicial repeal	−12	(10)	somewhat liberal	50.0	(10)

[a]Source: Erikson, Wright, and McIver (1993, ch. 2). The estimates of citizens' ideology in 48 states come from combining 122 CBS News/*New York Times* polls. Scores for each state were calculated by subtracting the percentage of conservative respondents from the percentage of liberal respondents. "Most liberal" states score −10% and higher, "somewhat liberal" states from −15 to −10.1%, "somewhat conservative" states from −20 to −15.1%, and "most conservative" states less than −20%. Erikson, Wright, and McIver excluded Alaska and Hawaii because no estimates were available and excluded Nevada because of a sampling problem.

[b]Source: Berry et al. (1998). Estimates of all 50 states' ideology run from 0 ("most conservative") to 100 ("most liberal").

places like Indiana, South Dakota, and Maine. None of these states have enacted nondiscrimination laws protecting gays yet.

However, as the next section makes clear, the fate of sodomy laws was linked closely to the campaign to revise the penal codes of the fifty states that took place over two decades after 1960. Penal code reform captured the imagination of the legal profession after World War II, and the reformers' recommendations gradually filtered into a number of state governments.

Early Legislative Repeal: The Role of Legal Reformers as Stakeholders

The great progress made in repealing sodomy laws from 1960 to 1980 owes much to legal professionals—lawyers, judges, and law professors, all of whom were important stakeholders in the debate over penal law reform. At stake for legal professionals are their professional interests and values in seeing that lawmakers design laws that the judicial system can enforce effectively and efficiently. Their expertise and practical experience with the law afford them influence. The opinions of professional legal organizations on these questions have a special credibility and legitimacy for legislators and judges, many of whom are lawyers themselves. Penal code reformers were critical for two reasons. First, they made the repeal of sodomy laws a small part of a more sweeping reform of the criminal law. In so doing, they packaged sodomy law repeal as a much broader set of reforms that reduced the salience of the sodomy law issue. Second, they defined the repeal issue as about the "overcriminalization" of "victimeless crimes" and of rational, good government reform. Thus, repeal did not become a "gay rights" issue.

Anglo-American criminal law codification has a long and distinguished history, beginning with the philosopher and legal scholar Jeremy Bentham. The American Law Institute (ALI) was responsible, more than any other organization, for legal reform and rationalization in the United States during the post–World War II decades (Kadish 1987). The ALI is a private organization of legal professionals founded in the 1920s by an elite group of jurists, lawyers, and legal academics, including William Howard Taft, Elihu Root, George Wickersham, Harlan Fiske Stone, Benjamin Cardozo, and Learned Hand. Famous judges, prominent lawyers from New York and Philadelphia, and law professors from Harvard and other elite universities dominated its ranks (Goodrich and Wolkin 1961). The ALI's stated purposes are to "promote the clarification and simplification of the law and its better adaptation to social needs, to secure the better administration of justice, and to encourage and carry on scholarly and scientific work" (quoted in Hazard 1994, 3; see also Frank 1998). Its status and legitimacy lay partly in its political independence from the legislative bodies whose work it evaluates (Kadish 1987, 234–40) and its expertise. The ALI has enlisted scores of law professors from throughout the country and assembled an extensive system of judges and prosecutors who review its work. The ALI has had the time, talent, and expertise to undertake major reforms of legal codes intended to apply generally across all fifty states.

The ALI received a grant in 1950 from the Rockefeller Foundation to study American criminal law to ascertain what kinds of behavior should be criminalized, how mental conditions and other circumstances should bear upon culpability, whether the classification of criminal offenses should be revised, and the appropriateness of particular forms of punishment and medical treatment (Goodrich and Wolkin 1961, 22–23). Under the leadership of Columbia University Professor Robert Weschler, the ALI embarked on a "fundamental reexamination, not only of the legal, but of the pertinent extra-legal bases of the criminal law as well as its aims, administration and effectiveness in action" (quoted in Frank 1998, 13). The ALI's investigation culminated in 1962 with publication of the *Model Penal Code*.

While it is full of reformist aspirations, the ALI sees itself, and others also see it as, an organization whose aim is to improve the legal establishment, not to challenge it. Its "conservative reformist outlook," as one observer describes it, reflects its adherence to careful judicial weighing of evidence (Hazard 1994, 11). In revising legal codes, ALI "reporters" place themselves in the position of a hypothetical "rational" legislator who seeks to develop "reasonable" and "realistic" rules based on logic and experience rather than emotion and prejudice. Its approach embodies the rational pragmatism of Progressive Era "good government" reformers whose chief aim was "to make law as rational and just as law can be" for the community and the individual (quoted in Kadish 1987, 237). In addition to legal experts, the ALI drew upon the burgeoning knowledge of social science and medicine in developing its *Model Penal Code*. It recruited sociologists, prison administrators, and psychiatrists to its advisory boards (Goodrich and Wolkin 1961, 23).

Out of its investigation, the ALI grew concerned about the "overcriminalization" of behavior that involved little or no harm to individuals, property, or government "or else highly intangible [harms] about which there is no genuine consensus or even no harms at all" (Kadish 1987, 21). Upon issuing commentaries and drafts of the *Model Penal Code* in the 1950s, and its final draft in 1962, the ALI urged legislatures to repeal sodomy laws and other victimless crimes, or at least reduce the penalties for them. It argued that sodomy laws were difficult to enforce; encouraged blackmail, entrapment, and discriminatory enforcement; discouraged homosexuals from seeking psychiatric help; and wasted the resources of the criminal justice system that could be put to better use (ALI 1955, 1962; Schwartz 1963, 676; Mitchell 1969, 79). The lack of the laws' enforcement undermined the public's respect for the law by fostering cynicism and a perception of hypocrisy. For example, the finding of Alfred Kinsey—that homosexuality was widespread—published in the well-known Kinsey Reports, suggested to the ALI that the laws were not effective in discouraging homosexual behavior (Kadish 1987, 23; Schwartz 1963, 674).

The ALI report also presented a normative case for doing away with sodomy laws based upon a respect for privacy rights. Embracing a liberal philosophical principle that John Stuart Mill asserted a century earlier, the ALI believed that consenting adults had the right to be protected against state interference in their acts of "private morality" that hurt no one except perhaps themselves (Mill 1859; Hart 1963; Schwartz 1963, 670). For Judge Learned Hand, sodomy was "a matter of morals, a matter very largely of taste" that the state had no business policing. Because the state's efforts to regulate private morals often sprang from religious convictions, such laws also raised First Amendment issues (Schwartz 1963, 674).[11] Restraining government from enforcing a particular moral consensus on matters of private personal conduct was particularly important, the ALI argued, in a diverse society like the United States, where "different individuals and groups have widely divergent views of the seriousness of various moral derelictions" (quoted in Schwartz 1963, 674). The criminal law was an inappropriate vehicle for society to use for controlling sexual behavior simply because it found it abhorrent: "no harm to the secular interests of the community is involved in a typical sex practice between consenting adult partners. The area of private morals is the distinctive concern of spiritual authorities" (quoted in Mitchell 1969, 79).

The ALI did not take an "anything goes" attitude towards sexual conduct, and it acknowledged that the community might form a moral consensus around perceived harms that are purely psychic. However, according to one of the drafters of the Model Penal Code, the ALI had "a general reluctance to extend penal controls of immorality to private behavior that disquiets people solely because they learn that things of this sort are going on" (Schwartz 1963, 675). The ALI recommended regulation of such conduct only if it involved minors or if it involved coercion, solicitation of sex for commercial purposes, loitering, or creating a public "nuisance." (Schwartz 1963, 675). Purely moral objections to such behavior were insufficient grounds for its criminalization.

The ALI voted in favor of the decriminalization of sodomy by a count of 35 to 24. The ALI was the most important professional group that endorsed the repeal of sodomy laws, but it was not the only one. In the early 1970s, when the largest number of states began to repeal their laws, the National Association for Mental Health, the American Psychiatric Association, the American Psychological Association, and the American Medical Association all removed homosexuality from their lists of mental disorders, which was an important rationale for enforcing sodomy laws against homosexuals (Barnett 1973, 294; Chauncey 2004a, 526). Other nations also decriminalized strictly private adult behavior. Continental European nations repealed their sodomy laws in the 1960s and 1970s, although many never had them or they were not as severe as those in the United States. Among major nations, only the United States and the former Soviet Union continued criminalizing same-sex acts between consenting adults (Barnett 1973, 293).[12]

The ALI's reform principles and recommendations received much recognition and acceptance in the United States and abroad (Hazard 1994, 8; Hull 1998). It played a decisive role in a majority of the states that repealed their sodomy statutes from 1960 to 1979. Even before its completion in 1962, the *Model Penal Code* had an impact on legislation and court opinions. Illinois was the first state, in 1961, to revise its penal code and eliminate its sodomy statute (Goodrich and Wolkin 1961, 24). Of the twenty-four states that repealed their sodomy laws in that period, sixteen of them, or two-thirds, repealed their sodomy laws as part of major overhauls of their state penal codes (Lewis 1999, 5). Thus, we can say confidently that the ALI figured prominently in the repeal of about one-third of the sodomy laws among the fifty states. Other states lowered the seriousness of the offense, for example, making sodomy a misdemeanor rather than a felony. Since the gay rights movement did not have sufficient political strength in the 1970s to accomplish repeal on its own, the opinions of legal and medical professionals probably had some impact on the eight other states that repealed their laws in this period.

Later Judicial Victories

The repeal of sodomy laws virtually ceased in the 1980s. Only Pennsylvania (through its courts) and Wisconsin (thorough its legislature) eliminated their laws in this decade. Conservative traditionalists and religious fundamentalists emerged to counter the gay rights movement in a number of states, especially within the Republican Party. The conservative backlash against gay rights began with Anita Bryant's crusade to overturn a Dade County, Florida, antidiscrimination ordinance in 1977 and gained momentum as evangelical Christians mobilized in the years that followed. Policymakers also did not want to appear to encourage sexual practices implicated in the spread of AIDS. Finally, the Supreme Court's ruling in *Bowers v. Hardwick* in 1986 upheld the constitutionality of sodomy laws and "removed one incentive" for state legislatures to enact reforms (Brantner 1992, 497). Some state courts and legislatures used *Bowers* to justify fending off efforts to repeal sodomy laws (Brantner 1992, 507–8; Leveno 1993–94, 1037). Because *Bowers* dealt only with the constitutionality of sodomy laws as the state used them against homosexuals, it also undercut legal efforts to build alliances with heterosexuals whom the police could also arrest under sodomy laws.

Rejected by the U.S. Supreme Court, advocates of repeal turned to state courts. State supreme courts invalidated the sodomy laws of seven of the next nine states to repeal their sodomy laws after Pennsylvania and Wisconsin had done so. Several close observers suggested that reformers would have more success at the state level in the wake of *Bowers* (Rubenfield 1986; Brantner 1992, 533; Leveno 1993–94; Cicchino, Deming, and Nicholson 1991). Unlike the U.S. Constitution, many state constitutions expressly contain a right of privacy, and some state courts define privacy differently than the majority in *Bowers* did (Leveno 1993–94, 1035–41, 1046).

FROM *BOWERS* TO *LAWRENCE*

In August 1982, police arrested Michael Hardwick, a bartender in Atlanta, when they found him having sex in his bedroom with another man in violation of Georgia's sodomy statute.[13] Twenty-four states had sodomy laws when the Supreme Court took up *Bowers v. Hardwick* in 1986. The Court's majority framed the issue as whether a "fundamental right" to engage in "homosexual sodomy" existed, even though Georgia's law was neutral as to the gender of the participants in the oral and anal sex acts that it prohibited. Hardwick's lawyers framed the issue as whether the state can interfere with adults' decisions about whether to engage in particular forms of private, consensual sexual activity. The Court acknowledged that earlier cases, like *Griswold v. Connecticut* and *Roe v. Wade,* recognized a right to privacy, but it argued that the privacy claim in those cases related to marriage, procreation, and raising children and that homosexual sodomy was not related to those issues. The Court argued that prior cases did not protect all consensual sexual conduct between adults undertaken in private. Adultery and incest, for example, remained crimes in many jurisdictions.

The Court's majority also asserted that for a fundamental right to exist, it must be "implicit in the concept of ordered liberty" or "deeply rooted in [the nation's] history and tradition" (*Bowers* 478, 191–92). "Homosexual sodomy" met neither of these criteria. As no such right existed, the state had to show only that it had a legitimate aim in outlawing such conduct. Thus, the appropriate basis for review of the Georgia law was whether the state had a "rational basis" for criminalizing same-sex conduct, not a stricter test that required "heightened scrutiny." The Court deemed that a community's moral values were a sufficient basis for meeting that standard.

Seventeen years later, the Court in *Lawrence* reframed the issue entirely. Arguing that *Bowers* failed "to appreciate the extent of the liberty at stake" when it defined the issue as whether there was a "fundamental right to homosexual sodomy," Justice Kennedy broadened the issue to "whether the petitioners were free as adults to engage in the private conduct in the exercise of their liberty under the Due Process Clause" (*Lawrence v. Texas*, 539 U.S. 564 [2003]). In refocusing the issue, he wrote, "To say that the issue in *Bowers* was simply the right to engage in certain sexual conduct demeans the claim the individual put forward, just as it would demean a married couple were it to be said marriage is simply about the right to have sexual intercourse" (539 U.S. 639). Kennedy eschewed conventional constitutional law methodology of explicitly categorizing certain *acts* as embodying a "fundamental right" and others as not. He chose, instead, to focus generally on how intimate sexual conduct is one way in which consenting adults express themselves in their *relationships* and how the substantive meaning of "liberty" in the Due Process Clause covers such conduct: "It suffices for us to acknowledge that adults may choose to enter upon this [intimate] relationship in the confines of their homes and their own private lives and still retain their dignity as free persons" (539 U.S. 565; see also Tribe 2004). Mere moral disapproval of homosexual conduct did not give the state a rational basis for criminalizing such relationships. As long as there was no "injury to a person or abuse of an institution the law protects," there was a strong presumption against government setting boundaries upon the kinds of intimate relationships individuals enter into (123 S. Ct. 2478).

In *Lawrence*, the Court recognized the powerfully negative symbolic force of sodomy laws when it wrote that the "continuance [of *Bowers*] as precedent demeans the lives of homosexual persons . . . [and] control[s] their destiny" (*Lawrence*, 123 S. Ct. at 2482, 2484). The Court did not simply decriminalize sexual acts that were closely associated with the gay "life-style" (although undertaken by heterosexuals as well). More importantly, it sought to combat the dehumanizing stereotype of same-sex couples' intimate relationships as nothing more than physical and erotic. According to Justice Kennedy, "when sexuality finds overt expression in intimate conduct with another person, the conduct can be but one element in a personal bond that is more enduring" (123 S. Ct. at 2478).[14]

The implications of *Lawrence* for gays in employment nondiscrimination, adoption, marriage, and other areas are only beginning to emerge. A number of experts and court observers have weighed in on this topic, particularly with regard to same-sex marriage. Opinions diverge widely, from those who see the decision as certain to open the door to further breakthroughs to those who see the substance of the decision (or the court system's capacity and inclination to use it) as much more limited. Little agreement exists about what *Lawrence*'s impacts will be or how long it will take for them to surface (see Hirsch 2005; *Harvard Law Review* 2005).

The Court's opinion in *Lawrence* listed several qualifications, noting that the case before it did not involve "minors[,] . . . persons who might be injured or coerced" and that the ruling did not "give formal recognition to any relationship that homosexual persons seek to enter" (539 U.S. 578). Evidence of the limited potential of *Lawrence* to further expand gay rights is found in the case *Lofton v. Secretary of the Department of Children and Family Services.* In that case, a federal appeals court upheld the constitutionality of Florida's ban on gays adopting children. It held that the state's rationale for the policy (promoting what the legislature deemed an "optimal family structure") could not be subject to a higher level of scrutiny because *Lawrence* had not conferred any "fundamental right" to "private sexual intimacy" (quoted in Parshall 2005, 258). On the other hand, state courts in Massachusetts, Washington, and New York have relied upon *Lawrence*, in part, to extend the right of marriage to same-sex couples (see Parshall 2005, 266–70).[15] The most far-reaching case so far has been the Massachusetts Supreme Judicial Court's ruling in *Goodridge v. Department of Public Health,* which held that the denial of marriage licenses to same-sex couples violated that state's constitution (798 N.E. 2d 941, Mass 2003).[16]

EXPLAINING THE COURT'S REVERSAL IN LAWRENCE

Why did the Supreme Court declare state sodomy laws unconstitutional after it concluded just the opposite seventeen years earlier? One explanation, particularly popular in the press after the Court handed down its ruling in *Lawrence*, gave considerable credit to the historical analyses presented in amicus curiae briefs that the American Civil Liberties Union, the Cato Institute, and a group of ten historians filed (Perlstein 2003; *New York Times* 2003; see also D'Emilio 2005, 5–7). The briefs supplied new information that was unavailable or overlooked in 1986 and that cast considerable doubt on key clams that Justice Byron R. White, writing for the majority, and Chief Justice Warren Burger, in a concurring opinion, made in *Bowers*. White and Burger argued that "homosexual sodomy" could not possibly be a right rooted in the country's laws and traditions because every state that ratified the Bill of Rights, and all but five states that ratified the Fourteenth Amendment, prohibited the conduct. Those state laws, in turn, had far more "ancient roots" in classical antiquity (478 U.S. 191–92, 196–97).

The historians' brief pointed out that there was no consistent pattern to the kinds of nonprocreative sexual acts that the state regulated during medieval and American colonial times and that the laws sometimes included same-sex partners and sometimes did not. "Sodomy" was not equivalent to homosexual conduct, as the *Bowers* majority implied. The laws targeted certain acts, not homosexuals as a group of people. States like Texas singled out homosexual sodomy for punishment only late in the twentieth century, just at the time when they decriminalized heterosexual sodomy. Hence, "neither millennia of moral teaching nor the American experience teach *any* consistent message about which sexual practices between consenting adults should be condemned and why. Rather, the unprecedented enactment in recent decades of sodomy laws that exclusively penalize homosexual conduct is one indication of the growth of a uniquely twentieth-century form of discrimination" (Chauncey 2004a, 519, 510–11).

Useful as the historians' brief may have been in helping the Court discredit *Bowers*, it is unlikely that it was decisive in shaping the outcome. Even one of its principal authors suspects that "the press exaggerated the importance of our intervention" (Chauncey 2004a, 503). Indeed, the majority in *Lawrence* went well beyond correcting the historical record. It redefined the issue altogether and formulated what Justice Antonin Scalia, in dissent, called an "unheard of" rationale and redefinition of the Due Process Clause that contained an expansive liberty interest.

The Court hinged its argument about such an interest on more than history and tradition. According to Justice Kennedy, quoting from his own concurring opinion in an earlier case (*County of Sacramento v. Lewis*, 523

U.S. 833, 857 [1998]), "history and tradition are the starting point but not in all cases the ending point of the substantive due process inquiry" (539 U.S. 11 [2003]). When he declared that "*Bowers* was not correct when it was decided and it is not correct today," he meant that, even with the historical record understood as it was in 1986, the *Bowers* Court had failed "to appreciate the extent of the liberty at stake" (539 U.S. 6 [2003]). Kennedy argued that the most relevant part of the record was *recent* history, which manifested an "emerging awareness" of the expansive meaning of liberty in the Constitution. He recounted a host of developments, starting with the ALI *Model Penal Code*'s recommendation to eliminate criminal penalties for consensual sexual relations. He proceeded to discuss the thirty-seven states that decriminalized sodomy since 1961, the European Court of Human Rights' repeal of sodomy laws, the Supreme Court's commitment to individual autonomy established in *Griswold v. Connecticut* and *Roe v. Wade* and affirmed in *Casey v. Planned Parenthood of Southeastern Pennsylvania*, and most recently, the Court's assertion of equal protection for gays and lesbians in *Romer v. Evans* (539 U.S. 11–13 [2003]). In sum, "the Nation's laws and traditions . . . show an emerging awareness that liberty gives substantial protection to adult persons in deciding how to conduct their private lives in matters pertaining to sex" (539 U.S. 11 [2003]).

Changes to the Supreme Court that took place after 1986 were more critical to its decision to reverse *Bowers* than the new historical analysis. Exactly how did the Court change in ways that pushed it to overturn *Bowers*? One possibility is that the Court was responding to public opinion, which had grown more positive toward gays and gay rights since 1986. Considerable evidence shows that shifts in public opinion affect Supreme Court decisions (Monroe 1979; Page and Shapiro 1983; Barnum 1985; Marshall 1989; Mishler and Sheehan 1993). One way that public opinion affects the Court is *indirectly*, when voters elect new presidents who fill vacancies on the Court that more or less reflect the ideological bent of the administration (Dahl 1957; Funston 1975; Segal and Spaeth 1993). According to this "ideological replacement" explanation, the Supreme Court reversed *Bowers* because it was a more liberal Court in 2003 than it was in 1986. Six justices who sat on the *Bowers* Court, including three of five in the majority, did not sit on the *Lawrence* Court in 2003.

Table 4.3 presents data on two measures of the ideological bent of the *Bowers* and *Lawrence* courts and the individual justices who sat on them. The first shows the percentage of liberal votes cast by each justice and for

Table 4.3 The U.S. Supreme Court and justices' ideology under *Bowers* and *Lawrence* (justices in the majority listed in *italics*)

Bowers Court (1986)	Ideology score[a]	% liberal votes, all cases[b]	% liberal votes, civil rights cases[c]	% liberal votes, civil liberties cases[f]	Ideology score, year[d]	Ideology score, career[e]
Blackmun	-0.77	54.3	62.1	52.8	-0.93	-0.11
Brennan	1.00	73.2	83.6	79.5	-3.38	-1.87
Burger	-0.77	35.6	37.3	29.6	1.95	1.80
Marshall	1.00	74.0	85.1	81.4	-4.11	-2.73
O'Connor	-0.17	39.7	44.4	35.7	1.29	0.89
Powell	-0.67	39.9	41.0	37.4	0.74	0.91
Rehnquist	-0.91	30.7	26.8	21.8	3.13	2.76
Stevens	-0.50	60.7	63.9	64.5	-0.58	-1.62
White	0.00	49.4	55.8	42.4	1.17	0.43
Entire Court:						
Median	-0.5	49.4	55.0	42.4	0.74	0.43
Mean	-0.2	50.8	55.5	49.5	-0.08	0.05
Majority:						
Mean	-0.5	39.1	41.1	33.4	1.65	1.36
Dissenters:						
Mean	0.18	65.6	73.6	69.6	-2.25	-1.58
Lawrence Court (2003)						
Breyer	-0.05	57.3	68.8	61.2	-1.22	-1.05
Ginsberg	0.36	59.6	65.6	64.6	-2.0	-1.33
Kennedy	-0.27	42.2	39.7	36.6	0.72	0.84

	a	b	c	d	e	f
O'Connor	-0.17	39.7	44.4	0.89	0.18	35.7
Rehnquist	-0.91	30.7	26.8	2.76	1.31	21.8
Scalia	-1.00	35.7	32.0	2.51	2.72	28.4
Souter	-0.34	57.1	62.7	-0.78	-1.85	60.8
Stevens	-0.5	60.7	63.9	-1.62	-2.78	64.5
Thomas	-0.68	32.5	22.3	3.26	3.43	25.1
Entire Court:						
Median:	-0.34	42.2	44.4	0.84	0.18	36.6
Mean:	-0.4	46.2	47.4	0.61	0.06	44.3
Majority:						
Mean:	-0.16	52.8	57.5	-0.51	-0.59	64.7
Dissenters:						
Mean:	-0.86	33.0	27.0	2.84	2.49	25.1
Bowers "leavers":						
Mean:	-.04	54.4	60.8	-0.26	-0.76	54.0
Lawrence "replacements":						
Mean:	-0.33	47.4	48.5	0.58	0.30	46.1

aFrom Epstein et al. (2003, 485, Table 6-1). Data are a measure of the judgments of newspaper editorials that characterize nominees before their confirmation as liberal or conservative on civil rights and liberties issues. Scores range from +1 (most liberal) to −1 (most conservative).

bThe percentage of justices' votes that are liberal in all cases from 1953 to 2001 except "interstate relations and miscellaneous." From Segal and Spaeth (2005, 320).

cPercentage of liberal decisions in civil rights, 1946–2003. From Epstein et al. (2003, 486–88) and the S. Sidney Ulmer Project, U.S. Supreme Court Databases, http://www.as.uky.edu/polisci/ulmerproject/sctdata.htm.

dIdeal point scores for 1986 and 2003 from Martin and Quinn (2002). 6 = most conservative; −6 = most liberal.

eIdeal point scores for justices' careers through 2004 from Martin and Quinn (2002). 6 = most conservative; −6 = most liberal.

fPercentage of liberal decisions in civil liberties cases, 1946–2001. From Epstein et al. (2003, 486–88).

the entire membership of each Court for all cases, civil rights cases, and civil liberties cases only. The second measure is an estimate of "ideal points" and assigns scores from 6 (for most conservative) to −6 (for most liberal) for each justice and each Court. Those scores are available for all cases only. The table provides little support for the ideological replacement hypothesis. The Court underwent no ideological shift between 1986 and 2003. Indeed, most of the measures indicate that the Court that ruled in *Lawrence* was *more* conservative, not less, than the one that handed down *Bowers*. Comparing the entire memberships of the *Bowers* and *Lawrence* courts, all six of the mean scores and four of the six median scores indicate that the *Lawrence* Court was more conservative than the *Bowers* Court. We get the same result when we compare the antirepeal majority in *Bowers* with the antirepeal dissenters in *Lawrence* and the prorepeal dissenters in Bowers with the prorepeal majority in *Lawrence*. The *Lawrence* Court is more conservative than the *Bowers* Court on every measure of these comparisons. The same conclusion holds when we compare the six justices who were on the Court in *Bowers* (and who departed before the Court ruled in *Lawrence*) with the six justices who replaced them. On every one of the measures, the six replacements involved in the *Lawrence* decision were, on average, more conservative than the justices they replaced on the *Bowers* Court.

Another possibility is that the *Lawrence* Court was more liberal *specifically* on gay rights issues, even though the Court had not undergone a broader ideological shift. One reason the Court might have become more hospitable to gay rights is that the new members of the Court who arrived after *Bowers* were from a younger generation that supports gay rights more than their predecessors. According to the "generational turnover" hypothesis, younger generations are subject to "cohort effects" in which salient social events and trends during the period when they come of age as teenagers and young adults have lasting effects on their political opinions throughout life. Alan Yang's (2003) study of public opinion change in gay rights shows clear cohort effects that explain the movement of aggregate public opinion in a more liberal direction on gay rights issues. Successive generations of Americans generally exhibit more liberal opinions on gay rights issues than do those who came before them.[17] Yang (2003, ch. 2) found significant differences between pre- and post–World War II age cohorts in their attitudes on gay rights issues, with the postwar generation registering significantly more liberal attitudes. Under this scenario, a younger cohort of justices with more tolerant opinions about gays and liberal opinions about gay rights replaced a less tolerant and more conservative older cohort.

The data are consistent with this hypothesis. Clearly, the Court in *Lawrence* was of a different generation than the one in *Bowers*. The entire membership of the *Bowers* Court was from the pre–World War II generation. By the time of *Lawrence*, five members of the postwar generation (Justices Stephen Breyer, Kennedy, Scalia, David Souter, and Clarence Thomas) sat on the Court and one other (Ruth Bader Ginsberg) straddled the two generations. Four of these postwar generation "replacement justices" were among the six-member majority in *Lawrence* (see table 4.4).

A third possibility is that some justices shifted their opinions on gay rights between 1986 (or whenever they joined the Court) and 2003. Unlike the ideological and generational replacement hypotheses, this scenario does not assume that justices' political opinions are fixed and unchanging by the time they join the Court. Instead, justices' political opinions can evolve during the years they sit on the Court. Under this "political adjustment" hypothesis, public opinion may have *direct* effects, even controlling for the Court's ideological composition, if justices defer to public opinion in order to preserve the Court's authority (see Mishler and Sheehan 1993).[18] Moderate justices are particularly prone to respond to public opinion and are more strongly responsive to it than justices with stronger ideological orientations (Mishler and Sheehan 1996). Alternatively, under the "conversion" hypothesis, justices' political opinions may change because of the "underlying social forces that set in motion those broad changes in public opinion" (Mishler and Sheehan, 1996, 174). The conversion hypothesis is consistent with "period effects" in which events and social trends shape changes in opinion over one's entire life. Yang (2003) found such period effects to go along with the cohort effects mentioned already. Specifically, he found that *all* generations of Americans have become more liberal on gay rights over recent decades. For example, when the Court decided *Bowers* in 1986, less than 40 percent of the pre–World War II cohort supported "allowing" gays to be college teachers. Their rate of approval rose to 57 percent by 2000. Their ranking on the "feeling thermometer," which measures negative and positive affect toward gays, was a cold score of 25 in 1986. That figure rose to almost 40 by 2000 (Yang 2003, 60, 74).

The data available do not permit us to distinguish between changes in justices' opinions due to political adjustment and those from conversion. The fact that public opinion has been split on the issue of legalizing

Table 4.4 Generational cohorts among justices of the *Bowers* and *Lawrence* courts (justices in the majority listed in *italics*)

Years in which justices were born:

Bowers Court		Generational Cohort
Brennan	1906	pre–World War II
Burger	1907	pre–World War II
Blackmun	1908	pre–World War II
Marshall	1908	pre–World War II
O'Connor	1930	pre–World War II
Powell	1907	pre–World War II
Rehnquist	1924	pre–World War II
Stevens	1920	pre–World War II
White	1917	pre–World War II
Entire Court:		
Median year	1908	pre–World War II
Mean year	1914	pre–World War II
Court Majority:		
Median year	1917	pre–World War II
Mean year	1917	pre–World War II

Lawrence Court		
Breyer	1938	post–World War II
Ginsberg	1933	borderline
Kennedy	1936	post–World War II
O'Connor	1930	pre–World War II
Rehnquist	1924	pre–World War II
Scalia	1936	post–World War II
Souter	1939	post–World War II
Stevens	1920	pre–World War II
Thomas	1948	post–World War II
Entire Court:		
Median year	1936	post–World War II
Mean year	1934	post–World War II
Court Majority:		
Median year	1933–36	borderline
Mean year	1933	borderline

homosexual relations casts doubt on the political adjustment hypothesis, although it is possible that the Court's majority was deferring to the public's more positive attitudes toward gays generally and toward other gay rights issues. Two of the key moderate justices in the *Lawrence* decision, Sandra Day O'Connor and Kennedy, compiled more liberal voting records over time (see figure 4.1).

O'Connor is the only justice who voted in the majority in *both* the *Bowers* and *Lawrence* decisions. Although O'Connor's vote was not as decisive in the 6–3 *Lawrence* decision as it was in 5–4 decisions, her reputation as a moderate conservative and the most pivotal swing vote in the Court under Chief Justice William Rehnquist made her a prime candidate for conversion. Conversion may have played a role in O'Connor's decision to vote with the majority in *Lawrence*, but the different facts in *Lawrence* and *Bowers* provided O'Connor with an opportunity to vote with the majority in both cases without indicating a change in her basic orientation to gay rights cases. Unlike in Georgia, the Texas law applied to homosexuals only. In her concurring opinion in *Lawrence*, O'Connor did not overrule *Bowers*. She argued instead that the Texas law failed to treat homosexuals and heterosexuals in the same manner. Since the discrimination was based simply on the state's desire to discriminate against an unpopular minority, O'Connor found the discrimination unwarranted (*Lawrence*, 123, S. Ct., O'Connor J., concurring, 2484–87). In adopting the equal protection rationale, O'Connor avoided embracing the majority's sweeping claims about due process rights.

Justice Kennedy was the other key moderate conservative who may have undergone a pro–gay rights conversion or deferred to the growing acceptance of gays in society since *Bowers*. Kennedy authored the Court's opinions in *Lawrence* and in *Romer v. Evans* in 1996, the other major victory for gays before the Supreme Court. Kennedy ranked as the median member of the Rehnquist Court in his ideology scores for all cases to come before the Court and for civil liberties cases in particular (see table 4.3). Indeed, as one observer put it, Kennedy's opinions reflect an "increasing acceptance of a methodology that gives an expansive interpretation of liberty shaped by evolving societal standards" (Parshall 2005, 237–38).

In sum, the Supreme Court's reversal of *Bowers v. Hardwick* was probably most strongly influenced by a combination of a younger, more gay friendly, generational cohort that sat on the Court in 2003 and the influence on more moderate justices of period effects in which the social climate had grown more tolerant toward gays and supportive of gay rights. Having

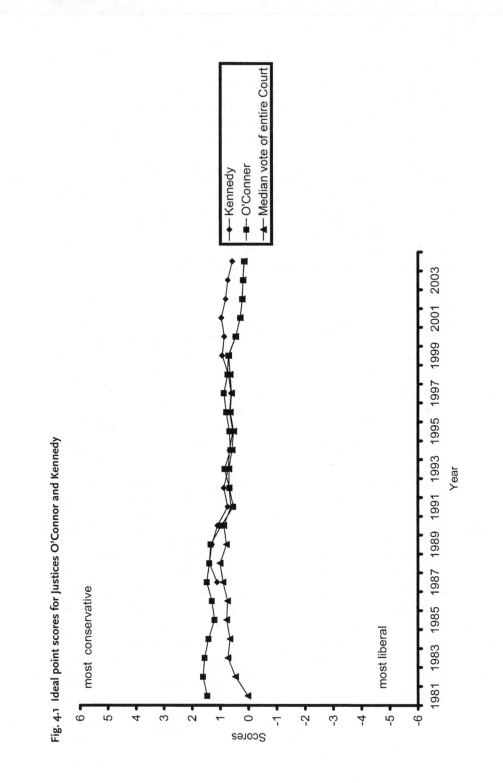

Fig. 4.1 Ideal point scores for Justices O'Connor and Kennedy

thus become predisposed to overturning *Bowers,* a majority of the Court in 2003 availed itself of new information on the history of sodomy laws that helped undermine many arguments used in *Bowers* to uphold the constitutionality of such statutes.

CONCLUSION

Our examination of the repeal of sodomy laws supports the hypotheses presented in chapter 1 for the most part. Despite the opinion of the public that was, at best, badly split over whether homosexual conduct should be legal, the gay rights movement has achieved total success on the issue of legalizing homosexual conduct. Three reasons account for this outcome: (1) reformers took advantage of variable conditions in the states that were often conducive to the spread of repeal from 1960 to 2000, a period in which the U.S. Supreme Court was uninvolved and later protective of sodomy laws in 1986; (2) the presence of influential stakeholders in the legal profession who favored repeal; and (3) eventual judicial cooperation in the repeal movement. The last two factors, in particular, point to the key role of liberal elites in the success of the LGBT rights movement when public opinion is cool toward gay rights.

To see the importance of state-level policymaking, we need only to imagine what likely would have happened if the locus of "morals legislation" was at the federal rather than state level of government. It is implausible (though conceivable) that Congress or the Supreme Court would have repealed a federal sodomy law. Congress never adopted a modern criminal code, and its failure to do so is the ALI's most glaring disappointment in its campaign to get the *Model Penal Code* adopted (Robinson and Dubber 1999, 6). Even if Congress had adopted such a code, it is not certain that it would have included the repeal of a federal sodomy law. Congress has a very poor record on gay rights, having yet to pass even minimal civil rights and hate crimes protections and to lift the ban on gays in the military—all changes that the public supports more strongly than the decriminalization of homosexual conduct. The federal government would have been the most ideologically suited to repeal a federal sodomy law when liberals were at their height of influence from the mid-1960s to the mid-1970s. But the gay rights movement had yet to come into its own, gay rights was not on the agenda, and public opinion was much more hostile toward gays. The U.S. Supreme Court's record in ruling in favor of gay petitioners was poor until the 1990s and then became mixed in the decade that followed.[19]

By contrast, almost half of the states eliminated their laws before 1980, including many of the largest, like California, New York, New Jersey, and Illinois. Only thirteen states still had sodomy laws on the books at the time of the *Lawrence* decision. Public opinion in the various states clearly had some role, particularly after 1980. By the time of *Lawrence,* all of the states of a moderate to liberal ideological bent, and virtually all in which public opinion supported legalization, had repealed their laws.

But more than variation in public opinion and ideology across states was at work. Public opinion did not favor the repeal of sodomy laws in many states where it occurred in the 1960–79 period, and there was no strong gay rights movement to push the issue onto the agenda. The fact that almost half of the states repealed their laws through legislative means is inconsistent with our expectation that it would be very difficult to expand gay rights through popular institutions in the absence of public support. The preferences of highly influential and respected legal and medical stakeholders, like the ALI and the American Psychiatric Association, converged neatly with repeal and helped to disseminate the idea of decriminalization of victimless crimes widely. Reformers absorbed sodomy law repeal into the broader issue of penal law reform and defined the problem as over-criminalization of victimless crimes, or more generally, good government reform, rather than gay rights. The low salience of gay rights issues from the 1960s to the mid-1970s, and the absence of a strong religious conservative movement in those years, made it possible for criminal code reformers to define repeal as a broad good government issue rather than a gay rights issue.

Although judicial involvement in the repeal process was limited until 1980, the courts played a major role in picking up the ball when legislative efforts stalled. Ten state supreme courts overturned their sodomy statutes from 1980 to 2002 (despite the U.S. Supreme Court's *Bowers* decision, which declared them constitutional). Once the Court reversed *Bowers* and swept aside the thirteen remaining sodomy laws in 2003, the number of sodomy laws eliminated through judicial means exceeded the number repealed legislatively. The Court's *Lawrence* decision was the critical endpoint in a long story with a consistent theme—a growing reluctance to use government to enforce prohibitions against adult consensual sexual behavior—that moved first down a legislative track, and then down a judicial one. *Lawrence's* significance lies not just in striking down the thirteen sodomy statutes that remained but also in shutting the door on such laws for good.

The finality of the Court's decision means that no political jurisdiction can enact laws prohibiting sexual expression between consenting adults in private. Insofar as the laws' branding of gays and lesbians as criminals legitimated and encouraged hostility and discrimination against gays and blocked progress in expanding gay rights, *Lawrence's* effects may be even more far reaching.[20]

Adoption

5

Barbara and Carole Fryberger met in 1983 and decided to make their home in Lancaster County, Pennsylvania. Carole gave birth to twin boys named Robby and Reese in 1997 after ten years of infertility treatments and in vitro fertilization. Barbara was a parent to the twins as much as Carole was, and the boys thought of her as one of their "mommies." The women sought to have Barbara become the boys' other legal parent so that the children would have greater emotional and financial security: The boys would not be eligible for Barbara's health insurance, Social Security survivors' benefits, and other entitlements without the adoption. Moreover, Barbara would have no legal claim on the boys if Carole were to die. The women found to their surprise that the adoption would not be automatic. The state approved the Frybergers' adoption only after a lengthy legal battle that culminated in a 2002 Supreme Court of Pennsylvania decision. Today, same-sex couples are routinely granted adoptions in Pennsylvania (Espenshade 2000a, 2002b).

Chad Long is an elementary school teacher, and Todd Berg supervises people who work with the disabled. They met in 1996, fell in love, and began a committed relationship. Five years later, they decided they wanted to become parents. Adopting a child who is under the custody of the state of North Dakota, where they live, was virtually impossible because the Department of Human Services (DHS) had a reputation for rejecting gays and lesbians as adoptive parents. The men worked instead with a private adoption agency, which found a birth mother who was willing to let them adopt her two-year-old son. The agency dropped their case, however, when the child's foster parents threatened to go to the media about the impending adoption and DHS appeared ready to block it. The men turned to another agency that was willing to work with them, helped to get the boy removed from the foster parents, and found ways to keep DHS from interfering in the adoption. Chad and Todd's determination was rewarded in 2001 when they became the proud parents of the little boy, whom they named Jensen (Cahill, Ellen, and Tobias 2002, 82–83).

Thousands of same-sex couples like Barbara and Carole and Chad and Todd across the United States have formed families and assumed the rights and responsibilities of parenthood. The rate at which gay couples have done so has risen rapidly since the start of the "gayby boom" in the 1990s. Lambda Legal estimates that 250,000 children are being raised by same-sex couples in the United States (Lambda Legal 2007; NGLTF 2003; Lotozo 2003; Gray 2001). Using data from the 2000 census, one study estimates that approximately 65,500 adopted children are being raised by gay parents. More than 4 percent of adopted children live in gay and lesbian households. Same-sex couples are raising 1 percent of all adopted children (Gates et al. 2007).

Gays and lesbians have parented children resulting from heterosexual marriages for years. What is new over the past two decades is that gays have adopted as *couples,* and courts and adoption agencies have viewed them increasingly as suitable parents (Ricketts and Achtenberg 1987, 92–93; Weston 1991, 165–67). Many of the children whom same-sex couples adopt have been in the foster care system, were given up for adoption by their biological mothers, or have serious problems that make them difficult to place in permanent homes. But as in Barbara and Carole's example, same sex-couples are not just adopting the unwanted offspring of people who are strangers to them. Artificial insemination and surrogate motherhood make it possible for gay and lesbian couples to have children who are biologically related to one of the partners. The partner who is not biologically related to the child can petition the court for a "second parent" adoption that is granted in an increasing number of jurisdictions (Gray 2001).

PROGRESS IN GAINING ADOPTION RIGHTS

States and counties across the United States have become increasingly favorable toward adoption by same-sex couples. Gay couples have secured the right to adopt statewide in ten states and the District of Columbia (see table 5.1). Some of these states are among the most populous in the nation: they account for 35 percent of the U.S. population and about 42 percent of the gay and lesbian population as estimated from the 2000 census.[1] Six of the ten states with the highest number of same-sex couple households

Table 5.1 Status of same-sex second-parent adoption rights in the United States

States in which right is legally secure or regularly granted[a]
10 states plus District of Columbia: CA, CO, CT, IL, IN, MA, NJ, NY, PA, VT

States in which right is available in some jurisdictions[b]
15 states: AL, AK, DE, HI, IA, LA, MD, MN, NH, NV, NM, OR, RI, TX, WA

States in which law is unclear and untested
18 states: AZ, AR, GA, ID, KS, KY, ME, MO, MT, NC, ND, OK, SC, SD, TN, VA, WV, WY

States in which same-sex couple adoption is prohibited or severely restricted[c]
7 states: FL, NE, MI, MS, OH, UT, WI

Sources: Adopted from issue maps "Adoption Laws in the U.S." and "Second Parent Adoption in the U.S." from the National Gay and Lesbian Task Force (http://www.thetaskforce.org/downloads/reports/issue_maps?adoption_laws_09_07_color.pdf; http://www.thetaskforce.org/downloads/reports/issue_maps/2nd_parent_adoption_05_07_color.pdf); and "Adoption Laws: State by State" from the Human Rights Campaign (http://www.hrc.org/issues/parenting/adoption/8464.htm).
[a]State allows second-parent or stepparent adoption by same-sex couples either by law or high court interpretation.
[b]In these states, no high court rulings have been made, but at least one trial-level court has ruled that the state's law permits same-sex second-parent adoptions. Some counties also grant joint adoptions.
[c]FL law prohibits gays and lesbians from adopting. MI, MS, and UT laws prohibit unmarried or same-sex couples from adopting. In NE, OH, and WI, a state court has ruled that the law does not allow adoption by same-sex couples.

reported in the census are included in this group (California, New York, Illinois, Pennsylvania, Massachusetts, and New Jersey) (Smith and Gates 2002). In fifteen other states, gay couples have been able to adopt in jurisdictions where at least one trial court has declared same-sex couple adoptions legal. Gays and lesbians living in these states often petition judges in the "gay friendly" counties, which are usually large urban centers that are known to grant the adoptions. These states, combined with the nine states in which gay couples have secured the right to adopt statewide, comprise well over half of the U.S. population (56 percent) and of gay and lesbian families living in the United States (63 percent).[2] Therefore, about two-thirds of the gay and lesbian population of the United States has a realistic chance of adopting children if they desire and are found to be suitable parents.

The process of granting adoption rights to gay couples is much more politically significant than the process whereby gay and lesbian individuals adopt children or parent their offspring from heterosexual marriages. When the state grants adoptions to gay couples, it explicitly acknowledges and legitimates same-sex spousal relationships. The couples cannot conceal their sexual orientation and their relationship, nor can society deny their existence.

The progress gays have made in adoption compared with marriage is striking. Only seven states allow marriage or civil unions or have a significant domestic partnership policy, compared with twenty-four that allow gays to adopt. Forty-four states have adopted bans on gay marriage, twenty-six of which contain the ban in their constitution. Only seven states prohibit or severely restrict gay adoption.[3] Virtually no state legislatures or ballot referenda have overturned court rulings permitting gay adoption, nor has any state changed its constitution to ban gays from adoption. When courts in several states began ruling in favor of adoption rights in the early 1990s, as many Americans opposed gay adoption as oppose gay marriage today. Almost three-quarters of Americans registered "strong" opposition to the idea of allowing gays to adopt (Wilcox and Wolpert 2000). And although the public has warmed somewhat to the idea of gay adoption over the past decade, public opinion remains about evenly split (see chapter 1; Sullivan 1993; Duncan 1994). Allowing gays to adopt remains far less popular than allowing gays to serve in the military and banning discrimination against them in employment. Given the much greater potential for adoption to provoke heterosexual anxieties than for protecting gays from discrimination in the workplace or in the housing market, it is striking that the gay rights movement has been almost as successful in gaining the spread of adoption rights as protections against discrimination in employment and housing.

What accounts for the relative political success gays and lesbians have experienced in this area? This chapter argues that particular institutional features of the process in which adoption policy is made and adoptions are adjudicated have had a significant impact. Adoption policymaking is highly decentralized, with numerous state and local judges afforded considerable discretion in deciding cases. Judges generally enjoy greater insulation from majority opinion than do legislators, and they address petitions for adoption as exercises in practical problem solving that involve weighing a number of factors that vary according to the facts of particular cases. The interests of important stakeholders like adoption agencies and social workers coincide with same-sex couples seeking adoption. The mission of the adoption system, changes in family structure and family law, and the political attitudes of adoption professionals are compatible with greater support for gay petitioners.

COURT-CENTERED POLICYMAKING

Courts have taken the lead in deciding whether to allow same-sex couples to adopt (Stashenko 2000). Courts in twenty-four states have ruled on whether the law permits same-sex couples to adopt, compared with only eight state legislatures that have passed laws in this area. In some of the eight legislative approval states, courts put the issue on the agenda, induced legislative action, and shaped the legislatures' decisions.[4] In others, the courts have been heavily involved in affirming or elaborating upon the applicability of the statutes.[5] In the eighteen remaining states, the law on adoption is unclear. Neither the legislature nor the courts have ruled on whether the law permits gay couples to adopt. Even in these eighteen states, however, courts are the key policymakers by default, as specific decisions about awarding children are always left up to "the informed and reasoned judgment of a family or probate court" (Shapiro 1995–96, 636). Thus, the influence of the courts on adoption policy stems from the absence of legislative involvement in setting policy and the need to rely upon judges as "street-level bureaucrats" to implement the law in specific cases (Lipsky 1980).

Judicial Support for Gay Adoption

Courts are more likely than legislatures to permit gay couples to adopt. Gay couples secured the right to adopt through the courts in eight of the ten states where it is permitted statewide. In the ninth state, Connecticut, a court decision precipitated legislative approval of second-parent adoptions. Only three of the legislatures of the ten states that permit adoption have followed up the court decisions with changes in their adoption statutes. Favorable trial court rulings have secured adoption rights in the fifteen other states where gay couples can adopt in certain jurisdictions. In his study of 163 adoption, custody, visitation, and foster care decisions of state appellate courts from 1981 to 2000, Pinello (2003, 16, 18) found that gay and lesbian petitioners prevailed more than half of the time and that their chances of success increased more than 50 percent over that period.

SELECTION OF STATE COURT JUDGES

Courts are more hospitable to gay couples because the methods used to select and retain judges afford them a degree of autonomy from constituency opinion that state legislators do not enjoy. The ten states that allow gay couples to adopt statewide are disproportionately states in which judges are appointed to office and do not have to run for reelection. Judges in four (or 40 percent) of these states and the District of Columbia do not have to worry about reelection, compared with only 12 percent of judges in the forty-one other states. Of the nine states and District of Columbia where judges do *not* run for reelection, all but one is a state in which gay adoption is secure statewide or at least one trial court judge has ruled in its favor (U.S. Department of Justice 1998).[6]

The vast majority of state court judges, or about 84 percent, must run for reelection, just as their legislative counterparts do. Judicial elections are notoriously low-salience contexts that heavily favor incumbents. Even so, given the controversy and visibility of gay rights issues, judges and legislators probably anticipate constituents' reactions to their decisions. Judges who have longer terms of office should have to worry less about the electoral consequences of their decisions. Indeed, the length of judges' terms of office appears to be an important predictor of judicial behavior (Songer 1995; Brace and Hall 1997, 1206). State appeals court judges serve 8 years and trial court judges 6.6 years, on average (U.S. Department of Justice 1998, 26–29, 34–49). By contrast, the average length of terms is 3.5 years for state senators and 2.2 years for state representatives (Silbey 1991, 436–37).

Pinello's (2003, 92) examination of hundreds of cases involving gay and lesbian rights at the state level revealed that state judges who enjoyed longer terms of office were more likely to render decisions in support of gay rights.[7] The data in table 5.2 confirm Pinello's broader finding for adoption policy specifically. It shows that states whose judges have ruled in favor of adoption rights enjoy longer terms of office than do judges in states that have not done so. The difference in the length of terms for appeals court judges in states in which high courts have ruled in favor of gay adoption, compared with those that have ruled to prohibit them, is more than four years, and almost three years for trial court judges. Appeals court judges who sit on courts that have ruled in favor have terms almost twice as long as in states that ruled to prohibit gay adoption.

**Table 5.2 Length of judicial terms of office and lesbian/gay/
bisexual adoption rights (number of states in parentheses)**

	Appeals courts mean length of term	Trial courts mean length of term
All states	8.0	6.6
States in which adoption rights are legally secure and regularly granted (10, plus District of Columbia)[a]	10.9	8.5
States in which adoption is permitted in some jurisdictions (15)[b]	8.0	7.2
States in which no court has ruled on gay adoption (18)	7.7	5.8
States that have prohibited or severely restricted gay adoption (7)	6.3	5.7
States in which a high court has prohibited or severely restricted gay adoption (4)	6.5	6.0

[a]Category includes Massachusetts, where judges may serve until 70 years old. The average length of term is estimated at 10 years, which is most likely conservative. Removing Massachusetts from the calculations does not affect the figure calculated for this category of 10.2 years.

[b]Category includes New Hampshire, where judges may serve until 70 years old, and Rhode Island, where they may serve for life. The average length of term is estimate at 10 years, which is most likely conservative. Removing New Hampshire and Rhode Island from the calculations reduces the calculation of the average term to 7.7.

CASE-BY-CASE DECISION MAKING

Since most states do not have clear policies on gay adoption, policy is made in a highly disaggregated fashion by judges who must consider the facts in specific cases. Case-based decision making is typical of how courts make policy, but the lack of guidance in most adoption statutes and the necessity for judges to take account of the specific circumstances of the petitioners and children involved in each case magnify its importance. Judges become very familiar with the parties to an adoption, aware of the practical consequences of their decisions and the limited options that are often available in finding suitable parents. This is advantageous for gay petitioners because judges' decisions are framed in terms of concrete, personal relationships and practical needs, rather than as statements of broad policy goals or pronouncements on cultural values (*New York Times* 1993a). Legislators' decisions, by contrast, are likely to reflect broad policy judgments and expressions of cultural values, even if they come in contact with constituents who are trying to adopt.

Judges may be more supportive of gay adoption rights than legislators for other reasons. Even judges who must run for reelection may perceive their role as stating what the law is rather than responding to majority opinion. In addition, judges may view the protection of minority rights as a chief function of the courts in a democratic system.[8]

Sources of Judicial Involvement

VAGUE STATUTES

Judicial dominance of policymaking is typical of most issues in family law. Legislatures have granted courts significant discretion in deciding what the law is and how it should be applied in specific circumstances.[9]

State laws are vague because decisions about adoptions must be made on a case-by-case basis after careful consideration of the facts in particular family contexts. Children differ greatly in their age; race; family history; physical, financial, and emotional needs; and relationships with the adults in their lives. Prospective parents differ in age, physical and emotional health, work demands, financial resources, capacities for nurturing and guidance, and support from family and friends. "Family law," according to a leading expert, "is characterized by more discretion than any other field of private law because of the need to tailor legal resolutions to the unique circumstances of each individual and family" (Glendon 1986, 1165).

Statutes dealing with adoption, custody, and visitation do not go much beyond stating the fundamental principle that decisions should be made "in the best interest of the child" and the goal of finding stable and permanent homes for as many children who need them. This gives courts wide latitude, if they choose to use it, in deciding what kinds of adoptions to permit (Padawer 2002). Most laws are also vague with regard to who is eligible to adopt. They stipulate typically that unmarried individuals and married couples can adopt but are silent about whether unmarried couples, gay or straight, can adopt.

For example, Michigan's adoption law states that "if a person desires to adopt a child . . . that person, together with his wife or her husband, if

married, should file a petition" (Associated Press 2002a). Judges and attorneys differ about whether that law permits gay and unmarried straight
couples to adopt. Some believe that the law only allows married couples
to adopt; others contend that a couple must adopt a child together if they
are married, but if they are not, each partner can "co-adopt" individually
(Associated Press 2002a). Illinois law states that someone may adopt if
he or she is "a reputable person of legal age and of either sex, provided
that if such person is married, his or her spouse shall be a party to the
adoption proceeding . . . in all of which cases the adoption shall be by both
spouses jointly." Until an appellate court ruled that it could construe the
word "person" as plural, judges disagreed about whether it permitted two
unmarried people to adopt jointly depending upon whether they thought
that "person" could include two unmarried individuals (Gitlin 1995; Bailey
1995a, 1995b; Duncan 1994). New York's law states that an "adult unmarried person or an adult husband and his adult wife together may adopt
another person."[10] Before New York's highest court ruled in favor of adoptions by unmarried couples, some judges thought this provision meant
that only an unmarried individual or a married couple could adopt. Others
held that an unmarried person whose partner already had custody of the
child could also adopt the child but that a married person only could adopt
along with their spouse (Florescue 1995, 3; Spencer 1995, 1).

Adoption laws typically include "relinquishment provisions" that bar individuals from adopting a child unless someone who is already the child's
legal parent gives up his or her parental rights. (Exceptions are made for
stepparents, who are married to the legal parent). These provisions ensure
that birth parents who put their children up for adoption cannot claim parental authority once others have adopted the child. If gay men and lesbians want to adopt their partner's child, courts may deny them under the
relinquishment requirement because (unlike stepparents) gay couples are
unable to marry or form civil unions in most states. Courts in some states
get around the relinquishment requirement by ruling that the law permits
second-parent adoptions. Some of these states permit unmarried couples
to adopt, or their courts have been persuaded by gay couples that second-
parent adoptions are in the best interest of children. Many courts recognize that the intended targets of relinquishment provisions are biological
and adoptive parents who are strangers and that it is absurd to insist that
a parent relinquish his or her own parental rights in order for the partner
to adopt his or her child (Litchman 2002, 1; Bleemer 1995, 9; *New York*

Times 1993c). Still, some courts have barred second-parent adoptions on the grounds that they are only permitted in cases where two people are married, regardless whether an adoption may be in the best interest of the child.[11]

Different rulings have arisen not only among states but from one county or judge to another within the same state.[12] Even in states where the high court has ruled against allowing second-parent adoptions, lower court judges have circumvented the rulings at times by interpreting the law as permitting adoptions by gay partners as single individuals. In Wisconsin, where that state's Supreme Court has barred second-parent adoptions, a lesbian described her adoption of a baby from China this way: "First I gave up my parental rights for about a nanosecond, otherwise Mary Jane [her partner] couldn't have adopted her. Then we both adopted her as single adults." According to her lawyer, "the law doesn't say you can't" (quoted in Ingersoll 2002). Other states, like Ohio, permit gay couples to enter into "cocustody" agreements in which the partner of a gay or lesbian parent shares parental authority (Thomas 1998, D10).

STRICT AND LIBERAL CONSTRUCTIONISTS

Adoption law is as much *judge* centered as it is court dominated. Stare decisis is usually a major constraint on court decisions, but it is not as important in adoption policy because of the relative absence of precedents on issues like second-parent adoptions. Judges are much freer to base their decisions on their judicial philosophies, their political attitudes, and voters' preferences.[13]

Judges' willingness to grant same-sex couple adoptions rests heavily upon whether they are "strict" or "liberal" constructionists. Strict constructionists make laws more restrictive by having them cover fewer situations; rely heavily upon the plain, literal meaning of the words of statutes; and defer to the legislature to define the law. Unless the law says that that two unmarried people can adopt, strict constructionist judges rule that they cannot (Gitlin 1995). Strict constructionists believe that legislatures should decide what is lawful and that judges who interpret the law loosely are usurping the role of legislators.[14] In disallowing gay couples to adopt, strict constructionists frequently argue that they are not judging the suitability of gays as parents. Some of them admit that gays can be fit parents but insist that the legislature must clarify the law to permit them to adopt. The appeals court judge who dissented in the 2–1 ruling that approved same-sex second-parent adoptions in New Jersey argued that "the matter before the court is one of statutory application; it is not about sexual orientation and it is not about approval or disapproval of the manner in which individuals live their lives" (quoted in Bleemer 1995, 9). Judges have made the same point in rulings against gay couples in Michigan, Massachusetts, Illinois, and other states.[15]

Liberal constructionists construe the language of statutes broadly, so that they apply to more situations. If the law is unclear or silent, they believe that judges should disregard it or look only to its general purpose. Family laws in many states were written decades before the sweeping social and technological changes in marriage, the family, and reproduction of the past half century (Florescue 1995, 3). Liberal constructionists argue that the fundamental purpose of adoption statutes is to make sure that children's physical and emotional needs are met and that legislatures have increasingly intended to promote adoption over foster care and other options. In a typical example, New York's highest court ruled to allow one gay partner to adopt the child of the other partner because the child "would be irrevocably deprived of the benefits and entitlements of having as her legal parents the two individuals who have already assumed that role in her life, simply as a consequence of her mother's sexual orientation" (Dao 1995). A few years later, the same court ruled that a lesbian couple could submit a joint petition to adopt a foster child instead of filing separately because their sexual orientation "is of no significance because the goal of the [adoption] statute is to 'encourage the adoption of as many children as possible'" (Dobbin 2004; Florescue 1995, 3).[16]

DECENTRALIZED POLICYMAKING

It is arguable whether we should characterize adoption as a strictly state-level policymaking function, as adoption policy decisions essentially fall to local courts in many states by default. Court interpretations and applications of adoption laws vary across states and across the counties within them. State supreme courts and appellate courts have set statewide policy on gay adoption in only twelve of the twenty-seven states in which the courts have become involved in making policy. Appellate courts routinely defer to the decisions of trial court judges in adoption, custody, visitation, and foster care cases because trial courts observe witnesses to ascertain their truthfulness and demeanor and evaluate other evidence directly. Since appellate court judges are at a disadvantage in these kinds of cases, "trial judges, accordingly, are particularly powerful" (Pinello 2003, 22). Thus, in several states, the availability of second-parent adoptions often varies from county to county and even judge to judge within particular counties.

Fourteen of Pennsylvania's sixty-two counties had permitted second-parent adoptions, while the others prohibited them or had no policy, until its Supreme Court ruled to allow them (Kelley 2000). Before an Illinois appellate court ruled on the issue, some of that state's courts permitted second-parent adoptions routinely for about four years while others did not (McDonough 1999). Before New York's highest court declared such adoptions legal in 1995, lower courts denied a gay male couple from Staten Island (who had been together for twenty-three years) the adoption of one of the men's eight-year-old daughter, while courts in Washington County decreed that two gay men jointly could adopt two boys who were the biological offspring of neither man. Courts granted several lesbian couples second-parent adoptions in Manhattan and Rochester at the same time that judges denied the petitions of other couples in Brooklyn, Westchester, Staten Island, and Putnam counties (Bruni 1995; Adams 1995). The different rulings reflected judges' preferences for literal or liberal interpretations (Anderson 1994). Before California decided to permit second-parent adoptions, one lawyer recalled that "depending upon what county you live in and what judge you get, it's either the adoption is granted because the judge believes it's in the best interest of the child, or the adoption is denied because the judge won't allow an unmarried couple to adopt" (Cheevers 1999). In New Jersey, before an appeals court in that state ruled that a lesbian could adopt her partner's child, decisions also varied from one locality and judge to another. In a few counties, the adoptions were "routinely granted for many years" according to the legal director for the New Jersey Civil Liberties Union (quoted in Bleemer 1995, 9).

Decentralization facilitates adoption for same-sex couples in three important ways. First, it permits advocates for same-sex adoption rights to take advantage of the prevalence of more liberal political attitudes found in some states and local communities. Second, it affords same-sex couples opportunities to "venue shop," thus increasing their chance for success. Third, it reduces the salience of the gay adoption issue to the disadvantage of its opponents.

Geographic Distribution of Political Attitudes and Resources

Wilcox and Wolpert (2000, 424) show that "moral traditionalism is an important source of [the public's] attitudes on adoption" and that support for greater "social equality" is "somewhat important." Assuming that judges' political attitudes influence their decisions at least somewhat (Spaeth 1995), we would expect judges in some jurisdictions to be more hospitable to gay rights than others. Judges in jurisdictions with higher proportions of liberals are more likely liberal as well, or they might feel compelled to follow the liberal opinions of the voters in their jurisdictions.

Table 5.3 divides states into the same four categories used in table 5.1, ranging from states in which gay adoption is legally secure statewide to those that have prohibited or severely restricted it. It uses Erikson, Wright, and McIver's (1993) and Berry et al.'s (1998) measures of citizens' ideology in the fifty states.[17] Table 5.3 shows a clear association between the ideological complexion of the states and their propensity to permit gays to adopt. States that allow second-parent adoptions, on average, score more than twice as high on the Erikson, Wright, and McIver liberalism measure than the states that prohibit it. Among the states in which adoption is legally secure, all but one falls into the "most liberal" or "liberal" categories. States that allow same-sex couples to adopt in at least some jurisdictions score lower on the liberalism score than the states in which it is secure statewide, yet a majority of these states also rate as "most liberal" or "liberal." By contrast, a majority of the states where second-parent adoptions are prohibited fall into the "most conservative" and "conservative" categories. The same is true for the states in which the law is unclear and untested. The results using the Berry et al. measure are similar. States that permit gays to adopt statewide register almost twenty points higher on the liberalism measure, and states in which adoption is permitted in some jurisdictions register about eight points higher than the states in which the law is untested or where gay adoptions are prohibited.

Another way to get at the role of ideology in adoption decisions involving gays is to look at religious affiliation. Moral traditionalism and fundamentalism are closely linked. Fundamentalists evaluate gays and lesbians much more negatively than the average person, and fundamentalism is a major predictor of opposition to expanding rights for lesbians and gays (Wilcox and Wolpert 2000, 417, 423, 427). Table 5.4 shows that all but one of the states in which gays and lesbians have secured adoption rights have low percentages of citizens who are members of fundamentalist Protestant denominations. States that prohibit or severely restrict gay adoption, and those in which the law has not been tested, have much higher percentages of citizens who are fundamentalists, about one-fifth of their popu-

Table 5.3 Ideological identification in the states and the status of same-sex second–parent adoption rights (Number of states in each category; Berry et al. measure in *italics*)

Ideological identification	Adoptions legally secure statewide	Adoption permitted in some jurisdictions	Law unclear and untested	Adoptions prohibited or severely restricted
Most liberal	7 *5*	4 *4*	1 *1*	1 *1*
Liberal	3 *3*	4 *5*	1 *2*	2 *2*
Conservative	1 *2*	1 *1*	10 *8*	2 *2*
Most conservative	0 *0*	3 *5*	6 *7*	2 *2*
Mean liberalism Score	−7.4 (n = 11)	−12.1 (n = 12)	−18.6 (n = 18)	−16.8 (n = 7)
Mean liberalism Score	*59.2 (n = 10)*	*49.6 (n = 15)*	*42.3 (n = 18)*	*42.5 (n = 7)*

Sources: Erikson, Wright, and McIver (1993, ch. 2). The estimates of citizens' ideology in 48 states and the District of Columbia come from combining 122 CBS News/*New York Times* polls. Scores for each state were calculated by subtracting the percentage of conservative respondents from the percentage of liberal respondents. Most liberal states score −10 and higher, liberal states from −15 to −10.1, conservative states from −20 to −15.1, and most conservative states less than −20. The District of Columbia is included in the table because its adoption policy is separate from that of any state. If the District is excluded from the calculations, the mean liberalism score for those states in which second–parent adoptions are legally secure statewide becomes −7.4, still within the "most liberal" category. Erikson, Wright, and McIver excluded Alaska because no estimates were available and excluded Nevada because of a sampling problem.

Berry et al. (1998) estimates of citizens' ideology in the 50 states (excluding the District of Columbia) range from 0 (most conservative) to 100 (most liberal). Categories are most liberal (55.0 and higher), liberal (45.1 to 54.9), conservative (39.4 to 45.0), and most conservative (0 to 39.3) from author's calculations based upon rankings of state scores and dividing them into quartiles.

Table 5.4 Membership in fundamentalist Protestant denominations and the status of same-sex second-parent adoption rights (number of states in each category)

	Adoptions legally secure statewide	Adoptions permitted in some jurisdictions	Law on adoptions unclear and untested	Adoptions prohibited or severely restricted
Rate of membership				
High	0	2	9	2
Moderate	1	3	5	2
Low	9	7	4	3
Mean percentage of fundamentalists	4.7	11.8	21.3	22.4

Source: Calculated from data supplied in Erikson, Wright, and McIver (1993, 67). Measures are the percentages of the state populations belonging to fundamentalist Protestant groups. high = more than 20%; moderate = 10.1–20%; low = 0–10%. Erikson, Wright, and McIver excluded Alaska because no estimates were available and excluded Nevada because of a sampling problem.

lation, compared with less than 5 percent of states where gays can adopt statewide.

States that permit gay and lesbian couples to adopt also have greater lesbian, gay, bisexual, and transgender (LGBT) political resources. States in which adoptions are legally secure statewide rank, on average, three times higher in political resource measures than states that prohibit or severely restrict adoptions as well as those in which the adoption laws are unclear and untested. Similarly, states in which adoptions are permitted in some jurisdictions rank about 50 percent higher among states in these measures than states in which gay adoptions are prohibited or in which the law is unclear and untested (see table 5.5).

Opportunities for Venue Shopping

Gay petitioners increase their chances for gaining adoption by seeking out the right people in the right places to help them. Usually with the aid of an attorney, adoption counselor, or local gay and lesbian organization, couples start by looking for an adoption agency that is willing to work with them to find children and support their petitions in court. Some adoption agencies have explicit nondiscrimination policies regarding sexual orienta-

Table 5.5 Level of LGBT political resources and the status of same-sex
second-parent adoption rights (number of states in each category)

	Adoptions legally secure statewide	Adoptions permitted in some jurisdictions	Law on adoptions unclear and untested	Adoptions prohibited or severely restricted
Level of resources				
High	8	7	3	0
Moderate	1	6	4	4
Low	1	2	11	3
Mean ranking in resources	10.8	20.9	34.2	33.4

Source: Calculated from data supplied in Haider-Markel (2000, 298–99). Measures are rankings of the states in size of membership of the National Gay and Lesbian Task Force per 100,000 population.

tion. Private agencies are more expensive to use than the public system, but they generally have "the flexibility to be more progressive in support of non-traditional adopters" (Women's Law Project 1995, 17). Alternatively, attorneys bypass adoption agencies and arrange private adoptions by seeking out women who are willing to give up their babies to same-sex couples (Dullea 1988; Feeney 1997).

Gay couples also shop for jurisdictions and judges who are known to grant adoptions to gay couples or who are open to the idea. One adoption attorney described the process as boiled down to "whether our judges can appreciate the importance to a child not to have a parent legally recognized" (quoted in Paquette 1996). Venue shopping for courts is most crucial outside of the approximately two dozen states that, according to the Human Rights Campaign (HRC), grant gay adoptions fairly routinely. As an HRC spokeswoman puts it, "People in these states who want to do this—do they live in the right county? Did they happen to get the right judge, the right social worker?" (quoted in Associated Press 2000, 3D). An American Civil Liberties Union attorney who handles gay and lesbian issues says that outside the approximately twenty states that routinely grant gay adoptions are others in which "there are scattered judges doing second-parent adoptions" (Tysver 2001). Couples' attorneys try to steer clear of judges whom they know or suspect to be bigoted, or the many state-level judges who have to run for reelection and may fear that their constituents will disapprove if they permit gay adoptions (see Paquette 1996).

In Texas, which permits unmarried couples to adopt, one Houston lawyer has assisted in more than 150 second-parent adoptions by filing petitions in Austin, Dallas, and San Antonio "rather than risk drawing a judge here [in Harris County] who might interpret the family code differently. All of the family court judges here are Republican" (Crowe 2004). In New York, between twenty and fifty gay and lesbian couples in the early 1990s regularly sought out sympathetic jurists like Manhattan Judge Eve Preminger before the state's highest court ruled that second-parent adoptions were permissible in the state (Sullivan 1992; Bruni 1995; Paquette 1996). Judges in Nassau and Suffolk counties on Long Island, however, were known as less politically liberal and did not permit same-sex couple applications before that time (Paquette 1996).

Gay couples also venue shop in states where adoption policy remains unclear and no trial court has rendered a decision on whether second-parent adoptions are legal. In Michigan, Judge Nancy Francis of Washtenaw County (which includes Ann Arbor, a liberal community) created "the Second Parent Program" in order to facilitate such adoptions. Gays and their attorneys seek out judges in the county to obtain the adoptions (Associated Press 2002a; 2002b). In South Carolina, some adoption agencies arrange adoptions for gay couples as well (Munday 2003).

Gay couples are sometimes able to "fly under the radar" even in states that have banned or restricted gay adoption. The story of Todd Berg and Chad Long from North Dakota at the beginning of this chapter is one such case. Despite a 1994 Wisconsin Supreme Court ruling that a Green Bay woman could not adopt the child of her partner, "several dozen" adoptions have taken place in Dane County, which encompasses the liberally minded community of Madison, where a substantial number of the state's gay and lesbian population live. Adoption attorneys there have persuaded judges to allow gay and lesbian partners to adopt simultaneously as single, unmarried individuals (Ingersoll 2002). Under California Governors George Deukemejian and Pete Wilson, the Department of Social Services decreed that unmarried couples were unfit as adoptive parents. Despite the policy, second-parent adoptions were common in cities like Los Angeles and San Francisco, where judges often ignored the policy and based their decisions on "home study" reports prepared by social workers. Similarly, once an adoption agency approved gays to adopt as single parents, an adoptions program manager working for Riverside County found lawyers who would recommend to judges adoptions for gay couples. "I think word trickled out that this was a place gay folk could get a fair shake," a close observer said (Zimmerman 2003). Such adoptions were rarely allowed in rural counties until the policy was changed under Governor Gray Davis to allow gay couples to adopt throughout the state (McKee 1995; Herscher 2000). Before New Jersey revoked its prohibition against adoption by unmarried couples, the Division of Youth and Family Services "essentially winked at its own restrictive policy, suggesting instead that one person adopt the child and his or her partner later petition the court for second-parent recognition" (Padawer 1997). Adoptions have also been known to occur in Ohio, despite high court rulings prohibiting them (Hoffman 2003).

Gays and lesbians can also venue shop outside their states of residence by petitioning courts in neighboring states or establishing their residency in them. Before Pennsylvania adopted a statewide policy of allowing second-parent adoptions, some gay couples living in the eastern part of the state moved across state lines to New Jersey, where such adoptions were permitted (Carpenter 2002). And gay couples in midwestern states who find it difficult to adopt look for adoption agencies located in Chicago or other large cities to help. Underscoring the importance of venue shopping, opponents of gay adoption like Professor Lynn Wardle of Brigham Young University in Provo, Utah, lament, "You find a friendly judge and friendly social worker and 'Bingo'" (quoted in Gehrke 2000).

Venue shopping is not always a practical strategy, and couples who expect their efforts to fail may be discouraged from trying to adopt (Bruni 1995; Paquette 1996). Even in states and counties where it is possible for gay couples to adopt, many adoption agencies refuse to facilitate them, and it may be difficult to find birth parents willing to accept gays as parents for their child.[18] Nevertheless, many more couples are able to adopt under a decentralized system than could do so under a centralized system that precluded venue shopping.

Low Issue Salience

Because scores of judges around the country make adoption decisions in a highly decentralized and case-by-case fashion, the vast majority of gay adoption cases escape national and statewide attention. Adoption is the gay rights issue that the print media covers the least (see chapter 1). The closed nature of the adoption process and sealed records that ensure the privacy of the biological and adoptive parents and children also reduce salience (Sullivan 1993). When the issue occasionally becomes more visible, as it did when the celebrity Rosie O'Donnell spoke out and gained considerable national media coverage for her criticism of Florida's ban on gay adoption, gay rights advocates worry that it will encourage other state legislatures to enact bans (Plohetski 2002; Associated Press 2002a).

PROFESSIONAL STAKEHOLDERS
IN FAVOR OF GAY ADOPTION

An extensive network of legal and child welfare professionals lies at the center of the adoption process. Judges, adoption agencies, social workers, and attorneys specializing in adoption are major stakeholders in the system, along with adoptive parents and children. How they view gay and lesbian couples who seek to adopt is of vital importance in whether the adoption system will be responsive to their petitions. Increasingly, these actors have been more favorable toward gays as prospective parents.

A study of more than 200 adoption agencies indicates a general willingness to place children with gays and lesbians (Brodzinsky, Patterson, and Vaziri 2002). More than 60 percent of agencies accept applications from gays and lesbians, and more than one-third report having made at least one adoption placement with a gay or lesbian adult in the preceding two-year period. Sixteen percent of the agencies actively seek gay couples or advertise themselves as "gay friendly." The agencies most likely to accept applications are those that are public, private secular, Jewish, and Lutheran and those that seek to place children with special needs (e.g., disabled children) and children from foreign countries. Anecdotal evidence also suggests that "adoption agencies, sperm banks and organizations that work with surrogate mothers have become more sensitive to gays and lesbians" (*New York Times* 2000b). In the mid-1990s, when polls revealed that two-thirds of Americans still were opposed to gay adoptions, the director of the National Center for Lesbian Rights reported that "many public and private agencies are now placing children with gays and lesbians" (quoted in Salter 1994, A9).

Social workers who work for adoption agencies and state and county departments of child welfare are another important group in the adoption process. They conduct the crucial home studies that collect and assess important information about prospective parents and the children they seek to adopt.[19] Judges rely heavily upon the studies in making their decisions about whether an adoption is in a child's best interest. Ample evidence suggests that many social workers, perhaps most, favor adoption rights for gays and lesbians. The National Association of Social Workers (NASW) in 1988 committed itself officially to work to end discrimination based upon sexual orientation in child custody, visitation, and adoption, before most jurisdictions that now permit same-sex second-parent adoptions did so. The NASW Code of Ethics states, "the social worker should not practice, condone, facilitate or collaborate with any form of discrimination on the basis of . . . sexual orientation" (NASW 1988, 161) and "the sex, gender identity or sexual orientation of natural or prospective adoptive or foster parents should not be the sole or primary variable considered in custody or placement" (quoted in Lowy 1999, A8). From the social workers' perspective, according to a Michigan attorney who has researched the legality of second-parent adoptions for judges, "they don't see anything wrong with same-sex parents. In fact, they may see it as beneficial." (Associated Press 2002b).

Professional stakeholders support adoptions by same-sex couples for several reasons: (1) the mission of their organizations is to find permanent homes for the many children in need of them, (2) family law has evolved to accommodate "nontraditional" parents, (3) empirical evidence on gay and lesbian parenting shows positive results, and (4) social workers' goal of finding suitable parents fits well with their liberal political leanings.

Organizational Mission and Society's Need

The adoption system's central goal is to promote legal adoption. Adoption provides children with the stability and commitment that they cannot obtain through foster care and other arrangements. The pressure to increase adoptions arises out of the large numbers of children in need of permanent homes, the costs associated with foster care, and a growing recognition of the disadvantages associated with it. Besides the immediate benefits of adoption, children who are raised in stable, loving homes are more likely to grow into healthy, well-adjusted adults who can contribute to society.

Once it became apparent in the 1980s that many children in foster care shuttle back and forth between their foster and biological parents, federal and state governments started to emphasize the need to adopt more children. Gays and lesbians represent a pool of prospective parents who can help meet this need and save taxpayers money. Advocates for gay and lesbian adoption frequently emphasize the many children who are unwanted.

According to the family policy director for the National Gay and Lesbian Task Force, the reason that adoption agencies have become much more receptive to having gays adopt is "the tremendous need for homes. Most agencies, either private or public, have realized that to cut an entire class of people out of the applicant pool creates a disaster in the system" (Huppke 2000; see also Hayes 2002).[20] In Ohio, where an appellate court has ruled that the state's adoption law does not allow second-parent adoptions by same-sex couples, adoption agencies have begun "A Child's Waiting Adoption Program" to deal with approximately 3,600 children who need parents in that state. According to one placement director in a Jewish agency, "the point of our recruitment [of gay and lesbian parents] was there was this large, untapped pool of men and women who would make great parents" (quoted in Hoffman 2003).

Adoption professionals find gay clients particularly attractive because they are willing to adopt a higher proportion of "special needs" children (Salter 1994). According to social worker Jill Johnson, "People want babies and they want kids without pasts and they want guarantees they weren't drug-exposed. When kids have histories people tend to shy away" (quoted in Zimmerman 2003). Dan Savage (2001), a gay commentator and adoptive parent, argues, "it is an open secret among social workers that gay and lesbian couples are often willing to adopt children whom most heterosexual couples won't touch: HIV-positive children, mixed-race children, disabled children and children who have been abused or neglected. . . . The real choice for children waiting to be adopted . . . isn't between gay and straight parents, but between parents and no parents."[21]

The need for suitable parents is not lost upon policymakers. According to one judge on the Pennsylvania Superior Court, "the reality of our society today is such that unwanted infants are left abandoned in dumpsters, and some married heterosexual parents are unfit to raise children whom they often grossly abuse or neglect. We should interpret the laws of our Commonwealth in such a way that adheres to the mandates of our Legislature and promotes the placement of children in stable families who can provide nurturing and supportive homes" (Kelley 2000). In New Hampshire, where a twelve-year ban on gay adoption was overturned in 1999, the existence of a large number of children awaiting adoption was the principal argument that the ban's opponents used in favor of lifting it. According to then Governor Jean Shaheen, "For too long, too many qualified families have been denied the opportunity to provide a child in need with a healthy, loving environment. This law will allow more children to be with supportive and nurturing families" (quoted in Love 1999). In Texas, a state without an official policy on gay adoption, the Department of Protective and Regulatory Services sometimes turns to gay and lesbian households when heterosexual homes cannot be found. The state had about 3,500 children in state custody awaiting adoption in a typical year in the 1990s, which was far more than the number of "approved" homes in which those children could be placed (Plohetski 2002).

Evolution of Family Law and Emergence of the "Best Interest" Standard

Children in need of people who are willing to adopt them have always existed. What has changed is society's view of who qualifies as a suitable parent. The United States and other Western nations underwent a shift in family structure, gender roles, and sexual mores starting in the 1960s arising out of greater affluence, the demographic bulge of the post–World War II baby boom, social and geographic mobility, and technological change (Abramson and Inglehart 1995; Inglehart 1990). Divorce, premarital sex, cohabitation, and out-of-wedlock birth increased and lost much of their stigma. Women participated in the workforce in greater numbers and gained more control over reproduction. New kinds of families emerged that did not conform to the structure and traditional gender roles of the nuclear family. They included single-parent families, "blended" families, and adults who were neither the mother nor father of the children they were parenting. As gays and lesbians came out of the closet and formed domestic partnerships, they too began constituting their own "families of choice" in greater numbers and more visibly than ever (Weeks, Heaphy, and Donovan 2001; Weston 1991). The stress in liberal ideology on individual autonomy, choice, and fulfillment buttressed these trends. As of the 2000 census, about 46 percent of Americans fifteen years of age and older were unmarried, and married heterosexual couples with children comprise less than one-quarter of households (Stacy 2001; Kreider and Simmons 2003).

These changes in family structure and social norms clashed with family law, which was preoccupied with regulating sexual activity between men and women. The law defined moral conduct in terms of prohibitions against premarital sex, contraception, abortion, and adultery. Family law, however, began to change in the 1960s and 1970s. Society began to remove moral judgments about sexual conduct from public policy and relegate them to

private life. This principle guided the adoption of "no fault" divorce, the legalization of contraception and abortion, and the gradual repeal of sodomy
statutes.

The new family law redefined moral considerations rather than jetti-
soned them. A new consensus concerning the moral purposes of family
life emerged that transcended the debate between conservative critics of
the trends that began in the sixties and their liberal defenders. The new
family law does not attempt to reconstitute the nuclear family and restore
the old prohibitions. Nor does it promote individual autonomy at the expense of familial obligations. Rather, it aims to make decisions about the
distribution of rights and responsibilities on the basis of how well they
contribute to the care of, support of, and commitment toward *children*.[22]
Among liberal feminists, conservatives, and communitarians alike, "there
is . . . an emerging consensus about the centrality of protecting children,
as perhaps *the* core value that should be promoted in family law" and that
there are "shared moral principles that support the protection and support
of children" (Murphy 1999, 1127–28, 1134).[23]

Family law is suffused now with the notion that what matters most is
children's welfare. The emphasis in the old law on punishing parents who
misbehave during marriage frequently worked against children's interests
(Murphy 1999, 1135). A major justification for no-fault divorce, for example, is to spare children the trauma of protracted and emotionally charged
litigation that often arose in order to determine the party at fault for the
dissolution of the marriage (National Conference of Commissioners on
Uniform State Laws 1995). Divorce, restraining orders, and alimony have
receded in importance since the 1980s (Bergin 2003). The lessening of
sexual misconduct as grounds for divorce under no-fault rules eventually
extended to decisions over custody and visitation. "Developments in custody law refined the best interest [of the child] standard to focus on factors
that more directly bear on children's well-being" than the parents' sexual
conduct, such as their ability to provide financial and emotional support to
their child (Murphy 1999, 1155). Courts no longer disqualify a parent from
visitation, custody, and adoption simply because they engaged in nonmarital sexual relationships. Courts use the "nexus test" instead to determine if
a parent's sexual conduct threatens or produces harm to their child (Murphy 1999, 1187; McCahey et al. 1996, sect. 10.12[2b]).[24]

The emphasis on children's welfare has had important implications for
adoption. First, adoption is viewed now as superior to foster care and re-

unification with a child's biological parents. Courts and child welfare agencies abandoned family reunification after they recognized that returning the child to his or her biological parents at almost any cost placed some children in danger and left many more to spend years shuttling back and forth between their foster and biological parents. Another idea that has mostly been dropped is matching children as closely as possible with adoptive parents' racial, ethnic, class, and educational characteristics. The growing shortage of non-special-needs children available for adoption makes matching less feasible, and the sociological characteristics of adoptive children and parents are mostly irrelevant to successful parenting and child development. White middle-class couples still prefer white American babies, but they have turned increasingly to black, Latino, or mixed-race babies and the number of international adoptions (mainly from Asia, Russia, and Latin America) has mushroomed (Pertman 2000, 23, 159).

Second, adoption is less exclusionary. Courts awarded children almost exclusively to heterosexual married couples in the past. Today, many agencies place children with nontraditional parents, including single individuals, disabled people, and unmarried heterosexual couples. Singles, mostly women, account for about one-third of adoptions in the United States, but the number of single men who are adoptive parents has risen because of positive experiences with divorced fathers raising their children as single parents (Crary 2003). Expanding the variety of individuals and families eligible to adopt helps reduce the number of children who remain in foster care and recognizes that the structure of a family is less important than whether it meets the children's needs.

The broad changes in family law and adoption practice have facilitated the burgeoning numbers of gay couples desiring to adopt. Under the old family law, homosexual conduct was considered such a serious moral transgression that it demanded punishing the offending parent by excluding him or her from custody and visitation rights, regardless of how well they parented the children and the effect the decision would have on them (Murphy 1999, 1153–54, 1186–88; Rivera 1986, 275, 329). By the mid-1990s, the courts in a majority of jurisdictions embraced the nexus test in cases involving the determination of whether a homosexual is fit to be a legal parent (Shapiro 1995–96, 635, 641). Once courts and legislatures swept away the moral basis of the old family law and its regulatory approach to sexual conduct, they opened the door to judging gay parents according to their record and ability to fulfill the parental role rather than their sexual orientation.

This seemingly liberal turn of events is aimed at promoting values that conservatives and communitarians wish to see families promote—stability, commitment, responsibility, and the protection and care of children within two-parent households.

Gay and lesbian adoption is also consistent with the expanding definition of what counts as a "family" and the inclusion of nontraditional parents. The idea that gays would be allowed to adopt seems less radical than it would have been before the trend toward greater diversity of adoptive parents and mixing of parents and children from different social backgrounds (Pertman 2000, 22–24, 30, 158, 161; Bergin 2003). Once people recognized that families that did not conform to the traditional nuclear family could meet children's needs and that the sociological characteristics of adoptive parents are of little relevance to parenting, the importance of the gender and sexual orientation of the couples seeking to adopt receded as criteria for adoption.

The emergence of the best interest standard has had a more profound impact for the politics of gay adoption than merely its use as a tool for deciding specific cases. It has helped to define the issue of gays adopting in terms of the practical needs of children rather than granting rights to individuals whose lifestyle is controversial. It frames the policy choice in terms of practical considerations that are amenable to rational analysis rather than symbolic meanings rooted in emotion. Opponents of having gays adopt may still argue that it is in no child's best interest to have gay parents. But they must bring to bear arguments and evidence on children's needs rather than arouse emotional reactions to whether homosexuals deserve rights and same-sex relationships should be legitimated. Mobilizing opposition against gay adoption is much more difficult as a result. Gay advocates of adoption rights realize this advantage. They cultivate the "doing what is best for kids" definition and downplay the "gay rights" definition of the issue. As one of the two men who won a landmark case granting them adoption rights in New Jersey explained, "This didn't start out as a gay rights call to arms. It was about two parents wanting to protect their son, two parents who happen to be gay" (quoted in Padawer 1997).[25]

Evidence on Gay Parenting

A number of empirical studies support the argument that gays and lesbians make suitable parents and that children of gay parents fare as well as children of heterosexuals across a range of indicators.[26] Children raised by gay parents have similar levels of popularity with peers, develop similar kinds of friendships, and are as likely to have satisfactory relationships with adults of both genders as children raised by heterosexuals (Patterson 1992; McCandlish 1987, 23–24; Tasker and Golombok 1991, 181, 187; Golombok, Spencer, and Rutter 1983; Gottman 1990, 177; Kirkpatrick, Smith, and Roy 1981). Children of lesbian mothers are more likely than those of divorced heterosexual mothers to have positive relationships with men and integrate them more thoroughly in their lives as friends (Kirkpatrick, Smith, and Roy 1981, 549). They do not seem to differ in their school performance, cognition and behavior, or social competence from children raised by married heterosexuals (Flaks et al. 1995, 109–10, 35). Children raised by divorced lesbian partners are no more likely to have emotional or behavioral problems or experience hyperactivity or unsociability than children raised by divorced heterosexual women, when followed to adulthood (Golombok, Spencer, and Rutter 1983, 565, 570; Gottman 1990). Adolescents parented by divorced lesbians living with same-sex partners have no less self-esteem than those parented by divorced heterosexual women living with opposite sex partners (Huggins 1989, 123, 131).

Children raised from birth in lesbian households do not differ from children generally in their levels of social competence or behavior problems (Patterson 1994, 156; Patterson 2000, 1062). They are no more likely to display aggression, antisocial behavior, or the desire to be the center of attention, and they are more likely to report "greater feelings of joy, contentedness and comfort with themselves than did children of heterosexual mothers" (Patterson 1994, 168). Children raised by gays and lesbians are at no greater risk of child abuse.[27] They are no more likely to grow up gay or lesbian, have difficulties establishing their sexual identity, or be unable to exhibit gender role behavior that is typical in the culture (Patterson 1994, 156, 169; Patterson 2000; Golombok, Spencer, and Rutter 1983, 551, 568; Gottman 1990, 177, 189; Kirkpatrick, Smith, and Roy 1981, 551; Green 1978, 692, 696; Green 1982; Green et al. 1986, 179–81; Hoeffer 1981, 542; Warren 1980, 692, 696). Only about 5 percent of children with an openly gay or lesbian parent report experiencing harassment because of their parents' sexual orientation, and these experiences do not seem to have any long-term psychological effects on them (Miller 1979, 544, 548; Green 1978, 695–96; Bozett 1989, 137, 143; Susoeff 1985, 852, 877–80).

Other studies reveal that gays and lesbians make good parents. Gays do not have a greater incidence of psychopathology than straight people

(Freedman 1971; Montagu 1978, 62, 66; Oberstone and Sukoneck 1976, 172, 183).[28] Gay parents develop parenting skills and practices and display levels of interest in their children that are at least as good as heterosexuals (Flaks et al. 1995, 105, 111; Hoeffer 1981, 536, 543; Kirkpatrick, Smith, and Roy 1981, 545, 550; Miller and Bigner 1981, 49, 55; Bigner and Jacobsen 1992, 99, 104; Stacey and Biblarz 2001, 164). Finally, lesbian relationships are no more transient than those of heterosexual women; fathers are apparently not essential for the healthy development of children; and heterosexual marriage is not necessary for effective fathering (Golombok, Spencer, and Rutter 1983, 551–72; Silverstein and Auerback 1997, 397–98; Peterson 1996).[29]

Few research findings in the social sciences categorically "prove" anything, and opponents of gay adoption have criticized these studies.[30] However, the researchers who have conducted the studies work at credible institutions, and no comparable set of studies shows that gays and lesbians parent less well than heterosexuals do.

What is not in doubt is the political impact of the studies. They have played an important role in gaining the endorsement of gay adoption by a long list of advocates and professionals in the fields of adoption and child welfare. Many professional organizations have endorsed same-sex second-parent adoptions, including the American Academy of Pediatrics, American Academy of Child and Adolescent Psychology, American Academy of Family Physicians, Child Welfare League of America, American Psychoanalytic Association, American Psychiatric Association, and American Psychological Association (Zimmerman 2003; *Tulsa World* 2003, A20), as has the American Bar Association (Crowe 2004). Many members of these organizations work closely with practitioners in the adoption process.

The endorsement of the American Academy of Pediatrics, representing about 55,000 pediatricians, is particularly noteworthy because of the wide respect and deference that group enjoys in courts and legislatures (Goode 2002). It frequently files amicus curiae briefs or lends moral support when gay adoption cases go to higher courts.[31] The professional groups uniformly define the issue in terms of children rather than gay rights: "This is really about the needs of children," said Dr. Joseph Hagan, chairman of the Academy's committee on psychosocial aspects of family health, which drafted the Academy's statement supporting second-parent adoptions (quoted in Goode 2002). The president of the American Bar Association, somewhat differently, defines the issue as one of "parents' rights and not gay rights" (Manson 2003).

The endorsement of gay adoption by so many professional organizations provides proponents of gay adoption with ammunition from credible authorities to counter the objections leveled by opponents about the risks posed by gays having close contact with children. By the early 1990s, the accumulating evidence was cited by judges who made rulings allowing same-sex couples to adopt.[32]

Perhaps as important as the statistical evidence is the more direct and anecdotal experience with gay parents that child care professionals in the adoption system have had. Gays have been adopting as single individuals in many locations for years (see Espenshade 2002c). As the director of the National Center for Lesbian Rights put it, "adoption agencies feel like they have a body of information, a consensus that says children do well in lesbian and gay families. Their experiences with gay families have by and large been very positive" (quoted in Salter 1994). Since gays have been adopting as single parents with generally positive experiences, it is more difficult to deny them the same privilege when they attempt to adopt as a couple. The widespread belief that it is better for children to have two parents looking after them than one makes the denial of opportunities for gay couples to adopt more difficult.

To dampen the possibility that biological parents or courts will reject gay prospective parents, agencies generally do not inquire into the sexual orientation of those they are investigating.[33] Some heterosexuals who put children up for adoption *prefer* gay and lesbian couples as parents.[34] Only about one-quarter of adoption agencies report that biological parents request that their child *not* be placed in a gay-headed household or object to such a placement when it is proposed. According to one study, only about half of adoption agencies routinely informed birth parents before placing a child with a gay adoptive parent (*Providence Journal-Bulletin* 2003).

It is not difficult for gays and lesbians to hide their sexual orientation. Gays have been able to adopt for many years because of the privacy surrounding adoption proceedings, where records are usually sealed. When gays try to adopt as *couples,* however, this strategy is much less feasible. The fact that two men or two women living together want to share parental authority over a child is prima facie evidence that they are in a relationship. This suggests that adoption professionals exhibit a higher level of acceptance of gays than they would have years ago.

Political Predispositions of Social Workers

Social workers' professional reasons for promoting gay adoption mesh with their political inclinations. Several studies have shown that feelings toward gays and support for gay rights are correlated with gender, political ideology, and party affiliation. Women generally have warmer feelings toward gays and lesbians and are more supportive of laws protecting gay rights.[35] Seventy-seven percent of social workers in one survey were found to be female (Garvin and Tropman 1998, 452). Social workers who are involved in politics are likely to be Democrats. A survey of the 171 social workers who hold federal, state, and local office finds that almost two-thirds are Democrats; another third are nonpartisan (a requirement in many states), are independent, or belong to a party other than the Democratic Party or the Republican Party; and only 5 percent are Republican (NASW 2003b). An examination of the NASW Web site (http://www.socialworkers.org) reveals a decidedly liberal tilt across a variety of issues. As one might expect, the organization strongly favors greater public spending on programs that help those in poverty, low-income workers, and others in need of help. The NASW has also been a strong supporter of gay and lesbian rights. According to the NASW's political arm, the organization "continues to diligently pursue enactment of ENDA [the Employment Non-Discrimination Act] through progressive coalition efforts with the Human Rights Campaign" (NASW 2003a, 5) It also supports hate crimes laws that cover LGBTs and supports proposals to allow gay marriage (NASW 2003a, 2004a, 2004b).

CONCLUSION

Gays and lesbians seeking to adopt have met with greater political success than one would expect from the relatively high level of threat that Americans perceive from gay adoption. A majority of gays and lesbians who have established families now live in places where adoptions are routinely granted or where they are a realistic possibility. The institutional characteristics of adoption are of decisive importance in advancing adoption rights. In this case, all three of the characteristics expected to dampen resistance to gay rights come together—high judicial involvement, state and local policymaking, and stakeholders whose interests coincide with those of gay rights advocates. Here again, as with the repeal of sodomy laws, liberal elites appear to play a crucial role in bringing about relative LGBT success. The legalization of homosexual conduct and adoption rights for gay and lesbian couples are very different policy issues, Yet, in both cases, policymakers, experts, and professionals with liberal or libertarian policy views have been key actors in helping the LGBT community circumvent a deeply ambivalent public and organized opponents to gay rights.

The dominance of state and local courts in an area of law noted for granting judges wide discretion makes it more likely that policy decisions will diverge from majority preferences. State legislatures generally have deferred to the courts in areas of family law where judgments must be made on the basis of detailed knowledge of the needs of particular children and the qualifications of parents, which vary widely from case to case. Judges are more responsive in states where they do not have to run for reelection, enjoy longer terms of office, and serve in jurisdictions with more liberal constituencies. The case-based nature of judicial decision making helps to frame decisions in terms of the practical needs of children rather than cultural symbols. The combination of judicial decision making, private adoption records, and the local venues of most policymaking reduces the salience and national media attention of the gay adoption issue. As a result, it is more difficult for opponents of gay rights to mobilize against adoption rights for gays and lesbians. The highly decentralized, disaggregated structure of decision making also facilitates venue shopping in the many states where no statewide policy permitting gays to adopt exists. Gays can seek out judges in jurisdictions where citizens are more politically liberal, fewer Protestant fundamentalists reside, and the LGBT community has greater political resources.

Finally, key professional stakeholders in adoption policy have strong political, organizational, and "good public policy" reasons to turn to gays and lesbians as prospective parents. Enlarging the pool of prospective parents promotes the missions of the major players in the adoption process who seek to cope with the shortage of suitable homes for the many children who need them. A variety of child welfare and adoption experts support opening adoption to gays and other nontraditional families. Gay adoption also fits well with the "children first" ethos of the new family law, which appeals across the ideological spectrum. These forces have turned a potentially contentious cultural issue into one in which the LGBT movement's aims are consistent with policymakers' desire to find a solution to the problem of children in need of parents who can care for them.

Military Service

Michelle Douglas joined the Canadian military in 1986 and graduated at the top of her class in basic training. Douglas became a lieutenant in the Air Force, which assigned her to a "special investigations" unit whose task, in part, was to root out suspected gays and lesbians. The military investigated Douglas herself in 1988 and found that she had a "close relationship" with another woman. Under false pretenses, two men took her to a hotel room and interrogated her about her sexual activities, compelled her to take a lie-detector test, and denied her request to seek legal advice. She admitted that she was gay and had engaged in same-sex conduct but refused to identify other homosexuals in the military. She was given a less sensitive job, lost her top-secret security clearance, and was recommended for dismissal. After she reluctantly accepted her release from the service, an independent government review committee investigated her case and found in her favor. She then launched a court case that led to a ruling by Canada's highest court that the policy under which the military dismissed her violated the Canadian Charter of Rights and Freedoms (Bindman 1992d).

Alastair Gamble studied German and Latin in high school and at Emory University in Atlanta, where he earned his bachelor's degree. As a specialist in the U.S. Army, he collected human intelligence. He completed interrogation training and won a Certificate of Commendation for his efforts in training officers to work with U.S. allies. He entered the Defense Language Institute in 2001, where he was halfway through a course of intensive training in Arabic and had earned grades at the top of the class. The government's need for Arabic linguists rose sharply after the attacks of September 11, 2001. During a surprise inspection in the middle of the night in April 2002, the military caught Gamble sleeping with his boyfriend, who was also in the military. A search of his room turned up nonpornographic gay-themed films; photographs of Gamble and his boyfriend in affectionate, nonsexual poses; and greeting cards expressing romantic sentiments. Gamble's unit undertook an investigation into his sexual orientation. A few weeks later, the military gave him and his boyfriend dishonorable discharges (Frank 2002). In the first ten years since Congress adopted its "don't ask, don't tell" policy, the military expelled fifty-four Arabic speakers and nine Farsi speakers for violating the ban on gays openly serving in the military (Associated Press 2005a).[1]

Virtually alone among developed democracies, the United States bans gays and lesbians from serving openly in the military. The failure to end the ban in the 1990s was a major political defeat for the gay rights movement and its allies. Congress not only left the ban intact but also made it harder to eliminate in the future by codifying it in law under the "Don't Ask, Don't Tell" policy. Eligibility for membership in the military is only partly about expanding employment opportunities. It is also about status and symbolism. Eligibility to join the defenses of the nation signifies citizenship. Exclusion from the privileges and responsibilities of military service diminishes the status of citizenship because society honors those who serve in the military for their patriotism, sacrifice, and bravery.

If the U.S. is an exception cross-nationally, it is also something of a mystery. The ban's opponents have had several reasons for optimism that they would see the ban lifted. First, most nations have eliminated their restrictions on gays serving in their militaries. At the time that the United States took up the issue in 1993, nineteen foreign militaries did not have policies excluding homosexuals or had lifted their bans (Gade, Segal, and Johnson 1996). They included Canada, Australia, Spain, Germany, France, Israel, Italy, the Netherlands, Belgium, Sweden, Norway, and Denmark. Great Britain followed suit in 2000 (Lancaster 1992; Riding 1992). Britain's Royal Air Force sponsored a float in London's 2004 gay pride parade and, with the Royal Navy, began targeting gays for recruitment in 2005 (Wise 2004; Barkham 2005). All of these countries are U.S. allies, and most are members of the North Atlantic Treaty Organization.

Second, most Americans are not particularly threatened by the prospect of gays serving openly in the military. Support among the public for allowing gays to serve has grown steadily from 51 percent in 1977 to 80 percent in 2003 (see chapter 2). Just before the issue reached the agenda in 1993, public support for lifting the ban stood in one poll at 57 percent (RAND

1993, 442, 446) and 61 percent in another (Wilcox and Wolpert 1996, 131). Once debate got started in 1993, however, some polls indicated a softening of support. Two *Newsweek* polls in the spring and summer of that year reported that between 37 and 42 percent approved while between 51 and 56 percent disapproved of lifting the ban on gays serving openly.[2] Other polls suggested continued support for lifting the ban. A Gallup poll and a National Election Survey indicated that support remained above 50 and 60 percent, respectively, and that the number who "strongly" supported lifting it had risen from the year before (Wilcox and Wolpert 1996, 130–31). Many people did not have firm preferences on the issue; a third or more respondents in polls that measured opinion strength only leaned in favor of or against ending the ban, or registered no opinion. Although support for lifting the ban was not broad or deep, the polls suggested none of the furious reaction that arose after the 1992 election. The level of support for admitting gays was higher than it had been for allowing racial integration of the armed forces in the late 1940s,[3] and it was as high as or higher than support for allowing gays to adopt children when courts began ruling in favor of gay petitioners in the 1990s.

Third, lifting the military ban received presidential support.[4] Although the issue barely registered during the 1992 campaign, Bill Clinton first made his campaign promise to lift the ban in response to a question posed at a Harvard University forum. Gay rights advocates greeted Clinton's pledge warmly and took his election as a sign that they had finally arrived on the national political scene as a legitimate and influential constituency. Due partly to the president's efforts, public support for lifting the ban may have increased over time as the debate unfolded during 1993. According to Wilcox and Wolpert (1996, 140, 135), "Clinton did have a persuasive effect on the attitudes of citizens who were not strongly homophobic," particularly women, those with a strong commitment to equality (including many blacks), and "especially among those with weak positions on the issue."

Finally, some conservative leaders, like the former chairman of the Senate Armed Services Committee, Senator Barry Goldwater (R-AZ), and commentators, like David Brooks, Andrew Sullivan, William Buckley, and George Will, came out in favor of lifting the ban (Goldwater 1993; Sullivan 1993; U.S. Congress, Senate 1993, S11201). Contrary to the impression that military leaders were uniformly against lifting the ban, a number of them, including retired Admiral William J. Crowe, Jr., gave their support (see U.S. Congress, Senate 1993, S11178–79, S11202).

What conditions and forces have blocked progress in this area despite these positive developments? Following the kind of analysis presented in the last two chapters, we focus our attention on the preferences of key policymakers and the institutional venue in which they addressed the military ban issue. Institutional advantages afforded gay rights opponents decisive leverage over the process and spelled defeat for Clinton and his supporters. First, the stakeholder in the policy debate—the military—was firmly and actively opposed to change. Second, the national government alone makes military policy, and courts have played a passive and deferential role. Despite having left the question of gays in the military up to the executive branch, Congress used its legislative powers and became the dominant actor in the military ban issue in the 1990s. Congress's independent powers and the conservative, promilitary orientations of key committee chairmen made it very receptive to the military and antigay groups that mobilized against Clinton's plan. After 1993, conservatives' dominance of Congress and the George H. W. Bush administration kept the issue off the agenda.

After presenting this explanation, we evaluate it further in light of the experience of foreign nations and other efforts to expand opportunities in the military for historically discriminated groups. We will see that most of the same institutional variables that explain the persistence of the ban on gays in the United States also explain the elimination of similar bans in other nations and the lifting of restrictions on the participation of blacks and women in the U.S. military. First, let us review the history of the military's treatment of gays and lesbians.

HISTORICAL BACKGROUND ON GAYS IN THE MILITARY

The relationship between gays and lesbians and the military has been a paradoxical one. The military has been among the most homophobic and repressive institutions in American society. Yet, within its sex-segregated organization, it has provided gays and lesbians with ample opportunities to develop homosexual relationships, and by bringing formerly isolated gay men and lesbians together, the military has fostered gay identity and community. Military service in World War II was instrumental in laying the foundation for the modern gay rights movement (Berube 1990).

Laws and regulations banning or punishing homosexuality in the military have existed since the American Revolution.[5] The first military law designating sodomy as a specific offense appeared shortly after World War I, on the heels of a scandal concerning the investigation of homosexual behavior at the Newport, Rhode Island, naval base.[6] For decades afterward, the policy targeted those who engaged in sodomy regardless of their sexual orientation. Congress included the ban on sodomy between same and opposite-sex couples when it enacted the Uniform Code of Military Justice in 1950.

Influenced by the field of psychiatry, the military gradually came around to the idea that homosexuals were an identifiable group defined by a "psychopathic personality disorder" (Manegold 1993). Congress added a vague proscription to the Uniform Code against "all disorders and neglects to the prejudice of good order and discipline in the armed forces" (Burelli 1994, 18). The military's efforts in World War II to screen conscripts who revealed or suggested homosexual tendencies were largely unsuccessful, however, and it continued to emphasize treatment and retention of soldiers and sailors whose homosexuality it discovered or suspected. As gay identity and the gay rights movement emerged in the post–World War II period, the military increasingly moved toward excluding and separating gays and lesbians by making the ban more explicit, restrictive, and targeted (Scott and Stanley 1994, xi; Stiehm 1994, 150–51). The basis for the exclusion policy moved completely away from a person's sexual behavior and toward his or her sexual orientation. The military targeted homosexuals for exclusion whether or not they engaged in same-sex sexual behavior (Berube 1990; Stiehm 1994).

The trend toward separating homosexuals from the military culminated near the end of the Jimmy Carter administration in the explicit policy statement that "homosexuality is incompatible with military service." Military authorities were to discharge personnel who engaged in homosexual conduct or who "by their statements, demonstrate a propensity to engage in homosexual conduct," as their activity "seriously impairs the accomplishment of the military mission." The military deemed homosexuality detrimental "to maintain discipline, good order, and morale; to foster mutual trust and confidence among service members; to ensure the integrity of the system of rank and command; to facilitate assignment and worldwide deployment of service members who frequently must live and work under close conditions affording minimal privacy; to recruit and retain members of the Military Services; to maintain the public acceptability of military service; and to prevent breaches of security" (U.S. Department of Defense 1982, 1).

The military discharged approximately 1,500 individuals each year between 1980 and 1990 for "homosexuality" (Scott and Stanley 1994, xi).[7]

Evidence of homosexual behavior resulted in immediate dismissal. Verbal admissions of homosexuality resulted in dismissal after an investigation in order to prevent false admissions of homosexuality by individuals wishing to avoid or end military service. The military generally gave honorable or general discharges to individuals separated from the military for their sexual orientation and issued dishonorable discharges only when there was a finding that an individual had committed a criminal act, such as using physical force or engaging in homosexual acts with a minor. This policy survived a series of court challenges based on a variety of legal and constitutional grounds.

Gays remain excluded from eligibility for service today under the current don't ask, don't tell policy and are subject to dismissal if military authorities find out about their orientation. From the point of view of gay rights advocates, don't ask, don't tell is, at best, only a marginal improvement, despite Clinton's characterization of it as a compromise between the previous policy and lifting the ban. While, pursuant to don't ask, don't tell, recruiters no longer ask recruits about their sexual orientation, the policy has major drawbacks. First, while the rate of dismissals from the military due to homosexuality is not as high under don't ask, don't tell as under the previous policy, the military has dismissed 9,488 service members since the policy began in 1994 and through fiscal year 2005 (Shanker 2007). Second, the policy retains the statement that "homosexual conduct is incompatible with military service" and adds that individuals have no constitutional right to serve in the armed forces. Third, it is much harder to get rid of the ban than before 1993 when it was possible to do so through executive order because Congress has codified the ban in law.

Finally, implementation of the policy has been plagued with problems and criticism. Don't ask, don't tell requires that gays and lesbians keep their sexuality secret and lie about it. Studies have shown that gays and lesbians incur substantial costs by remaining in the closet, including social isolation, reduced self-esteem, and the physical and emotional stresses that result from them (see Herek 1996b). Further, the policy tries to distinguish between homosexual status and conduct, based on the idea that some people who identify themselves as gay do not engage in homosexual conduct and some of those who engage in homosexual conduct do not identify as homosexuals (Lever and Kanouse 1996). The military is mandated to discharge individuals for conduct only. But the status-conduct distinction is difficult to maintain in practice and is frequently blurred under the presumption that a person engages in homosexual conduct, or has the propensity to do so, even if all that is known is the person's homosexual status. If a service member admits that he or she is gay, military authorities may require them to answer questions about their behavior and prove that they do not engage in, or do not intend to engage in, same-sex behavior (Zellman 1996, 283). The same conflation of status and conduct has been evident in court rulings on don't ask, don't tell (Jacobson 1996, 53–55; Halley 1996).

AN INSTITUTIONAL EXPLANATION FOR THE
PERSISTENCE OF A DISCRIMINATORY POLICY

Four institutional characteristics of decision making over the military issue have made it intractable to lifting the ban: national-level policymaking, the conservatism of the military, the independence and conservative dominance of Congress, and the deferential stance of the courts. The clash between President Clinton and Congress over the issue invited national media attention that increased the issue's salience, helping mobilize the ban's supporters, who were more numerous and intense than were Clinton and his allies (Rayside 1996, 171). The story dominated the news during the week that followed Clinton's first inauguration. Irate service members, their families, and members of the public opposed to lifting the ban deluged the Capitol with phone calls and letters.[8] As the major stakeholder in the debate, the military's adamant and overwhelming opposition to reform was critical in several respects. Its expertise on the issue allowed it to redefine the issue from "discrimination" to "military effectiveness." Its traditional masculine culture fostered a perception among its personnel that gays posed a threat to service members and their mission, spawning a vocal constituency that felt comfortable justifying the policy of exclusion. The military's interest in the issue, prestige, and influence tipped the balance of forces in favor of preserving the ban (Schmitt 1993a, 1993f, 1993h). Although advocates of lifting the ban, like Representative Barney Frank (D-MA), may have been correct that "the American people have, in fact, a greater capacity to deal with differences than people here give them credit for" (U.S. Congress, House 1993, H7069), many of the ordinary Americans who mattered most in the debate—soldiers, sailors, and air personnel—were not ready to deal with some of those differences. Congress was disposed to listen to the military's arguments and come to the aid of the military and its allies among veterans groups and the lineup of typically antigay religious and "family values" groups. Congressional opponents to allowing gays to serve openly in the military controlled key committee positions and joined with these groups to dominate the definition of the issue as one about unit cohesion and military effectiveness. In doing so, they softened the public's growing support for lifting the ban and further encouraged opposition to Clinton's proposal. With the courts adhering to their historically passive and promilitary position, Clinton was left isolated.

In breaking down this analysis, first, we discuss the military's role in the fight over lifting the ban in 1993 and the reasons for its opposition. Next, we examine the congressional response. Following that, we look at how reformers managed to overturn the ban in other nations and how they succeeded in the cases of race and gender integration in the United States.

The Military: A Conservative Institution

The military is at the center of the dispute over whether to allow gays into its ranks. We cannot understand the ban's existence and persistence without understanding the military. If the military were a different institution— a university or a high-technology industry, for example—its ban on gays would almost certainly no longer exist. Change has never been easy to accomplish in such a large, complex, and fragmented institution, with its many entrenched interests and strong political connections to Congress. The armed services have resisted efforts for many years to make their organization and operations more effective, efficient, and politically accountable.[9]

An area of perennial difficulty has been the military's personnel policies, beginning with the integration of blacks, and more recently, with women and gays. When Clinton proposed lifting the ban in 1993, the *Washington Post* reported that "rarely has the leadership of the U.S. military stood as united [against change] on a single issue" (Lancaster 1993). Military opponents included the Joint Chiefs of Staff, noncommissioned officers, ordinary enlisted men and women, and veterans groups (Price 1992; Schmitt 1993a). Military leaders testified against lifting the ban on Capitol Hill and concerned service members, their families and veterans groups swamped the Capitol switchboard with phone calls and letters.

The military invoked most of the same reasons for excluding gays and lesbians that it gave for resisting the integration of blacks and women (Karst 1991; Thomas and Thomas 1996): Lifting the ban would reduce the military's effectiveness, which requires cohesion within military units (see chapter 2). Servicemen and -women would react negatively to gays living openly among them, which would reduce the mutual trust and discipline upon which cohesion rests.[10] Heterosexual personnel would feel anxious about undressing and showering with gays, react abusively and violently toward them, and reject gay and lesbian officers (thus destroying "the integrity of rank and command"). Gays would prey upon younger men and women who are insecure in their sexuality, react with jealousy when jilted, and show favoritism toward subordinates when in positions of authority. Ultimately, a decline in trust and morale would make recruitment and retention of enlistees more difficult (Thomas and Thomas 1996).

Underpinning the argument in favor of keeping the ban in place was not the actual presence of gays, but rather how nongay personnel would *feel* about the presence of openly gay individuals and their expectations about how gays would treat them. According to one researcher who interviewed hundreds of service members, most supporters of the ban "agree that gays and lesbians are competent soldiers, but . . . [t]hey feel gays should be excluded because of their own feelings about homosexuality" (Miller 1994, 81). President Clinton also noted the central importance of service members' feelings in understanding the military's resistance to lifting the ban: "[T]hose who oppose lifting the ban are clearly focused not on the conduct of individual gay service members, but on how non-gay service members feel about gays in general and, in particular, those in the military service" (quoted in U.S. Congress, Senate 1993, S11199).

Surveys of military personnel at the time revealed firm opposition to lifting the ban. One of the issues with the widest gap between the opinions of military leaders and the public was whether the armed services should allow gays and lesbians to serve (Feaver and Kohn 2001). In one major survey, the public supported allowing gays to serve by 56 percent, to 37 percent against it, and military leaders opposed it 73 percent, to 18 percent against.[11] Sixty-five percent of military leaders said they would be more confident with a straight than a gay commander, and only 20 percent said that it would not matter to them. Military leaders oppose gay rights in other contexts as well: 42 percent of military leaders oppose allowing homosexuals to teach in public schools, about twice as high as for civilian leaders (Miller and Williams 2001).

Surveys of rank-and-file personnel conducted in the 1990s and news accounts during that time reveal a similar level of opposition to lifting the ban and a large gap between men and women in the military, with men registering much stronger opposition than women (Schmitt 1993f). In a survey of more than 3,600 Army soldiers, 75 percent of males and only 43 percent of females disagreed or strongly disagreed with lifting the ban. *Los Angeles Times* and Air Force polls produced similar results (Miller 1994, 71). A multiservice survey of 2,346 individuals revealed that 76 percent of men and 55 percent of women enlistees supported the ban. A more recent survey of 72 male Marines taken in the late 1990s found that 72 percent of them supported the ban (Estrada and Weiss 1999). The opinions of males in the military as a group carry greater weight, of course, as men constitute a much larger proportion of military personnel than do women.[12]

The intense hostility of military men toward having gays in their midst comes through clearly in studies that use interviews, discussion groups, and informal conversations. Laura Miller (1994) observed the "vehemence," "emotion," "raised voices," and "red faces" with which military men voiced their opposition to lifting the ban when she conducted hundreds of discussions with U.S. Army soldiers in 1992 and 1993. Some of the men "indicated they would be so offended by an infringement on their privacy that they would react with violence" (Miller 1994, 75, 79). Further, "Common in the interviews and written comments from men were statements like: 'It's not right,' 'It's sick,' 'It's despicable,' 'nauseating' and 'I'll kill them.'" A study of male Marines found that 63 percent thought that "male homosexuals are disgusting," and 41 percent believed that "lesbians are sick" (Estrada and Weiss 1999). Theodore Sarbin (1996, 181–82), who interviewed Navy officers about gays in the military, concluded that "the suspected or acknowledged homosexual person is perceived as a polluted specimen, the pollution forming an invisible and silent miasma. In the course of my interviews . . . nearly all said . . . that they would not be comfortable sharing sleeping quarters with a gay man." When Sarbin asked Navy officers if they feared that gays would assault them sexually, they said that they did not. Despite further probing, they gave no clear reason for their concern except for feeling uncomfortable. According to Sarbin, "Further discussion led to the inference that somehow the space would be polluted, not by germs, but by an unarticulated conception of the gay man as a tabooed object and a carrier of sin" (Sarbin 1996, 181–82).

REASONS FOR THE HOSTILITY OF MILITARY PERSONNEL TO LIFTING THE BAN

The political backgrounds of military personnel help to explain their intense opposition to allowing gays to serve. The gap in attitudes between the military and the public on gay rights issues comes as no surprise because the military is disproportionately male, conservative, and Republican, all groups with lower levels of support for gay rights. Military leaders identify as Republicans and conservatives more than do civilian leaders and the public. Sixty-four percent of military leaders in one survey identified themselves as Republicans, compared with 46 percent of civilian veteran leaders, 30 percent of civilian nonveteran leaders, 37 percent of veterans, and 29 percent of nonveterans in the public generally. Sixty-seven percent of military leaders identify as conservative, compared with 52 percent of civilian veteran leaders, 32 percent of civilian nonveteran leaders, and 50 percent of veterans and 39 percent of nonveterans in the general public (Holsti 2001, 28–33). While more than 70 percent of the men in the military opposed having openly gay and lesbian individuals serve in 1993–94, only 50 to 52 percent of males and 45 to 59 percent of Republicans among the public did so (*Time*/CNN/Yankelovich 1993–94). It is likely that the military attracts, or shapes, the antigay attitudes that are particularly strong among its personnel.[13]

Today's smaller military, made up of volunteers and careerists, is less representative of the public than in the past and less open to infusions of civilians and changes in their attitudes. According to one study, "the decline in the military participation ratio and Republican dominance of the South" explain most of the gaps found between civilians and service members on domestic policy issues (Desch 2001, 317; see also Moskos 1994, 63).

In a broader political context, support for a strong military establishment has been part of the conservative creed since the beginning of the Cold War. Liberals have been more distrustful of the military and less willing to spend money on defense at the same time that they have been the strongest supporters of gay rights. Although gay rights and defense issues may have little connection, the military has aligned itself with the conservative movement. Conservative opponents of lifting the ban emphasized Clinton's opposition to the Vietnam War and lack of military service as evidence that the country could not trust him to support the military (Herek 1996a, 11).

The military's opposition to lifting the ban appears rooted in psychological and cultural factors as well. The importance of the ban, according to Randy Shilts (1993, 6), is less about keeping gays out of the military "than with having people think there are no homosexuals in the service." Undoubtedly, the military's unique living and working arrangements help to trigger homophobic fears and thus a need to maintain the fiction that gays are absent from the military. Service men and women live and work in a close proximity that is largely absent in civilian employment. Service members' concern about a "loss of privacy" is a euphemism for their anxieties about exposing themselves to homosexuals. Nongay servicemen and -women fear having to shower and undress in front of individuals who may find them physically attractive. Given that gays and straights share dormitories, locker rooms, pools, and gyms throughout their lives, these fears would seem irrational (Stiehm 1994). Nevertheless, given deep-seated homophobic feelings throughout much of society, the military's close quarters sets the stage for many service members' active resistance to lifting the ban.

The objective circumstances of military life trigger antigay reactions, but they are not the source of them. If they were, military women would be as opposed to lifting the ban as their male comrades. But as we have noted, much of the opposition to gays in the military is gender based. Because the military remains predominately a male institution and the stigma that society assigns gays and lesbians is much more prevalent among men, the impact of those feelings is much greater in the military than elsewhere. In her interviews of service men and women, Miller (1994, 79) found that male soldiers appeared "much more emotional over lifting the ban than women. . . . Women generally made their points and then preferred to spend the rest of the discussion talking about harassment, childcare or job restrictions. In contrast, the issue consumed the [entire] interview with pro-ban male soldiers."[14]

More important than the predominance of males in the military is the construction of the military along gender lines and in a manner that is antithetical to homosexuality (Connell 1992; Adam 1994). As such, military service plays an important role in the formation of masculine identity. What lifting the ban *means* for many men is apparently critical. Maintaining the illusion of a homosexual-free zone of social interaction reduces male anxiety. Military service is not simply a job for many men in the military; it also helps to affirm and strengthen their masculine identity.

Most men see the achievement of manhood as essential to their identities. Recent psychoanalytic theory argues that, because men identify with their mothers who nurture them in their early years, they feel compelled to establish a male identity throughout their lives. They prove their manliness by escaping from, and rejecting, feminine identity (Stoller 1985). Men who struggle in this endeavor see themselves as failures to qualify fully as men. Men maintain their male identities through participation in social institutions that support an "ideology of masculinity"—a belief that power belongs to those who display traditionally masculine traits (Karst 1991). Many cultures, including that in the United States, identify military service with stereotypically masculine traits, such as strength, bravery, aggression, and emotional detachment. The military thus serves as a symbol of masculinity and the pursuit of manhood (Jeffords 1989; Enloe 1988; Elshtain 1987; Ehrenreich 1997, 123–31; Francke 1997, 155–57; Kovitz 2003; Hockey 2003). To maintain the military's function in the formation of masculine identity, it is important to exclude those who do not embrace stereotypical masculine identity or refuse to do so—women and gay men (Mead 1949, 160; Benecke and Dodge 1996, 81–84).

As Shilts (1993, 5) points out, "the presence of gay men—especially so many who are competent for military service–calls into question everything that manhood is supposed mean." The military's exclusion draws a bright line between "real men" and others, maintaining the military as a symbol of masculine power and superiority. The stigmatization and stereotyping of gay men serves to distinguish the real men from the others. With the help of psychiatrists in the 1940s, the military disseminated a construction of homosexuals as effeminate, passive, fearful, and exhibiting other traits antithetical to the stereotypical masculinity that it associated with "good" soldiers (Berube 1990; Lehring 2003, ch. 4). Assigning homosexuals to a deviant and outsider status reassures other members of the armed service that they rightfully belong to the organization and are "man enough" to be an insider. Thus, individuals' discomfort with gays and lesbians is not simply a homophobic reaction; it reflects the fear that the organization will change in ways that do not permit it to bolster masculine identity and sense of superiority (Karst 1991; Rolison and Nakayama 1994; Rimmerman 1996a, xxi).[15]

Maintaining the military as an institution that reinforces traditional male identity is as important to the military as it is to the individuals who inhabit it.[16] The military itself perceives male dominance as crucial to maintaining the close bonds that it needs to be effective. Admitting those who are not deemed masculine enough jeopardizes the bonding that is the basis for unit cohesion.[17]

While the military's hostility to lifting the ban is important, it is not a sufficient explanation for its continued existence. The same resistance to gays in the military has been common in most nations. Homophobia, disapproval of homosexuality, and negative stereotypes of homosexuals exist in many foreign militaries. But the United States is one of the few in which policy continues to reflect the military's preferences.[18] The United States is also unique in having a powerful, independent legislative branch of government willing to support the military.

A Powerful Ally: Congress

The central player in Congress in blocking President Clinton's efforts to lift the ban was Senator Sam Nunn (D-GA). Nunn was in an excellent position to challenge the president from his position as chair of the Senate Armed Services Committee. Committee chairs, especially in the Senate, had considerable influence even in the early 1990s, where they were less constrained by party leaders, caucuses, and subcommittee chairs than in the House of Representatives. The fact that the committee attracted disproportionately conservative senators who strongly supported the military also helped Nunn. Nunn could count on the support of most of the Southern Democrats and all of the Republicans on the committee. Nunn was particularly pivotal because his voting record was the most liberal on gay issues of any of the southerners (Rayside 1996, 152). Coupled with the great respect that he earned for his expertise in defense matters, his relative moderation on gay issues had "given cover for a lot of other people" to oppose it without having to "fear . . . being branded right-wing conservatives," according to one close conservative observer.[19]

Nunn had a long and close relationship with the military, which Rayside (1996, 155) describes as "providing Nunn with valuable political leverage in Washington, ensuring him his share of spending benefits specific to his district, and creating for him a valuable national constituency of enlisted service members and veterans. Appearing strong on defense issues and conservative on social issues also provided a degree of protection against electoral challenge from right wing forces in his home state of Georgia."[20]

Nunn had warned Clinton before and after the election that he was opposed to lifting the ban (Rayside 1996, 156). Congress held hearings in the spring of 1993, which the media covered extensively. Supporters of lifting the ban criticized the Senate hearings and the committee's report for their bias in favor of keeping it.[21] Colin Powell, the first African American chairman of the Joint Chiefs of Staff, and General Norman Schwarzkopf, the commander of the forces in the Persian Gulf War (1990–91), testified against lifting the ban. Schwarzkopf argued that the troops would be so disheartened by allowing openly gay service members that they would become like the demoralized Iraqis "who sat in the deserts of Kuwait" when American forces defeated them (Schmitt 1993b, A1). A dramatic moment came when Colonel Fred Peck announced that his son was gay and testified that he feared for his son's life if the president lifted the ban because of antigay prejudice in the military. Carefully staged visits to military installations, including naval bases, where committee members and television viewers could see the cramped quarters shared by Navy personnel, capped the hearings. Nunn pointed out "the closeness of the bunks and shower stalls and asked groups of sailors how they felt about the idea of 'open homosexuals' in the armed forces" (Bawer 1993, 60).

Congressional barons like Nunn were well aware of their powerful position vis-à-vis the president. According to Nunn, "The Constitution . . . makes it very clear that Congress has the responsibility to deal with matters of this nature affecting the Armed Forces of the United States. . . . It is the responsibility of Congress to ensure that policies of the Defense Department enhance good order and discipline, while providing for fair and equitable personnel policies. So the question of whether homosexuals should serve in the military is an issue on which Congress and the President share constitutional responsibility" (U.S. Congress, Senate 1993, S755). With the president on the defensive and many in his administration and Congress dismayed that the issue had become a major distraction from other important business, Clinton signaled his intention to abandon his plan to lift the ban. While he and Defense Secretary Les Aspin were in the midst of developing a compromise with Nunn and other legislative opponents in May 1993, Clinton announced that there was a "legitimate concern" that "our country does not appear to be endorsing a gay lifestyle" (quoted in Rayside 1996, 162; Schmitt 1993e). Nunn and Representative Ike Skelton (D-TX), the chair of the House subcommittee with jurisdiction over the issue, made clear their intentions to legislate on the matter under a defense reauthorization bill that would have been difficult for Clinton to veto (Schmitt 1993c).

With the writing on the wall, Aspin and the White House came out favoring a "compromise" close to the version of don't ask, don't tell favored by Nunn and the military and closer to the existing policy than what Clinton originally proposed (Schmitt 1993b, Schmitt 1993d).[22] As long as personnel did not reveal their homosexuality or bisexuality through their statements or conduct, the military would not ask questions about their sexuality. The House rejected Representative Barney Frank's (D-MA) effort to craft an alternative that would permit individuals to engage in homosexual conduct and participate in gay-related activities when they were off base and out of uniform. Both houses of Congress passed the don't ask, don't tell compromise by comfortable margins.

If our argument about the key role of legislative power and preferences is correct, we should find a very different institutional context in nations that have dropped their bans on gays in their militaries. Comparative analysis may also suggest other institutional reasons for why the ban in the United States persists.

The (Ir)Relevance of International Experience

The experiences of Canada, Australia, and Great Britain are perhaps most instructive for the United States among the nations that have dropped their bans on gays in the military. All three countries share a common cultural heritage and language with the United States. Like the United States, these nations had long-standing bans against homosexuals serving in the armed forces, discouraged homosexuals from entering the service, and expelled those who entered. Britain discharged approximately 60 to 70 personnel every year in the years preceding the ban's elimination. Like the United States, Canada and Britain had all-volunteer forces.[23] Opponents of lifting the bans in these countries voiced the same concerns about gays serving openly: the unique circumstances of military service necessitated suspending individuals' civil liberties; homosexuality was seen as immoral; homophobic personnel would subject openly gay personnel to abuse and physical risk; and above all, the presence of openly gay soldiers, sailors, and air personnel would compromise morale, discipline, cohesion, and effectiveness and harm recruitment.[24] As in the United States, the issue was politically contentious and there was stiff and overwhelming opposition from military leaders, veterans groups, and rank-and-file personnel.[25] The British military believed that letting gays serve openly would pose a threat to masculine culture (Booth 1999; MacMillan 1999). British polls reported that 90 and 77 percent of service personnel opposed lifting the ban in 1996 and 1998, respectively (Clark 1998). As in the United States, there was reluctance and resistance among elected politicians to lift the ban (Walsh 1992; Connolly 1992c). And like the United States, the public supported or was indifferent to gays serving in the military (Associated Press 1992b; *Toronto Star* 1992b; Lancaster 1992).[26]

At the same time, a similar set of institutional conditions conducive to change runs through the three nations that lifted their bans discussed here:

(1) the absence of independent legislative power with which the military could align itself, (2) national or supranational judicial and quasi-judicial institutions that challenged the ban and forced the politicians to act, and (3) a willingness to draw lessons from international experience with allowing gays to serve.

CANADA

The first stirrings of Canada's movement toward lifting its ban on gays in the military began in 1986 when the Canadian Justice Department concluded that the ban was unconstitutional (*Toronto Star* 1992a). However, neither the military nor the government in power were eager to change policy. Military leaders continued to support the ban because they knew that rank-and-file members of the armed forces wanted it kept in place, and the government's majority in Parliament depended upon conservative support to stay in power. The military eased up its policy in 1987 by refraining from automatically forcing out servicemen and women whom it discovered were gay, but it prohibited them from training courses and promotions, which had the effect of halting their careers (Bindman 1992c; Lancaster 1992).

In 1990, the Security Intelligence Committee, an independent governmental watchdog organization, ruled in favor of a female air force lieutenant, Michelle Douglas, whom the military dismissed when it discovered that she was a lesbian (Bindman 1990) (her story begins this chapter). The committee ruled that the ban on gays violated Canada's Charter of Rights and Freedoms, a document similar to the U.S. Bill of Rights. But social conservatives had enough votes to bring down the Brian Mulroney government, then in power, if the ban were lifted (Morton 1992; *Hamilton Spectator* 1992), and the Canadian Supreme Court ruled that the Security Intelligence Committee's findings were not binding on the government and could be ignored (Bindman 1992a, 1992b).

Nevertheless, Canadian courts and quasi-judicial commissions became increasingly active in expanding gay rights in the 1990s. According to one observer, the success of Canadian gays has had less to do with a highly organized, coherent pressure group strategy than with "individual gays and lesbians fighting court battles on their own" (Walsh 1992). In 1990, a federal court ruled that gay prisoners had to be accorded the same treatment in conjugal visits as straight prisoners (Walsh 1992). In 1992, the Ontario Court of Appeal ruled the Canadian Human Rights Act unconstitutional because of its failure to include gays and lesbians in its provisions protecting citizens against discrimination (Pugliese 1992). And Canada's well-developed structure of federal and provincial human rights commissions issued a series of rulings in the area of domestic partner law that led to court cases and culminated in marriage rights for gays a decade or so later. The Ontario Human Rights Code included sexual orientation as a category protected against discrimination, but the Canadian Human Rights Act did not. Because only federal law covered the Canadian military, it continued to maintain restrictions on gays in the military (Vienneau and Lakey 1992). A few months later, a Canadian federal court in Toronto ruled just before the Douglas case went to trial that the military's restrictions on gays violated the Charter of Rights and Freedoms. That decision led the Canadian military to abandon all remaining restrictions on gays serving in its ranks and pay $100,000 to settle the Douglas case (Jacobs 1992; Vienneau and Lakey 1992).

The military's decision reveals the deference paid to the courts in Canada and to its lack of confidence in being able to persuade the courts of the same arguments that the U.S. military used effectively in Congress. Leaders of the Canadian military realized that they lacked a credible case to put before the courts concerning any adverse effects on military effectiveness of letting gays serve. According to a retired brigadier general who was the director general for personnel policy in the armed forces at the time, "we would not have been able to prove that it [homosexuality] had that deleterious effect on cohesion and morale that everyone talked about. Basically we realized that we didn't have the evidentiary foundation. . . . It just wasn't there, I mean, you can't use the old cohesion and morale arguments just based on folklore. You have to be able to prove this stuff" (quoted in Lancaster 1992).

AUSTRALIA

Australia's ban gays in the military dated back to the nineteenth-century British colonial period. When Australia decriminalized homosexuality in the 1970s, it wrote the ban into its military regulations (Spencer 1992). A female sergeant whom the military dismissed when it identified her as a lesbian took her case before the country's Human Rights Commission and won (Connolly 1992a). The ruling set off a contentious debate at the center of the Australian government. Australia's military chiefs were deadlocked for weeks but finally decided to uphold the ban (Connolly

1992b; AAPA US News 1992). Cabinet ministers were also split over the issue. The Defence Department secretary opposed lifting the ban, while the attorney general and the minister of Defence, Science and Personnel favored lifting it (Connolly 1992b, 1992e). A caucus committee within the ruling Labour Party took up the issue (*Hobart Mercury* 1992b). The caucus reached a compromise that lifted the ban at the same time that it strengthened regulations to protect individuals against unwelcome sexual advances from members of either sex and gave greater authority to officers to punish those who engaged in such behavior (United Press International 1992). Following the decision of their civilian superiors, the military quietly, if reluctantly, fell into line behind the new policy (Laidlaw 1992b; Associated Press 1992a).

GREAT BRITAIN

The British case is particularly important because Britain has a large military and is deeply involved in international affairs. It has been the most active ally of the United States in the Iraq War (2003–present) and the broader war on terrorism. Britain had one of the strictest policies on gays in the West and enforced it rigorously (*Economist* 1999; Cullen 1999). Once Britain lifted its ban, the United States and Turkey were the only North Atlantic Treaty Organization nations left with a ban in place against gays in the armed forces.

In 1995, the House of Commons, controlled by Conservatives, voted overwhelmingly against lifting the ban (Clark 1998). Members of Parliament are not required to follow the preferences of their party on "moral questions," and they enjoy "free votes." Gay and lesbian military personnel, unlike their counterparts in Canada and Australia, were unable to petition their nation's courts. British service members are subject to military courts of law with no appeal to civilian courts (Riding 1992). When Tony Blair and the Labour Party came to power in 1997, they pledged to eliminate the ban but were stymied by opposition from military leaders, much the same as Bill Clinton faced in 1993 (*Agence France Presse* 1999; Morris 2000). And as in the United States, British courts had supported the military (Cullen 1999).

The path to overturning the ban in Britain began when several former military personnel filed complaints of discrimination with the European Court of Human Rights, arguing that their expulsion from the Royal Air Force was illegal under the European Convention on Human Rights (Purnell 1999). In 1999, the court ruled unanimously that the British military expulsions violated Article 8 of the convention, which guarantees a right to privacy. The investigations into the sexual behavior of the expelled service members that led to the expulsions were, according to the court, "exceptionally intrusive" and had a "profound effect" on their careers. Governments can infringe on individual rights only if a real threat exists to the operation and effectiveness of their militaries. The British government rested its case on the argument that gays openly serving posed a threat to the military's morale because of the "negative attitudes of heterosexual personnel" toward gays and lesbians in the services. However, the court said that such attitudes did not justify discrimination against gays any more than it had against women and racial minorities and that the government failed to show why it could not integrate homosexuals into the armed services in the same way that women and racial minorities had been (Meade 1999; see also Leeman 1999).

Although the European Court of Human Rights had no authority to force Britain to change its law, as a signatory to the European Convention on Human Rights, Britain was obligated to abide by the court's rulings even if that required changing its laws (Lyall 1999). The British Defence minister immediately suspended all expulsions in order to study the implications of the ruling, but he also made clear that the British government accepted the ruling and prepared legislation to lift the ban (Hennessy and Annells 1999). The British always have complied with the court's decisions in such cases. For example, the British Parliament agreed to follow a 1997 European Court ruling that ordered it to lower the age of gay consensual conduct to sixteen years old (*Agence France Presse* 1999). Parliament passed a law that incorporated the convention into British law in October 2000, made domestic laws compatible with the convention and rulings by the court, and obligated British judges to interpret civil rights laws in accord with the convention (Cullen 1999).

In the end, the British replaced their ban with the same policy that Clinton had proposed in the United States—one that permitted gays to serve openly in the military while toughening restrictions on inappropriate sexual behavior (by either homosexuals or heterosexuals) that compromised military effectiveness (Johnson 2000). Great Britain has come the farthest perhaps of any country that has lifted its ban, from strictly banning gay personnel to actively recruiting gays into its ranks, within just a few years (Lyall 2005).

INTERNATIONAL INTERVENTION AND LESSON DRAWING

The international environment was an important element in British and Australian efforts to lift their bans. Governments in the two countries were obliged to uphold international norms and agreements and were open to learning from the experiences of other nations. An important argument that reformers used in Australia was that continued discrimination against gays in the military violated international agreements that Australia had signed and was obligated to uphold (Allen 1992). Nations that had signed the International Labour Convention had agreed not to discriminate in the workplace on the basis of sexual orientation (AAPA US News 1992; Connolly 1992e). For the Australian attorney general in particular, "that was a powerful additional argument" (Charlton 1992b). Australia seems to have been more open to the international environment in another way: according to one observer, "opinion within the government has been strongly divided, but has given a push by the lifting of a similar ban by Canada" a short time earlier and "has taken the debate on the issue in the United States as a signal for change" (Munro 1992)—President Clinton's efforts to lift the U.S. ban occurred during the same period as the debate in Australia.

Britain was one of the last remaining European nations to keep its ban in place (Cullen 1999; *New York Times* 2000a). For Britain, the abandonment of its ban was a logical step in following trends among its European neighbors and former Commonwealth nations. After talking to his counterparts in other European nations where no bans on gays existed, Air Chief Marshal Sir David Cousins, the head of the Royal Air Force, member of the Joint Chiefs of Staff, and a leading military adviser to Prime Minister Tony Blair, announced his support for lifting the ban (Clark 1998). International influence is apparent also in the kinds of policy alternatives that foreign nations consider. Britain modeled its policy on those that the Australians adopted: stricter rules against sexual harassment and conduct would accompany lifting the ban (Waugh 1999). Perhaps most importantly, the chief lesson learned from the experience of other nations was that the sky did not fall once the government lifted the ban. No evidence suggests that having gays serve openly compromises military effectiveness or creates other problems. This may be the result of most gays remaining closeted, but it undermines the main argument of the opponents (Summerskill 2000; Lyall 2005; Lancaster 1992).

International constraints and lesson drawing were absent from the American debate. The United States is not a signatory to the International

Labour Convention and is not subject to the decisions of supranational in-stitutions with sovereign powers akin to those held by European Union authorities.[27] Of course, the United States could still have drawn lessons from foreign experience. Some American supporters of lifting the ban have pointed to other nations to show that their decision to lift their bans did not produce adverse consequences. In response, the ban's supporters argue that the power and role of the U.S. military around the world is uniquely vital to world peace and that, therefore, there can be "no room for error." Part of the resistance, however, is plainly a defiant attitude that the United States has nothing to learn from other countries and does not defer to their policy judgments (see Lancaster 1992).[28]

Judicial and Legislative Behavior in the U.S. Case

The very different institutional context in the United States from other countries has served to block efforts to lift the ban, as we have seen. In its willingness to challenge the president, Congress has played a critical role in perpetuating the ban and blocking efforts to abolish it. Students of comparative politics have long recognized the considerable independ-ence and power of Congress vis-à-vis the executive that is unrivaled in any other democracy. In the post-Vietnam, post-Watergate era, congressional assertiveness in military affairs grew. Although the level of party discipline under Republican presidents has grown, it has been much more limited under Democratic presidents. When Clinton tried to lift the ban, he still faced a fragmented institution that gave considerable influence to con-gressional barons like Sam Nunn and a party majority that was hard to keep together on controversial issues. The system afforded legislators who might have supported Clinton none of the "cover" that parties and party leaders provide their members on unpopular votes in parliamentary sys-tems (Rayside 1996, 148–51).

The United States is also distinctive in the role of the courts vis-à-vis the military. The law exempts the military from many lawsuits, and the rights of military personnel are severely restricted. Courts have traditionally taken a passive and deferential role even when litigants have charged the military with discrimination in its personnel policies (Burelli and Dale 2005, 14–16; Brewer, Kaib, and O'Connor 2000, 393).[29] In his study of judicial decision making across several policy areas related to gay and lesbian rights, Pinel-lo (2003, 10) found that gays and lesbians fared worst in military cases, prevailing in less than one-quarter of cases from 1981 to 2000. The U.S.

Supreme Court's ruling in *Matlovich v. Secretary of the Air Force* (591 F.2nd 852, D.C. Circ. 1978) began a string of losses for gay rights organizations and individuals who challenged the ban (Pacelle 1996, 209–16). The Court typically has declined to hear appeals of service members who were discharged after admitting or being found guilty of engaging in sodomy, as in *Hatheway v. Secretary of the Army* (641 F. 2nd 1376 9th Circ. 1981) and *Beller v. Middendorf* (632 F. 2nd 788 9th Circ. 1981) (Brewer, Kaib, and O'Connor 2000, 387). The Court refused to stay an injunction against the don't ask, don't tell policy in *United States v. Meinhold* (510 U.S. 939 1993) and refused to review the five federal appeals court rulings in which the policy has been upheld (*Thomasson v. Perry* [895 F. Supp. 850 1996], *Thorne v. U.S. Department of Defense* [916 F. Supp. 1358 1996], *Richenberg v. Perry* [97 F. 3rd 256 8th Circ. 1996], *Phillips v. Perry* [106 F. 3rd 1429 1997], and *Able v. United States* [986 F. Supp. 865 1998]) (Burelli and Dale 2005, 16–18).[30]

The Court's ruling in *Bowers v. Hardwick* (1986), that state antisodomy laws were constitutional, served as the basis for the finding in these cases. The prevailing doctrine has been that the military's need to maintain cohesion and discipline provides a "rational basis" for discrimination. Opinions differ about whether the Court's ruling in *Lawrence v. Texas* (2003), which overruled *Bowers,* will strengthen legal challenges to don't ask, don't tell. Opponents of the ban argue that it is incompatible with the Court's finding in *Lawrence* that a fundamental interest in liberty protects homosexual behavior and trumps the government's broad assertion that the ban is necessary to maintain cohesion and discipline. Others argue that *Lawrence* does not apply to the military, given the long string of precedents in which the courts have deferred to the judgment of Congress and the military in curtailing individual rights (Burelli and Dale 2005, 18–19).

Comparisons with Racial and Gender Integration

The military has a long history of discrimination against particular groups in its personnel policies. Although no exact parallel to the ban on gays and lesbians exists, the segregation of blacks and the exclusion of women from most jobs in the military represent similar instances of struggles for equality within the military. Advocates of racial integration and gender inclusion encountered a great deal of resistance from opponents who argued that integrating blacks and women would be detrimental to military effectiveness, just as opponents of lifting the ban on gays make today (see Bianco 1996; Karst 1991). Nevertheless, the military ended racial segregation and makes many more opportunities available to women today than they enjoyed in the past.

The African American and female integration cases provide further support for the political-institutional explanation for the persistence of the ban on gays in the military. Many of the same institutional actors and arrangements that have been important in the struggle over the ban on gays and lesbians serving openly in the military also figured prominently in the struggles over blacks and women in the military. Resistance to the integration of blacks and women came from the military and conservative elements in society, but the political and institutional constraints were less strong and weakened over time, which has not yet happened in the gay and lesbian case.

RACIAL INTEGRATION

A critical juncture in the history of black civil rights came in 1948 when President Harry Truman ordered the integration of the armed forces. A key question is why Congress did not block Truman, as it blocked Clinton forty-five years later in his effort to lift the ban on gays. According to two historians, Congress "largely ignored" Truman's executive order (Mershon and Schlossman 1998, 184). Many whites, especially in the South, opposed integration of the military as fiercely as social and religious conservatives oppose lifting the ban on gays. Public opposition to integration in the military was strong (63 percent in one poll), higher than the opposition to maintaining the ban on gay personnel (Mershon and Schlossman 1998, 177–78; RAND 1993 as quoted in U.S. Congress, Senate 1993). And having inherited the office upon Roosevelt's death, Truman had yet to win election for the presidency.

Part of the explanation for the different outcomes is that Truman issued an executive order to integrate blacks, while Clinton demurred from issuing an order to lift the ban on gays. By issuing an executive order, Truman bypassed Congress. The opponents of integration had little means to resist. The main weapon of the Southern opponents of civil rights was the Senate's filibuster. Although the filibuster was a highly effective tool for blocking civil rights legislation after World War II, it was of no use when opponents needed to pass legislation overturning an executive order (McCoy and Ruetten 1973, ch. 6; Lawson 1991, 35–36).

For Craig Rimmerman (1996b, 112), Clinton's failure to "demonstrate resolve and principle" is a major part of the reason for his failure to get the ban lifted and for accepting a compromise that fell far short of his campaign pledge. Besides refusing to issue an executive order, Clinton failed to work with gay advocacy groups, pursue an effective legislative strategy, and use the presidency's bully pulpit to educate the public about why the ban should have been abolished.

Although Truman's boldness in issuing an executive order was certainly part of the reason for his success, Clinton could not have resolved the issue of gays in the military by issuing such an order because he was in no position to have it carried out.[31] Issuing an order would have emboldened Clinton's opponents further to pass legislation codifying the ban. Even if Clinton had been less prone to compromise, had a greater commitment to lifting the ban, and was willing to spend more of his political capital, it seems very unlikely that he would have gotten his way. The final vote to codify the Nunn policy indicates that Congress would have had enough votes to override a Clinton veto of the don't ask, don't tell compromise. A vote to rescind an executive order eliminating the ban altogether would likely have received even more votes, given that Congress would have been reacting to a president whose aim was to evade Congress.

Clinton was more assertive on this issue than were his counterparts in nations that have lifted their bans. Those leaders either did not support lifting their bans or did not become active supporters until other actors compelled them to do so.[32] Clinton may have generated more support for lifting the ban had he tried harder. One analysis of the trend in opinion over the course of the debate found that the president did help to educate the public.[33] Yet it is very doubtful that Clinton would have generated a level of support from ordinary Americans that would to make the issue paramount for most of them. His efforts were as likely to mobilize substantial numbers of people who were strongly against lifting the ban as those fewer citizens who were strongly in favor of lifting it (Rayside 1996, 171). No matter how much more receptive the public may have become to lifting the ban, few legislators would have worried that voters would punish them at the polls if they did not support the president on this issue.

Truman's success and Clinton's failure were due to the very different situations that the two presidents faced within and between the two major political parties and with the military. These differences induced Truman to act favorably toward racial integration and reduced the chances that Congress would resist his initiative. In contrast, they led Clinton to act cautiously and increased the probability that Congress would greet his proposal with effective resistance.

The debates over race and gender took place during a period when liberals were much stronger and the Republican Party was not closely associated with the social conservatism rooted in the South. Ending racial segregation would not have been possible without the strength of liberals in Congress and civil rights advocates in both parties in the late 1940s. In 1948, the issue of racial integration in the armed forces was part of the broader struggle for gaining civil rights for blacks and was a highly contentious issue within the Democratic Party.

The 1948 presidential election promised to be close. Blacks and white liberals pressured Truman to push for civil rights, but doing so inflamed white southerners, another important Democratic constituency party (Mershon and Schlossman 1998, 179; Gropman 1998, 74–79).[34] Truman tried to navigate this divide at the Democratic National Convention by offering a vague statement in the platform about supporting civil rights generally but avoiding specific policy commitments.[35] His strategy failed to appease the dominant liberal faction, however, which pushed through stronger language that induced many Southern Democrats at the convention to desert the party (Mershon and Schlossman 1998, 180–84; Dalfiume 1969, 169–70).

At the same time, the Republican Party was still a moderate, northern-dominated party that afforded blacks a credible alternative to the Democrats. Wendell Willkie, Franklin Roosevelt's Republican opponent in 1940, for example, openly supported civil rights and attracted black votes (MacGregor 1981, 19). Truman's Republican opponent, New York governor Thomas E. Dewey, also supported civil rights. The GOP platform expressed opposition to the military's segregation and "increased pressure on Truman to do something more than talk about civil rights" (Gropman 1998, 78–79, 82; see also Dalfiume 1969, 167–68; Mershon and Schlossman 1998, 170–71). Truman's need for black votes, his loss of control of the convention, the triumphs of the procivil rights liberals, and the threat of Republicans out-flanking him on civil rights pushed him to issue his executive order a few weeks after the convention (Lawson 1991, 32–40).

Even before Truman issued his executive order, signs surfaced that he would not encounter the kind of effective opposition that Clinton later did in his bid to end the military's ban on gays. The Senate defeated an effort by Senator Richard Russell (D-GA) to amend the Selective Service bill to block any presidential effort to end desegregation in the military through executive order (Mershon and Schlossman 1998, 181–82). Because Republicans held the majority in the Senate, Southern Democrats did not control key committee chairmanships (Donaldson 1991, 133). In the end, Congress facilitated the implementation of Truman's order. As an increasing number of members announced their support for integration, the different services interpreted that as a signal that the military's support for desegregation would be an important consideration in making appropriations decisions for the Cold War (Donaldson 1991, 137).

In contrast, first, the debate over lifting the ban on gays and lesbians took place during a period of conservative ascendancy in Congress. Clinton and gay rights organizations would have needed to expend large amounts of political capital to overcome the formidable political opposition they encountered. Even if they could have mustered greater resources and resolve and correctly anticipated the strength of the opposition, it is unlikely that they could have prevailed.

Second, as the key stakeholder in the policy debate, the military was not uniformly opposed to racial desegregation, as it was to lifting the ban on gays. Military planners realized that segregation was costly and hindered the full use of black manpower, concerns that lasted through World War II and into the Cold War that emerged in the late 1940s (Mershon and Schlossman 1998, ch. 6; Astor 1998, 331; Donaldson 1991, 134). In the broader geopolitical context of a worsening Cold War, racial segregation made it more difficult for the United States to exert international leadership (Mershon and Schlossman 1998, 159). Even before Truman issued his executive order, some elements within the military favored integration or did not oppose it strongly; specifically, the Navy supported it, the Army and Marine Corps opposed it, and the Air Force was divided. The Navy removed most of the legal barriers to racial segregation in 1946, more than two years before the executive order.

What seems to account for the different positions of the services is whether they had leaders with a commitment to integration on practical, political, or moral grounds (MacGregor 1981, chs. 2–3; McCoy and Ruetten 1973, ch. 11).[36] After Truman issued the order, white southerners in Congress came to the support of General Omar Bradley, who announced that the Army would continue to segregate as long as segregation existed in society. But the southerners did not have the strength to do more than that. Bradley's overt opposition was isolated among the top brass of the military, and he quickly retreated from his stand (Mershon and Schlossman 1988, 185; Astor 1998, 330–31; Dalfiume 1969, 173). Shortly after Truman issued his order, "it was clear that the Army was to be in the minority in fighting to retain its policy of segregation" and the civilian leadership fell in line to implement the order (Dalfiume 1969, 175). Thus, unlike the solid opposition to allowing gays in the military across different branches of the armed services, supporters of racial integration found a much more congenial situation.

GENDER INCLUSION

The inclusion of women in the armed forces is approaching the inclusion of African Americans as nearly complete. Women's inclusion was far more gradual than blacks' inclusion, with no single breakthrough on the scale of Truman's executive order. Women participated in the military in great numbers during World War II, but afterward Congress limited women to 2 percent of total enlistments and restricted promotions above the rank of lieutenant colonel. Congress eliminated these ceilings in 1967 and opened new career fields to women when it ended the draft and inaugurated the all-volunteer force in 1973. It ended the separate women's auxiliary corps in 1978 and allowed women to be eligible for all noncombat jobs. Women comprised 14 percent of the U.S. armed forces in 2002 (NATO 2002). The major hurdle has been allowing women into combat. Because combat is the core function of the armed services and the military categorizes many jobs under that rubric, exclusion from combat roles decreases women's status and restricts their employment. Congress and the Defense Department started opening combat roles to women in the early 1990s, and today women are allowed to fill more than 90 percent of the career fields in the armed services (NATO 2002).

What accounts for this record of significant progress for women? First, the military benefits much more from allowing women greater participation than allowing gays to serve openly. Women's sheer numbers make them more valuable, particularly whenever human resource shortages occur, as they did during World War II and after the Vietnam War. The nation's shift to an all-volunteer service after Vietnam made it imperative that the military turn to women as a source of enlistments (Enloe 1994, 86; Moskos 1994, 60; Thomas and Thomas 1996, 66). Since the 1970s, undersecretaries of Defense for Manpower and Logistics, including those under Republican administrations, have "generally supported the proposition that the military needed women to enlist and re-enlist" (Enloe 1994, 92). By emphasizing human resource shortages, the supporters of female inclusion were able to define the issue as one of "military effectiveness" as much as civil rights, defining the issue in the same manner as opponents of lifting the ban on gays today.

It has been much easier for women to use their visibility to make people aware of their contributions to the military than it has been for gays, who must remain in the closet. The exemplary participation of a growing number of military women in Operation Desert Storm during the Persian Gulf War in the early 1990s led people to realize that women were as exposed to danger as the men who fought in combat, which reduced concerns about women's competence in battle and their ability to survive capture. Their performance drew applause from then Defense Secretary Dick Cheney and General Norman Schwartzkopf, the latter an ardent opponent of allowing gays to serve openly in the military (Stiehm 1994, 159).

As with efforts to end racial segregation, some of the service branches have been more receptive to women than have others. The more receptive branches include the Army, with its large number of jobs to fill for which women are eligible, and the Air Force, which found that female recruitment did not threaten the all-male elite fighter pilots under the combat exclusion (Enloe 1994, 93–95).

The second reason for women's progress in this arena is that women have enjoyed official representation within the military, which has afforded them legitimacy and access to decision makers, a situation that is unthinkable for gays and lesbians. Women, like blacks, have always had an open and acknowledged role in the military, no matter how limited or second class that role may have been. The question has not been *whether* women should have a place in the military, but how much equality they should enjoy with men.

In the early 1950s, the Pentagon created the Defense Advisory Committee on Women in the Armed Services (DACOWITS), which reports directly to the secretary of Defense. DACOWITS advocated on behalf of women in order to reduce harassment and expand their employment opportunities. During the Cold War, DACOWITS consistently sought to define the issue of women's advancement in terms of optimizing "military readiness" and worked to cultivate a construction of military women as professionalized, patriotic soldiers rather than support personnel or victims of the "poverty draft." These efforts paid off during Desert Storm, when the media and military projected that image to the public (Enloe 1994, 91–97, 102). Furthermore, women have benefited from female career officers who have spearheaded efforts to end discrimination and expand opportunities. More confident, better connected, and having a long-term stake in the institution, these women developed political networks with women's rights groups and liberals in Congress to pursue their aims (Enloe 1994, 95).

Third, the courts have been much more willing to intervene on behalf of women against the military than on behalf of gays. The success of female litigants has been limited but real, and it serves as an exception to the court's general deference to the military (Stiehm 1989, 110–133). In *Frontiero v. Richardson* (411 U.S. 677 1973), the Supreme Court ruled that women were entitled to the same housing, medical, and other benefits as men in the military. In *Crawford v. Cushman* (531 F. 2nd 1114 1976) and related cases, it said that the military could not discharge women because of pregnancy. In *Owens v. Brown* (455 F. Supp. 291 1978), the Court decided that the Navy's ban on women serving onboard most ships was too broad. And in *Craig v. Boren* (1976), the Court ruled that any sex discrimination had to be "substantially related to an important governmental objective." The Court has stopped short, however, of striking down prohibitions against women serving in combat.

Finally, several military women's breakthroughs came during a period (1967–78) in which conservatives were much less powerful than they were in the 1990s when gays tried to break down barriers. In short, the military has not been uniformly opposed to having women play a greater role, much as with blacks in the post–World War II years, and the courts and Congress in the 1970s were much more willing to challenge the military's policy than they have been more recently on behalf of gays and lesbians.

CONCLUSION

The dispute over gays in the military is our third case of a mismatch between public opinion and public policy. The military case is in crucial respects the reverse image of the sodomy repeal and adoption cases. Despite public support for lifting the ban, it remains in place. Opponents rebuffed the only serious effort to get the ban removed and have kept the issue off the agenda ever since. Conservative elites and traditionalist veto groups have been able to thwart or dampen growing public support for lifting the ban.

Critical to the outcome is the institutional locus of decision making and the preferences of the key institutional actors. The same factors that led to the defeat of Clinton's effort to lift the ban also account for opponents' ability to keep the issue off the agenda since 1993. As the stakeholder in the debate, the military's opposition to reform is deeply rooted in the political backgrounds of military personnel and the institution's masculine culture. The military cultivates and evokes homophobic feelings and the intense opposition to gay rights that those feelings inspire. Reformers must address at the national level the issue of whether to lift the ban, with Congress now playing the decisive role in policymaking. Congress undertook this role as a legislature with independent powers and under the control of conservative forces. Centered in the Senate Armed Services Committee, opponents redefined the issue from "discrimination" to "military effectiveness." In the process, they softened public support for lifting the ban and mobilized opposition among enlisted personnel, veterans, and the usual social conservative and fundamentalist opponents of gay rights. The courts have deferred to the judgment of the military and Congress. The salience of the dramatic clash between president and Congress in the 1990s, coupled with the easy access afforded to the military and social conservatives, gave opponents a decisive advantage over the process.

Comparisons with how other nations addressed the issue of gays in the military and with discrimination in the U.S. military against blacks and women support the analysis presented in this chapter. In Canada, Britain, and Australia, courts and independent, quasi-judicial bodies put the issue on the agenda and forced politicians to act. In the United States, a president led the effort to lift the ban who had not received a majority of the popular vote, did not have military credentials, and was seen as motivated by the need to fulfill a campaign pledge. The integration of blacks succeeded largely because President Truman faced a much more hospitable set of conditions in Congress and in the party system, which induced him to act and ensured that Congress would not challenge him effectively. Elements within the military favored or were ambivalent toward integration. Women's progress remains incomplete, but to the extent that they have succeeded, it is because the courts have helped, the military perceives expanding women's opportunities as somewhat beneficial to its goals, and women have had a legitimate presence in the military for a long time.

Institutional resistance to lifting the ban on gays serving openly may recede with Democratic control of Congress after the 2006 and 2008 elections. Given the public's support for lifting the ban, signs of rising acceptance among younger service members, and a lack of adverse consequences from the lifting of bans in most other countries, a good chance exists that the United States will lift its ban eventually, but only when advocates overcome all of the institutional hurdles.

7

The three preceding chapters demonstrated the critical role of institutions in the legalization of homosexual conduct and gay adoption and in the failure to lift the ban on gays in the military. Institutions mediated the impact of public opinion by dampening and circumventing potential and actual resistance to the repeal of sodomy laws and gay adoption and by encouraging and accommodating resistance to lifting the military ban. What about the policy responses to gay rights advocates' demands for same-sex marriage, civil unions, employment nondiscrimination, and hate crimes legislation? Have institutions had important impacts on these issues as well?

At first glance, it hardly seems necessary to take into account the role of institutions in these cases. The very different levels of threat that the public perceives from demands for marriage, workplace nondiscrimination, and hate crimes protection provide a parsimonious explanation for the relative success or failure of gay rights advocates. Because the public overwhelmingly supports covering gays under hate crimes and civil rights statutes, most states have adopted hate crimes laws, and more than half of the U.S. population lives in jurisdictions that protect gays from discrimination. As most Americans firmly oppose same-sex marriage, not surprisingly, only two states permit it and the vast majority of states and the federal government prohibit it.

This chapter argues that the level of public support for gay rights on these issues only partly explains public policy outcomes in each of them. Explanations rooted in public opinion and institutional arrangements are not mutually exclusive. First, institutions have played a crucial role in facilitating success in hate crimes and nondiscrimination and have contributed to the limited success in marriage. Second, a focus on institutions helps us to understand why public policy deviates from the public's preferences in particular instances. Although the public overwhelmingly supports protecting gays under hate crimes and nondiscrimination laws, the laws still do not cover many Americans. Although Americans oppose gay marriage, some states have resisted the tide to enact bans on same-sex marriage. Despite polls showing that more than half of the public supports civil unions and domestic partnership benefits, only a handful of states provide these alternatives to marriage, and many states have policies that prohibit them.[1] Most Americans do not support gay rights intensely enough to become active, while opponents continue to mobilize against them in many instances. Institutions create the possibility for these deviations from national public opinion to occur.

This chapter presents findings for each case for the three main institutional variables, starting with an examination of the role of third-party stakeholders. Next, we examine the impact of the federal system, followed by the influence of legislative and judicial policymaking. The findings from these cases confirm most of the expectations discussed in chapter 1 and are consistent with most, but not all, of the patterns found for the cases examined in chapters 4–6.

STAKEHOLDERS

As we saw in the other chapters, third-party stakeholders are crucial actors in the politics of gay rights. Because gays and lesbians are a small, controversial minority, they depend on third parties who have an incentive to support their cause. Stakeholders' presence varies considerably across hate crimes, civil rights, and same-sex marriage. Stakeholders are most in evidence in the struggle for hate crimes legislation, less so in efforts to secure nondiscrimination policies, and least visible in the fight for gay marriage and other kinds of partner recognition. These cases support the hypothesis that the presence of stakeholders who champion gay rights increases the prospect of lesbian, gay, bisexual, and transgender (LGBT) political success.

Hate Crimes

Gays and lesbians share the goal of protection against hate crimes with racial, ethnic, and religious minorities and other groups who have been targets of bias attacks. They have built broad coalitions with African Americans, Jews, women, and other victim groups (Haider-Markel 2000, 305–06; Haider-Markel 1998; Jenness 1999). These coalitions make up

the "anti–hate crimes movement" that emerged when the civil rights movements of the 1960s and 1970s melded with the crime victims' movement
that arose in the late 1970s (Jenness 1995; Jenness and Broad 1997; Jenness and Grattet 2001; Maroney 1998).

In New York, the Anti-Defamation League of B'nai B'rith (ADL), Urban League, National Association for the Advancement of Colored People
(NAACP), and Order of the Sons of Italy joined with the Empire State Pride
Agenda and other gay rights groups to push for that state's hate crimes
law (*Post Standard* 1995; Finnegan 1997). In Illinois, gays organized a coalition that included the ADL and the National Organization for Women
(NOW), and a coalition organized in Oklahoma included African American and Jewish groups (Haider-Markel 2000, 305–6). In Washington state,
gays and lesbians joined with Asian American, Jewish, and Arab American
groups (Mar 1992; Robinson 1991a). In Pennsylvania, New Hampshire,
and Colorado, the ADL was the key coalition partner (Motley 1992; Hastings 1990; Sarche 2001; Paulson 2005).

In Texas, the anti–hate crimes coalition included the NAACP, American
Jewish Congress, and League of United Latin American Citizens (Jacobs
2001); in Tennessee, the ADL and NOW got behind hate crimes legislation (Miller 1999); in Idaho, the Idaho Women's Network and the NAACP
helped form a coalition (Warbis 1999); in Hawaii, the Japanese American
Citizens League and a number of other civil rights groups allied to support
the cause (Song 2001; Dunford 2001); in New Mexico, the ADL, the New
Mexico Black Leadership Conference, and a variety of Hispanic organizations joined gays and lesbians (Archuleta 1999; Seemann 1997; Domrzalski 1996); and in Louisiana, it was the ADL and NAACP (*Advocate* 1995;
Times-Picayune 1998).[2]

Rounding out the coalitions are churches and other religious groups,
state and local human rights commissions, nonprofit organizations, and a
few businesses. In Illinois, supporters of hate crimes legislation included
organizations that are usually on opposite sides of the political fence—
Planned Parenthood and the Illinois Catholic Conference. In New York
state and in cities across the country like St. Louis, the Catholic Church split
from social and religious conservatives to support hate crimes protection for
gays and lesbians (Tipton 1991). John Cardinal O'Connor's efforts to pass
New York's law were decisive in getting the legislature to approve it (*Daily
News* 2000). In Colorado, the Interfaith Alliance of mainline Protestant
churches, Muslim leaders, and Catholic leaders supported the legislation

(Sanko 2002). In Oklahoma, gay rights supporters received backing from the National Conference of Christians and Jews. In Hawaii, the coalition included the American Civil Liberties Union (ACLU) and the state's Civil Rights Commission (Dunford 2001); in Idaho, groups as diverse as the Idaho Human Rights Commission, the ACLU, and Hewlett-Packard and other high-tech businesses backed the legislation (Warbis 1999); in Texas, it was the ACLU and a variety of religious groups (Jacobs 2001).[3]

Coalition partners help to get gays and lesbians covered under hate crimes legislation in several ways. First, acting in concert with other groups, gay and lesbian organizations augment the resources that they bring to bear upon the political process. Gay rights organizations typically press their demands on other issues with a few allies who feel as strongly about the need to change policy. Women, blacks, and religious minorities, for example, have already won nondiscrimination policies in employment, public accommodations, and housing, and society has not denied them the right to marry or adopt children.[4] But in battles over hate crimes laws, these groups or others frequently seek the same protection.

In addition, advocates argue that it is illogical for society to withhold hate crimes protection from gays when society grants the protection to other groups; further, they say perpetrators may view the exclusion of gays from hate crimes laws as tacit permission to commit violence against them. Also helpful to LGBT hate crimes law advocates is that the public feels more positively toward other victim groups than towards gays. In surveys that measure Americans' affect toward different groups on the "feeling thermometer," people register "colder" scores for gays than for blacks, welfare recipients, and Jews, for example (Sherrill 1996, 470). Legislators who vote for hate crimes laws can argue that the inclusion of protection for gays was part of a broader proposal to extend hate crimes protection to the nongay groups. They did not want to "throw out the baby with the bathwater."

Second, when a diverse set of groups claims that it needs hate crimes protection, debate focuses on general arguments for and against it that apply to *any group* that is the target of hate-motivated violence. The debate focuses upon widely shared values such as public safety, tolerance for diversity, equal treatment before the law, and freedom of expression, rather than upon gay rights and whether gays and lesbians deserve protection specifically. Supporters of hate crimes legislation frame their case mostly in terms of tolerance for social diversity or in terms of "law and order"—that the extra penalties are appropriate justice for victims and help to deter crimes that threaten entire communities (see chapter 2). Denying victim groups hate crimes protection is more difficult once other groups receive it because the applicable general arguments do not differentiate among groups.

Other victim groups are also an important source of tactics for anti–hate crimes advocates to raise awareness, educate the public and policymakers, and mobilize support for broadening hate crimes legislation (Rasky 1990). For example, gay rights organizations learned about the effectiveness of collecting data on hate crimes and publicizing shocking crimes from the ADL and NAACP.[5] The murder of gay University of Wyoming student Matthew Sheppard received national attention and spurred advocates to push the issue on the agenda, just as similar attacks on blacks and Jews have done. Less well-known attacks on gays in other states had the same effect.[6] The publicity surrounding horrific crimes can turn opponents into supporters of hate crimes legislation. U.S. Senator John Warner (R-VA), the minority leader of the Virginia House of Delegates, and the speaker of the Arkansas House opposed hate crimes legislation until they learned about attacks like the one committed against Sheppard (Associated Press 2000, 2001c).

Another important stakeholder in the hate crimes arena has been law enforcement organizations and officials. Police and prosecutors are responsible for maintaining law and order and bringing criminals to justice. Groups that seek hate crimes protection often monitor police and prosecutors, pressure them to make greater efforts to recognize bias-related attacks and pursue perpetrators, and seek their endorsement of proposed legislation. Law enforcement provides credibility and legitimacy to arguments in favor of expanding hate crimes protection. The image of police and prosecutors that the media and politicians disseminate is generally positive—public servants who stand between vulnerable citizens and dangerous criminals, often putting their own lives on the line, and speaking with authority on issues of crime and punishment. Police and/or prosecutors have supported covering gays and lesbians under hate crimes legislation in Florida, Oregon, Wisconsin, Maryland (Berrill 1992; Cohen 1993), Illinois (Haider-Markel 2000), Louisiana (Anderson 1995; Times-Picayune 1998), Arkansas (Rowett 2003), Colorado (Scanlon 2005), Texas (Stockwell 1999; Jacobs 2001), Maine (Cosby and Malmude 1994), Washington (Mar 1992; Dunnewind 1992; Simon 1991; Robinson 1991a, 1991b), New Mexico (Fletcher 1997; Archuleta 1999; Hill 1996; Domrzalski 1996; Eichstaedt 1997), Georgia (Teepen 1991), and at the federal level (Palmer 1997;

Tsong 1998; Pandolfi 1999; Holland 2002; U.S. Congress, House 2004a, H7690–91, H7697).[7]

Law enforcement officials also redefine the issue in a way that helps to garner broad, bipartisan support from the public and policymakers. When police and prosecutors are active in debates over hate crimes proposals, they frame the issue in law and order terms, which steers debate away from giving gays and lesbians "special rights" and "condoning homosexuality." Fighting crime historically has ranked high on the political agendas of more conservative parties and politicians. Thus, the law and order definition has the potential to broaden the appeal of hate crimes measures across the political spectrum. Furthermore, politicians know that legislating harsher and more certain sentences is popular with voters on a highly salient issue like crime. Much as they seek to enhance their prospects for reelection by delivering tax cuts and spending programs to their constituents, elected officials find it attractive to show voters that they are helping to fight crime and "getting tough" with criminals (Murakawa 2005). Opponents of hate crimes legislation risk having people brand them as "soft on crime."

Building coalitions with other victim groups and enlisting the support of law enforcement increase the likelihood of passing hate crimes legislation, but these measures do not guarantee success (Haider-Markel 2000). Thirty-two states' laws include hate crimes based upon sexual orientation, but thirteen others have laws that exclude gays and lesbians (NGLTF 2007b).[8] Dozens of organizations representing stakeholders back federal hate crimes legislation, yet they have not succeeded so far.[9] Resistance to the inclusion of sexual orientation sometimes requires dropping sexual orientation from the list of categories included in the proposed hate crimes legislation[10] and often has delayed the adoption of hate crimes laws (see Daley 1990; New York Times 1990; Rasky 1990; Atlanta Journal and Constitution 1994; Shen 1991; Daily News 2000).

Civil Rights

The impact of stakeholders in battles over nondiscrimination policies is less clear than on other issues because stakeholders have not lined up as uniformly with LGBT rights advocates as they have on other issues. Liberal civil rights and liberties groups, churches, and human rights commissions usually support these measures, but small businesses and landlords have often stood in opposition. The presence of stakeholders on both sides of the issue may counteract the impact of each of them.

Gay and lesbian rights groups pushing for nondiscrimination policies usually try to court many of the same liberal civil rights organizations and human rights commissions that join them in efforts to gain hate crimes legislation. The ACLU; black civil rights groups like the NAACP; NOW and other women's groups; and the Metropolitan Community Church, Unitarians, Quakers, and mainline Protestant denominations often become active. Human rights commissions and boards grew out of the black civil rights struggle of the 1960s, and one can find them in almost every state and local community (Button, Rienzo, and Wald 1997, 88). The boards are quasi-governmental entities consisting of representatives of a broad spectrum of minority groups in the community that investigate alleged discrimination, publicize their findings, and make recommendations on behalf of minorities whom they have found to be victims of discrimination (Button Rienzo, and Wald 1997, 66). As such, they speak with a degree of visibility, authority, and legitimacy that gay rights organizations, acting on their own, do not possess.

Business opposition to covering gays under nondiscrimination policies arises out of an ideological antipathy toward government and concerns about regulatory burdens. Business opposition constrains the number of localities that adopt civil rights protections. Many localities cover only public-sector employees because extending them to cover private-sector employees engenders business opposition (Button, Rienzo, and Wald 1997, 125). At the same time, business opposition is secondary and sporadic compared with the resistance that comes from social and religious conservatives (Button, Rienzo, and Wald 1997, 176–77, 187–89). Rather than attempt to block nondiscrimination policies, business tries to shape the regulations and the enforcement of the ordinances so that they are less burdensome. Finally, business opposition to nondiscrimination policies is not as effective in communities with liberal attitudes and those whose major employers are large national and multinational corporations (Button, Rienzo, and Wald 1997, 189).

Business opposition to nondiscrimination policies may be waning. At one time, Cincinnati was the largest major American city that banned the enactment of laws based upon sexual orientation and whose corporate community Button, Rienzo, and Wald (1997, 189) once described as "the strongest instance of business influence arrayed against the gay rights movement." However, Cincinnati changed its policy. Proctor and Gamble, the city's best-known company; Federated Department Stores; and others supported a successful effort to repeal the ban in 2004 (Sloat 2004). In arguing in favor of the repeal, Cincinnati's corporate and political leaders cited Americans' changed attitudes about gays and lesbians and the economic costs of continuing the ban in lost tourism dollars and harmed employee recruitment (Nolan 2004; Associated Press 2004). At the federal level, growing support for the Employment Non-Discrimination Act (ENDA) from large companies helps to counter opposition from smaller firms. Large corporations, particularly in high-tech and service sectors, view nondiscrimination policies as good for productivity and recruitment. Many have instituted their own policies. Dozens of corporations support ENDA, and many have testified before Congress in favor of it (Stachelberg 2002).[11]

The net impact of stakeholders in the civil rights arena is difficult to gauge because of the potentially offsetting activities of liberal civil rights allies and business opponents. It is plausible that many fewer local communities have adopted nondiscrimination policies in communities where liberal and civil rights groups are weakly organized and where business opposition has been stronger (or it took much longer to adopt such policies).

Marriage and Partner Recognition

Stakeholders are relatively scarce in the struggle over gay marriage and partner recognition. None of the victim groups, professional organizations, or occupational constituencies with claims of special expertise or material interests is evident in partner recognition, as they are on other gay rights issues. While many employers provide domestic partner benefits through contracts with their employees, they are not usually key players in public policy conflicts over same-sex partner recognition. The ACLU, a supporter of gay marriage and partner rights, files lawsuits on behalf of gay and lesbian couples (see http://www.aclu.org/getequal/caseprofiles.htm). The ACLU's impact is relatively modest, however. The landmark gay marriage cases in Hawaii, Vermont, and Massachusetts were undertaken by the Gay and Lesbian Defenders, not the ACLU (Chauncey 2004b, 123–36). It would be difficult for any stakeholder to champion successfully a cause as controversial and salient as gay marriage, and one that has inspired a determined grassroots opposition. The ACLU's interest in gay marriage is not as central to its mission as is the interest of other stakeholders on other gay rights issues. Its agenda encompasses a wide array of civil liberties and human rights issues, and its work on gay rights includes nondiscrimination cases unrelated to same-sex partners. The ACLU has a reputation in many quarters as an organization with an ideological axe to grind rather than as a source of nonpartisan expertise or as an actor with a legitimate material interest. Finally, like any organization that pursues its political activity through litigation, the ACLU's victories are piecemeal because they are applicable to particular fact situations and jurisdictions.

In sum, these cases are largely consistent with the hypothesis that the presence of sympathetic stakeholders makes success more likely for gay rights supporters. Gays have been highly successful in gaining hate crimes legislation, in part, because they have forged alliances with other victim groups and law enforcement officials. They have been least successful in marriage, an issue that includes no significant stakeholders. Stakeholders play an important role in civil rights battles, but their net effects are more uncertain because they have been active on both sides of the issue.

DECENTRALIZED POLICYMAKING

The three cases lend considerable support to the proposition that gay rights advocates are more successful when state and local governments are the venues for policymaking. The gay rights movement owes much of its progress in civil rights and hate crimes protection to the federal system. Thirty-two states provide protection against hate crimes, and twenty provide protection against discrimination, including California, New York, and Illinois, in addition to well over 200 local governments (Van der Meide 2000). In contrast, Congress and the president have done virtually nothing to advance gay rights. Thirty-five years after the first local governments passed civil rights protections, twenty-five years after the first states followed their lead, and twenty-three years after the first state passed a hate crimes law covering sexual orientation, Congress has yet to enact any major piece of gay rights legislation.[12] The federal hate crimes law currently covers crimes motivated by bias toward a person's race, religion, and ethnicity. The House and Senate passed hate crimes legislation covering sexual orientation twice, but conference committees stripped the provision from the final legislation (Dewar 2000, 2004a).[13] The Senate failed to pass the Employment Non-Discrimination Act in 1996 by one vote. The House approved ENDA in 2007, but the Senate has failed to act. Even in recognition of same-sex relationships, the states have performed better than has the federal government. Seven states have refused to ban gay marriage and a small but growing number have instituted marriage, civil unions, or domestic partner benefits. In comparison, Congress passed the Defense of Marriage

Act (DOMA), which permitted states to refuse to recognize other states' legal sanction of same-sex partnerships and limited marriage to one man and one woman for the purpose of federal benefits.

Is it likely that gays and lesbians would have made as much (or more) progress in the absence of state and local authority to make laws? To probe the impact of federalism on gay rights further, let us try to imagine the status of gay rights if the United States had a unitary system of government instead. We can never be certain how gay rights advocates would fare under a unitary system because such a radical change could have other political ramifications. In the absence of state and local authority to make policy in marriage, civil rights, and hate crimes, interest groups would channel the resources aimed currently at states and localities to the national level. Policymakers in Washington also might feel a greater need to enact such policies. With those caveats in mind, we can make some informed guesses.

Gay Rights without Federalism

MARRIAGE AND PARTNER RECOGNITION

Gays and lesbians certainly would have made less progress in marriage, civil unions, and domestic partnerships under a unitary system of government. States that now have marriage, civil unions, and broad domestic partner laws—California, Connecticut, Massachusetts, Vermont, New Hampshire, Oregon, and New Jersey—cover about 20 percent of the population (more than 57 million Americans), a sizable minority. These policies would not exist if only Washington made policy. Because states would not have authority to ban same-sex marriage, Congress would have been even more likely to pass the federal DOMA and may have approved a constitutional amendment limiting marriage to opposite-sex couples. DOMA's opponents could not have argued that the federal government should leave issues about marriage up to the states.[14]

CIVIL RIGHTS

Passage of the Employment Non-Discrimination Act would have been unlikely under a unitary system. Gay rights supporters have reintroduced ENDA in almost every recent Congress. ENDA had 194 cosponsors in 2002 and had 180 in 2003, for example, which constituted between 41 and 44 percent of House seats and represented almost the same percentage of the population (more than 48 percent) covered by state and local nondiscrimination laws at the time. Supporters would have needed between twen-

Table 7.1 Support for legislation favored by gay rights advocates
in the U.S. House, 107th–109th Congresses (2001–6)[a]

	Median Members from states with civil rights protections	Entire House	Difference	Mean Members from states with civil rights protections	Entire House	Difference
107th Congress	100	33	67	68	51	17
108th Congress	88	22	66	63	40	23
109th Congress	88	25	63	61	40	21

[a]From the Human Rights Campaign, *Congressional Scorecard*, 107th, 108th, and 109th
Congresses, www.hrc.org/.

ty and forty additional votes to pass ENDA, but reaching that number would
have been difficult. With Republicans in control of the House from 1994 to
2006, and with Democrats comprising 90 percent of ENDA's cosponsors,
little chance existed that the legislation would come up for a vote.

Even if ENDA had come up for a vote, it is unlikely that it would have
passed. Using scores that the Human Rights Campaign (HRC) assigns
based upon "key votes" cast by members of Congress from 2001 to 2006,
table 7.1 shows the difference in levels of support for gay rights legislation
between the House as a whole and the delegations of the seventeen states
that granted civil rights protections for gays and lesbians as of 2006.[15] The
two groups are substantially different, particularly when we compare the
median House member with the median member from the seventeen
states with civil rights protections. The scores of members from the states
that make it illegal to discriminate on sexual orientation, ranging from 88
percent to 100 percent for the 107th through 109th Congresses, are considerably higher than the median scores for the entire chamber in those years,
which ran only between 22 and 33 percent.

Although the new Democratic majority that took over Congress in 2007
has passed such legislation in the House of Representatives, a filibuster in
the Senate or a presidential veto could defeat it. We can surmise with some
degree of confidence, therefore, that no gays and lesbians in the United

States would have been protected through at least 2008 if the issue had been solely left up to the federal government, whereas more than half of the population is currently covered under state and local governments.

HATE CRIMES

Hate crimes legislation would have the best chance of gaining federal approval under a unitary system, as thirty-two states currently cover sexual orientation, and the absence of state authority to make law would place greater pressure on Congress to enact federal legislation. Even so, it is unlikely that Congress would have acted. The history of efforts to pass such legislation reveals the great difficulty with passing *any* gay-friendly legislation at the federal level and shows that institutional rules privilege antigay forces even when a majority of the public and members of Congress disagree with them. A proposal to include sexual orientation under the federal hate crimes law died in the Senate in 2001 and 2002 when its supporters failed to impose cloture to end filibusters (Shepard 2002; U.S. Congress, Senate 2004a, S6766). In 1999, 2000, and 2004, the House and Senate approved hate crimes legislation, but conference committees thwarted that legislation (Sandalow 2000; Raum 2000; Dewar 2004b).

In their role of reconciling differences between bills passed by the House and Senate, conference committees exert significant influence on the final content of legislation (Shepsle and Weingast 1987). Specifically, conference committees move legislation in a more extreme ideological direction than the versions originally passed by their parent chambers (Vander Wielen 2006). For example, the Senate passed hate crimes legislation 57 to 42 in 2000. The House voted 232 to 192 to instruct their conferees to accept the Senate-passed bill and defeated an effort to derail the instructions 196 to 227 (Human Rights Campaign 2000a, 2000b). Four years later, the Senate again passed hate crimes legislation, by a vote of 65 to 33, as an amendment to a defense authorization bill, and the House followed suit, voting 213 to 186 to instruct House conferees to accept the amendment (Human Rights Campaign 2004). Both times, conservative Republican leaders appointed members of conference committees who stripped the provision out of the final legislation that they presented to the House and Senate (U.S. Congress, Senate 2004a, S6766, S6775; U.S. Congress, House 2004a, H9054; *Post Standard* 2000).

The party leaders' appointment of conferees who were not representative of Congress led to the defeat of hate crimes legislation. Table 7.2 shows

Table 7.2 Support for gay rights among conference committee members considering federal hate crimes legislation in the 106th and 108th Congresses

| | 106th Congress (1999–2000) | | | | 108th Congress (2003–4) | | | |
| | House | | Senate | | House | | Senate | |
	Mean	Median	Mean	Median	Mean	Median	Mean	Median
All conferees	31.1	10	50.9	36	29.4	22	40.6	25
Republican conferees	6.0	0	17.2	0	8.7	0	11.6	0
Democratic conferees	65.7	80	92.1	100	56.7	50	71.1	75
All members	48.9	40	50.7	50	40	22	42.3	38
All Republican members	16.1	10	20.4	14	8.6	0	10.4	0
All Democratic members	85.5	90	87.6	100	76.2	88	75	75

Sources: The Human Rights Campaign (HRC) reports scores of key votes and cosponsorships of legislation in each Congress for every member of the U.S. House and Senate. Scores range from 0 to 100, with 100 reflecting members who vote and cosponsor in support of the HRC's position in every instance. Scorecards for the 106th and 108th Congresses are obtained from www.hrc.org. Data on conference committee membership are obtained from the Government Printing Office Web site, http://www.gpoaccess.gov/calendars/senate/search.html.

that members of the conference committees supported gay rights less often than the memberships of the House and Senate as a whole. Lower mean and median scores reflect less support for gay rights on the HRC's score-card of members' key votes in Congress during 2000 and 2004, the two most recent years hate crimes legislation reached the conference commit-tee stage. Conference committee members in most instances have lower scores than the average and median members of the House and Senate, including House Democrats. The differences are particularly large for the House conferees and for 2000. Because Republicans held a majority of the seats on these committees, the key comparison is between the scores of Re-publican conferees and the members of the House and Senate as a whole. The median HRC score for Republican members of the conference com-mittees from both the House and Senate was zero, or between twenty-two and fifty points lower than the scores for the median members of the entire House and Senate. The mean scores for the same comparison groups were also considerably lower than for the median legislator, particularly in the House. Thus, while it is more likely that the federal government would have adopted hate crimes protections for gays and lesbians under a uni-tary system than other gay rights proposals, it remains doubtful. Under Democratic majorities, Congress may pass such legislation, but whether a Republican president would sign it into law is uncertain.

How Federalism Matters

A number of conditions and forces that shape policy outcomes vary con-siderably across state and local governments. Jurisdictions differ dramati-cally in public support for gay rights; general political ideology; size, social diversity, education levels, and resources of the gay and lesbian commu-nity; political party competition; and opportunities available for citizens to vote on gay rights through the initiative process.

MARRIAGE AND PARTNER RECOGNITION

One reason that some states grant at least some form of same-sex partner recognition (or have not banned partner recognition policies) is that public opinion in these states tends to be much more moderate on the question of gay marriage. Ten states currently grant same-sex marriages or civil un-ions or at least some domestic partner rights and benefits (Massachusetts, Vermont, Connecticut, California, Oregon, Washington state, Maine, New Hampshire, Hawaii, and New Jersey), and two others have no law or court ruling adverse to same-sex marriage (Rhode Island and New Mexico). Using a logit analysis conducted by Lewis and Oh (2006, 33) of state-level poll results on whether individuals favor or oppose gay marriage, nine of these states rank among the top fifteen in public support for same-sex marriage. All except Hawaii scored higher than Pennsylvania, the "reference state" that tends to have typical attitudes on gay rights, which ranks twenty-first, with 31 percent of residents in support of gay marriage. Lewis and Oh found, for example, that Massachusetts residents ranked first in support for gay marriage (46 percent), Rhode Island residents ranked second (44 percent), Vermont residents ranked sixth (41 percent), and Connecticut residents ranked seventh (41 percent), all of which were considerably higher than Pennsylvania.

The twelve states that grant legal recognition to same-sex relationships or have no law or court ruling adverse to such recognition are also overwhelmingly states with the highest levels of LGBT political resources (as calculated by Haider-Markel 2000, 298–99).[16] Ninety-two percent of these states ranked in the top third of states with the greatest LGBT resources, compared with 50 percent of states with DOMA laws and only 8 percent of states with DOMA constitutional amendments, or "super-DOMAs," that forbid civil unions and other forms of partner recognition in addition to marriage.

The opponents of same-sex marriage have used the ballot initiative extensively and successfully to get voters to approve bans on gay marriage. Voter initiatives increase the salience of issues considerably. By 2007, forty-four states banned gay marriage, twenty-six of them enshrined bans in their constitutions, and seventeen of the bans included super-DOMAs. Twenty-seven states, or almost two-thirds, enacted their bans through the ballot box. Arizona is the only state in which voters defeated a marriage ban when it was on the ballot in 2006.[17]

The initiative is an effective weapon for banning not only gay marriage but also alternatives to it, like civil unions. Twenty-six states fall into one of three "most restrictive" categories: (1) they ban not only marriage but also civil unions and other forms of partnership recognition (super-DOMAs), (2) they enshrine their ban on same-sex marriage in their state constitution, or (3) they enshrine their super-DOMA in their constitutions. Eighteen states have "restrictive" same-sex partner policies that ban same-sex marriage through statute or a high court ruling that holds that the state does not have to permit same-sex couples to marry but have not prohibited other forms of partner recognition. Finally, twelve states and the District of Columbia fall into the "least restrictive" category—two of them have marriage (Massachusetts and California), four have civil unions (Connecticut, New Jersey, New Hampshire, and Vermont), four afford at least some partner benefits (Oregon, Washington state, Hawaii, and Maine), and two have no law or high court ruling on marriage and same-sex partnerships (New Mexico and Rhode Island).[18]

States that make it easier for citizens to vote directly on the legal status of same-sex unions should have policies that are more restrictive.[19] As Haider-Markel and Meier (1996) have shown in their study of employment nondiscrimination policies, LGBT rights advocates' chances for victory decline when gay rights issues became salient and the scope of conflict expands. In that case, it becomes easier for their opponents to define the conflict in the highly symbolic terms that are the hallmark of "morality politics." Voter initiative campaigns greatly broaden the scope of conflict and increase the salience of the gay marriage issue, challenging LGBT advocates to educate voters, for example, on the differences between regular DOMAs and super-DOMAs, and hope that they will be sufficiently attentive and discerning to differentiate between them. Gay marriage advocates may find states that do not have the direct initiative less challenging. Legislative policymaking is usually less salient than voter initiatives and offers a better opportunity for compromise and careful deliberation. In the manner of interest group politics, gay marriage supporters can lobby sympathetic legislators to bottle up DOMA proposals in a committee or develop compromise measures that avoid the sweeping prohibitions on partner recognition contained in super-DOMAs.

States vary widely in the opportunities they afford citizens to participate directly in public policymaking through the ballot box. States that allow voters to propose and vote on laws or constitutional amendments directly, without going through state legislatures, have higher levels of direct democracy. Table 7.3 shows that states that have the direct initiative process tend to have partnership recognition policies that are more restrictive than states without it. Seventy percent of the "high" direct democracy states had most restrictive policies, compared with 29 percent of the "moderate" direct democracy states and 31 percent of the "low" direct democracy states. And twice as many states with the most restrictive policies have high direct democracy as those with the least restrictive policies (62 to 31 percent).

The relationship between the initiative and the restrictiveness of same-sex partnership recognition holds when we control for citizen and elite ideology among states and the prevalence of Protestant fundamentalists. Conserva-

Table 7.3 Restrictive same-sex partner recognition policies and direct democracy

Percentage of states with "most restrictive" same-sex partner recognition policies in each category:

	%	N[a]
High direct democracy	70	(16/23)
Moderate direct democracy	29	(2/7)
Low direct democracy	31	(8/26)

Of all states with "most restrictive" same-sex partner recognition policies, percentages falling into each category:

	%	N
High direct democracy	62	(16/26)
Moderate direct democracy	8	(2/26)
Low direct democracy	31	(8/26)

Notes: High direct democracy = direct initiative amendment , when constitutional amendments proposed by the people are directly placed on the ballot and then submitted to the people for their approval or rejection; direct initiative statute , when laws proposed by the people are directly placed on the ballot and then submitted to the people for their approval.

Moderate direct democracy = indirect initiative amendment , when constitutional amendments proposed by the people must first be submitted to the state legislature during a regular session; indirect initiative statute , when laws proposed by the people must first be submitted to the state legislature during a regular session; popular referendum , the power to refer to the ballot, through a petition, specific legislation that was enacted by the legislature for voters' approval or rejection.

Low direct democracy = the legislative referendum , when a state legislature places an amendment or a statute on the ballot for voter approval or rejection (every state but Delaware requires state constitutional amendments to be placed on the ballot for voter approval or rejection) (Initiative & Referendum Institute, University of Southern California School of Law, Los Angeles, www.iandrinstitute.org/.

Sources: Data on state laws and constitutions from the National Gay and Lesbian Task Force (2007a, 2008), the Human Rights Campaign (www.hrc.org), and Peterson (2004).

[a]The total number of observations equals 56 for these calculations because California, Hawaii, Oregon, New Hampshire and Maine have both banned same sex marriage and provide same-sex couples with partner benefits. The California Supreme Court recently overturned the ban (not reflected in the table) and voters will vote on a constitutional amendment to ban same-sex marriage in 2008.

tism and Protestant fundamentalism are associated with less support for gay rights policies (Wilcox and Wolpert 2000). According to table 7.4, states with greater direct democracy are more likely to have more restrictive policies than states without the initiative, whether they are liberal or conservative. The same is true when we distinguish states on the fundamentalism

Table 7.4 Levels of direct democracy and the restrictiveness of same-sex partner policies

Percentage of states in each category of direct democracy that have:

	Most restrictive policies[a]	Restrictive policies[b]	Least restrictive policies[c]
Liberal states[d]			
High direct democracy	50 (5/10)	20 (2/10)	30 (3/10)
Low direct democracy	0 (0/13)	62 (8/13)	38 (5/13)
Conservative states			
High direct democracy	82 (9/11)	18 (2/11)	0 (0/11)
Low direct democracy	73 (8/11)	27 (3/11)	0 (0/11)
Low fundamentalism states			
High direct democracy	64 (7/11)	18 (2/11)	18 (2/11)
Low direct democracy	8 (1/13)	54 (7/13)	38 (5/13)
High fundamentalism states			
High direct democracy	100 (5/5)	0 (0/4)	0 (0/3)
Low direct democracy	66 (4/6)	33 (2/6)	0 (0/6)
High LGBT resources[e]			
High direct democracy	20 (1/5)	40 (2/5)	40 (2/5)
Low direct democracy	8 (1/12)	40 (5/12)	50 (6/12)
Low LGBT resources			
High direct democracy	89 (8/9)	11 (1/9)	0 (0/9)
Low direct democracy	50 (3/6)	50 (3/6)	0 (0/0)

measure. States that permit greater direct democracy have policies that are more restrictive, whether their populations include large or small numbers of fundamentalists. All of the states with the most restrictive partner recognition policies *and* that do not have the direct initiative are conservative states. For states that make it harder for citizens to change policy, only those with determined conservative majorities (and a minority of such states at that), have been able to circumvent the legislative filter on nondeliberative public opinion. The presence or absence of the direct initiative has its greatest impact in more liberal states and states with fewer fundamentalists. Fifty percent of the liberal states with the initiative have most restrictive policies, but none of the non-initiative liberal states falls into the most restrictive policy category. Similarly, of the states with fewer fundamentalists, 64 percent of the direct initiative states had most restrictive partner recognition policies, compared with only 8 percent of the low fundamentalism states without the direct initiative. Thus, institutions mediate the impacts of ideology. The level of direct democracy also has an effect when we control for the level of LGBT political resources in the states. Among states high in LGBT resources, those that have the direct initiative have more than twice the chance of having a most restrictive policy. Among states low in LGBT resources, those that have the direct initiative have almost twice the chance of having a most restrictive policy (see table 7.4).

The size of states' population, in turn, mediates somewhat the impact of the direct initiative on policy. Consistent with other research (Donovan and Bowler 1998), the population size of a state moderates the effects of direct democracy on the restrictiveness of same-sex partner recognition policies. Large states are more likely to be more socially diverse. Diversity makes it more difficult for a monolithic majority to coalesce and fosters greater efforts to build tolerance. Therefore, large states are less likely to have highly restrictive partner recognition policies (see table 7.4). California and Washington, for example, are states that score high on direct democracy but have not adopted super-DOMAs or enshrined their bans on marriage in their constitutions. (A constitutional amendment to ban same-sex marriage is on the ballot in California in 2008.) At the same time, some large states, including Michigan, Ohio, Florida, and Missouri, have adopted most restrictive policies.

The main finding in this section—that greater direct democracy usually leads to more restrictive bans on same-sex partner recognition—suggests, ironically, that the direct initiative's greater openness to popular participation may lead to policy results that are less reflective of public opinion than when policy is made by legislators, much as James Madison might have

Table 7.5 Population and coverage of civil rights laws for gays and lesbians

	2006	2000	1995	1990	1985	1980
% of U.S. population covered by civil rights laws including sexual orientation	48.9	40.7	37.7	24.8	16.8	12.4
% of U.S. population covered by *state* civil rights laws that include sexual orientation	40.5	24.3	23.6	16.3	12.5	10.4
% of U.S. population covered by *local* civil right laws in states without such laws	8.3	16.4	14.1	8.4	4.3	1.9
Population covered by *state* laws as a % of total population covered	82.9	59.7	62.5	66.0	74.6	84.6
Population covered by *local* laws in states without such laws as % of total population covered	17.1	40.3	37.4	34.0	25.4	15.4

Sources: Population data are from U.S. Census Bureau (2006a, 2006b, 2006c, 2006d). States and localities covered by civil rights laws that include sexual orientation are from NGLTF (2005, 2007c); Eskridge (1999), appendix B2; and Lambda Lega (2006).

predicted. The public's opposition to marriage coexists with its increasing support for civil unions and growing support for giving gay couples many of the specific rights that married couples enjoy. Polls show that public support for civil unions rose from 43 percent in 2001 to 53 percent in 2005 (Egan, Persily, and Wallsten 2006, 31) and even higher margins for giving same-sex partners inheritance and hospital visitation rights, social security benefits, and similar specific benefits (AEI 2004, 33–35). Yet super-DOMAs make it impossible to grant civil unions and much more difficult to provide the specific rights and benefits connected with marriage.

CIVIL RIGHTS

In their study of state-level civil rights politics, Haider-Markel and Meier (1996) found that the politics of civil rights for gays and lesbians followed a pattern of "interest group politics" in which the issue did not become salient. In that scenario, states that adopted civil rights protections in employment, public accommodations, and housing had larger and more active gay and lesbian communities, populations that are more educated, sympathetic elites, and historical legacies of support for civil rights.[20] However, as conflict over the adoption of nondiscrimination measures became more salient, policymaking resembled "morality politics," and the prospects for victory for gay rights declined.[21] In that scenario, gay rights forces lost in states with larger numbers of Protestant fundamentalists and greater support for the Republican Party. Higher levels of education remained a strong predictor of success for gay rights forces, however.

States also vary significantly in the general ideological leaning of their populaces. Using the liberalism-conservatism measures of state-level public opinion developed by Erikson, Wright, and McIver (1993), we find that opinion in states that have adopted nondiscrimination policies are, on average, much more liberal than in states that do not offer gays and lesbians such protection. Erickson, Wright, and McIver also measure the percentage of the states' populations belonging to fundamentalist Protestant sects, a measure that should be particularly relevant for support for gay rights. States that have nondiscrimination laws covering gays cluster in the Northeast and Pacific Coast, regions that have more liberal opinions and lower proportions of fundamentalist Protestants than states in the South and rural West. The average ideological score for the twenty states (as of 2007) with nondiscrimination laws covering gays is –8.3, or more than twice as liberal as states without such laws (–18.4). (Their scale runs from 0, most liberal, to –28, most conservative.) The average percentage of Protestant fundamentalists in states with such laws is 5.9, which is less than one-third of the percentage (21.4) for the states without them. An alternative measure of state ideology developed by Berry et al. (1998) also shows that states with nondiscrimination laws are more liberal than states without them. Their measure runs from 0 (most conservative) to 100 (most liberal), with an average score of 58.2 for the twenty states with such laws, compared with 41.0 for the states without them.

The federal system has helped the passage of civil rights protections because *local* governments share with states the authority to adopt nondiscrimination laws. Many gays and lesbians would have no legal protection from discrimination except for their local government. From 1990 to 2000, local nondiscrimination ordinances covered from more than one-third to 40 percent of the population (or between 21 million and 46 million people) in states that did not have such laws (see table 7.5). Local ordinances protected gay and lesbian residents of New York City, Chicago/Cook County, Seattle, and many other communities until their state governments passed antidiscrimination laws after 2000. Many gays and lesbians also live in Philadelphia, Pittsburgh, Cleveland, Columbus, Detroit, Tampa, Denver, and many other local jurisdictions in Pennsylvania, Ohio, Michigan, Florida, Colorado, and other states that have not passed nondiscrimination laws covering sexual orientation.

Urbanism—measured as the size, density, and diversity of a community—has had a profound effect in helping to promote gay rights. Cities have fostered the development of gay subcultures that are crucial to the emergence of a gay identity, community building, and political mobilization (Bailey 1999; Chauncey 1994; Boswell 1980; D'Emilio 1983; Berube 1990). Large, dense, urban areas provide a "safe space" where large numbers of gays and lesbians come in close contact and establish neighborhoods, community organizations, and businesses. At the same time, nongay urban residents, many of whom belong to other minority groups, develop a permissive attitude toward gays and lesbians (Wilson 1995). These conditions, in turn, encourage additional migration of gays to urban centers. Studies by the National Opinion Research Center; Voter Research and Survey national exit poll data; and mailing lists of donors, subscribers, and activists in gay political and social organizations reveal that gay men and lesbians in larger cities are more likely to self-identify as gay and participate in organizational life (Bailey 1999, 54–59).

Wald, Button, and Rienzo (1996) found that population size was the most important determinant of whether a community had a civil rights policy covering gays and lesbians. Size predicted best the *absence* of such a policy—most small communities do not have them. Among larger communities (more than 250,000 in population), the number of nonfamily households in a city, the level of organization and political activity of the gay community, the presence of sympathetic political elites, and the number of Protestant fundamentalists are other significant predictors of the adoption of a nondiscrimination policy. After population size, localities with higher levels of gay organization and activity, nonfamily households, and education; fewer fundamentalists; and a member of Congress who had cosponsored gay rights measures, in that order, were more likely to have gay rights ordinances.[22] Haeberle (1996) reported similar findings. The density of urban areas mattered most, followed by levels of education and the size and level of political mobilization of the gay community. As higher density brings people with diverse backgrounds into closer contact, it leads to the adoption of civil rights ordinances. The ordinances reflect higher levels of tolerance where people from diverse groups get to know each other, or alternatively, more densely populated communities adopt these policies in an effort to discourage conflict that might arise from the closer contact.

Institutional differences among local governments also affect the chances for adoption of local ordinances. Although the conventional wisdom is that single-member-district systems are preferable to at-large districts for minority representation, this may be accurate only under certain conditions. Gays and lesbians may gain rights more easily in at-large districts with preference or cumulative voting (Rosenblum 1996; Segura 1999).

Gay rights opponents have tried to use the initiative process to repeal, legalize, or prevent bans on discrimination against gays and lesbians in employment, housing, public accommodations, and credit. Unlike their success in banning gay marriage, these efforts met with mixed success and have had no lasting impact.[23] Figure 7.1 shows the number of state and local nonmarriage gay civil rights measures that appeared on the ballot through 2006 and whether gays won or lost the contests. Most of the measures appeared between the early 1990s and early 2000s. After 2002, the number of measures trailed off considerably as gay rights forces began winning ballot contests and opponents shifted their efforts to enacting bans on marriage.

Voters in six states have weighed in on fourteen initiatives. Gay rights forces have prevailed in half of them (see table 7.6). Since 1997, only Maine has rejected a nondiscrimination law, and it later reversed itself and approved a nondiscrimination law it in 2005. Antigay initiatives in Oregon were defeated in 1992 and 1994 and in Idaho in 1994, and the U.S. Supreme Court's ruling in *Romer v. Evans* (1996) struck down Colorado's Amendment 2, which had prohibited local governments from passing nondiscrimination laws protecting gays. Voters rebuffed gay rights supporters in Washington state in 1997 when they asked voters to approve a nondiscrimination law, but gay rights opponents have failed to qualify their own ballot measures in 1994, 1995, and, most importantly, in 2006, after the state legislature passed a nondiscrimination law. In addition, between 1992 and 2006, antigay rights initiatives failed to qualify at least fourteen times in nine states. Thus, opponents ultimately have not been able to use the direct initiative to block adoption of nondiscrimination laws and have been able to use it only to delay adoption in a few states.

The story is much the same at the local level. The early and mid-1990s were the high-water mark for local initiatives intended to roll back or prevent

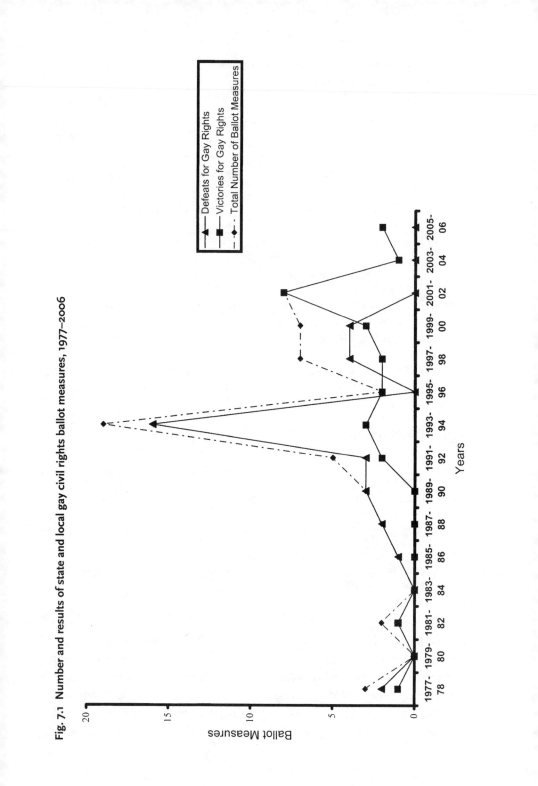

Fig. 7.1 Number and results of state and local gay civil rights ballot measures, 1977–2006

Table 7.6 Results of state ballot measures related to gay nondiscrimination laws, 1978–2006

State	Measure	Year	Pass/fail	Outcome as defeat/victory for gay rights
CA	School employees can be fired for homosexuality	1978	Fail	Victory
OR	Repeal ban on sexual orientation discrimination	1988	Pass	Defeat
CO	Repeal/prevent local laws banning sexual orientation discrimination	1992	Pass	Defeat
OR	Government to discourage homosexual behavior	1992	Fail	Victory
ID	Repeal/block laws prohibiting discrimination against gays	1994	Fail	Victory
OR	Prevent legal classifications based upon sexual orientation	1994	Fail	Victory
ME	Limit protected classes to exclude sexual orientation	1995	Fail	Victory
WA	Add sexual orientation to civil rights laws	1997	Fail	Defeat
ME	Repeal law prohibiting discrimination based on sexual orientation	1998	Pass	Defeat
OR	Prohibit public education on homosexuality	2000	Fail	Victory
ME	Ban discrimination based on sexual orientation	2000	Fail	Defeat
ME	Limit protected classes to exclude sexual orientation	2005	Fail	Victory

Sources: Witt and McCorkle (1997); Prichard (2003); www.gaydemographics.org/; LexisNexis Academic newspaper search.

extending civil rights to gays and lesbians. Twenty-nine measures appeared on the ballot from 1977 to 1994 in cities and towns in nine different states.[24] Gay rights opponents won all but three of those contests. Twenty-one measures appeared from 1994 to 2006, and gay rights supporters prevailed in 71 percent of them. Gay rights backers have won the last ten local contests (from 2001–06), which took place in Kalamazoo, Traverse City,

Huntington Woods, and Ypsilanti, Michigan; Miami and Sarasota, Florida; Tacoma, Washington; Westbrook, Maine; Topeka, Kansas; and Cincinnati, Ohio. Some of these communities, most notably Cincinnati, had repealed or blocked nondiscrimination ordinances in the past. Even before 1995, the success of antigay rights forces in local initiative campaigns was more apparent than real. Measures put on the ballot in more than a dozen local communities in Oregon almost completely account for the spike in measures from 1992 to 1994 (see figure 7.1). Oregon Citizens Alliance placed "toned down" versions of failed statewide anti-gay-rights measures that it sponsored in 1992 and 1994 on the ballot in small, mostly rural, local communities that were more inclined to support their cause. Given the modest proportion of the state's population that these communities comprised, the piecemeal victories were as much a concession of defeat as a sign of victory at the state level (Egan 1993; Martinis 1994).

Hence, while ballot initiatives have had a significant adverse impact on efforts to gain adoption of gay marriage and other forms of same-sex partner recognition, they have had only modest and short-term impacts on the struggle for protection against nondiscrimination. In short, direct democracy is problematic for gay rights only on salient issues that the public perceives as threatening.

HATE CRIMES

Fewer studies have examined why states adopt hate crimes policies, but according to Haider-Markel (2000, 305), "adoption of these laws is driven by many of the same forces driving state adoption of antidiscrimination laws," such as the relative strength of gay rights groups and, more importantly, higher levels of party competition.[25] States that include sexual orientation under their hate crimes laws also tend to be more liberal and have lower rates of Protestant fundamentalism than those that do not. States with laws covering sexual orientation are almost twice as liberal as those that do not, at a rate of –11.7 compared with –20.2 on the Erikson, Wright, and McIver (1993) ideology measure. The proportion of their populations that belong to Protestant fundamentalist denominations (10.2 percent) is, on average, less than half of the proportion (25.2 percent) for states that do not cover antigay bias.

Ideology and Protestant fundamentalism do not appear as important in hate crimes as in civil rights, however. If we compare states whose hate crimes laws cover sexual orientation but do not have nondiscrimination laws covering sexual orientation with all states, we find that the two groups resemble one another. The average ideology score for states with only hate crimes laws is –14.9, almost identical to the –14.3 for all states; the average percentage of Protestant fundamentalists for states with only hate crimes laws is 14.7 percent, slightly less than 15.6 percent for all states. Indeed, several states—including Kentucky, Texas, Tennessee, and Missouri—that protect gays and lesbians under their hate crimes laws also score very high on conservative ideology and have proportions of their populations that are well above the mean for Protestant fundamentalism. This finding suggests that ideology and religious affiliation are less important than other factors identified earlier as contributing to the widespread adoption of hate crimes statutes covering sexual orientation, such as the formation of broad coalitions. Because advocates for hate crimes laws can frame them as a law and order issue, they hold out the prospect for building coalitions with law enforcement organizations, political moderates, and some conservatives.

LEGISLATIVE AND JUDICIAL POLICYMAKING

Legislative and ballot initiative processes at the state and local levels have been the chief institutional venues for decision making in marriage, hate crimes, and civil rights. State legislatures and/or voters have banned marriage in forty-four states and enacted hate crimes statutes covering gays in thirty-two of them. Twenty state legislatures and about 100 municipalities outside of those states have adopted nondiscrimination laws and ordinances. These outcomes broadly reflect public opinion on all three issues, but legislators and voters act more quickly and decisively when the heterosexual majority's interest in protecting marriage is at stake than when the homosexual minority's interest in hate crimes and civil rights is the issue. A larger majority of states approved marriage bans in a shorter period than enacted hate crimes and civil rights statutes over a much longer period. States approved virtually all of their marriage bans within a decade, from the mid-1990s to the mid-2000s. In contrast, it took relatively liberal states like Massachusetts, Minnesota, and Washington seventeen years, twenty years, and twenty-nine years, respectively, to pass nondiscrimination laws covering gays (Longcope 1989; Whereatt 1993; McGann 2006). Likewise, it took several years to pass hate crimes laws in many states (Sarche 2001), and opponents continue to block efforts in several states.[26] As much as the public supports extending hate crimes and civil rights protections to gays and lesbians, advocates often face serious opposition from social conservatives and religious opponents who see any legal protections for gays as an endorsement of homosexuality and the start of a slide down a slippery slope that eventually will end with the approval of gay marriage. Gay rights advocates succeed very gradually in popularly democratic arenas when the public is behind them; they fail much more rapidly when the public opposes them.

When we examined gay adoption, the military ban, and the legalization of homosexual conduct in the previous chapters, we found support for the hypothesis that gay rights advocates are more successful when courts are the primary institutional venue for making policy decisions. Civil rights, hate crimes, and marriage offer much less support for this hypothesis, however. For issues on which large majorities of the public support gay rights, judicial involvement clearly is *not* necessary for gay rights advocates to achieve policy success. Gay rights advocates have enjoyed a good measure of success in getting state and local legislative bodies to enact hate crimes and civil rights measures.

The Courts' Impact
CIVIL RIGHTS AND HATE CRIMES LAWS

Courts have been important in the enforcement of civil rights laws after legislative bodies have enacted them. Courts have applied civil rights protections in myriad specific instances, ruling in favor of numerous gay and lesbian petitioners who allege discrimination in public accommodations, business transactions, employment, and housing (for examples, see www.lambdalegal.org and www.aclu.org). Courts also have facilitated the spread and implementation of hate crimes laws by declaring them constitutional (Jacobs and Potter 1998, 121–28).[27]

Yet the courts have not been particularly helpful to gay and lesbian petitioners in discrimination cases. In his study of seventy-seven sexual orientation discrimination cases from 1981 to 2000, Pinello (2003, 10, 48) found that federal and state appellate courts ruled in favor of gay petitioners less than half of the time, and only about 14 percent of the time in federal cases. Two well-known defeats are Supreme Court rulings in *Boy Scouts of America v. Dale* (530 U.S. 640 2000) and *Hurley v. Irish-American Gay, Lesbian and Bisexual Group of Boston* (515 U.S. 557 1995), which, respectively, permit the Boy Scouts to exclude gay males and parade organizers to exclude gays and lesbians who want to march under their own banner. The Supreme Court's decision in *Romer v. Evans* (517 U.S. 620 1996) was an important victory for gays because it forbade states from barring local governments from enacting antidiscrimination policies. However, *Romer* promoted gay equality in the political process rather than in society. And the Court used the "rational basis" standard in its ruling rather than more equality-enhancing standards of review that offer "heightened scrutiny" to alleged discrimination against racial and gender groups. Finally, litigation is a limited tool for fighting discrimination because most cases apply to specific-fact situations rather than set broad policy.

MARRIAGE AND PARTNER RECOGNITION

There is little doubt that the courts have played a key role in the politics of same-sex marriage and partner recognition. Courts put the issue on the agenda in the early 1990s, prompted legislators and voters to respond, and have helped to keep it there ever since. State courts ruled in favor of same-sex petitioners in Hawaii, Vermont, Massachusetts, and New Jersey, resulting in the adoption of marriage, civil unions, or domestic partner benefits. Had the courts refused to hear these cases, or had they ruled against the same-sex couples that brought the lawsuits, it is doubtful that their state legislatures would have adopted partner recognition policies, or certainly not as quickly or extensively as they have. (California's Supreme Court ruled in favor of gay marriage after the state had adopted partner benefits.)

Across the nation as a whole, however, courts have not been especially active in the marriage debate. Courts in twenty-eight states, the largest category of those displayed in table 7.7, have not ruled in favor of either side. When the courts have weighed in, they have ruled against same-sex plaintiffs more often than they have ruled in their favor. Courts have ordered marriage or an equivalent status for same-sex couples in five states, but they have ruled that states are not compelled to issue marriage licenses or provide equivalent rights to gay couples in eight others (New York, Washington, Arizona, Maryland, Indiana, Louisiana, Georgia, and Nebraska). In six states, where the courts have not ruled on the constitutionality of same-sex unions, they have supported gay marriage opponents by qualifying their antimarriage measures for the ballot or enjoining local authorities from issuing marriage licenses to same-sex couples.

Most importantly perhaps, court decisions in Hawaii, Vermont, and Massachusetts set off a backlash against same-sex partner recognition. Voters and elected officials greeted the Hawaii and Massachusetts decisions, in particular, with grassroots campaigns to enact DOMA laws and constitutional amendments. Figure 7.2 shows the number of DOMA laws

Table 7.7 The courts and same-sex marriage/partnership recognition in the fifty states

Declared in favor of same-sex marriage or similar status	5 states (CA, HA, MA, NJ, VT)
Upheld laws/constitutions banning same-sex marriage or rejected arguments that denial of marriage licenses illegal/ unconstitutional	8 states (AZ, GA, IN, MD, LA, NE, NY, WA)[a]
Declared in favor of same-sex marriage opponents but did not rule on whether ban is legal/constitutional	6 states (AR, CT, NM, OR, TN, WV)[b]
States with cases pending as of June 2008	3 states (AK, IA, OK)
States with no cases decided or pending	28 states (AL, CO, DE, FL, ID, IL, KN, KY, ME, MI, MN, MO, MS, MT, NV, NH, NC, ND, OH, PA, RI, SC, SD, TX, UT, VA, WI, WY)

Sources: Lambda Legal, "In Your State," lists the current status of same-sex marriage and partnership recognition rights in each state (http://www.lambdalegal.org/cgi-bin/iowa/states/index.html; accessed September 12, 2006). See also Steves (2005); Davenport (2004); DeAgostino (2005); Associated Press (2006); Gyan (2005).

[a]In Nebraska, a challenge to that state's ban on same-sex marriages was brought before the federal courts and was upheld by a district court and the U.S. Court of Appeals for the 8th Circuit.

[b]Courts in Arkansas and Tennessee ruled against efforts to prevent opponents from placing same-sex marriage bans on the ballot. Courts in Oregon and New Mexico stopped local authorities from issuing marriage licenses to same-sex couples. A court in Connecticut ruled that the state was not compelled to call civil unions "marriage." The high court in West Virginia refused to hear a challenge to that state's same-sex marriage ban.

and amendments adopted since 1993, when Hawaii's Supreme Court announced its decision. It shows that fifteen such measures (including the federal DOMA) gained approval in 1996 and eight more gained approval in 1997. The number of new bans dropped to six in 1998 and between zero and four from 1999 to 2003. After the *Goodridge v. Department of Public Health* (798 N.E. 2nd 941 Mass 2003) decision in Massachusetts in 2003, another flurry of measures passed, this time mostly in the form of constitutional provisions and super-DOMA prohibitions against all forms of same-sex partner recognition. Voters and legislatures adopted eighteen bans in 2004–05 and seven more in 2006.[28]

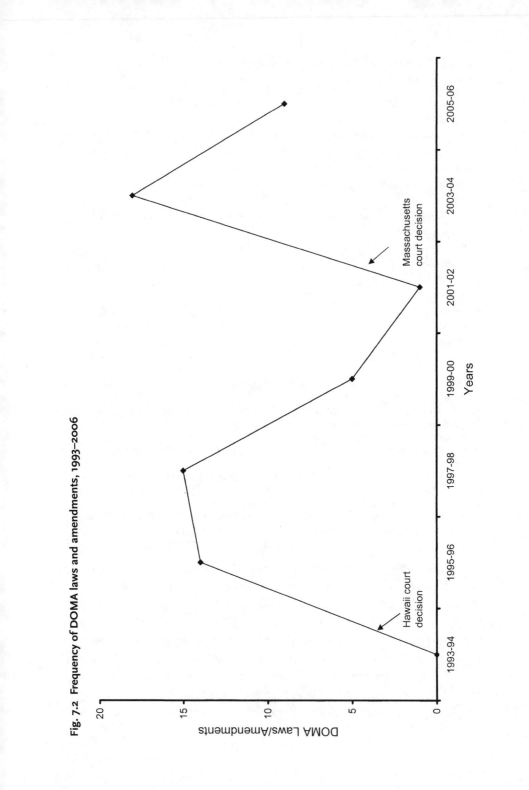

Fig. 7.2 Frequency of DOMA laws and amendments, 1993–2006

Future court rulings in favor of gay couples should set off less oppo-sition if only because the novelty of them has worn off and increasing numbers of states have amended their constitutions to ban marriage (or in fewer cases, have adopted some form of partner recognition). The New Jersey and California Supreme Courts' 2006 and 2008 rulings in favor of same-sex couples did not have the dramatic impact of earlier court rulings.

CONCLUSION

Because most Americans support protecting gays and lesbians against hate crimes and discrimination but find same-sex marriage threatening, gay rights advocates have achieved notable success in securing the former and have fallen far short of gaining the latter. Unlike what we saw in the preceding three chapters, these cases are not about liberal or conservative elites and constituencies going around public opinion, but about harness-ing public opinion and taking advantage of institutional opportunities to translate opinion into policy.

Public opinion influences not only which side prevails in gay rights struggles but also the *pace* of policy change. In that respect, public opinion has heavily favored gay rights opponents. When majority opinion sup-ports the position of gay rights opponents, policy change occurs more quickly than when it favors gay rights advocates. High levels of opposition to gay marriage led most states to enact marriage bans within a decade. Protecting gays against hate crimes and discrimination in the workplace has taken much longer to achieve. Fewer states have hate crimes and civil rights laws that cover gays than ban gay marriage, despite similar levels of public support for all three policies. The adoption of civil unions and partnership benefits has also been more limited than one would expect given the moderate levels of public support for those policies. In short, a threatened majority is more likely to act quickly to protect its own per-ceived self-interest than an unthreatened majority is to protect the inter-ests of a minority.

Institutions also have shaped policy outcomes in these three issues, and they help us to identify which institutional arrangements most consistently pattern the policy fortunes of gay rights advocates. Where they are active, stakeholders play a critical role in influencing which side wins. Just as stake-holders sympathetic to gay rights helped overcome potential resistance to gay adoption and the legalization of homosexual conduct, victim groups, civil rights organizations, and law enforcement organizations have helped build support for hate crimes laws. Civil rights groups have been indispensable allies in struggles for nondiscrimination policies, while business opponents have impeded their adoption.

The federal system, on balance, is advantageous for gay rights advocates. Federalism disaggregates and distributes public opinion unevenly across fifty separate jurisdictions and allows jurisdictions to regulate how much direct influence organized groups and voters have over policy. Just as policymaking at the state and local levels has helped the causes of gay adoption and the legalization of homosexual behavior, it has helped to achieve moderate to high levels of success in civil rights and hate crimes protection and made it possible for some states to recognize same-sex partnerships. Federalism also accounts for why some states *deviate* from public opinion, such as those that have failed to enact hate crimes laws and that ban gay marriage, or have approved same-sex marriage or super-DOMAs that ban all forms of same-sex partner recognition. Just as legislative majorities at the national level thwarted the public's support for lifting the military ban, they have done the same in passing a federal DOMA and blocking federal civil rights and anti–hate crimes measures.

These cases provide much less support for the proposition that judicial policymaking is more conducive to success for gay rights advocates than when policymaking is undertaken in legislative venues. To the extent that courts have been involved, they have a mixed record in helping to expand protections against discrimination and bringing about same-sex marriage and civil unions. Although many legislative bodies have enacted bans on gay marriage, they have also facilitated the translation of public support for civil rights and hate crimes protections into policy. Ballot initiative processes, where they exist, have contributed significantly to the spread of more restrictive policies against marriage and civil unions. As this example shows, public opinion often shapes the general direction of public policy, but institutions influence *specific* policy responses.

Finally, institutions illuminate why policy success varies when we control for levels of public support for gay rights. Gay rights advocates have experienced greater levels of success in passing hate crimes laws than in passing civil rights protections at the state level, even though the public overwhelmingly supports both kinds of measures. Most states have hate crimes laws covering gays and lesbians; most do not have laws against discrimination. Stakeholders are more numerous and more uniformly on the side of LGBT rights groups in seeking hate crimes protection, and the ability of LGBT activists to secure protections against employment nondiscrimination at the local level reduces the need to focus LGBT resources at the state level.

While public opinion and institutional arrangements help to explain the different levels of success that LGBT advocates have encountered across issues, substantive differences among issues shape levels of public support for policies and the kinds of institutional venues and actors that play a central role in policymaking. Varying levels of support for policies reflect different issue characteristics, as we saw in chapter 2. Issues embody different kinds of demands and concerns on both sides of the debates. For example, while ballot initiatives have had a significant adverse impact on efforts to gain adoption of gay marriage and other forms of same-sex partner recognition, they have had a modest and short-lived impact on the struggle for protection against nondiscrimination, a very different LGBT demand that the public does not find threatening. Likewise, issue differences influence what kinds of stakeholders and other coalition partners will become active in policymaking. Debate over hate crimes laws attracts a large number of stakeholders aligned with LGBT advocates. Many victim groups have not yet attained hate crimes protection, and many of them, along with law enforcement organizations, have tangible stakes in seeing such laws adopted. Debate over employment nondiscrimination attracts stakeholders on both sides of the issue because antidiscrimination laws potentially burden businesses financially. Meanwhile, the civil rights organizations in support of these laws for gays and lesbians have mainly an ideological interest in the cause because the groups they support have already won these protections. Debate over marriage includes few stakeholders because it addresses a deprivation that almost uniquely affects gays and lesbians and because its controversial nature expands the scope of conflict beyond the range of the immediate interests involved.

Conclusion

This book stands an old question on its head. Instead of asking, When can a nation's politics bring about social change? it has asked, Why does social change sometimes succeed and sometimes fail to help a group's political fortunes? Gays and lesbians have attained an unprecedented and significant level of visibility and acceptance in society. The more positive image and treatment of gays in everyday life and the mass media has contributed to political gains as well. Yet, political progress has been highly variable. Major parts of the gay rights agenda remain totally or partially unfulfilled, while others have been adopted as public policy.

The gay rights movement wages its political battles across a set of distinct issues that reflect its diverse goals.[1] The extent to which Americans perceive its goals as threatening and how political institutions mediate the resistance that arises from those perceptions shape the movement's chances for success. The movement's public policy fortunes, thus, lie at the nexus of public opinion and political institutions within each issue arena. This chapter begins by summarizing and integrating the study's main findings, which generally support the expectations put forward in chapter 1 concerning the impacts of stakeholders, federalism, and judicial policymaking. Taken as a whole, the analysis suggests two alternative pathways to political success for the lesbian, gay, bisexual, and transgender (LGBT) rights movement—"liberal pluralist" or "liberal elitist"—depending upon whether public opinion and institutional arrangements, or institutions alone, are hospitable to the movement's goals. It also shows why the movement has failed (or experienced only meager success) in reaching its other policy goals.

Next, the chapter assesses several broader implications of the study. First, it examines the relevance of the cases for our understanding of the role of the courts in minority politics. Under what conditions are the courts more likely to expand rights for minority groups? Following that, we explore the study's implications for social movement theory. Specifically, how does an analytical framework centered on issue differences help us understand patterns of success and failure in other social movements? Finally, we look at the study's implications for the future of gay rights and the LGBT movement's strategies and tactics. On which issues, in which places, and under what conditions can we expect the movement to make progress in the future? What kinds of strategies should LGBT leaders and activists pursue that might hasten the achievement of their goals?

EXPLAINING LGBT MOVEMENT SUCCESS AND FAILURE

We begin by summarizing the study's findings. What has been the impact of our main institutional variables on LGBT-related policy fortunes? Are stakeholders crucial to LGBT fortunes, and how do they contribute to political success or failure? Do the chances for LGBT success vary with the federal or state and local level of government and with judicial or legislative venues for policymaking?

Stakeholders

Stakeholders play a major role in all of the issues we examined except for gay marriage. As expected, the fortunes of gay rights advocates are linked closely to the goals and preferences of third-party stakeholders. Success for gay rights advocates increases when stakeholder support for gay rights is stronger, is more one-sided, and includes more than the usual liberal and civil rights groups. Adoption agencies and adoption lawyers, social workers, and many family court judges have supported the petitions of gay couples seeking to adopt. Penal code reformers were crucial to advancing the repeal of sodomy laws through state legislatures and the courts. The endorsement of hate crimes laws to cover sexual orientation by racial, ethnic, and religious victim groups and law enforcement organizations have aided in their adoption in many states. On the other hand, opposition from military leaders and ordinary service members has been a major impediment to lifting the ban on gays serving openly in the armed services. Liberal civil rights "conscience constituents" have played an important role in helping gays and lesbians secure nondiscrimination policies as they did earlier for other social movements, but business opposition blunts their impacts in some localities and at the federal level where liberalism has fallen out of fashion since the 1970s. The lack of support from any significant stakeholder in the marriage debate means that the LGBT movement has largely fought that difficult battle on its own and come out mostly on the losing end.

Stakeholders shape policy outcomes, first, by bringing attention to issues and placing them on the agenda. Penal code reformers pushed state legislatures to consider decriminalizing sodomy as part of overhauls of criminal law as far back as the 1950s and 1960s. Human rights commissions and civil rights groups have documented the need for nondiscrimination ordinances. Victim groups and civil rights organizations gather statistics on the incidence of hate crimes and publicize dramatic attacks on gay and lesbians.

Second, stakeholders redefine issues in ways that help or hinder the cause of gay rights. Because stakeholders usually have more credibility than the more partisan pro- or anti–gay rights advocates, their efforts to reframe issues have a greater chance of success. The credibility of a source is crucial for successfully reframing issues (Druckman 2001). Stakeholders transcend debates over "gay rights versus traditional values" by redefining them in ways in which it is easier to find common ground. Military leaders transformed an issue of equal employment opportunities and social inclusion into one about unit cohesion and "military effectiveness." Legal reformers turned an issue about "sin" and "gay rights" into one about rationalizing the criminal code and doing away with the "overcriminalization of victimless crimes." Family court judges, adoption agencies, and social workers, using evidence-based criteria and rational-legal processes, cast gay adoption in terms of finding suitable parents and doing what is in the "best interest of children." Police, prosecutors, and victim groups articulate the expansion of hate crimes laws to cover gays as an issue of "law and order," justice for victims, and tolerance for diversity. Liberal civil rights and religious groups frame issues about discrimination against gays in employment and housing as part of the nation's long struggle to fulfill the "American ideals" of freedom and social equality.

Finally, stakeholders provide valuable political resources. Sympathetic adoption agencies and lawyers steer gay parents to judges and jurisdictions that are more disposed to rule in their favor. Rank-and-file members of the armed services flooded Capitol Hill with vocal objections to President Bill Clinton's plan to let gays serve openly in the military. Stakeholders are often more persuasive than LGBT advocates and traditional values proponents because they may be perceived as nonpartisan experts (such as penal code reformers) or groups with a legitimate interest in the outcome (such as the military). By doing so, they provide political cover for policymakers who must take positions on contentious issues.

Federalism and Decentralized Policymaking

Gay rights supporters fare better, on balance, when state and local levels of government address their concerns than when they go to Washington. A conservative-dominated Congress in the 1990s defeated the president's proposal to lift the ban on gays serving in the armed services and kept the issue off the agenda afterward. Congress has refused to approve protection for gays and lesbians under federal civil rights and hate crimes laws and passed the Defense of Marriage Act. The federal courts have been much less inclined to support gay and lesbian plaintiffs than their counterparts at the state level (Pinello 2003). While the U.S. Supreme Court's record is mixed, its most important decision to enlarge gay rights—*Lawrence v. Texas* in 2003—came after most states had repealed their sodomy laws and almost two decades after it had decided in *Bowers* to uphold them. Although one cannot know for sure, it is implausible that gay rights advocates would have fared as well under a unitary system of government than they have under the federal system.

The new president and Congress that take power in 2009 may be more helpful to gays and lesbians, particularly in extending federal hate crimes and nondiscrimination protection and in lifting the ban on gays openly serving in the military. Even if they are, the federal government's inaction on gay rights issues over the past half century is a major reason that making progress in advancing the gay rights movement has varied so much across many issues. At the same time, state and local jurisdictions have played a critical role in their advancement, starting with the repeal of sodomy laws in 1960 and the adoption of nondiscrimination policies in 1972.

Federalism facilitates access to government for gay and lesbian groups and stakeholders sympathetic to their cause. States and localities with more moderate and liberal elite and mass opinion, higher levels of LGBT political organization, more educated populations, and legacies of tolerance toward minorities are more likely to adopt and preserve gay rights laws. These communities create an atmosphere in which gays and lesbians feel more comfortable to come out of the closet and become active politically. As other gays and lesbians migrate to these locales, the size and strength of LGBT political organizations increases, as does, in turn, elite responsiveness to their demands (Wald, Button, and Rienzo 1996).

Since federalism fosters and legitimates political diversity, people are more willing to accept that some parts of the country will adopt more liberal policies protecting gays and lesbians than they might accept in their own states and local communities. Policymaking at the subnational levels also has the advantages of lowering issue salience and incremental policymaking. Policy changes at the state and local levels often escape national media coverage, making them seem less threatening than more sweeping, winner-take-all policy changes at the national level. Gay rights organizations can win geographically limited victories, gradually extending hate crimes and civil rights protections, repealing prohibitions on sodomy, and permitting gay adoption.

Fears of government intrusion and regulatory burdens may be less intense at state and local levels, where citizens have practical expectations about the role of government in solving social problems and where ideological resistance to expanding civil rights and hate crimes laws is less acute than it is in Washington. Stakeholders with little access in Washington may have a good deal more in Sacramento, Boston, Chicago, and other urban areas and state capitals. Liberal civil rights groups and other gay and lesbian allies, whose influence declined in Washington after the 1970s, maintained influence in many cities, college towns, and the Northeast and Pacific coast.

Judicial Policymaking

The hypothesis that gay rights advocates are more successful when courts are the primary institutional venue for resolving conflict has more mixed support. Surveying hundreds of gay rights cases across a wide range of issues at the federal and state levels, Pinello (2003, 10) found that courts support gay and lesbian petitioners only about half of the time. While the courts occasionally have been important defenders of nondiscrimination policies, as in the Supreme Court's *Romer v. Evans* decision, and in maintaining the constitutionality of hate crimes laws, as in *Mitchell v. Wisconsin,* Pinello (2003, 10) found that courts support gay and lesbian supporters less than half of the time in rulings on sexual orientation discrimination cases. Importantly, the U.S. Supreme Court has never accorded sexual orientation discrimination the "heightened levels of scrutiny" that it has applied to instances of racial and gender discrimination. Court rulings on marriage set off a serious backlash. Court decisions in Hawaii and Massachusetts, coupled with the 2003 Supreme Court's ruling in *Lawrence v. Texas,* provoked grassroots campaigns that resulted in bans on marriage—and, increasingly, other forms of partner recognition—in forty-four states. Furthermore, high courts have ruled against same-sex couples' marriage claims more often than they have ruled in their favor. Looked at from this perspective, the courts' involvement has been, at best, a mixed blessing for the cause of gay marriage.

Judicial involvement is clearly not a necessary condition for gays and lesbians to make progress. While high judicial involvement seems to benefit the cause of gay rights on some issues, low involvement does not preclude success on others. Almost as many state legislatures repealed sodomy laws as were those laws invalidated by state courts and the Supreme Court. State and local legislative bodies have enacted hundreds of hate crimes and civil rights measures, and legislative and executive officials have been the main actors on these issues.

At the same time, gays and lesbians would not have progressed politically as far or as fast as they have without courts ruling in their favor. LGBT advocates have encountered considerable success in two areas where courts have been highly involved—the repeal of sodomy laws and granting adoption rights. Same-sex couples have the opportunity to adopt children in at least some jurisdictions in almost half of the states because courts, in most cases, have granted them joint and second-parent adoptions. Given the state of public opinion and the strength of "family values" groups, it seems unlikely that legislatures would have acted as favorably toward same-sex couples seeking to adopt as the courts have been. Same-sex behavior is no longer criminal because courts declared sodomy laws unconstitutional in more than half of the states. The elimination of sodomy laws not only created a zone of privacy for gay people but it also removed an important impediment to gaining other legal rights. After the rise of the antigay rights opposition and the AIDS crisis in the 1980s, legislative repeal of sodomy laws ceased. It took the Supreme Court's *Lawrence* decision to sweep away the remaining sodomy laws, mostly in conservative southern and midwestern states. Courts have not ruled consistently on the side of gay and lesbian petitioners on these issues (less than a majority of state high courts have declared same-sex couples eligible for adoption statewide, for example). Yet it is implausible that fulfillment of the gay rights agenda would be as far along today if the courts had stayed out of these areas and deferred to the judgments of the other branches of government.

In addition, courts have played an exceedingly important role in getting same-sex marriage on the agenda, and some of the states that have adopted marriage or civil unions did so in response to judicial prodding. At the same time, the low level of judicial involvement overall and the lack of LGBT political success on the marriage issue provides further support for the hypothesis that gays are more successful when courts play a central role. The courts have not been the primary institutional venue for resolving the issue in most of the country. Most state high courts have not been involved in ruling on the issue, and most states have enacted marriage bans through legislative action or ballot initiatives. Similarly, the courts' *lack* of involvement in military policy has shut off the possibility of a judicial remedy for the discrimination experienced by gay service members under the "don't ask, don't tell" policy. The courts' deference to the legislative and executive branches on the ban on gays serving openly has contributed to the failure of LGBT rights advocates to eliminate the ban.

In sum, institutions have had a decisive impact on policy outcomes in three of the six cases examined. Despite the relative lack of public support for legalizing homosexual conduct and permitting gays and lesbians to adopt children, a set of supportive stakeholders and state and local judicial policymaking has dampened much of the resistance to these policies. As a result, gay rights advocates have made more progress than one might have expected. Conversely, despite public support for lifting the ban on gays in the military, conservative elites in Congress and the military have worked with social and religious conservatives to maintain the ban.

For the other three cases we examined, the parsimonious explanation for the outcomes is the level of threat that Americans perceive from LGBT demands. Most Americans support extending protections against hate crimes and discrimination in the marketplace, oppose same-sex marriage, and are divided over civil unions. Even in these cases, however, institutional arrangements—stakeholders and state and local policymaking in the hate crimes and nondiscrimination cases and the availability of the ballot initiative in gay marriage—play an important role in bringing about policies that are consistent with the opinions of a majority of citizens.

Alternative Causal Pathways to LGBT Policy Success

The 2 × 2 matrix presented in table 8.1 integrates the study's findings on the successes and failures of the gay rights movement on six issues. The

Table 8.1 Typology of social movement issues

		Perceived threat from social movement demands	
		High	Low
Balance of resources and political opportunity structures favors	Movement supporters	**Liberal elitist issues** (adoption; legalization of sexual conduct)	**Liberal pluralist issues** (hate crimes; civil rights)
	Movement opponents	**Traditional populist issues** (marriage)	**Traditional veto group issues** (military ban)

vertical axis distinguishes among cases according to whether the *balance of political opportunities and resources* favors the pro– or anti–gay rights movement. Included on this dimension are institutional authority structures, rules and procedures that either dampen or encourage resistance to gay rights, the party affiliations and political ideologies of key policymakers, pro– and anti–gay rights supporters' and opponents' financial and organizational resources, and the support that the movements can garner from stakeholders and coalition partners. LGBT rights advocates succeed only when the balance of political opportunities and resources is in their favor. The horizontal axis distinguishes among cases according to the *level of threat from extending gay rights perceived by the public*. The intersection of these variables yields four categories of LGBT issues reflecting different combinations of perceived threat and the balance of political opportunities and resources: liberal elitist, liberal pluralist, traditional populist, and traditional veto group issues. Because issues often evolve over time, the categorization of cases may change in response to changes in levels of public support, political opportunity structures, and resources at the disposal of the pro– and anti–gay rights forces.

The typology suggests two causal pathways to success for gay rights advocates. The *liberal elitist* path features supportive stakeholders and judicial policymaking at the state and local levels primarily. LGBT rights advocates have achieved a good measure of success despite a divided public on these issues because elites with liberal attitudes on particular LGBT issues control policymaking. Institutions help to reduce issue salience, dampen resistance to LGBT demands, and insulate policymakers from opposition mounted against them. Courts and other institutions that enjoy some autonomy from opposition forces and public opinion play a pivotal role in the resolution of these issues. Stakeholders whose goals are consistent with those of the movement enjoy access to these policymakers.

Gay rights advocates have followed the liberal elitist path in expanding adoption rights and the legalization of homosexual conduct. Courts dominate policymaking in both cases. State legislatures give enormous discretion to state courts and local family and probate judges, most of whom either do not run for reelection or enjoy relatively long terms of office and noncompetitive races. Local judges work closely with adoption agencies, lawyers, and social workers, who increasingly regard gays and lesbians as suitable parents, particularly for hard-to-place children. Decentralized decision making and the privacy that surrounds adoptions reduce the salience of the issue of having gay couples adopt children, sheltering judges from public exposure and mobilization by gay rights opponents. Courts also eliminated a majority of state sodomy laws. Although the Supreme Court's *Lawrence* decision was highly salient, most states got rid of their sodomy laws very gradually over a period of forty-three years before the *Lawrence* decision through state legislative repeal and state court rulings. About half of the states repealed their laws *before* the emergence of a strong anti–gay rights movement emerged in the late 1970s. Reformers legalized homosexual conduct in a context of low issue salience—as part of a large rationalization of the penal code that obscured the repeal of sodomy laws. Even after gay rights became a controversial cultural issue, penal code reformers continued to have influence and served as respected authorities for advocates of the repeal of sodomy laws.

The *liberal pluralist* path to LGBT success features supportive stakeholders and public opinion and legislative policymaking at the state and local levels. Gay rights advocates succeed when the public perceives little threat from LGBT advocates' demands and when institutions deflect or dampen resistance to their efforts to extend rights. The legislative bodies that consider the issues reflect the public acquiescence in extending gay rights, although it may take several years to enact these policy changes. The lack of opposition from the public encourages elected officials to put these issues on the agenda, but whether legislative bodies adopt the policies and how long it takes to adopt them depends upon gay rights organizations' ability to rally sufficient resources, stakeholders, and other sympathetic coalition partners to their cause. Gay rights advocates and policymakers limit the scope of conflict in these cases to conventional "insider" interest group politics, in which the side that musters the greatest resources prevails.

Gay rights advocates have followed the liberal pluralist path in gaining hate crimes protection for more than three-quarters of the U.S. population and civil rights protections for more than half. They have taken advantage of broad public support for banning hate crimes and discrimination directed at gays; large numbers of politically active gays and lesbians located in larger urban areas; communities with more educated populations; fewer Protestant fundamentalists; and liberal public opinion in states on the East and West coasts and in parts of the Midwest. They have enjoyed the support of stakeholders (e.g., victim groups and law enforcement organizations) and liberal civil rights groups.

Politics in the seven states that a have adopted marriage, civil unions, or an equivalent set of benefits resembles the liberal elitist model, the liberal pluralist model, or a blend of the two. The gradual building of legislative support for civil unions and domestic partnerships in Connecticut, Oregon, California, and New Hampshire, for example reflects the liberal pluralist model. The dominant role of the courts in the politics of Vermont and Massachusetts (and California in 2008) typifies the liberal elitist model, although legislative policymaking also played an important role in developing the specific policy responses to the court rulings in those states.

Where LGBT advocates have largely failed, one or more of the elements critical to the liberal elitist and liberal pluralist pathways is absent. Advocates are most likely to fail when Americans perceive their demands as threatening and when institutional arrangements facilitate the resistance that arises from those perceptions. *Traditional populist* issues combine high salience, a high level of perceived threat, and a configuration of political opportunities and resources that favor anti–gay rights forces. These conditions drastically reduce the prospects for expanding LGBT rights. Most citizens are firmly opposed to these LGBT demands or are sharply divided over them. Policymakers address these issues within institutional venues that leave them highly exposed to gay rights opponents' grassroots campaigns to mobilize voters and legislators against them. Opponents push the issues onto legislative agendas and the ballot box in states that have the direct initiative. Stakeholders sympathetic to gay rights are scarce or cannot exert significant influence once the issues become highly salient and the scope of conflict expands.[2]

States and localities where efforts to enact nondiscrimination laws have failed or where such laws have been repealed, such as the city of Cincinnati, may often resemble the traditional populist pattern. The adoption of state and federal defense of marriage acts also fits in this category. Substantial and stable majorities of Americans oppose gay marriage, major stakeholders are absent, and the courts have stayed out of the conflict in most states and at the federal level. Public opposition to permitting gays and lesbians to share in a traditional social and religious institution linked closely to heterosexual privilege and identity fueled a determined grassroots effort to get legislators and voters to ban same-sex marriage in forty-four states (including seventeen that have banned civil unions and other forms of same-sex partner recognition along with marriage).

One of the most important ways to defeat policies of benefit to relatively powerless groups is to keep issues off the agenda as "nondecisions" (Bachrach and Baratz 1970). Undoubtedly, many "defeats" for LGBT rights are those in which the local climate of opinion is so unreceptive that LGBT advocates are discouraged from even presenting their demands for protection against hate crimes and discrimination and for partner recognition.

Finally, the public is not highly threatened by demands for gay rights in struggles over *traditional veto group* issues, but gay rights opponents enjoy greater political opportunities and resources than gay rights advocates. Conservative elites, allied with stakeholders and oppositional groups, dominate policymaking in these arenas. With public support for LGBT demands often shallow and unstable in these cases, elites can ignore it or push public opinion in a negative direction. The failed effort to lift the ban on gays serving openly in the military fits this pattern. The national government has exclusive control over military policies; the major stakeholder in the dispute over whether to permit gay service members to serve—the military itself—is opposed to lifting the ban; and the courts have deferred to the executive and legislative branches. A conservative coalition of Republicans and Democrats, dominant in the powerful armed services committees in Congress, worked closely with military leaders, rank-and-file service men and women fearful of openly gay colleagues, and social conservatives to defeat President Clinton's plan to end the ban. Although polls showed majorities of the public in support of lifting the ban before and after Clinton's failed attempt, opponents launched an effective media and lobbying campaign to redefine the issue and raise concerns about how lifting the ban would affect military effectiveness, which caused support to drop at the time that the issue was decided.

The analysis may also hold up for cases not examined in this book. For example, the gay rights movement was largely unsuccessful in getting the federal government to respond in a timely and effective manner to the HIV/AIDS crisis (Rimmerman 2002, 86–110; Andriote 1999). Only the federal government had the regulatory authority and financial resources that were vital to stemming the tide of the crisis. Not until several years into the crisis did President Ronald Reagan even acknowledge it publicly. The Reagan and George H. W. Bush administrations discouraged the surgeon general of the United States from speaking out about the problem and from making it a top priority of the Centers for Disease Control, and they failed to prevent discrimination against people with AIDS. It took years to educate the public on the crisis, develop and approve new AIDS drugs, and fund AIDS treatment and prevention services at levels sufficient to attack the problem seriously. Not until late in the Clinton administration was the Ryan White Comprehensive AIDS Resources Emergency (CARE) Act, passed in 1990, fully funded. Nonprofit AIDS service organizations bore the brunt of the crisis.

AIDS resembles most of the characteristics of a traditional veto group issue. The public supported stronger federal efforts and more resources to help fight the AIDS crisis,[3] but support declined when asked explicitly about "homosexuals" or "gays" as the beneficiaries of the assistance.[4] However, the institutional context favored doing less rather than more. Conservative politicians at the national level who were influenced by fiscally and socially conservative constituencies, particularly in the Republican party, dominated policymaking, and the courts were largely out of the picture. These forces were strong enough to resist the stakeholder that wanted a more vigorous response to the epidemic—public health authorities—until the epidemic had led to thousands of deaths (Andriote 1999, 138–45).

BROADER IMPLICATIONS OF THE STUDY

Our analysis of gay and lesbian politics sheds light on topics of broader relevance. One area of inquiry that arises is what these findings tell us about how well courts promote the expansion of minority rights and under what conditions they exert greater influence. The findings also speak to our understanding of how social movements succeed or fail in the public policy arena. This section addresses each of these concerns in turn.

Gay Rights, Minority Rights, and the Courts

What do our findings about gay rights suggest about the impact of the courts on minority rights? Skeptics argue that little evidence suggests that the courts serve as bulwarks for minority rights and that the faith placed in them by some civil rights advocates is misplaced (Rosenberg 1991; Pacelle 1996; Spann 1993). Recently, John D'Emilio (2007) has applied this argument specifically to the struggle for LGBT rights. Expecting courts to usher in sweeping social changes across a wide range of issues in a system designed to disperse and constrain governmental authority would seem a "hollow hope" indeed. Critics, however, may be overly dismissive about the importance of the courts. Even if they do not bring about thorough social reformation, courts can play a significant role in the advancement of minority rights. The experience with gay rights suggests that broad generalizations about the role and importance of the courts in the advancement of minority rights are difficult to make. The courts' impacts are complex and vary across issues and historical periods. Our findings are consistent with Pinello's (2003, 10), which showed that gay and lesbian petitioners' success rates in the courts vary significantly according to the issue area. Gay litigants succeed more than half of the time in family-related and sodomy/privacy cases, for example, but in less than a quarter of suits against the military.

If courts are not a panacea for those seeking to advance gay rights, neither are they ciphers. Courts have been catalysts for getting issues on the agenda, producers of new policies, and enforcers of policies crafted by legislatures. They are indispensable to social movement success in some instances, impediments to progress in others, and of lesser relevance in still others. The issues for which the courts have contributed significantly to the advancement of gay rights—the legalization of homosexual conduct, adoption, and (to a much lesser extent) partner recognition—share three essential characteristics: *a legacy of judicial involvement borne of legislative reluctance to address issues or difficulty in developing a legislative consensus; independence from other political actors in order to authorize or implement court decisions; and policymaking at the state court level.*[5]

Courts have been major players in gay adoption, gay marriage, and the repeal of sodomy laws (after 1980) partly by default. Sexual conduct, relationship, and family issues make legislators uncomfortable, threaten many of their constituents, and incite intense opposition from conservative family and religious groups. Legislative leaders willing to push these controversial issues must build majorities through an arduous process of negotiation that is susceptible to stalemate. Legislators' disinclination to address these issues provides an opening for courts to intervene. The courts have the greatest potential impact on those issues for which public support is weakest. Legislatures have given substantial discretion to courts in adoption, custody and visitation, and (until recently) marriage laws, making court rulings on these issues more likely. The courts in these cases did not simply "place their imprimatur on trends already well under way" (D'Emilio 2007, 57). State courts clearly have been in the vanguard in extending the right to adopt children to gays and lesbians. State courts and the U.S. Supreme Court, in the absence of much public support, repealed a majority of state sodomy laws. Rather than riding a wave of social approval and legislative action, the courts picked up the ball when legislative repeal efforts stalled after 1980.

The courts have been more successful in expanding gay rights where they have not needed to rely upon other authorities to authorize or carry out their decisions. For example, judges serve as both the makers and the implementers of adoption policy. Because all but a handful of state statutes either expressly permit or prohibit awarding adoptions to same-sex couples, family court judges are largely free to grant the petitions to people they deem suitable. Similarly, the courts' rulings to invalidate sodomy laws were essentially self-executing. Police and prosecutors stopped enforcing the laws or judges dismissed charges. Even if courts lack the ability to compel state authorities to issue marriage licenses to same-sex couples, they have been catalysts to legislative action.

The skeptical view of the courts as defenders of minority rights has focused exclusively on the federal courts, and the Supreme Court in particular. Outside of the legalization of homosexual conduct, the federal courts have not done much to further gay rights, as the skeptics would predict. They have ruled against gay plaintiffs in a large majority of cases and have deferred to Congress and the military in upholding the ban on gay service members. While state courts have not been consistent defenders of gay rights, they have a record that is superior to the federal courts (Pinello 2003, 9–10).[6] Gays have been more successful in state than federal courts partly for the same reasons they are more successful at state and local levels of government generally: State court judges who rule in favor of LGBT rights tend to enjoy longer terms of office and preside in states with more moderate and liberal opinions. Most sitting federal judges are appointees of conservative Republican administrations. State supreme courts repealed more sodomy laws that the U.S. Supreme Court did in the *Lawrence* decision. Family and probate court judges award adoptions in a highly decentralized system of thousands of counties whose records are usually sealed. These conditions reduce the salience of adoption, making it difficult to monitor probate judges and mobilize opinion against gay adoption.

An Issue-Based Approach to Social Movement Studies

All of the major theoretical perspectives on social movements—resource mobilization, political opportunity structure, and cultural framing—have probed the forces and conditions for social movement success. Most of the literature presents broad theoretical treatments and refinements of resource mobilization, political process, and framing approaches or assesses their usefulness for explaining the success or failure of particular social movements.[7] A systematic focus on issue differences is a useful strategy for organizing our knowledge by collating and categorizing cases drawn from a number of studies. It helps build empirical generalizations about what conditions determine social movement success by bringing different cases in relation to one another using a common set of concepts and variables.

A recurrent problem in social movement theory is the assumption of a single source of social movement success. Depending upon the theory, success comes to those movements that mobilize the most resources and pursue the most astute strategies, that enjoy a political opportunity structure that provides access to sympathetic elites and coalition partners, or that possess a repertoire of cultural frames that key political actors find compelling. The issue-based approach, in contrast, sees the possibility of different paths to social movement success within the agendas of social movements as well as across movements. Success may come from a sympathetic set of relatively autonomous elites, group mobilization and coalition building, appeals to the public for support, or some combination of these.

A focus on issues is a useful strategy for building generalizations because it focuses our attention on critical political properties that issues share *across social movements.* We are more likely to find political properties that are important for explaining success that are common to issues across movements than across issues that encompass the agenda of a single social movement. For example, the conditions that led to extending the voting franchise to women may bear a closer resemblance to the conditions conducive to protecting gays and lesbians and African Americans from nondiscrimination than to the conditions that led to success on other women's rights issues, like abortion and inclusion in the military. Likewise, abortion politics may bear a closer resemblance to the politics of gay adoption, gay marriage, and busing to achieve racial integration than to women's suffrage.

The typology presented earlier is useful for understanding the pattern of successes and failures of other social movements. While we cannot fully explore the utility of this approach for building generalizations applicable across social movements, a review of some examples from the women's and black civil rights movements illustrates the potential of this approach. Despite differences among these movements and historical contexts, many of the same general forces have operated to shape their policy fortunes.

Women's suffrage and black civil rights in employment, public accommodations, and voting are examples of liberal pluralist issues. Suffrage pitted women's rights organizations and their allies against liquor, brewing, railroad, and manufacturing interests and urban political machines. Suffrage groups developed an array of strategies and tactics that included public education and grassroots organizing referenda campaigns, professional lobbying, and confrontational tactics. They received critical support from stakeholders and coalition partners, including abolitionists, temperance workers, populists, and progressives, all of which supplied a repertoire of strategies and tactics and all of whose political goals meshed well with those of suffrage. The battle for suffrage, which lasted for decades, was first won in many western and midwestern states, where the populist and progressive movements were strong, before the federal government finally granted women the right to vote in 1920 (Banaszak 1996). Gauging the level of public support for women's suffrage is difficult because opinion polls did not exist, but state referenda on giving women the right to vote garnered, on average, half of the male population (plus, presumably, support from most women).

The black civil rights movement grew in the years before and after World War II along with economic and demographic changes in the South, particularly the urbanization of the black population, the growth of black churches, and the black middle class (Goldfield 1997, 262–95; McAdam 1982; Morris 1984; Piven and Cloward 1977). Black ministers; college students; and liberal religious, human rights, and labor activists coalesced and employed a number of different tactics, including demonstrations and confrontation with their opponents, much like women's suffrage groups did decades earlier. The public perceived this first wave of civil rights policies

—nondiscrimination in employment and public accommodations and voting rights—as "color blind." Public support, especially among northern whites, rose rapidly between 1963 and congressional passage of the Civil Rights Act of 1964 and the Voting Rights Act of 1965 (Schuman, Steeh, and Bobo 1985, 22–27; Erskine 1967, 486). The public and political elites, including President John Kennedy, recoiled against the brutality launched by southern segregationists in their effort to repress the movement, which intensified the demands and militancy of the protesters and charismatic leaders like Dr. Martin Luther King. Kennedy's assassination gave further impetus to efforts to enact the Civil Rights Act, and Lyndon Johnson's landslide election in 1964 ushered in large Democratic majorities.

Abortion politics, the integration of blacks in the military, and school busing to achieve racial integration exemplify liberal elitist issues. Like gay adoption and the legalization of homosexual conduct, the public was opposed to the integration of African Americans in the military and busing to achieve racial desegregation, and it remains sharply divided over abortion policy.[8] The courts' role was as pivotal in abortion and busing as it was in approving adoption rights for gays and sweeping aside sodomy laws. The U.S. Supreme Court has adhered to the core of its 1973 *Roe v. Wade* decision that women have a right to choose abortion, although the Court's dominant role has made abortion much more salient and controversial than the gay rights cases that fit under this category. The federal courts were politically isolated in pursuing busing. Building upon *Brown v. Board of Education* and a series of cases that followed, the Burger Court in the 1970s declared busing a legitimate tool for pursing the mandate to desegregate schools as thoroughly and rapidly as possible (Orfield 1978, 1–15). Although busing orders met with stiff resistance and were much less successful than their supporters had hoped, courts pursued the policy vigorously in many communities for several years. The political opportunity structure similarly favored the integration of blacks in the military. President Harry Truman was able to issue an executive order on his own, had the support of some branches of the military, and faced a likely rebellion in his own party from blacks and white liberals (who outnumbered white southerners) and the possible nomination of a pro–civil rights Republican to run against him.

The politics of the Equal Rights Amendment (ERA) resembles a traditional veto group issue. Throughout the debate over the ERA, a stable majority of Americans, averaging 57 percent, supported it. Majorities in the

U.S. House and Senate passed the ERA, and a significant majority of states (thirty-five) ratified it. But the political opportunity structure tilted in favor of the anti-ERA side. Constitutional amendments require ratification by three-quarters of the states, a formidable institutional obstacle that ERA supporters could not overcome in the face of a threatened and determined minority of social conservatives and religious fundamentalists who were strong in rural and southern states. The anti-ERA forces succeeded in redefining the issue as one of upending the traditional roles of men and women that could have radical social implications. Public support at the national level masked declining support over the course of the campaign in the non-ratified states. Coalitions of "right wing" and "mainstream conservative" state politicians who controlled many of the state legislatures also encountered conservative local businesses that worried about how the ERA might empower the federal courts (Mansbridge 1986).[9]

The issue-based approach helps us understand better why some social movements experience greater success (or experience it more rapidly) than others. Because political opportunity structures, social movements' resources, and public opinion vary across issues, a social movement's overall success depends upon the kinds of issues on its agenda. Hence, the distribution of issues among the four categories determines the rate of success that a movement experiences. The agendas of successful social movements include mainly liberal elitist and liberal pluralist issues. Because social movements help to shape their agendas, they have some control over their chances for success. Successful social movements avoid traditional populist and traditional veto group issues, or they reframe them and steer them toward institutional venues that are compatible with liberal elitist or liberal pluralist issues.

WHITHER LGBT RIGHTS?

What might the future hold for the politics of gay and lesbian rights? Predicting political trends and events is hazardous. Who in the 1960s would have envisioned the spread of civil rights ordinances protecting gays in the decades that followed? Who knew that the AIDS crisis would eventually strengthen the gay rights movement? How many people in 1990 anticipated that gay marriage would become a serious topic of debate just a few years later? John D'Emilio (2000) describes the history of the gay rights movement as a series of "leaps and creeps"—periods of drift and slow progress punctuated by rapid, large-scale advancement. Some of the conditions that shape the policy fortunes of social movements are difficult to predict and often change abruptly. Which party controls the government can change from one election to the next. Focusing events like the AIDS crisis and the murder of Matthew Sheppard in Wyoming occur unexpectedly and capture attention. Other events—like demographic and attitudinal change—take longer. It is not clear when changes conducive to advancing gay rights will occur, how long they will last, or if they will have the impacts that advocates expect.

Despite uncertainty, it is not hard to see that some outcomes are more likely than others in the short to medium term. Let us first consider what might happen at the national level before turning our attention to the states.

Prospects at the National Level

We have seen that gay rights advocates have experienced meager success in Washington. Social conservatives have dominated national politics since the late 1970s. Policy battles in Washington are more salient because of the media's attention and the winner-take-all nature of national policymaking. Governmental solutions to social problems at the national level incur greater ideological resistance. Although these hurdles are not easy to overcome, social movements made progress in Washington during the 1960s and 1970s and in other periods. The chances for advancing progressive legislation and minority group interests at the national level are historically contingent. The election of Democratic majorities to Congress in 2006 and 2008 should help to get gay rights legislation back on the agenda. If the Democrats can enlarge their majorities in the House and Senate, and take over the White House (or work with a socially moderate Republican president), further breakthroughs appear on the horizon.

Advancing gay rights in Washington is far more efficient than having to wage a multitude of separate battles at the state and local levels. Further progress in the states and localities may be more difficult as states and communities that have already adopted gay rights policies tend to be more politically moderate. Finally, only action at the federal level can lift the ban on gays in the military.

Chances for future success vary across issues, as we have seen. Gay rights advocates in Washington face their best prospects for gaining hate crimes and civil rights protections (Toner 2007; Murray 2007)—goals that enjoy high levels of public support because they do not appear to sanction same-sex conduct and relationships. Hate crimes protection is the most politically feasible goal. Such a law would merely extend the existing federal hate crimes statute to gays, women, and the disabled. Even many people who do not condone homosexuality are willing to levy extra penalties for bias-motivated attacks. Supporters can portray hate crimes protection as a law and order issue rather than a gay rights issue. With Democrats in control of Congress, Republican leaders are no longer able to kill hate crimes legislation in conference committees as they did earlier. The House and Senate approved the measure in 2000, 2004, and 2007, but the George W. Bush administration is threatening a veto as this book goes to press (Bell 2007b; Simon 2007; Murray 2007).

Most Americans also support equal treatment for gays in employment, housing, and public accommodations. The House passed the Employment Non-Discrimination Act (ENDA) for the first time in 2007 (although without protection for transgendered persons) by a vote of 235–184 (Neuman 2007). ENDA came within a single vote of passage in 1996 in the Senate. Over a decade of generational turnover favorable to gays and lesbians has occurred since the Senate voted. President Bush has threatened a veto of the measure if it reaches his desk. State and local nondiscrimination laws cover about half of the population, more than were covered in 1996. A compelling argument for other jurisdictions to adopt such laws is the lack of problems that have arisen in jurisdictions that have adopted them. This issue poses greater obstacles to passage than hate crimes legislation, however, because gay rights opponents will claim that it is a stepping-stone to gay marriage and small businesses will complain that ENDA will spur litigation and federal regulation.

Lifting the military ban will be more difficult than enacting anti–hate crimes and nondiscrimination policies because of opposition from the military and the deference that Congress pays to its judgments. Prospects for lifting the ban have improved, however, since the issue was on the agenda fourteen years ago. Public support for permitting gays to serve in the military is about as high as it is for hate crimes and employment nondiscrimination laws, about 80 percent (AEI 2004, 13). On the specific question of allowing gays to serve "openly," support has risen from 52 percent in 1994 to 56 percent in 2000 and 60 percent in 2006 (Henry J. Kaiser 2001; *USA*

Today 2007). Gay and lesbian former service members have built larger organizations devoted to their cause than in the past, such as the Service Members Legal Defense Network. Most importantly, younger generations of military service members appear more accepting of gays than their predecessors were a decade or more ago (Alvarez 2006), just as younger cohorts in the civilian population are more tolerant and relaxed about homosexuality. In a recent poll of troops who served in Iraq and Afghanistan, 73 percent said they were "comfortable serving in the presence of gays" (*USA Today* 2007). [10] Most nations have lifted their bans, including America's closest ally, Great Britain. The United States is one of only three democracies that still have a ban.[11] Foreign experience provides a clear lesson—allowing gays to be open in the military does not create disruptions.[12] Finally, the military's human resource needs make a more inclusive personnel policy more imperative if recruitment levels continue to lag and the demands upon U.S. forces persist from the war on terror and other threats (Alvarez 2006).

Favorable legislation and court rulings at the national level are a long way off in family and relationship issues. Matters related to children will remain squarely state and local concerns. Congress and the president are not about to approve gay marriage or civil unions, and it does not seem likely that the Supreme Court will invalidate state bans on same-sex marriage in the near to medium term. Gaining same-sex partner eligibility for federal benefits, such as Social Security, appears far off in the future. The best that one can expect is that Congress will continue to refrain from passing a federal constitutional amendment prohibiting gay marriage and allow the states to make their own choices in this area.

In the wake of the *Lawrence* decision, close observers of the Supreme Court speculated about the ruling's impact on other LGBT issues, particularly gay marriage. Despite Justice Anthony Kennedy's admonition that *Lawrence* did not involve same-sex marriage, a wide range of observers, from Justice Antonin Scalia to Harvard Law Professor Lawrence Tribe, predicted that the decision would pave the way to marriage. Other experts believe that the impacts of *Lawrence* are unclear and probably far off (see Parshall 2005; *Harvard Law Review* 2005; Eskridge 2004; Harcourt 2004; Tribe 2004; Kelman 2005; Hirsch 2005). Since the Court ruled in *Lawrence,* a conservative Republican president has appointed two new justices who, so far, appear to align themselves usually with the Court's conservative bloc. President Bush may make additional appointments to the Court (albeit with Democrats in charge of the Senate) and so, too, may his successor. All one can say with any certainty is that the current Court would seem an unlikely champion of same-sex partnership recognition.

Prospects at the State Level

Because it will take bipartisanship in Congress and presidential support to gain adoption of gay rights measures in Washington, states and localities will remain the key venues for policymaking on marriage and family issues. Breakthroughs at the national level, with their broad implications and high salience, may set off a backlash. This is why the Democrats who took control of Congress in 2007 have been cautious so far in advancing their agenda on cultural issues (Toner 2007). Citizens are less likely to notice, and more likely to accept, policy breakthroughs at the subnational levels. The public hardly seems to notice slow but steady progress in the spread of progay employment nondiscrimination, adoption, and hate crimes policies.

If social and demographic trends continue to reflect a gradual building of tolerance and acceptance of gays and lesbians among the public, and if political conditions in the states are favorable, the number of states with progay policies should increase. Research on gay rights at the state level provides clues about which states might adopt civil rights protections for gays and lesbians next. States and localities with more liberal and moderate elites and mass publics, fewer fundamentalists, higher education levels, and higher levels of resources among gay rights interest groups are those most likely to adopt gay rights measures in the future. Which states might be next to pass such a law? Consider the thirty-three states that did not have antidiscrimination laws covering sexual orientation as of 2006. Five of those states—Pennsylvania, Michigan, Colorado, Delaware, and Oregon—ranked among the top ten states on at least four of these five measures: elite and citizen ideology, Protestant fundamentalism, gay rights groups' resources, and education levels.[13] They were the most likely to adopt antidiscrimination laws. Oregon and Colorado, in addition to Iowa, enacted their laws in 2007.[14] Adding Oregon, Colorado, and Iowa to the seventeen others that already had nondiscrimination laws has increased the proportion of Americans covered to more than half of the population.

Opinions differ on whether the LGBT movement is likely to win the struggle over gay marriage in the long run, but the battle is resolved in the vast majority of states for the near future.[15] What remains to be determined is how many states adopt civil unions or a package of partner benefits that approximates them. Lewis and Oh (2006) collected state-level public opinion data on support for gay marriage that serve as a proxy for gauging support for civil unions and domestic partner benefit policies. Levels of support for gay marriage in states that have nondiscrimination laws covering sexual orientation, like Rhode Island, New York, New Hampshire, Maine, Washington, Nevada, New Mexico, Minnesota, Maryland, and Illinois, are similar to the levels in certain states that have marriage, civil unions or significant partner benefit packages (Vermont, Connecticut, California, and New Jersey) (Lewis and Oh 2006, 33). These ten states are the most likely candidates to adopt civil unions or partner benefits in the near future. With Democrats making gains across the country in the 2006 election, two of them—New Hampshire and Washington state—in addition to Oregon adopted civil unions or similar policies in 2007.[16]

RECONSIDERING LGBT MOVEMENT
STRATEGIES AND TACTICS

Gay rights organizations face significant constraints in coordinating their activities and influencing government. The movement is a loose collection of organizations that serves a socially diverse constituency, including many closeted individuals.[17] Broader political forces and conditions also constrain the movement. A decentralized government affords advocates on both sides multiple points of access to policymakers and makes it hard for the movement's leaders to pursue coherent strategies. For example, the judicial victories of a handful of progay marriage plaintiffs in a few states had a profound nationwide impact on the LGBT movement's agenda. Dramatic events like the Hawaii and Massachusetts court rulings on marriage, the AIDS crisis, and hate crime murders create pressure on movement leaders to reorient priorities and allocate scarce resources to those issues. Movement leaders must often wait until gays face life-threatening situations, such as the AIDS crisis and hate crimes outbreaks, to induce grassroots mobilization and build their organizations (Andriote 1999).

These constraints are not so strong that they render the movement irrelevant, however. Social movements succeed only when they mobilize supporters and challenge dominant interests. A strong, mobilized gay rights movement is not a sufficient condition for political success, but it is almost certainly a necessary one in politics today. Gay rights supporters cannot take mobilization for granted, as the failed effort to lift the ban on gays in the military makes clear (Rimmerman 1996b). LGBT organizations must continue to build their strength at the grassroots by offering opportunities for participation and pursuing issues that ordinary gays and lesbians care about.

This section presents recommendations for how LGBT rights organizations might increase their chances for success in the public policy arena. Some observers have presented ambitious plans to reorient the movement's goals and strategies, arguing that the movement should move beyond identity-based goals, mainstream institutions, and "insider" strategies of assimilation. Instead, it should pursue broader aims of social equality, liberation, cultural transformation, and "outsider" strategies of influence.[18] These recommendations may have merit, but it is not clear that they would be politically feasible or that the movement's political effectiveness would improve. The recommendations offered here are drawn from the findings of this study, with political realism and effectiveness in mind. Some LGBT activists undoubtedly know about and employ these strategies and tactics already; this discussion affirms what they are doing and points others in a new direction.

Strategies Related to the Institutional Context

The movement's chances for success should improve if it adopts strategies and tactics that build support with stakeholders and that shift conflict resolution, where feasible, to institutional venues that are more hospitable to their demands.

CULTIVATING STAKEHOLDERS' SUPPORT

Gay rights advocates often succeed when they secure the support of crucial stakeholders and encourage their active engagement in the policymaking process. Advocates can educate potential coalition partners about the deprivations that gays, lesbians, and transgendered people suffer and how joining with them can serve the interests of their constituencies as well. Gay rights leaders and activists should be attuned to the policy goals and preferences of potential allies and the kinds of appeals that will attract them. LGBT advocates should continue to court sympathetic stakeholders—like adoption agencies, social workers, victim groups, law enforcement officers, and liberal civil rights organizations—in the relevant policy arenas in which their support is critical. Enlisting the support of the military may seem daunting, but the time is auspicious for reaching out to military leaders and ordinary service members to help lift the ban. Younger service members are more willing to permit gays to serve openly, as are some military leaders (Shalikashvili 2007; Spiegel 2007).

Same-sex marriage is the only issue for which cultivating stakeholders' support may not be a viable strategy, as no such groups have emerged. But if gays and lesbians are willing to settle for legal recognition of their partnerships short of marriage, then the LGBT movement might build alliances with other demographic groups that, like lesbians and gays, are disadvantaged by policies that currently privilege heterosexual marriage. The activist group BeyondMarriage.org (2006) points out that most Americans no longer live in traditional nuclear families and that a wide variety of nontraditional families and relationships and kinship networks exist. Gays and lesbians might find common cause with senior citizens living with and caring for each other, adult children living with and caring for their parents, grandparents and other relatives raising children, single-parent households, and cohabitating heterosexuals that could benefit from the same kind of recognition and entitlement status for government benefits that currently only go to married people. These potential allies might be harder to organize than other stakeholders, but gays and lesbians have successfully formed alliances with similar grassroots constituencies in struggles to gain the adoption of hate crimes and employment nondiscrimination measures.

VENUE CHANGE

Where feasible, advocates should channel their demands to institutional venues that might improve their chances for success. Advocates frequently have little or no choice about the institutional venue in which to pursue their policy goals, but sometimes they do. Because advocates have been successful in gaining legislative adoption of hate crimes and civil rights protections and the courts have limited ability to expand those protections in the absence of statutes, they should continue that course. Further, because Congress codified the ban on gays serving openly in 1993, advocates can no longer simply lobby the president to issue an executive order to lift the ban. Getting the judiciary to overturn the ban is unlikely because courts generally defer to the military and most courts are reluctant to apply anything more stringent than the "rational basis" test to cases of sexual orientation discrimination. The Democrats' current control of Congress raises the possibility that a legislative strategy might work, and they plan to hold hearings on the issue (Bell 2007a).

Proponents of gay marriage should reconsider their strategy of seeking to secure marriage rights and civil unions through the courts.[19] Their preference for a litigation strategy is understandable because they have made some progress through the courts and numerous legislatures have passed bans on same-sex marriage. However, going through the courts is no guarantee of victory, and such efforts can backfire (D'Emilio 2007, 52–61). First, more state courts have refused to rule in favor of same-sex couples than have ruled in their favor. Second, the experience with favorable same-sex marriage court rulings, such as those in Hawaii and Massachusetts, shows that LGBT advocates must be careful in seeking redress through the courts on highly salient issues where they face intractable public opposition. The backlashes that judicial victories ignited led to broad statutory and constitutional bans that jeopardize civil unions and domestic partnership policies along with marriage. Advocates should stop basing decisions about whether to litigate primarily on the prospects for winning cases in particular jurisdictions. Instead, they should carefully assess the broader political ramifications if they are victorious. Before going to the courts, or in place of litigation, gay rights activists should more carefully plan their legal strategies and do considerably more political groundwork than they have done. Heterosexuals' exclusive claim on marriage is so rooted in history and social convention that it is unrealistic to think that LGBT activists could recast marriage in such a fundamental way through court orders alone (D'Emilio 2007, 58).

Judges do not enjoy the same level of democratic legitimacy as popularly elected officeholders. Gay rights opponents use "judicial activism" to whip up support for measures that outlaw marriage and other forms of partner recognition. Because court decisions are more likely to be perceived to produce a final victory for one side, they are likely to evoke fierce resistance from anti-same-sex marriage opponents. Legislative solutions are more likely to produce compromises, which may realistically be the best that gay rights advocates can accomplish on such a contentious subject at this time.

In its reliance on the assertion of rights claims, the judicial strategy diminishes the importance of other kinds of claims that may be more politically appealing, such as the ways in which policies that improve the lives of gays can benefit the community or some large segment of it. The rights-based model works well for issues relevant to impersonal social contexts that treat gays as individuals, like discrimination in the workplace. It is less appropriate for issues that directly raise the issue of the moral and social status of homosexual conduct and relationships, such as marriage and children's welfare. The legislative strategy is much less likely to ignite a backlash that could spread to other states. An increasing number of states—Connecticut, New Hampshire, and Oregon, for example—demonstrate that it is possible to gain the adoption of civil unions or domestic partnership policies without court orders, while keeping litigation as a reserve strategy (Killian 2006). While steadily building public and legislative support for civil unions may work best in small- to medium-size "blue" states,[20] plenty of these states currently do not provide same-sex partners with such benefits.

Although gay couples seeking to adopt children have been reasonably successful within the decentralized, low-salience context of state and local courts, gay adoption supporters many consider lobbying state legislatures. Many of the states in which adoption is available to gay couples require the couples to venue shop. Legislation would make adoption available across the state regardless of which county the couples reside. Although many Americans remain wary of gay parenting, support for it has risen since the early 1990s. The fact that many state laws neither allow nor prohibit gays to adopt means that legislators inclined to permit gay couples to adopt will not need to reverse an existing prohibition, and many states have large numbers of foster children who await permanent homes. A growing number of studies indicate that gay parents are as qualified as straight ones, and virtually all medical and child welfare professional organizations endorse gay adoption. States and counties that permit gay adoption provide models for how gay and lesbian parents can contribute to reducing the number of children awaiting adoption for jurisdictions without such laws.

Strategies to Win Over Public Opinion

Social movement organizations help to shape public opinion on issues of relevance to them. They play a key role in educating the public and framing issues for the media, policymakers, and citizens. Gay rights leaders and their allies in government should frame their issues differently than how they usually frame them. Changing issue definition strategies and tactics might improve the chances for winning the public over to gay rights and reducing Americans' fears and concerns. In particular, gay rights advocates should better reflect how those citizens most acutely affected by discrimination feel about them. In her study of how same-sex couples discuss same-sex marriage, Kathleen Hull (2006, 191) was struck by "how the public debates omit or distort the views and concerns of average gays and lesbians." The views of ordinary gays and lesbians have a ring of authenticity to them that are most likely to resonate with heterosexuals as well as directly challenge unwarranted heterosexist assumptions.

FULL EQUALITY VERSUS PRACTICAL NEEDS AND RECOGNITION

The importance that many gays and lesbians assign to marriage is no surprise, given the "cultural power of law" that Hull found. In addition to their interest in acquiring the tangible legal rights and benefits that come with marriage, many of Hull's informants called attention to the "social legitimacy that legal marriage would bring to same-sex relationships, the sense that legal recognition would render same-sex couples socially normal and culturally equal to heterosexual married people" (Hull 2006, 3).

Many gays and lesbians will view any strategy that retreats from marriage, and that focuses instead upon obtaining the rights and benefits associated with it, as "separate but equal." While neither the major LGBT organizations nor ordinary gays and lesbians are as preoccupied with the fight for marriage as are gay rights opponents and the media (see chapter 1), marriage is important to many gays and lesbians, particularly younger ones. In her interviews of more than seventy members of same-sex couples, Hull (2006, 24) reports that most same-sex couples believe that legal recognition for them "should take the form of marriage rather than domestic partnerships or civil unions." Opinion surveys indicate that about half of gays and lesbians do not consider civil unions the same as marriage, and more than three-quarters of gays and lesbians would want to get legally married if they were in a committed relationship. According to Egan and Sherrill (2005a, 231), "same-sex marriage appears to be an issue that resonates with everyday LGBT people to a degree even stronger than it does with elites—and it is reminiscent of the younger . . . activists who overcame the reluctance of older, more traditional LGBTs to develop new goals and tactics in the days after the Stonewall Rebellion." "Civil marriage" ranks particularly high among the priorities of LGBTs in the 18–25 and 26–44 age groups. Thus, gays' desire to be married and the cultural status of marriage will not diminish even if, as BeyondMarriage.org (2006) advocates recommend, the government grants legal recognition and benefits to non-marital households and nontraditional families and policymakers sever the legal entitlement to benefits from marital status.

Nevertheless, a sensible political strategy would avoid making "the perfect the enemy of the good." The reality is that the campaign for "full marriage equality" has boomeranged to the point that it endangers all forms of same-sex partner recognition, and a strategy that focuses on civil unions and domestic partner benefits promises real gains. Legally and culturally, marriage as the union of a man and a woman has been a fixed feature in our society, even though other aspects of marriage have changed substantially over the years. Groups in the United States that have tried to challenge this norm, such as the early Mormons, met stiff resistance and failed (see D'Emilio 2007, 58). It is difficult to think of an issue that holds out less possibility of success for a minority group in the United States. Borrowing a page from President Lyndon Johnson, gay and lesbian activists should ask themselves if they want "an issue" or tangible benefits and a legitimization of their relationships. As the BeyondMarrriage.org (2006) critics argue, the movement should stop making same-sex marriage a high priority and instead work to end the privileged position of marriage in legal entitlements and push for new legal arrangements that recognize and protect the majority of Americans who live in committed nonmarital relationships by separating government benefits and legal recognition from marital status. Many of the feelings of inferiority and disrespect that gay and lesbian couples experience arise from practical problems in daily life—like being denied control over medical decisions or having to pay inheritance taxes—and would be remedied with gaining civil unions or comprehensive packages of partner benefits.

In framing the relationship recognition issue, the most effective response that supporters of same-sex marriage can make to their opponents' arguments that gay rights threaten tradition and social order is *not* necessarily that legitimizing same-sex relationships is consistent with liberal principles like freedom and equality. Instead, they should frame these issues as specific, concrete, practical needs. Americans are more likely to find arguments that point out the practical effects of social policy on people's lives more compelling than ideological appeals. The financial, time, and emotional burdens on gays and lesbians (and their families and employers) from a lack of partner rights and benefits are significant and numerous (Riggle and Rostosky 2007). Heterosexuals should be asked to consider how they would respond if it were *their children* who were not covered by a partner's health insurance or Social Security survivor's benefits, or if it were *their spouse* who could not visit them in the hospital or who had to pay thousands of dollars in inheritance taxes.

In the analysis of arguments advanced for lifting the military ban in chapter 3, arguments about practical impacts, such as the contributions that gays and lesbians make to the military; the costs of enforcing the don't ask, don't tell policy; and the experience of foreign militaries that have lifted their bans all ranked behind principled arguments about civil rights. Similarly, in the debate over marriage, the practical impacts of the lack of partner recognition and benefits have taken a backseat to arguments about equality and nondiscrimination. Hull's (2006) analysis found that many gays and lesbians are willing to compromise on the issue of marriage, but that this point mostly gets lost in the highly polarized debate in which advocates only present "marriage" or "no marriage" as the available options.

Emphasizing practical needs over broad principles meshes nicely with an incremental strategy. Incremental policy change is always less salient and perceived as less threatening than wholesale changes. Same-sex partner recognition lends itself to incrementalism by transforming a highly symbolic issue like same-sex marriage, giving it a label that does not tap into people's emotions, and disaggregating it into myriad legal and material components about which it is easier to find common political ground. Opinion polls show that the public has greater support for civil unions than for marriage, and that it supports giving gays specific, concrete rights and benefits more than civil unions (AEI 2004). Emphasizing the practical needs involved in partner recognition and parental rights transforms a seemingly broad, radical, highly symbolic, and threatening demand into a set of limited, specific, and practical reforms that most people will not find threatening and to which most heterosexuals can relate. Thus, advocates should focus on securing particular rights and benefits for same-sex couples, such as to hospital visitation and health care decisions for partners, inheritance rights, and eligibility for other benefits provided by government.

SOCIAL RECOGNITION, SHARED VALUES, AND GAINS FOR SOCIETY

LGBT advocates should stop ceding discourse over the moral aspects of homosexuality and gay rights to their opponents and make their own explicit moral arguments. The LGBT rights movement's "secular liberal identity" makes it difficult for its spokespersons to enter into conversations about morality and religious teaching (Shaiko 2007). The conventional liberal position that maintains neutrality about the morality of private consensual conduct is problematic for debates over gay marriage and family-related issues (Ball 2003). Whether advocates champion marriage or more politically obtainable domestic partner recognition, they should make clear that they are demanding legitimacy for their lives and relationships as much as gaining tangible rights and benefits (see Hull 2006, 126–32). Advocates must go beyond demanding equal and fair treatment to address the moral *reasons* that make such recognition appropriate. They should make clear that same-sex partnerships and parental relationships can be as deeply loving, committed, and respectful as those of heterosexuals, and that the difference between same-sex and opposite-sex relationships—mainly whether the genitals of the partners are the same or different—is morally irrelevant. Because same-sex couples are deserving of society's validation, and marriage validates the legitimacy of spousal relationships, society must accord same-sex relationships the same or an equivalent civil status.

Moral considerations must include more than judgments about the legitimacy of individuals' conduct and relationships. They must also include whether legal recognition of same-sex relationships promotes good for society. Battles over gay rights are not only about gays and lesbians. Gay activists should avoid talking about the needs of gays and lesbians as if they exist in isolation from the rest of society and talk more about how awarding gays and lesbians new rights and opportunities contributes to broadly shared social goals. A crucial strategy for framing gay rights issues is to transform them from divisive issues over competing values—tradition and order versus freedom and social equality—into valence issues about which most people approve. Because many gays and lesbians have decided that they want to serve in the military and enter into marriage or a similar state-sanctioned status, they must convince policymakers and citizens that they are willing to uphold the values that these institutions purport to promote.

Some LGBT activists may be uncomfortable with incorporating inherently conservative values like social stability and assimilation in their appeals for marriage and other forms of partner recognition. Appeals based upon stability and assimilation and social equality are not mutually exclusive, however. Ultimately, advocates must decide whether it is more important to broaden support for partner and parental rights and for reforming the military than to maintain ideological purity.[21] Embracing conservative values as a strategy for gaining support does not mean that the movement needs to adopt tactics that are deferential or excessively polite to the heterosexual majority. Advocates should not shrink from pointing out the hypocrisy of divorce and the lax standards for who qualifies for heterosexual marriage, for example.

Here again, Hull (2006) found a gap between advocates' public rhetoric and the sentiments expressed by ordinary same-sex couples. Proponents of same-sex marriage in the debates that she examined failed to "mount an argument for same-sex marriage as a substantive moral good" (Hull 2006, 191). The data presented in chapter 3 of this book confirm Hull's findings, and they suggest that LGBT advocates are more successful when they emphasize definitions that transform gay rights issues into valence issues, calling attention to how expanding rights for gays and lesbians benefits society as a whole. For example, advocates of gay adoption frame the issue foremost in terms of promoting children's welfare, not as fairness to gays. Proponents of gay marriage and of allowing gays to serve openly in the military, in contrast, frame those issues overwhelmingly in terms of the wrongness of discrimination and the violation of gays and lesbians' civil rights, or they try to evade discussing the substantive merits altogether by making procedural or purely partisan points. Arguments about how gays contribute to national defense through their valor and sacrifice and about the high costs of investigating and prosecuting gay service members and of training their replacements lag far behind in the policy debate. Supporters of gay marriage similarly emphasize egalitarian definitions instead of how society benefits from having stronger, more committed spousal relationships.

A strong justification for allowing gays to marry or enter into civil unions is that society benefits when it treats gay relationships as equivalent to those of heterosexuals. Proponents should stress that people should judge relationships between same-sex partners according to the same criteria that we judge heterosexual relationships—how they contribute to social welfare, in addition to the partners' mutual love, respect, and support. Such unions, whether same sex or opposite sex, when given the support and official recognition of the state, benefit not just the individuals who constitute them but also the entire society by stabilizing relationships so that the partners can provide support for each other and the children who are in their care. Fortifying families helps society by reducing the financial, emotional, and other costs associated with strained and weak family relationships. Just as businesses justify providing partner benefits to their same-sex employees on the grounds that attracting and retaining their workers helps the bottom line (and not simply out of "fairness" to them), advocates should talk more about how same-sex partner recognition reduces social isolation and promiscuity and strengthens families (Eskridge 1996; Sullivan 1996; Feldblum 1998).

Two examples of this kind of discourse come from legislative hearings in Connecticut and floor debate in Minnesota on same-sex partner recognition:[22]

> Marriage is more than a bundle of rights. It also promotes stability in relationships. . . . These couples do not seek to weaken marriage in any way. On the contrary, they want to pledge themselves to adhere to all of its great criteria and ideals. Love, fidelity, intimacy, financial support, health care responsibility, mutuality. Marriage needs more of that kind of commitment, not less. (Connecticut General Assembly 2002, 129)

> We should be encouraging people to make these life-long commitments. We should be proud that people want to do that. . . . I want to defend marriage too. If others want to be married, I like to see commitments like that. That is what we are as human beings: People who have the capacity to love and care for others. . . . (Minnesota Senate 1997)

INTERPERSONAL APPEALS

Because issues concerning sexual orientation are about private, personal conduct, what people think about gays and lesbians as individuals is important. Sexual orientation is a fundamental aspect of a person's identity; thus, even sympathetic heterosexuals may find it difficult to fully comprehend and empathize with gays and lesbians. As with the women's movement, LGBT rights advocates realize that "the personal is political." Much evidence indicates that people who know gays and lesbians personally tend to be less homophobic and more supportive of gay rights, including same-sex marriage and civil unions (see Wilcox et al. 2007, 236–37).

Dispassionate legal analyses and dry statistical studies increase knowledge about the problems that gays and lesbians face, but they cannot create empathy and counter negative stereotypes about gays and lesbians. Rather than merely assert abstract claims about "rights," "equality," and other broad principles, gay and lesbian activists and their families should convey directly to policymakers how they live their lives and the values they cherish as partners, parents, and members of the community (Fajer 1992; Henderson 1987). Gay marriage and adoption advocates cannot avoid addressing the desires of policymakers and citizens for reassurances that gays and lesbians are capable of loving and respectful relationships and that they genuinely care about, and take responsibility for, one another and their children.

Policymakers glean information about the character and competence of gay partners and parents by communicating with constituents and through personal experience. Legislative advocates call attention to the importance of personal testimonies and other interpersonal interactions in building understanding and trust. As a chief supporter of civil unions in the Connecticut Senate put it at a public hearing on the subject, "For those of you who would like to talk to your legislators individually, I would encourage you to seek out your representatives and senators and share with them your personal stories. That is, in fact, one of the most powerful educational tools that you could employ in your positions and in advance of the cause that you've testified on behalf today" (Connecticut General Assembly 2003, 141).

State Senator (and lesbian) Kate Brown (2007) cites personal testimony as critical for getting Oregon's legislature to adopt partner benefits: "I know that we changed hearts and minds and votes by the testimony that we gave on the Senate floor. I do believe that us sharing our personal stories really helps people understand, helps people connect, and helps people become supportive of the issues that we feel so strongly about."

Some of the most persuasive argumentation in favor of gay rights comes from openly gay public officials (see Rom 2007, 19). A Minnesota state representative (and lesbian) who helped lead her state's effort to adopt its nondiscrimination law similarly emphasized the importance of face-to-face encounters between gay and lesbian individuals and legislators (Clark 2001): "While speeches in the legislative bodies are important . . . a great deal of persuasion that enabled passage of Minnesota's law happened in one-to-one meetings with legislators and their constituents and in one-to-one meetings that both Sen. Spear [a gay man and the prime sponsor in the Senate] and I had with our colleagues over many years and occasions. The personal context was, in my opinion, much more formative in my colleagues' decision-making process than any great speech that I may or may not have made."

Adoption policy debates, in particular, afford gays and lesbians opportunities for pursuing interpersonal appeals. The best advocates for gay adoption are gay and lesbian parents, not lawyers, lobbyists, and social workers.

Gay parents convey the emotional attachment and devotion they feel toward their children in the most compelling manner. An important component of the political strategy to gain second-parent adoption has been to normalize gay parenting by constructing positive images of gays and lesbians to counter negative stereotypes of them as poor role models and harmful to children. Legislators, judges, and other policymakers learn about gay mothers and fathers and prospective parents from their experiences with family, friends, political supporters, and staff members; through informal contacts with constituents; and in legislative hearings. Adoption lawyers and agencies for gay clients advise gays and lesbians to tell their personal stories to judges and legislators in hearings and home study investigations of adoption applicants. Such settings permit policymakers to view gays and lesbians as fellow parents, stepparents, and grandparents rather than as members of pressure groups.

The message that gays and lesbians convey in telling their stories is that "we are like you": responsible, caring, loving, and struggling to overcome challenges that parents typically face. Gay parents show that they embrace mainstream values of home and hearth, God and country, like their straight peers.[23] As one gay parent and advocate from Washington, D.C., puts it, "Most people know someone who's lesbian or gay, in their communities, through their kids' schools. It is through those interactions that people come to understand we all want the same things—to create safe, loving environments for our kids" (quoted in Crary 2003).

Love Makes a Family, a grassroots coalition that lobbied the Connecticut legislature for second-parent adoptions, claims that the appearances of gay parents at legislative hearings and legislators' visits to their homes convinced legislators to support changes in the adoption law (Tuhus 2000).[24] Chapter 3 presents additional examples of this sort of testimony:

> I won't try to tell you that the first bottle feedings, diaper changes or baby baths went smoothly. Like most new parents we felt like dumb and dumber. Those first few nights were sleepless for us, not for our son. We were too nervous to sleep, too excited. We were quite smitten. Couldn't stop holding him, talking to him, singing to him. He felt like our son. Gradually it sank in, he is our son . . . My parents thought they would never have grandchildren. Jess [the child] has brought them the joy that only a grandchild can bring. We love Jess and raise him as our son. We have baptized him in our church. He has the

blessings of our church, our families, our community, our friends. Is it too much to ask for our state's blessing too? We ask you to do what's right for Jess. We ask you to do what is in his best interest.[25]

Gay couples have given similar personal testimonies to advance the cause of same-sex marriage and partner recognition. Whatever the forum in which they convey their testimonies, they reveal the deep commitment and mutual respect of these couples and the important role public policy can play in stabilizing their families. Personal stories should be encouraged and disseminated as a major tactic in educating the public and building support on this issue. Likewise, gay, lesbian, and bisexual former military service members have told stories of their desire to serve their country; their valor and exemplary conduct; the unfairness and indignities suffered under the don't ask, don't tell policy; and the loss to the nation by dismissing gay personnel and discouraging qualified individuals to join.

No one should underestimate the hard work and time that even incremental efforts entail. Gay rights advocates have only limited control over the public policy fortunes of their movement. Nevertheless, advocates can hasten success if they have a clear understanding of the constraints they face, devise strategies and tactics to mitigate them, and are ready when auspicious historical moments hold out realistic possibilities for reform.

Notes

1. In this book I use the terms "gay and lesbian," "homosexual," and "heterosexual" because they are the categories used overwhelmingly in American political discourse. I do not endorse these as "real" or "essential" categories as opposed to socially constructed.

I also use "LGBT," "gay," or "gay and lesbian" as shorthand for "gay, lesbian, bisexual, and transgendered." Gay rights organizations typically include transgendered persons among the groups they represent. According to a report by the National Gay and Lesbian Task Force, "the struggle to establish civil rights protections for transgendered people cannot be separated from the struggle to win freedom and equality for gay, lesbian and bisexual people" (Green 2000a, 6). The movements for gay rights and transgendered rights have been closely aligned. Although sexual orientation and sexual identity are distinct phenomena, many people who are transgendered are also gay. Further, as sexual minorities, both groups have suffered many of the same kinds of treatment. They have been socially ostracized and victims of hate crimes and discrimination in employment, housing, education, and parental rights. At the same time, the agendas of the gay rights and transgendered rights movements do not overlap completely. For example, the long process of transitioning from one gender to another requires access to expensive medical treatment, which may be difficult for transgendered persons to obtain. This issue has been of much greater concern to the transgendered community than to most gays, lesbians, and bisexuals. All books must draw boundaries about what they cover, and I have decided to focus on issues that are common concerns to the different constituencies of the LGBT movement.

The LGBT rights movement has been significantly less successful in gaining rights and protections for transgendered individuals than for gay men, lesbians, and bisexuals. Many gay rights laws and judicial rulings apply only to gays, lesbians, and bisexuals, although the transgendered movement has made some significant progress recently at the state and local levels. For example, twenty states have employment nondiscrimination laws that cover sexual orientation, but only thirteen states' laws cover gender identity as a protected category; thirty-two states cover sexual orientation in their hate crimes laws, but only ten cover gender identity. I do not investigate why efforts to promote the rights of the transgendered community have lagged behind those of gays, lesbians, and bisexuals. This topic is important in its own right and deserves a separate investigation. In particular, it demands an examination of the internal politics of the LGBT rights movement and of how policymakers treat demands for including sexual identity in civil rights laws and other public policies differently than they treat demands for including sexual orientation. Including transgendered individuals in proposed measures to protect gays, lesbians, and bisexuals can make it more difficult to gain their adoption, as failed efforts to include sexual identity under the Employment Non-Discrimination Act in the U.S. House of Representatives illustrate (Currah and Minter 2000; Neuman 2007).

2. A study released in 2006 by Caitlin Ryan of San Francisco State University reports that teenagers are coming out at about thirteen years of age on average (Advocate.com 2006).

3. See Yang (2003) and American Enterprise Institute (2004).

4. See Chasin (2000) and Gluckman and Reed (1997).

5. According to the Human Rights Campaign (2006a), 253 Fortune 500 companies (51 percent) offer domestic partners health insurance benefits and 430 (86 percent) include sexual orientation in their nondiscrimination policies.

6. See Gamson (1998) and Walters (2001).

7. The reference to "the gay rights movement," "the LGBT movement," etc., throughout this book is not meant to imply that it is a monolithic entity. Rimmerman (2002, 1), following Franklin Kameny, argues that multiple gay rights *movements* exist. In addition to the movement's organizational diversity and fragmentation, gay rights activists have disagreed about whether, for example, the movement should pursue assimilation or seek to transform American culture.

8. For a discussion of the evolution of the goals of the gay rights movement over the most recent decades, see D'Emilio (2000).

9. For a discussion of media coverage as an indicator of change in policy agendas, see Baumgartner and Jones (1993, 48–51, 253–59). Media coverage of issues appears to correspond to governmental concern with them, particularly when looking at agenda change in broad issue areas over long periods of time. Different indexes of media attention to issues reveal similar patterns of attention.

10. According to D'Emilio (2000, 45), "it would be very hard to dispute the claim that the overwhelming majority of activists—and probably a large majority of gay men and lesbians—agree that the following set of goals are highly desirable: the repeal of sodomy statutes criminalizing homosexual behavior; the removal of the medical classification of homosexuality as a disease; the elimination of discriminatory provisions and practices at every level of government and in every institution of civil society; fair and accurate presentation of gay life and gay issues in the media; due process of law, especially in relationship to the behavior of law enforcement

personnel toward lesbians and gays; recognition of family relationships; and protection against hate-motivated violence." Except for the removal of homosexuality as a mental disease and fair and accurate portrayals of gays in the media, *which are not public policy issues,* D'Emilio's list of goals is essentially the same as the ones examined in this study.

11. Each of the Web sites includes a list of issues that it deems of major importance to the LGBT movement. As of July 2006, "health/HIV-AIDS" was the only issue other than the six examined in this work that appears on the lists of all three organizations. This study excludes HIV-AIDS and other health issues because they are not about securing rights for gays and lesbians. HIV is prevalent among many groups besides gay men, and few lesbians have the disease. Other issues appeared on one or two of the organizations' Web sites: treatment of elderly gays (NGLTF, Lambda Legal); treatment of LGBT youth in schools and LGBT issues in educational curricula (NGLTF, Lambda Legal); immigration (HRC, Lambda Legal); and social and economic inequality (NGLTF). The remaining issues appearing on the Web sites concern how gays are treated on university campuses (NGTLF) and in organized religion (NGTLF, Lambda Legal). Finally, some of the issues on the NGTLF and HRC Web sites are not policy problems but are about political processes, such as upcoming elections, ballot measures (NGTLF), and judicial nominations (HRC). See www.thetaskforce.org, www.hrc.org, and www.lambdalegal.org.

12. Many other gay rights groups organized around specific issues mobilize at the national, state, and local levels. It is reasonable to expect that the pattern of attention that the NGLTF and the HRC pay to issues roughly mirrors the levels of attention of gay rights organizations in the aggregate, or at least gives us some indication of their priorities.

13. The sample was diverse, but it was not representative of the LGBT community as a whole (young people and women were overrepresented).

14. The results of the 2003 Harris Interactive poll are reported in Egan and Sherrill (2005a). The Harris Interactive model's scientific status is in dispute, but Harris asserts that it weights its data in a way that produces a representative sample (see http://harrisinteractive.com/partner/methodology.asp) .

15. The Stonewall riots, when patrons at a gay bar in Greenwich Village, New York City, responded violently to police harassment, marked the first time that homosexuals forcibly resisted their oppression.

16. "Civil rights" is used in this book interchangeably with laws against discrimination in employment, housing, and public accommodations.

17. Some of these issues may be less critical than others in the sense that gays and lesbians may enjoy a particular benefit (or enjoy it conditionally) even in the

absence of public policy change. For example, marriage, adoption, and custody confer benefits, rights, and responsibilities that gays and lesbians enjoy only if society grants them through public policy. These include, for example, inheritance rights, tax and welfare state benefits, spousal claims over property, and authority over children. Antidiscrimination policies, by contrast, do not confer new privileges and benefits. They merely protect gays and lesbians from bias-motivated actions of employers and others. Homosexuals can serve in the military and remain employed even in the most hostile work environments (as long as they keep their sexual orientation secret) without civil rights protections.

18. These and related points are discussed more fully in chapter 6.

19. The movement's organizations have developed dramatically as well. Since its emergence as a "homophile" movement in the 1950s and the Stonewall Rebellion in 1969, the gay rights movement has built an impressive set of organizations to pursue its political goals. The Human Rights Campaign and the National Gay and Lesbian Task Force, for example, have tens of thousands of members, large professional staffs, and multimillion-dollar budgets that raise campaign donations and carry out lobbying efforts. Lambda Legal and the American Civil Liberties Union devote substantial resources to litigating gay rights cases in federal and state courts. A multitude of other organizations pursue more circumscribed goals and operate at the state or local level. Still others are arms of the major political parties. At the same time, a formidable set of conservative and religious opponents emerged in the 1970s that grew size and influence, especially at the national level and in many parts of the United States.

20. Determining the success of a social movement according to how well it attains its stated goals has a long history; see, for example, Gamson (1975) and Piven and Cloward (1977). Amenta and Young (1999) propose measuring movement success according to the "potential collective goods" (material or symbolic) that the movement attains for the group that it is trying to benefit. This approach has drawbacks, however. First, unlike a movement's policy preferences, which are stated by movement organizations, the researcher has to decide what constitutes a potential good for the group to ascertain whether the movement has obtained collective goods. Merely counting how many members of the group are eligible for a benefit may not be a valid measure unless we know how much value members place on the benefit. For example, some gays and lesbians may think that marriage is very important, while others may think that it is of little importance or count it as a "cost" of a misguided effort to assimilate in mainstream culture. Second, some benefits may not be possible to quantify. It may be relatively easy to ascertain who would benefit and by how much from a program of old-age pensions (Amenta and

Young's example), but it is far more difficult to ascertain for many of the collective goods sought by gay rights organizations. One cannot ascertain, for example, how many more gays and lesbians would join or stay in the military if the ban were lifted (rates of discharge for violations of the current policy would include only some of these individuals) or how many gays and lesbians would gain jobs, promotions, and psychological comfort from nondiscrimination laws. For a discussion of different kinds of social movement success, see Staggenborg (1995).

21. Included here are policies that leave the movement's constituency worse off than before the government took action; see Amenta and Young (1999).

22. For works that examine these goals in the context of other social movements, see McAdam (1988, 1999), Taylor and Raeburn (1995), and Taylor and Whittier (1992). On the gay rights movement, see Hertzog (1996).

23. Gay and lesbian organizations help gay men and lesbians come out of the closet, encourage schools and the media to cultivate positive and realistic images of gays, provide support groups for the families and friends of gays and lesbians, and persuade employers to provide partner benefits and nondiscrimination policies. These activities benefit gays and lesbians directly and create a political climate that is more conducive to gay rights. For discussions of the cultural goals and impacts of social movements, see d'Anjou (1996), Rochon (1998), and McAdam (1994), and for the relative neglect of the study of these impacts in the social movement literature, see Earl (2000) and McAdam (1994).

24. Some impacts—like how many gay couples receive marriage licenses—are easy to verify, but some effects are much more difficult to ascertain, for example, whether a decline in discrimination or hate crimes is the result of public policy. Many outcomes are hard to observe because firm estimates of the size of the gay and lesbian population, which serves as the baseline for measuring the proportion of gays who benefit from a policy, do not exist. It is also difficult to use available data to make inferences about how severe problems are and whether gay rights laws ameliorate them. For example, an increase in reported hate crimes might indicate either that more crimes are being committed or that victims are more willing to report them. Similarly, polls that report more tolerant attitudes toward gays may be due to the deterrent and educational impacts of nondiscrimination laws or to the greater contact that people have with gays and lesbians.

25. Dufour (1998) examines four issues, but only for Chicago and the state of Illinois.

26. As public support for laws protecting gays against employment discrimination has grown, more jurisdictions have adopted such laws (Yang 1997; Lewis and Rogers 1999). On the other hand, opinion polls also have shown regularly that the

public favors allowing gays to serve openly in the military and is against gay adoption (Yang 1997; Wilcox and Wolpert 2000), which is the opposite of what one would expect if politicians were simply following the public's preferences.

27. Mooney and Schuldt (2006, 10–11) surveyed several hundred Illinois residents to see if they distinguished gay marriage and abortion regulation, two issues often said to exhibit "morality politics," from other issues (capital punishment, casino gambling, civil liberties versus homeland security, national health insurance versus tax cuts, and campaign contribution limits). They found that residents reported believing "that decisions about gay marriage and abortion policy could be best made by simply applying their basic values rather than by gathering more information" and that "their 'religious or moral beliefs and values' influenced their 'thinking on this issue'" in higher proportions than on the other issues.

28. The central concern of social movement theories has been how politically powerless groups emerge, overcome obstacles to collective action, and maintain organizations. Many theorists also address why movements succeed or fail in reaching their goals. For works that compare social movement theories, see Giugni (1999) and Crossley (2002). Political process and resource mobilization theories are often presented as alternative and competing theories of social movements (McAdam 1982), but they are not mutually exclusive. Particularly when resource mobilization theorists try to explain the success of social movements, some of their interpretations include changes in the political opportunities and the rules governing institutions that appear very similar to the political process approach. See, in particular, Jenkins (1983, 546–49) and Tilly (1978, 213–14). For a discussion of whether social movements are essentially the same as, or different from, interest groups, see Burstein (1998).

29. This model has been used to explain the successes and failures of urban protest movements (Schumaker 1975; Lipsky 1968), farm workers (Jenkins and Perrow 1977), and the women's movement (Freeman 1975).

30. Studies of the antinuclear (Kitschelt 1986), women's (Costain 1992; Banaszak 1996), black civil rights (McAdam 1982; Morris 1993), and redistributionist protest movements of the 1930s and 1960s (Amenta, Dunleavy, and Bernstein 1994; Eisinger 1973) adopt this approach.

31. Eisinger (1973) found that open systems tend to assimilate and co-opt the movements.

32. New social movements refer to those that emerged in the 1960s and 1970s around race, gender, and sexuality in contrast to those that organized earlier around class and material interests. New social movement theory appears less relevant to understanding public policy outcomes. It argues that individuals who participate

in these movements primarily aim to develop and express a collective identity and to change the culture, which those individuals view as more effective than change through political activity.

33. For figure 1.2, for the line indicating support for nondiscrimination against gays, in 1982, 1989, and 2007 Gallup asked, "In general, do you think homosexuals should or should not have equal rights in terms of job opportunities?" Princeton Survey Research Associates/Newsweek asked the same question for the remaining years on the chart (AEI 2004, 12; Roper Center 2008c). For the line indicating support for nondiscrimination laws, in 1983 and 1985, the *Los Angeles Times* asked "Do you favor or oppose laws to protect homosexuals against job discrimination?" and in 1989, 1992 and 1996 the National Election Survey asked the same question (Yang 1997, 497); in 2000 the Kaiser Family Foundation asked, "Do you think there should or should not be laws to protect gays and lesbians from prejudice and discrimination in job opportunities?" (Kaiser, November 2000, 9); in 2004, the *Los Angeles Times* asked "Do you favor or oppose laws to protect gays against job discrimination?" (American Enterprise Institute 2004, 12, 14).

34. The question asked by Princeton Survey Research Associates/Pew Research Center in 1994 and 2006 was, "As I list some programs and proposals that are being discussed in this country today, please tell me whether you strongly favor, favor, oppose or strongly oppose . . . allowing gays and lesbians to serve openly in the military?" (AEI 2006, 13). When given a choice between allowing gays "to serve openly in the military," to "serve under the current policy," or not allow them "to serve under any circumstances," the number of respondents who support allowing gays to serve openly drops to 46 percent, while a majority of 51 percent prefer either the current policy or an outright ban (Roper Center 2008e).

35. The question asked by Gallup in 1999 was, "If a hate law were enacted in your state, which of the following groups do you think should be covered? . . . How about homosexuals?" (http://www.gallup.com/poll/content/default.aspx?ci=3943; accessed 7/1/05, hard copy in possession of the author). The question asked by the Kaiser Family Foundation (2000) of adults ages 18–24 stated, "As you may know, there is a federal law that mandates increased penalties for people who commit crimes against blacks and other minorities out of prejudice against them. Would you favor or oppose a similar federal law that would mandate increased penalties for people who commit hate crimes out of prejudice toward gays and lesbians?"

36. The question routinely asked for decades by a variety of polls is, "Do you think homosexual relations between consenting adults should or should not be legal?" Support rises when the question asks about "two men" or "two women" having "sex with each other in their own home." (AEI 2004, 5–6; Roper Center 2008f).

37. Since 2000, Gallup has asked, "Would you favor or oppose a law that would allow homosexual couples to legally form civil unions, giving them some of the legal rights of married couples?" The percentage in favor stayed in the 41–46 percent range from 2000 to 2002, rose to 49 percent, then fell to 40 percent in 2003, and rose again to 54 percent in 2004. Some poll questions use the words "civil unions," while others describe the status. In addition, when the poll question gives respondents a choice between allowing gays "to get married," allowing "legal partnerships," or offering "no legal recognition," support for gay rights increases. Thirty percent support marriage, 30 percent support legal partnerships, and 32 percent want no legal recognition (Fox News/Opinion Dynamics 2006) (see AEI 2004, 27–30; Egan, Persily, and Wallsten 2006, 31; Roper Center 2008h).

38. For example, in 2006, 54 percent of respondents to a Princeton Survey Research Associates/Pew poll responded that they favored "allowing gay and lesbian couples to enter into legal agreements with each other that would give them many of the same rights as married couples." However, an ABC News poll in 2006 found that only 41 percent agreed that "homosexual couples should be allowed to form legally recognized unions, giving them the legal rights of married couples in areas such as health insurance, inheritance and pension coverage" (AEI 2006, 31, 33).

39. During the 1992–94 period, 28–29 percent of respondents supported gay adoption. The figure rose to 46 percent in 2001, about the same percentage (47) of people who reject it (Henry J. Kaiser 2001, 10: "Do you think there should or should NOT be adoption rights for gay and lesbian couples so they can legally adopt children?"). Results shown in figure 1.3 are from 1992–93 from the National Elections Studies conducted during those years and 1994 from Yankelovich ("Do you think gay or lesbian couples, in other words homosexual couples, should be legally permitted to adopt children?") Results shown in figure 1.3 are from 1996–98 from Princeton Survey Research Associates ("Do you think there should or should not be equal rights for gays in terms of adoption rights for gay spouses?") The 49 percent 2006 figure in figure 1.3 is from ABC News/*Time*: "Would you favor or oppose allowing gay and lesbian couples to adopt a child?"; the 42 percent 2006 figure is from SRB/Pew Research Center: "Do you strongly favor, favor, oppose or strongly oppose allowing gays and lesbians to adopt children?"(AEI 2006, 40–41).

40. Of course, the kind and level of threat varies among *individuals* as well as issues.

41. As one Minnesota legislator put it during a debate over that state's nondiscrimination law, "As I have wrestled with this issue, I would say to . . . members of the gay and lesbian community, as a Norwegian Lutheran, I do not understand your lifestyle. . . . But at the same time, I am reminded of the oath I took . . . that

said that I would uphold the Constitution of the United States as well as the State of Minnesota. . . . If we pass this legislation it's because it is the right thing to do. Not because we totally understand, but because we want to be a state that does not discriminate against its people" (Minnesota Senate 1993).

42. Being an acknowledged homosexual still may be enough to disqualify a parent from custody and visitation rights with their biological child in some places (Rivera 1986; Murphy 1999). Other situations involving gays in contact with children also raise fears. Although the public firmly supports workplace nondiscrimination, support declines when people are asked whether "homosexuals should or should not be hired as elementary school teachers." Support ranged between 56 and 61 percent in Gallup polls taken from 2001 to 2003, about 25–30 points lower than for nondiscrimination in employment generally and in other occupations (AEI 2004, 12). Laws against employment discrimination that cover sexual orientation frequently exempt schools in their hiring of teachers.

43. Most gays and lesbians remain closeted in many work environments if they sense heterosexual discomfort with openly gay colleagues.

44. According to two gay adoptive parents, "Having children legitimizes gay relationships. I think that's what general society fears" (quoted in Zimmerman 2003). Similarly, gay rights opponent and law professor Lynn Wardle argues that efforts by gays to gain adoption rights have to do with gaining "legal acceptance for a family lifestyle, a homosexual lifestyle" (quoted in Gehrke 2000).

45. As Senator Robert Byrd (D-WV), an opponent of gay marriage, put it, "Obviously, human beings enter into a variety of relationships. Business partnerships, friendships, alliances for mutual benefits, and team memberships all depend upon emotional unions of one degree or another. . . . However, in no case, has anyone suggested that these relationships deserve the *special recognition* or the designation commonly understood as 'marriage.'" (U.S. Congress, Senate 1996b, S10109, emphasis added). Vincent McCarthy stated before the Connecticut General Assembly (2001) that "Underlying all the arguments for a right to have same sex relationships recognized as marriages, is the assumption that no difference exists between the same sex relationship and the committed sexual union of a man and a woman. Thus the difference that does exist goes to the heart of the State's primary interest for recognizing and encouraging marriage."

46. Single-parent families, blended families, and families in which grandparents or aunts and uncles take the primary parental role exist along with the nuclear family.

47. On the importance of examining the opposition to social movements, see Klandermans (1991) and Tarrow (1992).

48. On the importance of institutional "venue" and "context" for policymaking, see Baumgartner and Jones (1993) and Mucciaroni (1995).

49. For a discussion of institutions as organizational structures and purposive actors, see the literature on state-centered theories of policymaking in Skocpol, Evans, and Rueschemeyer (1985).

50. See also Nyberg and Alston (1976); Levitt and Klassen (1974); Irwin and Thompson (1977); Bobo and Licari (1989).

51. For the marriage case as an example, see Killian (2006). When the threat level is sufficiently high, "anti-diffusion" may occur (Klawitter and Hammer 1999), 35.

52. A study of an anti-illegal immigrant initiative in California suggests that support varied widely with the level of racial and ethnic diversity at the county level (Tolbert and Hero 1996).

53. This section draws considerably upon Rosenberg (1991, ch. 1).

54. On the role of the courts in racial integration, see Hochschild (1984).

55. See also Rostow (1952); Monti (1980); Neier (1982); *Harvard Law Review* (1977); Sax (1971).

56. See also Monroe (1979); Barnum (1985); Marshall (1989).

57. According to Cain (2000, 282–86), gay rights advocates face four additional hurdles in the courts. First, the lack of "respect" that courts show to gay petitioners is evidenced by the Supreme Court's ruling in *Bowers v. Hardwick* (1986), which validated state laws that criminalized gay behavior. Even *Plessy v. Ferguson* assumed that blacks deserved equal treatment (as long as it was in a segregated environment). Second, the courts have refused to accord gays the "heightened" or "strict scrutiny," the levels of review accorded to women and other minorities when they decide discrimination cases. Third, the Court's embrace of "new federalism," which accords states more autonomy and restrains federal power, means that gay rights advocates must fight their battles state by state. Finally, gay rights advocates avoid talking about sex because of discomfort with the topic. Cain's first point is moot given the Court's overturning of *Bowers* in *Lawrence v. Texas* (2003). The second obstacle is important, but it does not preclude courts from deciding in favor of gay petitioners, as they did in *Lawrence*. The embrace of new federalism, as we shall see, is not necessarily disadvantageous for the cause of gay rights and must be assessed in comparison with the chances for gay petitioners to succeed in federal courts. The courts are hardly alone in their discomfort with talking about sex. The same is true of the other branches of government (see Campbell and Davidson 2000).

58. According to Smith (1993, 149), "Rosenberg's study . . . focused only upon the question of whether judicial action caused '*significant* social reform' or 'policy change with nationwide impact.'" (Emphasis in original.)

59. One of Rosenberg's (1991) key pieces of evidence of the Court's lack of impact in the black civil rights movement is that activists did not cite *Brown v. Board of Education* as a factor that motivated them and that the public was generally unaware of the decision. Cain (2000, 8) argues that major Supreme Court decisions in women's rights and gay rights have had a direct impact on the policy debate because the political environment is much more saturated by the mass media than it was during the 1950s and 1960s.

60. According to Cain (2000, 7–8), "Without the [*Brown v. Board of Education*] decision, or if the decision had gone the other way, surely school desegregation would have taken much longer. . . . [A]lthough *Brown* may not have accomplished immediate desegregation or a significant reduction in racism, the decision did make material differences in people's individual lives . . . not only the lives of those who were the direct beneficiaries of the decision . . . but also individuals for whom the decision created new visions of the possibility of equality. . . . Statistics cannot capture these defining moments in individual people's lives. . . . The statistics show that desegregation occurred slowly, but, in the end, due in large part to the continuing efforts of NAACP lawyers, the *Brown* decision was implemented, city by city, school district by school district, university by university."

61. Denying the government's petition to exercise prior restraint over a newspaper about to publish material that the government does not want published would be an example of a self-executing ruling. Desegregating schools would be an example of a ruling that requires the cooperation of others to implement it.

62. If, instead, the lawsuit succeeded and the lobbying campaign failed, we might interpret that as a disconfirmation of the resource mobilization hypothesis. In fact, it may be evidence that the LGBT movement succeeds when it chooses the judicial strategy over the legislative one.

CHAPTER 2. DEFINING THE THREATS FROM GAY RIGHTS

1. Or, as Deborah Stone (1981, 10) puts it, politics is a struggle "for the control of ambiguity."

2. For example, higher proportions of the population today than in the 1970s believe that "having sexual relations with someone other than" a person's wife or husband is "always wrong" (79 percent in 2002 compared with 70 percent in 1973). And although the proportion of those who think that premarital sex is always wrong has fallen from 37 to 27 percent, the decline is less sharp than for disapproval of homosexual conduct (AEI 2004, 46–47).

3. Gay rights supporters do the same when they argue that the question of gay marriage ought to be resolved at the state level without "federal interference."

4. For example, as marriage has always been a state-level responsibility, state legislators and judges will not argue that marriage should be left up to the federal government.

5. Local legislators and judges may demur from legislating and adjudicating gay rights issues involving employment and housing discrimination, for example, by arguing that the federal government (or the states) should act first. But they cannot deny that all levels of government have the authority and responsibility for protecting civil rights.

6. On the social construction of groups in politics and their policy implications, see Schneider and Ingram (1993).

7. Most of the debates that are analyzed are floor debates because verbatim accounts are more readily available for these than for committee hearings. Except for the debates over employment/housing nondiscrimination and same-sex marriage, all of the speakers were federal and state legislators. For the debates over nondiscrimination policies, legislators made the vast majority of speeches recorded (275 of 354, or 78 percent). Citizens who spoke at public hearings in Ithaca, New York, and Palm Beach County, Florida, council meetings accounted for five of fourteen speeches in Ithaca in 1984, forty-four of fifty-one speeches in Palm Beach County in 1990, and thirty of thirty-four speeches in 1995. For debates over same-sex marriage in Connecticut, citizens made the majority of speeches recorded (133 of 230, or 59 percent).

8. The debates led to passage of the legislation in Ithaca (1984), the Massachusetts House (1989), Palm Beach County (1990), Maryland (2001), the Minnesota House and Senate (1993), and the Rhode Island House and Senate (1995). The debates led to defeats of the legislation in the Rhode Island House (1990) and Palm Beach County (1995).

9. For Scott Lively, quoted by the Associated Press, "if the state doesn't have even a legitimate interest in criminalizing sodomy . . . how can the state continue to regulate against . . . sadomasochism, sex between brothers and sisters, sex with animals and sex with corpses?" (Associated Press 2003).

10. These results may be somewhat skewed by the salience of the gay marriage issue at the time that the *Lawrence* case was decided. However, gay marriage has been on the agenda since the mid-1990s. One can expect that it would have colored every debate over the repeal of sodomy laws since Hawaii's Supreme Court issued the first ruling that found state laws banning gay marriage unconstitutional.

11. Opponents of gay marriage in the U.S. Senate debate emphasized most often the need for the federal government to protect the states from efforts to establish gay marriage. (See U.S. Congress, Senate, 1996b; S10100-29, S10552, S12015.)

This procedural definition aside, the major *substantive* argument in the debates as a whole spoke to the adverse impact on marriage and the family. (See U.S. Congress, House, 1996, H7273-7495, E1346; U.S. Congress, Senate, 1996b, 10100-10117, 10552.)

12. In table 2.3, these include "gay marriage threatens family, marriage and family," "gay marriage ends special status of heterosexual marriage," and, under "other," "slippery slope—will lead to more radical forms of marriage."

13. Other examples include the following: "The bills before this committee would elevate the status of same sex unions to the legal equivalent of marriage in Connecticut. . . . The traditional institution of marriage with all the social and ethical benefits it imparts, would be seriously eroded and perhaps destroyed"(Rabbi Daniel Greer, Connecticut General Assembly 2002, 59). "Marriage forms families, and families form societies. Strong families form strong societies. . . . Same-sex unions do not make strong families." (Sen. Lauch Faircloth, R-GA, U.S. Congress, Senate, 1996b, S10117).

14. The bafflement is reflected in this exchange on the House floor between Representatives Barney Frank (D-MA) and Steve Largent (R-OK) in the debate over the federal DOMA:

> *Frank:* How does the fact that I love another man and live in a committed
> relationship with him threaten your marriage? Are your relations with
> your spouses of such fragility that the fact that I have a committed, loving
> relationship with another man jeopardizes them? What is attacking
> you? . . . I will yield to the gentleman from Oklahoma [Mr. Largent] if he
> will tell me what threatens his marriage.
> *Largent:* I would just submit . . . that the relationship of the gentleman
> from Massachusetts [Mr. Frank] with another man does not threaten my
> marriage whatsoever, my marriage of 21 years with the same woman.
> *Frank:* Mr. Speaker, whose marriage does it threaten?
> *Largent:* It threatens the *institution* of marriage the gentleman is trying to
> redefine [emphasis added].
> *Frank:* It does not threaten the gentleman's marriage. It does not threaten
> anybody's marriage. It threatens the institution of marriage; that argument
> ought to be made by someone in an institution because it has no logical
> basis whatsoever. (U.S. Congress, House 1996, H7278).

15. Another example of this point: "The traditional [i.e., heterosexual] family . . . was worth giving *special status* above all other contracts in terms of a relationship among people" (U.S. Congress, Senate 1996b, S10105, emphasis added).

16. Remarks of the Reverend Howard Nash.

17. Other examples include the following: "The institution of marriage sets a necessary and high *standard*. Anything that lowers this standard as same-sex 'marriages' do, inevitably belittles marriage" (Rep. Lamar S. Smith, R-TX, U.S. Congress, House 1996, H7494, emphasis added). "[W]e've got to remember, there have to be *standards*, you have to go by the standards. Once you just bend a little bit, you lose everything and that's what we're doing here [with civil unions]" (Robert E. Muckle, Sr., Connecticut General Assembly 2003, 28, emphasis added). "[W]e, as an American people, do not and cannot accept same sex unions as a *standard*" (Sr. Suzanne Gross, Connecticut General Assembly 2001, 47, emphasis added).

18. Remarks of Rabbi Daniel Cohen.

19. In the Connecticut debate, speakers argued from a natural law perspective that same-sex relationships are inferior because gay partners cannot produce offspring. For example, "By its nature, marriage is ordered to the well-being of the spouses and to the procreation and the upbringing of children. Only such a union can be recognized and ratified as a marriage in society" (Connecticut General Assembly 2001). Remarks of Bishop Daniel A. Hart.

20. Remarks of John Sweeny.

21. DOMA's supporters in Congress were so opposed to homosexual and heterosexual relationships being accorded equality that they blocked an amendment merely asking the Government Accountability Office to study the differences between the rights and benefits under marriage and under domestic partnership policies. According to Representative Henry Hyde (R-IL), "putting [a mandated GAO study] in the statute gives it an equivalence to the marriage institution that we do not think is appropriate now" (U.S. Congress, House 1996, H7504).

Some opponents of gay marriage acknowledge the practical difficulties and unfairness that gays encounter by not being able to marry and suggest piecemeal reforms, for example, regarding inheritance taxes and hospital visitation and consultation. As the following exchange between Representative Mike Lawlor (D–East Haven) and Brian Brown, executive director of the Family Institute of Connecticut, makes clear, these reforms must never be mistaken for marriage or a surrogate for it:

Rep. Lawlor: Is there a compromise that you can envision that wouldn't undermine the fundamental structure of marriage?

Brown: Anything that doesn't create a separate institution, that doesn't give the State's imprimatur upon a separate social form, something, for example, that would expand contractual arrangements. Those sorts of things don't deal with marriage explicitly. Those sorts of things aren't undermining marriage and therefore, on a case-by-case basis, if we sought legislation, then yes. I mean, there is a chance to support those. (Connecticut General Assembly 2003, 88)

22. In Connecticut, the debate culminated in the passage of legislation to allow homosexual and unmarried heterosexual couples to adopt children.

23. In another editorial, Samuel P. Woodward (1995) argued that "the question before the people of this state today is whether we will continue to give our children to homosexuals in adoption and foster care, or whether we will instead protect children from people who practice deviant behavior, are poor role models and have the highest rate of sexually transmitted diseases."

24. The *South Bend* (IN) *Tribune* (1998) quoted Dr. Jeffrey Satinover, a psychiatrist, as follows: "Research reveals overwhelming evidence of damage done to a child by the absence of either a mother or a father. A homosexual household will either never have a mother or never have a father; that absence is what makes homosexual roommates unfit parents." And according to Linda Smith, a representative of Catholic Charities in Hartford, Connecticut, testifying before the Connecticut General Assembly (2000c) Judiciary Committee, "We believe strongly . . . that children grow and thrive best in the environment of a stable home with a mother and father who are in a lawfully sanctioned committed relationship and can act as appropriate role models for the child." Further comments by Representative Peter A. Nystrom included, "No matter how you cut it, I think a child in that relationship . . . I think something will be missing in that child's life as they grow up" (Connecticut General Assembly 2000b, 241.)

25. Testimony of Frank Nicoll; see also Espenshade (2002a, 2002b).

26. Gallup reported support for lifting the ban at 60 percent in 1989 and at 57 percent in 1992; PSRA/*Newsweek* reported 59 percent support in 1992. Shortly after Clinton's election to president in November 1992, Gallup reported 48 percent support, NBC/*Wall Street Journal* reported 47 percent support in June 1993, and *Newsweek* reported 42 percent support in April 1993 and 37 percent in July 1993. See AEI (2004) and Wilcox and Wolpert (1996).

27. Another example includes, "Homosexuality is incompatible with military service. Lifting the ban would have a negative impact on readiness, discipline, and morale" (U.S. Congress, House 1993, H7066, remarks of Rep. Floyd D. Spence, R-SC). See U.S. Congress, House (1993, H3913, H6061, H6066–67, H6074–76, H7070, H7078, H7084–85, H7087–89) and U.S. Congress, Senate (1993, S7603, S11031, S11035, S11176, S11189, S11191, S11227).

28. Remarks of Representative Ike Skelton (D-MO).

29. Remarks of Senator Dan Coats (R-IN).

30. Examples include, "In my view, the [Armed Services] committee elected to support the men and women of the Armed Forces on this issue. The polls I have seen indicate that service members are overwhelmingly in favor of continuing the ban on homosexuals in the military" (U.S. Congress, House 1993, H6061, H7067, remarks of Rep. Skelton) and, according to Representative Marilyn Lloyd (D-TN), "Every service member I have spoken with has expressed uneasiness over any changes to the policy banning service by homosexuals. The slightest distraction to any serviceperson in any military situation could be fatal" (U.S. Congress, House 1993, H7089). See also U.S. Congress, House (1993, H6061, H6070, H6074, H7066, H7081, H7085, H7088–89) and U.S. Congress, Senate (1993, S868, S6833, S7604, S11172, S11193, S11227).

31. In a *Los Angeles Times* poll, 74 percent of service members "disapproved" of lifting the ban; in an Air Force telephone survey, 67 percent "agreed" with "the current policy of separating known homosexuals from the military"; and in Laura Miller's survey, 75 percent "strongly disagreed or disagreed" with "allowing gays and lesbians to enter and remain in the military." See Healy (1993, 1). The *Los Angeles Times* polled 2,346 enlistees and reflected the demographic background characteristics of the military as a whole. The Air Force telephone survey, conducted in January 1993, of approximately 800 enlistees as reported in Miller (1994, 70), was based upon results of survey questionnaires of 2,000 male and 1,700 female enlistees. The only other issue that appeared to evoke as much concern from enlistees as lifting the ban was the consequences of the impending downsizing of the military in the wake of the end of the Cold War. See Healy (1993) and Air Force survey results cited in Miller (1994).

32. Remarks of Representative Randy Cunningham, (R-CA); see also U.S. Congress, House 1993, H6070, H7067, H7081, H7084, H7088 and U.S. Congress, Senate (1993, S1334, S6833, S7604, S11178, S11191, S11227).

33. Remarks of Senator Coats.

34. Remarks of Senator Sam Nunn (D-GA).

35. Remarks of Senator Slade Gorton (R-WA).

36. For examples of these arguments in congressional debate, see the remarks of Representatives Walter Jones (R-NC), Tom Feeney (R-FL), and Mike Pence (R-IN) in U.S. Congress, House (2004b, H7692–93 and H7695).

37. For other examples in the press, see Florio (1998).

38. Remarks of Senator Orrin Hatch (R-UT).

39. Remarks of Senator Paul Coverdell (R-GA). See also U.S. Congress, Senate (1996a, 9988-99, 10003-05, 10131-38, 12016).

40. Remarks of Senator Trent Lott (R-MS).

41. Remarks of Senator Norman R. Stone, Jr. (D), from Harford County.

42. Remarks of Rhode Island State Representative Read.

43. Saying that the issue is about condoning homosexuality is ambiguous because the negative implications are less clear than if speakers use terms like "immoral" and "sinful." People may think it is a bad idea for the state to condone homosexuality on moral grounds, but they may think so for other reasons as well, such as a belief that homosexual relationships are unstable or that homosexuals are at a higher risk of spreading AIDS.

44. Remarks of Representative Ray Flynn.

45. Remarks of Senator Neville.

46. These results may not be inconsistent with those reported in Mooney and Schuldt (2006, 10–11) on gay marriage reported in chapter 1. Their data came from a survey of citizens rather than observing how policymakers debate issues and the definitions that appear in print media. It is possible that citizens think about gay rights issues, or at least marriage, in moral terms more than political elites and advocates or that, for strategic reasons, policymakers and advocates are less likely to frame these issues in moral terms. Also, some of Mooney and Schuldt's survey questions asked citizens about their *perception* of whether moral values influenced their thinking on gay marriage. Citizens may assume that those values have a great impact on their thinking even though they may not.

CHAPTER 3. ADVOCATING GAY RIGHTS

1. For other examples, see U.S. Congress, Senate (2000a, 2003a, 2003c, 2003d, 2003e, 2004a, 2004b; S27, S3602, S4333–34, S5253–54, S5256, S5334, S5336, S5337, S5341–42, S5346, S5347, S5432–33, S5652, S6712, S6764–65, S6766, S6866–67, S7976, S9286, S9287, S9287, S10949, S12779); U.S. Congress, House (2003, 2004b; H7524, H7528, H7530; H7532, H7535, H7689, H7691, H7693, H7694, H7696, H7697, H7698, H3738, E620).

2. For other examples, see U.S. Congress, Senate (2000a, 2004b, S5334, S5336, S5337, S5345, S5346, S5432, S5433–34, S5652, S6712, S6764, S6764–65, S6769, S6775, S6776, S6866–67, S10948, S12779); U.S. Congress, House (2004b, H7691, H7692, H7693, H7694–95, H7697, H7678, H5728).

3. For other examples, see U.S. Congress, Senate (1999, 2000a, 2000c, 2003a, 2003b, 2003e, 2004c; S123, S3602, S5334, S5337, S5341–42, S5345, S5432, S5433, S6764, S6764–65, S6769, S7976, S10819, S6712, S12779); U.S. Congress, House (2003, 2004b, H7689, H7693, H7694–95, H7696, H3738).

4. For other examples, see U.S. Congress, Senate (2000b, 2000c, 2003a, 2003b, 2003e, 2004c; S123, S3602, S5334, S5432–33, S6775, S7976, S9286, S10819,

S12779); U.S. Congress, House (2003, 2004b, H3738, H7689, H7693, H7694–95, H7696–97, H7697, H7697–98).

5. For other examples from the U.S. Senate debate over the Employment Non-Discrimination Act, see U.S. Congress, Senate (1996, S9986, S9987, S9989, S9991, S9994, S9999, S10001, S10002, S10054, S10056, S10129, S10130, S10131, S10132, S10133, S10134, S10135, S10138, S10712, S8502).

6. See U.S. Congress, House (1993, H7040, H6059, H6072, H7066, H7068, H7071, H7073, H7075–76, H7078, H7080–81, H7083–84) and U.S. Congress, Senate (1993, S11170, S11175, S11177–180, S11193, S11204–206, S11226–27).

7. Senator Barbara Boxer (D-CA).

8. Senator Russ Feingold (D-WI).

9. Representative Gerry Studds (D-MA).

10. Representative Norman Mineta (D-CA).

11. Representative Martin Meehan (D-MA). For other examples, see U.S. Congress, House (1993, H6072, H7066, H7068, H7070, H7071, H7075, H7076, H7080, H7081, H7087, E2305); U.S. Congress, Senate (1993, S11168, S11174, S11180, S11193, S11204, S11205, S11206, S11226).

12. Senator Claiborne Pell (R-RI). For other examples, see U.S. Congress, House (1993, H7068–69, H7073, H7078–81, H7088, E2305) and U.S. Congress, Senate (1993, S11168, S11170, S11178, S11180, S11204–205, S11226–227).

13. Representative Tom Foglietta (D-PA). For other examples, see U.S. Congress, House (1993, H7066, H7069, H7071–72, H7075–76, H7079–84, H7087) and U.S. Congress, Senate (1993, S11168, S11174, S11193, S11204–205, S11213, S11216, S11226).

14. For other examples, see Associated Press (2003), *Intelligencer Journal* (2003), *Pittsburgh Post-Gazette* (2003), *Daily News* (2003), *Evening Sun* (2003), Safire (2003), *Roanoke Times* 2005), *Birmingham News* (2003), Ivins (2003).

15. For other examples, see Ivins (2003); Kidd (2003); Nethaway (2003); *Herald-Sun* (2003, A3); Murray (2003); *Alameda Times-Star* (2003); Manzanares (2003); Guevara (2003).

16. For other examples, see U.S. Congress, Senate (1996b, S10101, S10104, S10107, S10112, S10117, S10120, S10121, S10123, S10124, S10129); U.S. Congress, House (1996, H7273, H7274, H7276, H7278, H7442, H7446, H7447, H7448, H7449, H7481, H7481, H8482, H7485, H7486, H7487, H7488, H7489, H7491, H7492, H7496, H7497, H7498, H7499).

17. For other examples, see U.S. Congress, Senate (1996b, S10101, S10106, 10107, S10113, S10117, S10579); U.S. Congress, House (1996, H7270, H7275, H7277, H7278, H7442, H7443, H7444, H7445, H7446, H7447, H7448, H7483,

H7485, H7486, H7487, H7488, H7489, H7491, H7492, H7496, H7497, H7498, H7531, E1299).

18. For other examples, see Connecticut General Assembly (2002, 39, 42); Connecticut General Assembly (2003, 29, 117, 55, 66–67); Connecticut General Assembly (2001, 10, 14, 17, 23, 73, 80, 81, 88, 99, 116, 119); Connecticut General Assembly (2002, 7, 34, 39, 40, 42, 81, 85, 98, 110, 114, 117, 121, 128, 129); Connecticut General Assembly (2003, 3, 7, 10, 15, 29, 55–56, 82, 85, 101, 113, 114, 117, 119, 122, 125, 128, 129, 132, 135, 139); U.S. Congress, Senate (1996b, S10104, S10108, S10122); U.S. Congress, House (1996, H7177, H7442, H7443, H7444, H7445, H7446, H7447, H7448, H7486, H7491, 7497, 7531, E1299); Minnesota Senate (1997, Senator Allan Spear).

19. For other examples, see U.S. Congress, Senate (1996b, S10123, S10124), U.S. Congress, House (1996, H7273, H7275, H7278, H7442, H7443, H7445, H7446, H7448, H7486, H7492, H7499, 7504, 7531).

20. For other examples, see Connecticut General Assembly (2001, 22, 76, 89, 99, 122; Connecticut General Assembly (2002, 9, 35, 40, 41, 43, 85); Connecticut General Assembly (2003, 33, 85, 92, 122, 128, 132, 136).

21. Another good example: "It is the capacity of the individuals to love and protect the child that determines their adequacy as parents, not their sexual preference" (*Pittsburgh Post-Gazette* 2002a).

22. For other examples, see *Pennsylvania Law Weekly* (2002), Carpenter (2002), Espenshade (2002b), *Intelligence Journal* (2002a, A7; 2002b, A8), *Pittsburgh Post-Gazette* (2002b), Manson (2003), Associated Press (1999); *New York Law Journal* (1994), Wright (1997), *New York Law Journal* (1995).

23. The stories that gay and lesbian parents tell also point out what can happen to children without the protection of second-parent adoption. For instance, one story was told about a child of lesbian partners whose relationship had ended. According to the attorney appointed for the child, both women shared the emotional and financial responsibilities for raising the child but only one was recognized as the legal parent:

> When Jessica's parents separated, there was a great deal of anger and hurt and as often happens, the child suffered the most. For purely practical, but mostly financial purposes, it was not the primary care giver that held the position of legal parent. Therefore, when Jessica's legal mother took advantage of her status and regularly and continually denied the primary care taker visitation with Jessica, it was particularly devastating for her in that she was deprived of the relationship with the parent who woke her in the morning, who put her to bed at night, who bathed her, who made sure she had Halloween

costumes, she made sure she had cupcakes for school on her birthday. After many attempts to settle the matter without legal intervention, Jessica's other mother was forced to file suit to merely be able to see her daughter. Jessica is an adorable and articulate child. She had suffered so many losses and to see her suffer the loss of yet another mother, was unconscionable and yet so avoidable. (testimony of Kate Rizzo (2000), attorney at law, before the Judiciary Committee of the Connecticut General Assembly).

These kinds of "horror stories" dramatize the real costs that children and families incur when one parent is not able to secure the legal rights and responsibilities of parenthood.

CHAPTER 4. LEGALIZING HOMOSEXUAL CONDUCT

1. Quoted in Carpenter (2004, 1479).

2. The authorities later charged the person who called in the gun report with filing a false report.

3. "Allegedly" because at least one credible account raises questions about whether the police observed the two men having sex (see Carpenter 2004).

4. The U.S. Constitution does not explicitly mention a "right to privacy," but the concept is deeply rooted in American jurisprudence. Justice Lewis D. Brandeis articulated the right of privacy as "the right to be let alone—the most comprehensive of rights and the right most valued by civilized men" (Warren and Brandeis 1890; Olmstead v. United States 1928).

5. For a review of this literature, see Goldstein (1988).

6. On the history of urban America in this period, see also Rotundo (1993) and Smith-Rosenberg (1985).

7. These states were Arkansas, Kansas, Kentucky, Missouri, Montana, Nevada, and Texas (see Leveno 1993–94, 1029, note 2).

8. According to Eskridge (1997, 1069), "Whether through police vice squads and morals divisions, local or state censorship boards, national customs and post office censors, private juries and arbiters of decency, alcoholic beverage commissions, immigration officials and doctors in the Public Health Service, examining physicians for the Selective Service, or commanders, investigators, and medics in the armed forces, the homosexual found herself interrogated, investigated, censored, censured, jailed, and hospitalized in ways that only Kafka could have imagined."

9. According to Chauncy (2004a, 521–22), more than 50,000 men were arrested for violating New York City's law against "loitering about any public place [for] soliciting men for the purpose of committing a crime against nature or other lewdness," until Mayor John Lindsay halted such arrests.

10. Table 4.1 lists the thirteen states.

11. Mohr (1988) has made the same point more recently.

12. In England, the Wolfenden Committee, which issued its report around the same time as the ALI's *Model Penal Code,* also recommended in favor of decriminalizing sodomy. As in the United States, the legal profession in the United Kingdom spearheaded the effort to rationalize the criminal law (Mitchell 1969, 16, 78, 83).

13. Hardwick and his lover spent ten hours in jail. Jail employees joked to the other men in the cell that the two gay men would sexually assault them (Goldstein 1988, 1074). The police had initially visited Hardwick's home to deliver a warrant for an arrest, and a guest admitted them. Hardwick had failed to make a court appearance after the city had issued him a ticket for drinking in public, even though he had paid the ticket three weeks before his arrest. Although the district attorney declined to prosecute Hardwick, his American Civil Liberties Union attorneys brought their case before a federal district court judge, who ruled against him. Hardwick won his case before the 11th Circuit Court of Appeals, which found that the U.S. Constitution protected his behavior (Brantner 1992, 502–504).

14. For a discussion of the Court's reasoning in *Lawrence* and the implications of its ruling, see Koppelman (2002).

15. The progay marriage rulings in Washington state and New York were later reversed by their highest courts.

16. For a review of scholarly interpretations of *Lawrence* and its implications for future gay rights cases, see Parshall (2005, 271–80) and *Harvard Law Review* (2005, 2859–81); for specific interpretations, see Eskridge (2004), Harcourt (2004), Tribe (2004), and Kelman (2005).

17. For example, Yang (2003, ch. 2) points out that the generation that came of age from 1965 to 1973 is more liberal on gay issues than older generations and that the youngest generation that he studied (1992–2000) is usually the most liberal of all. Generations are not always progressively more liberal than their predecessors were or more liberal in the same magnitude as comparisons of other generations. For example, the generation that came of age during 1982–91 is sometimes no more liberal, or even less so, than some older generations.

18. Of course, it is possible for public opinion to affect Court decisions both indirectly and directly (see Mishler and Sheehan 1996).

19. The Court ruled favorably in *Romer v. Evans* (1996), but it delivered setbacks in *Hurley v. Irish American Gay, Lesbian and Bisexual Group of Boston* (1995) and in *Dale v. Boy Scouts of America* (2000).

20. For a discussion of the long-term implications of *Lawrence,* see Parshall (2005), Tribe (2004), and Hunter (2004).

CHAPTER 5. ADOPTION

1. Calculated from data supplied in Smith and Gates (2001, 4) and U.S. Census Bureau (2006a).

2. Calculated from data supplied in Smith and Gates (2001, 4) and U.S. Census Bureau (2006a).

3. The growth in gay parenting and adoption has been an important catalyst for getting gay marriage on the agenda. Many gay partners want their children to be afforded the benefits and protection that come with parents whose union is legally sanctioned (Crary 2004; Chauncey 2004b).

4. That is what happened, for example, in Connecticut and Massachusetts. See Gorlick (2000).

5. For California, see Morin and Hayasaki (2003). For Florida, see Farrington (2001).

6. The states in which state court judges do not run for reelection are Hawaii, Delaware, Connecticut, Massachusetts, New Jersey, Maine, New Hampshire, Rhode Island, and Vermont.

7. Pinello (2003) generally did not find a correlation between the methods used to select judges (election versus appointment) and support for gay rights, however.

8. Sharp differences of opinion remain on this point among students of the courts. The minority rights justification for judicial review has been advanced by Choper (1980), Ely (1980), and Bickel (1962). Empirical studies include Dahl (1957), Casper (1976), and Adamany (1973).

9. Family law includes the regulation of adoption, marriage, divorce, foster care, custody, and visitation rights.

10. New York Domestic Relations law, section 110.

11. For Nebraska, see Tysver (2002). For Wisconsin, see Segall (1994).

12. For example, judges in Pennsylvania's Erie and Montgomery counties ruled against second-parent adoptions on the grounds that "the Legislature has not seen fit to specifically sanction such adoptions [and that] the court is not legally empowered to grant the petition for adoption" (Judge Shad Connelly quoted in Associated Press 1999). These judges said that the law limits adoptions by stipulating that if two people seek to adopt, one must be the other's "spouse." Judges in York and other counties, by contrast, argued that same-sex couples were not disqualified because the Adoption Act does not specifically disqualify them and, in fact, states that "Any individual may become an adopting parent." Judges in Allegheny County allowed both second-parent and joint adoptions by gay couples. See Carpenter (2002).

13. On the influence of judges' attitudes generally, see Segal and Spaeth (1993), and Tate (1981).

14. For example, the majority in the appellate-level Pennsylvania Superior Court denied second-parent adoptions on the basis that "it is for the Legislature, not the courts, to determine whether same-sex adoptions are permissible" (quoted in Kelley 2000).

15. A Michigan judge disallowed unwed couples to adopt on the grounds that such adoptions were prohibited by law, not because he judged the gay parents unfit. See Associated Press (2002b); see also *New York Times* (1993b) and O'Donnell (1994).

16. For the same ruling by the Pennsylvania Supreme Court, see Carpenter (2002) and (Litchman 2002, 1).

17. The two measures correlate well.

18. As one adoption agency official puts it, "When people are making a decision about adoption, they want the ideal [i.e., a husband and wife]." Quoted in Espenshade (2002c).

19. Social workers talk to the child (if he or she is old enough); talk to the biological and adoptive parents; investigate the backgrounds of the prospective parents; assess the length and quality of their relationship; evaluate the relationship of the child with both parents (in the case of second-parent adoptions); consider the relationship of the child with the extended families of both parents; and often talk to teachers, physicians, and other important figures in the child's life.

20. According to the director of Families Like Ours, a nonprofit organization that caters to gay couples seeking to adopt, "agencies and states are realizing, 'Look, you've got two choices.' Either these kids stay in foster care and are never adopted, so they never have a family, or we actively go out and find them a family without prejudice. It's wink-wink, nudge-nudge" (quoted in Hayes 2002). According to a spokesperson for the Gay and Lesbian Alliance against Defamation, "So many children are desperate for families to love and care for them, I would argue [agencies] have an obligation to look at loving family environments without regard to sexual orientation" (quoted in *Connecticut Post* 2003).

21. Some judges have ruled that the Florida ban on adoption is unconstitutional because the clear need to find homes for so many children is evidence of the lack of a rational basis for the law. See Malmgren (2002). See also the argument of the American Civil Liberties Union (ACLU) before a federal appeals court concerning the Florida ban in Cunningham (2003, A1), where one of the ACLU's attorneys argued that about 3,400 children in the foster care system in Florida had no permanent adoptive home and yet Florida excluded a segment of the population from applying to adopt them.

22. For an argument in favor of a "new morality" that is "grounded in the values of caring and stability, against a background of fairness and equality," see Cahn (1997, 270).

23. Emphasis in original on page 1128. Ideological clashes remain over other issues such as divorce, abortion, and gay marriage.

24. Other policies reveal the heightened concern for children and for those who are responsible for taking care of them, such as placing a greater emphasis on joint custody agreements, parenting classes, and parenting plans; giving children a "voice" and legal representation in court proceedings; designating a "primary" caretaker; imposing stricter laws and enforcement of child support; giving greater attention to the impact of domestic violence toward parents and children (Murphy 1999, 1180–97); and according children born and raised in families outside of marriage (who had been ignored or condemned by the law) substantially equal rights to support and other benefits (Glendon 1989, 285; see also Krause 1993, 116–20). Legal and technological advances in determining paternity facilitated these changes.

25. For an Oregon couple's same argument, see Sullivan (2002).

26. For reviews of this literature, see Demo and Cox (2000), Elovitz (1995), Goleman (1992), and Sullivan (2002). See also a study of 256 families in thirty-four states by Nanette Silverman, who works with the Johnson and O'Connor National Survey of gay and lesbian parents at Dowling College in Oakdale, New York, reviewed in Davidson (2001).

27. Sexual abusers are disproportionately heterosexual men. See Groth (1978); Herek (1991, 133, 156); Jenny, Roesler, and Poyer (1994); Newton (1978); Sam Houston State University Criminal Justice Center (1980); Human Development Service (1982).

28. The American Psychiatric Association, the National Association for Mental Health, and the Office of the Surgeon General concluded that sexual orientation in and of itself does not constitute a mental illness. See American Psychiatric Association (1980, 380); Silverstein (1976–77, 153, 157); and Conger (1979, 501, 532); Conger (1977, 408, 432).

29. Although not focused on gay parents, a comparison of five different family structures, including adoptive and single-parent families, showed that there was no difference in well-being or parental relationships across different structures; see Lanford, Abbey, and Stewart (2001).

30. For a review and critique of conservative challenges to the research, see Elovitz (1995, 220–24).

31. For example, the Support Center for Child Advocates supported the ruling of the Pennsylvania Supreme Court granting second-parent adoption. See Carpenter (2002).

32. For example, Judge Preminger cited such evidence in her opinion that opened the door for such adoptions. See Adams (1992, 1).

33. See Polikoff (1989–90, 466–67). "If you don't bring up the fact that you are gay, nobody asks," according to Roberta Achtenberg, an attorney for the Lesbian Rights Project in San Francisco (quoted in Dullea 1988, 26). According to the publisher of *Gay Parent* magazine, "I think that agencies are willing to work with gay people if they don't have to do it publicly. It's sort of a don't ask, don't tell kind of a policy." According to the owner of a Vermont agency, "a lot of agencies [in other states] will say, 'Oh, you're gay? Wink, wink. Okay, a single person'" (quoted in Malmgren (2002). In South Carolina, the Department of Social Services does not check the sexual orientation of prospective adoptive and foster parents when investigating them. "We're looking for a safe and stable home for a child. The sexual practices of the parent are not something that is questioned," according to a spokesperson for the agency (quoted in Munday 2003, 5A). And according to the leader of a gay and lesbian parenting support group, "There is a level of discrimination, [but] many of those involved in the adoption are supportive and turn a blind eye that they are working with a gay couple" (quoted in Paquette 1996).

34. According to a gay parent from New York, "Ironically, she [the biological mother] chose us knowing we were gay. In her judgment we could offer the best. She had offers from heterosexual couples and singles. It's hard to choose a gay couple. She didn't have much education, but she saw through the prejudice, she saw the loving and caring" (Quoted in Paquette 1996). As a North Dakota couple related, "At the conclusion of our home study visit . . . our social worker shared some incredible news with us. She wanted to show our portfolio to a North Dakota birth mother who was interested in choosing a same-sex family to adopt her two-week-old son who was in temporary foster care. . . . On April 6, 2001, we received a phone call from our local agency that the birth mother had made a decision. She wanted us to adopt her son!" (quoted in Cahill, Ellen, and Tobias 2002, 82–83).

35. "Warmth" is measured on a "feeling thermometer" that asks respondents to rate homosexuals on a scale from 0 to 100. See Wilcox and Wolpert (2000, 418, 426). See also Herek (1988) and Pratte (1993).

CHAPTER 6. MILITARY SERVICE

1. Unless indicated otherwise, references to "lifting the ban" or "the military ban" in this chapter refer to the prohibition against gays serving in the military *openly*, which reflects the current "don't ask, don't tell" policy.

2. The *Newsweek* results are reported in Wilcox and Wolpert (1996, 143, note 7). A *Wall Street Journal*/NBC News poll in June 1993 found that only 21 percent of

registered voters opposed allowing homosexuals to serve under any circumstances, 38 percent favored service as long as sexual orientation was kept private, and 40 percent were in favor of homosexuals serving openly (reported in Rand 1993, reprinted in U.S. Congress, Senate 1993, S11185).

3. Polls of servicemen conducted in the 1940s showed that 88 percent of whites and 38 percent of blacks opposed integration (U.S. Congress, House 1993, H7072; also reported in Rand 1993, reprinted in U.S. Congress, Senate 1993, S11185).

4. This section draws upon Rimmerman (1996a, 1996b), Rayside (1996), and Herek (1996a).

5. On the history of gays and lesbians in the military, see Burelli (1994), Berube (1990), Shilts (1993), and Humphrey (1990).

6. For a discussion of how the military's investigation of a gay male subculture on the naval base created problems for the military, see Chauncey (1999).

7. The figure is from a Government Accountability Office report with data supplied by the Department of Defense, cited in D'Amico (1996, 7).

8. See Schmalz (1993) and the remarks of Senator Frank Murkowski (R-AK), January 28, S868; Senator Bob Dole (R-KS), U.S. Congress, Senate 1993, S1334).

9. The American military has resisted change in its structure and operations in many ways that are unrelated to its personnel policies, like other institutions in which interests, organizational cultures, and routines become entrenched.

10. Most in the military apparently no longer believe that gays lack the physical strength and aggressive disposition to come to the aid of colleagues (see Miller 1994).

11. It is possible that the public and members of the military are much closer in their levels of support for other gay rights issues. The only other question that this Triangle poll asked for, by which we can compare military leaders and Americans, generally concerned whether homosexuals should be allowed "to teach in the public schools." Forty-two percent of military leaders supported barring homosexuals from being hired as teachers, about the same percentage as Americans who generally favor barring homosexuals from teaching in "elementary schools" (AEI 2004, 12).

12. While all of these surveys have flaws, they all show similar results.

13. Studies of military cadets' attitudes on defense issues conducted to ascertain whether self-selection or socialization is more important in determining these attitudes suggests that both are important, but especially the self-selection (Bachman et al. 2000).

14. According to Miller (1994, 84), women are less opposed to the ban on gays for two reasons. First, they share with gays and lesbians membership in an "out"

group that needed to challenge a male-dominated and sometimes crudely sexist institution (recall, e.g., the Tailhook sex scandal, which involved Navy pilots who abused female military personnel at a convention in Las Vegas in 1991). Second, historically, women have had to learn how to fend off the sexual advances from men, so having to do the same from lesbians is not a novel issue for them.

15. According to Rolison and Nakayama (1994, 111), "The fusion of military effectiveness with masculinity and concomitant demonization of femininity and homosexuality has become so fundamental a part of the military psyche that the prospect of gays in the military stimulates a psychological panic rooted in fear of loss of the self." Similarly, according to Miller (1994, 83), in the gays-in-the-military debate, "heterosexuality, masculinity and the rules governing gender interaction are at stake. Cultural warfare of this sort therefore entails a struggle for cultural dominance. Compromise is unacceptable and losing outright is unthinkable. Winning is crucial because the worldview extends beyond the issue at hand and gives meaning to the entire structure of people's lives."

16. Barry Adam (1994, 112–13) goes farther in arguing that the military's masculine ideology is also connected to the United States' "national identity" as a superpower. Thus, the military's aversion to homosexuality is related to American identity as well as a feminized construction of homosexuality that rejects manhood.

17. A number of studies cast doubt upon whether social diversity reduces the level of bonding and cohesion necessary to carry out military operations effectively and whether cohesion is relevant (or even counterproductive) for military effectiveness (see MacCoun 1993; Janis 1982; Harrell and Miller 1997; Gade, Segal, and Johnson 1996; Belkin and Levitt 2000; Belkin and McNichol 2000a, 2000b).

18. For discussion of Canada, see Park (1994, 174, 176); for discussion of Israel, see Gal (1994, 186); see article by Anne Swardson, "Canada: No Problem with Gays in Ranks," reprinted in U.S. Congress, Senate (1993, S11214); see testimony of Lawrence Korb before Senate Armed Services Committee, reprinted in U.S. Congress, Senate (1993, S11202), where he says "some 80 percent of the Canadian armed forces opposed dropping the ban before the Canadian military decided it had no empirical or rational basis to fight the ban in court. Since the ban was dropped, the Canadians have not reported any morale or cohesion problems."

19. Bob Knight, spokesperson for the Family Research Council, a conservative group, quoted in Price (1992).

20. Rayside (1966, 155) also argues that Nunn had an antigay voting record, was unwilling to defend gay staff members, and may have been disappointed that Clinton passed him over to become secretary of Defense.

21. See Rayside (1996, 157) and the criticisms of Senator Edward Kennedy in U.S. Congress, Senate (1993, S11194).

22. While the don't ask, don't tell compromise was much closer to what the ban's supporters sought than its opponents, supporters have used it to portray U.S. policy as more lenient and respectful of individuals' privacy than the outright ban that existed (*Agence France Presse* 2000).

23. Other nations, which mostly used conscripts, found it more difficult to exclude a class of citizens from the service (Riding 1992).

24. For Australia, see Charlton (1992a), Laidlaw (1992a), Connolly (1992d), and Charlton (1992b). For Britain, see *Daily Mail* (1999), Leeman (1999), *Agence France Presse* (1999), Cullen (1999), Megowan (1999), and Settle (2000).

25. For Canada, see Morton (1992) and *Hamilton Spectator* (1992); for Australia, see Connolly (1992a, 1992c), *Sunday Herald Sun* (1992), *Hobart Mercury* (1992a), Connolly (1992e), United Press International (1992), Associated Press (1992a, 1992b), and Allen (1992); for Britain, see Booth (1999), Branswell (1999), Lyall (1999), MacMillan (1999), and Lyall (2005).

26. According to Segal, Gade, and Johnson (1994, 45), "the pattern of American public opinion toward homosexuality is similar to the one that seems to prevail in most other Western nations: aversion toward homosexual behavior, but respect for the rights of homosexuals."

27. See International Labour Organization, conventions on the "elimination of discrimination in respect of employment and occupation," http://www.ilo.org.

28. For example, as Senator Bob Dole (R-KS) put it during debate on the ban, "Americans are telling us that they don't care what happens in the French Army. They do not care what the Dutch, or any other country does with its armies. . . . What some other country does with its armies, that is their business. But what Americans care about is America's Army and America's Armed Forces (U.S. Congress, Senate 1993, S1334).

29. Statements by Chief Justices Warren Burger and William Rehnquist that articulated judicial deference to the military and to Congress on military matters can be found in Stiehm (1989, 109, 111, 123).

30. The Supreme Court also has been reluctant to overturn instances of gender discrimination in the military, such as in *Rostker v. Goldberg* (453 US 57 1981) and discrimination against gays and lesbians in the foreign service and Central Intelligence Agency, such as in *Webster v. Doe* (486 U.S. 592 1988) and *KRC v. United States Information Agency* (989 F. 2nd 1211 1994) (Brewer, Kaib, and O'Connor 2000, 393–94).

31. Rimmerman (1996b) attributes Clinton's ineffectiveness to his leadership style, which stressed compromise and fit well with his strategy to portray himself as a moderate, New Democrat and his concern about alienating the military (in light of his avoidance of the draft and opposition to the Vietnam War). He also points out that Clinton understood that he lacked the votes to overturn the ban in Congress and could not justify spending scarce political resources on the highly controversial issue.

32. Rimmerman (1996b) also blames the gay rights movement's mistakes and lack of resolve for Clinton's failed effort. Leaders in the movement believed that having a gay-friendly president who promised to lift the ban was all that would be necessary to reach their goal. Inexperienced in the ways of Washington, they did not anticipate the stiff resistance that opponents of ending the ban would muster and "assumed that access to power was tantamount to having direct influence over public policy" (Rimmerman 1996b, 112; see also Schmalz 1993). After interviews with some leaders before Clinton took office, who revealed a shocking naiveté about the controversial nature of the issue, Randy Shilts concluded, "My God, what planet are you people living on? It's such an archetypal conflict, of course it's going to be a huge deal!" (quoted in Yarbrough 1993, 36). Because the issue had never been high on the movement's agenda, its leaders were slow to mount a grass roots organizing drive. Other critics have questioned the particular tactics that the movement adopted after it mobilized. For example, Katzenstein (1996) argues that proponents of lifting the ban should have dramatized gays and lesbians in the armed forces by discussing those who had died for their country, not simply those who served competently and honorably but who did not sacrifice their lives. Although accurate, this interpretation appears to place too much emphasis on the unrealized potential of gay rights organizations to act as agents of change. The gay rights movement would still have engendered formidable resistance even if it possessed greater political savvy and had mobilized earlier and more energetically.

33. According to Wilcox and Wolpert (1996, 142), "Clinton and others who argued for lifting the ban persuaded many Americans to support the policy."

34. On the mobilization of blacks and white liberals for civil rights and military integration specifically in the period immediately after World War II, see Mershon Schlossman (1998, 168–175) and Dalfiume (1969, 169).

35. Before the convention, Truman made statements about his support of civil rights, created the President's Committee on Civil Rights, and endorsed its report (*To Secure These Rights*), which recommended a sweeping agenda to expand blacks' civil rights, including the right to serve in the military (Gropman 1998, 73–78).

All of these actions antagonized the South. Historians are divided about whether Truman's support of civil rights reflected his political calculations or personal convictions (for a review of the literature and an interpretation sympathetic to both views, see Mershon and Schlossman 1998, 159–60).

36. President Franklin Roosevelt took an active role in the Navy's personnel policy, the Navy Special Program's unit of the Bureau of Naval Personnel was headed by an ardent foe of segregation named Christopher Sargent, Navy Secretary James Forrestal saw the problems with segregation and its unfairness, and he had some support of the Chief of Naval Operations, Admiral Ernest King. See MacGregor (1981, ch. 3). In contrast, Army Secretary Kenneth Royall sought to block or slow down efforts at integration. See McCoy and Ruetten (1973, 225–29).

CHAPTER 7. MARRIAGE, CIVIL RIGHTS, AND HATE CRIMES

1. Although these policies do not have the status of marriage, are not portable across most state lines, and exclude the many federal benefits available to married couples, their adoption would give same-sex couples far more benefits than they have without them.

2. Other examples include Utah, where Utahans Together Against Hate consisted of the NAACP, Asian Leadership Coalition, Legislative Coalition for People with Disabilities, Japanese American Citizens League, Governor's Hispanic Council, and a variety of others (Equality Utah 2005; Guidos 2004; Dobner 2003; Bulkeley 2005); Montana and West Virginia, where gays joined with advocates for the disabled, such as Montanans with Disabilities for Equal Access (Cooke 2005; McCormick 2002; Seiler 2001; Wallace 2002); and Arkansas, where the Coalition Against Hate included members of the American Jewish Committee (Osher 2001).

3. Other examples include Utah, where an array of mainline Christian, Islamic, and Buddhist representatives; nonprofit organizations; and most notably, the Church of Jesus Christ of Latter Day Saints (the Mormons) endorsed the legislation (Equality Utah 2005); and West Virginia, where it was the Human Rights Commission, National Association of Social Workers, American Federation of State and Municipal Employees, Trial Lawyers Association, and West Virginia Interfaith Center for Public Policy (Finn 2001; Wallace 2002; Seiler 2001). Similarly broad-based coalitions support adding sexual orientation to federal hate crimes legislation (Toner 1990; Cohen 1993) and filed briefs when the U.S. Supreme Court ruled on the constitutionality of state hate crimes laws in 1993 (Grene 1993). The ACLU and other groups argued that hate crimes laws do not infringe on free expression protected by the First Amendment.

4. The ban on interracial marriage is an obvious exception to this point, but it is an example of a right that blacks have already won.

5. Groups typically compile and disseminate statistics on the number of reported hate crimes, or they push to get authorization for law enforcement agencies to do so.

6. The attacks include those committed against Fred Martinez in Colorado (Paulson 2005); Mark Bangeter in Idaho (Whittig 1999); Andrew Franks-Ongoy (Cooke 2005); Danny Lee Overstreet in Virginia (Heyser 2005); Arthur Warren in West Virginia (Fischer 2000); James Bailey, Billy Jack Gaither; and Billy Sanford in Alabama (Chandler 2002; Associated Press 2005b); and twenty gay campers on a beach in Hawaii (Song 2001). Although these crimes helped put the issue on the agenda in these states, only Colorado and Hawaii have enacted hate crimes laws covering gays.

7. In earlier work, Haider-Markel (1998) hypothesized that law enforcement bureaucracies would oppose expanding the scope and coverage of hate crimes laws because of the "relatively conservative nature" of law enforcement. However, he did not find evidence that the influence of law enforcement bureaucracies (measured as the size of the law enforcement bureaucracies in each state) influenced the number of groups covered under hate crimes laws.

8. For example, Alabama and Utah have hate crimes laws covering race, ethnicity, and religion, but not sexual orientation (see *Atlanta Journal and Constitution* 1994; *St. Petersburg Times*, 1992). In addition, law enforcement sometimes remains neutral or opposes hate crimes laws, as it did in Hawaii (Song 2001) and West Virginia (Bundy 2001).

9. They include the ADL, NOW, the National Coalition against Domestic Violence, the National Education Association, the Disability Rights Education Fund, the American-Arab Anti-Discrimination Committee, the Police Foundation, the National Sheriffs Association, the International Association of Chiefs of Police, the Police Executive Research Forum, and the Federal Law Enforcement Officers Association.

10. For examples, see Haider-Markel (2000, 306), McCormick (2002), Associated Press (1998b), and (Osher 2001).

11. As drafted, ENDA also exempts businesses with fewer than fifteen employers, which helps to lessen business opposition.

12. East Lansing, Michigan, was the first local community to enact a nondiscrimination ordinance covering gays in 1972; Wisconsin was the first state to do so in 1982. The first state to enact hate crimes legislation was California in 1983.

13. The House also passed hate crimes legislation by a vote of 223 to 195 in 2005 as part of the Child Safety Act, but it was defeated in the Senate Judiciary Committee (Young 2005; www.thomas.gov, bill summary and status for H.R. 3132).

14. As it was clear that most states were against legalizing same-sex marriage, this argument may have kept more members of Congress from voting for the DOMA.

15. As of May 2007, the number of states with nondiscrimination laws covering sexual orientation was twenty.

16. Haider-Markel (2000) calculated rankings of states based upon the number of National Gay and Lesbian Task Force members per 100,000 residents.

17. Supporters of same-sex partner recognition tried to use the ballot box to adopt civil unions or partner benefits on one occasion (Colorado in 2006), but voters rejected it.

18. A few states, like Hawaii, fall into more than one category, banning gay marriage, for example, as well as providing other kinds of partner recognition.

19. States have a variety of arrangements for allowing citizens to vote on laws and constitutional amendments, but most states fall into one of two categories: "direct initiative" states, which permit citizens to place proposed laws and/or amendments directly on the ballot, and "legislative referendum" states, which require legislative approval of measures (usually in more than one session and requiring supermajorities) before they can be put on the ballot. Twenty states have the direct initiative, six states have the indirect initiative (state legislatures must first pass citizen-proposed measures before they appear on the ballot) or the popular referendum (citizens can have legislation passed by the legislature put on the ballot), and twenty-four states have the legislative referendum only.

20. Haider-Markel and Meier (1996, 336–37) measured interest group resources as the number of members of the National Gay and Lesbian Task Force (NGLTF) per 100,000 population and the average dollar contribution per member made by NGLTF members. To measure the presence of sympathetic elites, they used support for gay rights on votes in the 100th Congress through the 103rd Congress that the NGLTF designated as significant votes.

21. This finding applied only to nondiscrimination in private employment (Haider-Markel and Meier 1996).

22. According to Wald, Button, and Rienzo (1996, 1168), smaller communities with gay rights ordinances, like Ann Arbor, Michigan, and Berkeley, California, tend to have highly educated populations and high college enrollments.

23. Former Miss America Anita Bryant led the first effort to overturn a local ordinance in Miami-Dade County, Florida, in 1977.

24. A search revealed that fifty local ballot measures appeared dealing with non-discrimination in employment, housing, public accommodations, and credit during the 1977–2006 period. Others may also have appeared.

25. Haider-Markel (2000) also found that passage of hate crimes laws is associated with support from law enforcement officials and opportunities to build broad coalitions with other victim groups seeking hate crimes protection, points that were explored earlier in this chapter.

26. This has happened, for example, in South Carolina (*Herald* 1997), Alabama (Chandler 2002), Idaho (Warbis 1999), Montana (Anez 1999), Virginia (Heyser 2000), and West Virginia (Wallace 2002; McCormick 2002).

27. The major case on constitutionality was the U.S. Supreme Court's decision upholding hate crimes laws in 1993 in the case of *Wisconsin v. Mitchell* (113 S. Ct. 2194).

28. Many commentators attributed Senator John Kerry's loss in the 2004 presidential election to the antimarriage backlash, which other observers later disputed (see Cahill 2005; Klein 2005).

CHAPTER 8. CONCLUSION

1. Gay rights organizations pursue multiple issues simultaneously and serially, but whichever approach is considered, the arenas in which they pursue them are largely separate and distinct.

2. Haider-Markel and Meier (1996) found that debates over whether to cover gays and lesbians under nondiscrimination laws fall into "interest group" or "morality politics" models depending upon whether the issue became salient and the scope of conflict broadened. Gay rights forces were more likely to fail when the issue became salient, conflict broadened, and the debate took on the tone of morality politics.

3. For example, a Roper survey in 1987 revealed that 62 percent of the public thought that "the federal government should be doing more with the problem of AIDS," compared with 31 percent who thought that the government was "doing all they can." Other Roper surveys in 1987 and 1991 showed that 53 and 50 percent of respondents, respectively, agreed that "the government isn't doing enough to prevent discrimination against people with AIDS" and 37 and 39 percent disagreed. An ABC News survey in 1990 showed that 53 percent agreed that "the government is not spending enough money on finding a cure for AIDS," and 24 percent disagreed. A CBS News/*New York Times* poll in 1993 found that 57 percent of the public felt that the federal government "pays too little attention to the needs and problems of people who have AIDS," compared with 35 percent who thought the attention was

the "right amount" or "too much." NBC News/*Wall Street Journal* polls in 1987 and 1988 found that 60 and 64 percent of respondents, respectively, thought that "the federal government is doing not enough about AIDS" and 25 percent thought that the government was doing "just about right" or "too much." (iPoll databank, http:// roperweb.ropercenter.uconn.edu/cgi-bin/hsrun.exe/Roperweb/ipoll/stateID/ ReoOi . . .; accessed 11/16/07, hard copy in possession of the author).

4. For example, *Los Angeles Times* polls in 1985 and 1987 showed that 39 percent and 45 percent of respondents, respectively, favored having "the government spend more money than it does now on AIDS research" if the disease "mostly affected people who were heterosexual, or straight, rather than people who were homosexual, or gay." A CBS News/*New York Times* poll in 1988 showed that only 36 percent of respondents had "some" or "a lot" of "sympathy for people who get AIDS from homosexual activity," compared with 60 percent who said that they had "none" or "not much." Polls by *Rolling Stone* magazine in 1988 and *Newsweek* in 1994 also revealed that the AIDS epidemic made more Americans "less sympathetic toward gays" than "more sympathetic" toward them (iPoll databank, http://roperweb. ropercenter.uconn.edu/cgi-bin/hsrun.exe/Roperweb/ipoll/stateID/ReoOi . . .; accessed 11/16/07, hard copy in possession of the author).

5. Even some of the skeptics suggest that courts can help secure minority rights under certain conditions (Rosenberg 1991).

6. Pinello (2003) found that courts ruled in favor of gay and lesbian petitioners in more than 57 percent of the cases that he examined.

7. Students of public opinion have noted the importance of issue differences on race more than those who study social movements. See Sniderman and Piazza (1993).

8. About 63 percent of the public opposed integrating the races in the military when President Harry Truman issued his executive order for the armed forces to do so (Mershon and Schlossman 1998, 177–78). For the past thirty years, about half of Americans support abortion rights "under some circumstances," about the same number combined either feel there should be no restrictions on abortion or no abortions permitted in any circumstances (O'Connor 1996, 12; Gallup 2000). Americans' division over abortion is also indicated by their responses to the question, "Are you satisfied with the nation's policies regarding the abortion issue?" Forty-five percent say that they are "satisfied," and 46 percent say that they are "dissatisfied" (Gallup 2004). Busing has consistently garnered only between 10 and 25 percent support among the public (Mayer 1992, 372–73).

9. Additional categories could emerge from adding more social movement issues to the analysis. For example, some issues might better fit a traditional elitist

pattern in which the public has little ability to block social movement demands that it finds highly threatening. However, elites with a commitment to traditional values may be able to prevent or repeal policies favored by the movement's supporters. Affirmative action may fit this pattern, for example. When the federal courts became more conservative, they curtailed the scope and methods of the policy.

10. A Zogby International survey of 545 service members who served in Iraq or Afghanistan found that 37 percent said they were opposed to allowing gays to serve openly in the military and 19 percent stated that they were uncomfortable having gays in their midst (reported in Spiegel 2007).

11. Portugal and Turkey are the other two.

12. The lack of disruption may be the result of most gays and lesbians remaining in the closet after nations lifted their bans.

13. The measure of educational attainment (persons twenty-five years old and over with a bachelor's degree or more in 2004 is from the U.S. Census Bureau (2006e). The measure of gay rights groups' resources (membership in the National Gay and Lesbian Task Force per 100,000 state population) is from Haider-Markel (2000). The measure of state citizen ideology and Protestant fundamentalism is from Erikson, Wright, and McIver (1993), and the measure of state elite ideology is from Berry et al. (1998).

14. These states also perform similar to or better on these measures than several states that have already adopted civil rights protections for gays, such as Maine, New Mexico, Wisconsin, New Hampshire, and Nevada.

15. For somewhat different assessments of the long-term future of gay marriage, see D'Emilio (2007) and Wilcox et al. (2007).

16. PBS *Newshour* broadcast, May 9, 2007, on Oregon gives credit to the Democratic takeover of the state government after the election with enacting that state's comprehensive benefits package.

17. For an exhaustive list of the constraints that the gay rights movement faces, some of which uniquely disadvantage it, see Sherrill (1993).

18. For example, Rimmerman (2002, chapter 6) advocates moving away from a "narrow politics of identity" and "civil rights approach" toward building broader political coalitions capable of addressing a larger set of social inequalities that exist in a variety of institutional settings. See also Gamson (1995), Vaid (1995), Warner (1999), and Seidman (2002).

19. Given the preferred strategy of many gay rights activists to work through the courts, a large literature has emerged arguing that the U.S. Constitution protects the right to same-sex marriage and prescribing particular legal doctrines and arguments

that litigators representing LGBT clients should pursue (see, for example, Koppelman 2006; Koppelman 2002, chapters 5–6; Gerstmann 2004; Sunstein 1999).

20. Blue is the color assigned by the media to Democratic strongholds; red represents Republican states.

21. For a discussion of these points within the gay and lesbian community, see Hirsch (2005, ch. 14).

22. For similar statements by legislators and witnesses, see also Connecticut General Assembly 2003, 125, 132; Connecticut General Assembly 2001, 76, 117, 123; Minnesota House Judiciary Committee 1997, tape 1; Minnesota House 1997, tape 3).

23. According to Shapiro (1995–96, 624), "Many people, including many judges, perceive lesbians and gay men as exclusively sexual beings, while heterosexual parents are perceived as people who, along with many other activities in their lives, occasionally engage in sex." See also Fajer (1992).

24. The legislative change in Connecticut was initiated by the Connecticut Supreme Court, which ruled that it could not allow a woman in an lesbian relationship to adopt her partner's baby despite overwhelming evidence that it would be best for the child and invited the state legislature to change the law (see Frisman 2000).

25. Testimony of Syd Phillips to the Connecticut General Assembly (2000c, 120).

Bibliography

Abramson, Paul, and Ronald Inglehart. 1995. *Value Change in Global Perspective.* Ann Arbor: University of Michigan Press.

Adam, Barry D. 1994. "Anatomy of a Panic: State Voyeurism, Gender Politics and the Cult of Americanism." In *Gays and Lesbians in the Military: Issues Concerns and Contrasts,* ed. Wilbur J. Scott and Sandra Carson Stanley, 103–18. New York: Aldine De Gruyter.

Adamany, David. 1973. "Legitimacy, Realigning Elections and the Supreme Court." *Wisconsin Law Review* 3 (September): 790–846.

Adams, Edward A. 1992. "Lesbian Parent Allowed to Adopt: Surrogate Grants Equal Rights to Child's Mother, Her Life Partner." *New York Law Journal,* January 31, 1.

———. 1995. "Lesbian Partner Denied Adoption: Appellate Panel Cites Unmarried Status, Domestic Relations Law." *New York Law Journal,* April 5.

Advocate, The. 1995. "La. Should Have Hate Crime Law" *The Advocate,* August 14, 6B.

Advocate.com. 2006. "Coming Out Process Still Complicated for Gay Youths." October 12. http://www.advocate.com/news_detail_ektid37444.asp.

Agence France Presse. 1999. "Britain Moves to Accept Gays in Army after Court Condemnation." September 27.

———. 2000. "No Rebellion in Ranks over Gays: British Defense Secretary." January 28.

Alameda Times-Star. 2003. "Gay Pride Parade Hails Court Ruling" *Alameda Times-Star,* June 30.

Allen, Rod. 1992. "Military Gay Ban Axed." *Courier-Mail* (Brisbane, Australia), November 24.

Alvarez, Lizette. 2006. "Gay Groups Renew Drive against 'Don't Ask, Don't Tell.'" *New York Times,* September 14, A18.

Amar, Akhil Reed. 1991. "Parity as a Constitutional Question." *Boston University Law Review* 71:645–50.

Amenta, Edwin. 2005. "Political Contexts, Challenger Strategies, and Mobilization: Explaining the Impact of the Townsend Plan." In *Routing the Opposition: Social Movements, Public Policy, and Democracy,* ed. David S. Meyer, Valerie Jenness, and Helen Ingram, 29–64. Minneapolis: University of Minnesota Press.

Amenta, Edwin, Kathleen Dunleavy, and Mary Bernstein. 1994. "Stolen Thunder? Huey Long's 'Share Our Wealth,' Political Mediation, and the Second New Deal." *American Sociological Review* 59 (October): 678–702.

Amenta, Edwin, and Michael P. Young. 1999. "Making and Impact: Conceptual and Methodological Implications of the Collective Goods Criterion." In *How Social Movements Matter,* ed. Marco Giugni, Doug McAdam, and Charles Tilly, 22–41. Minneapolis: University of Minnesota Press.

American Enterprise Institute (AEI). 2004. *Attitudes about Homosexuality and Gay Marriage.* Washington, DC: AEI Studies in Public Opinion.

———. 2006. *Attitudes about Homosexuality and Gay Marriage.* Washington, DC: AEI Studies in Public Opinion.

American Law Institute (ALI). 1955. "Comments to Section 207.5. Tentative Draft Number 4 to the *Model Penal Code.*" Philadelphia: American Law Institute.

———. 1962. "Proposed Official Draft to the *Model Penal Code.*" Sect. 213.2. Philadelphia: American Law Institute.

American Psychiatric Association. 1980. *Diagnostic and Statistical Manual of Mental Disorders,* 3rd ed. Washington, DC: American Psychiatric Association.

Anderson, Cerisse. 1994. "Recent Rulings Divide on Lesbian Adoptions." *New York Law Journal,* January 25.

Anderson, Ed. 1995. "Hate Crimes Legislation Passes Senate." *Times-Picayune* (New Orleans), May 18, A14.

Andriote, John-Manuel. 1999. *Victory Deferred: How AIDS Changed Gay Life in America.* Chicago: University of Chicago Press.

Anez, Bob. 1999. "Committee Advances Bill Abolishing Hate-Crimes Law." *Associated Press State and Local Wire,* January 25.

AAPA US News. 1992. "Defense Ban on Homosexuals." June 19.

Arceneaux, Kevin. 2002. "Direct Democracy and the Link between Public Opinion and State Abortion Policy." *State Politics and Policy Quarterly* 2 (4): 372–87.

Archuleta, Tim. 1999. "Hate-crimes Bill Now Goes to Public Arena." *Albuquerque Tribune,* February 11, A1.

Associated Press. 1992a. "Veterans and War Hero Angry over Lifting of Gay Ban." *Associated Press,* November 24.

———. 1992b. "Lifting of Gay Ban Softens Australia's Tough Man Image." *Associated Press,* December 9.

———. 1998a. "Bill Would Allow Gays and Lesbians to Adopt." *State and Local Wire,* December 31.

———. 1998b. "AG Calls for Gays to Be Included in Hate Crime Legislation." *Associated Press State and Local Wire,* October 13.

———. 1999. "Court Blocks Erie Gay Couple's Adoption Plans." *Associated Press State and Local Wire*, July 4.

———. 2000. "Gilmore Opposes Expanding Hate Crimes Law to Include Sexual Orientation." *Associated Press State and Local Wire*, September 28.

———. 2001a. "Anti-Gay Adoption Law Faces Court Challenge." *Charleston* (WV) *Gazette*, June 4, P3D.

———. 2001b. "Florida's Gay Adoption Ban Is Upheld." *Deseret News* (Salt Lake City, UT), August 31, A2.

———. 2001c. "Three House Speakers Agree Hate-Crimes Legislation Needed." *Associated Press State and Local Wire*, July 9.

———. 2002a. "Gay Adoption Advocates, Opponents, Seek Clarification of Law." *Associated Press State and Local Wire*, March 24.

———. 2002b. "Judge Blocks Last Adoption Hope for Gay, Unwed Couples." *Associated Press State and Local Wire*, June 5.

———. 2003. "Missouri Anti-Sodomy Law Similar to Texas Statute." *Associated Press State and Local Wire*, June 26.

———. 2004. "Family-Values Organizations Call for Boycott of 2 P&G Products." *Associated Press State and Local Wire*, September 17.

———. 2005a. "Report: One Gay Arabic Military Linguist Discharged in '04." *Associated Press State and Local Wire*, November 16.

———. 2005b. "Recent Attacks Fuel Debate on Hate Crimes." *Associated Press State and Local Wire*, December 5.

Astor, Gerald. 1998. *The Right to Fight: A History of African Americans in the Military*. Novato, CA: Presidio Press.

Atlanta Journal and Constitution. 1994. "Around the South: Feeling Left Out." January 29, A3.

Bachman, Jerald G., Peter Freedman-Doan, David R. Segal, Patrick M. O'Malley. 2000. "Distinctive Military Attitudes among U.S. Enlistees, 1976–1997: Self-Selection versus Socialization." *Armed Forces and Society* 26 (4): 561–85.

Bachrach, Peter, and Morton S. Baratz. 1970. *Power and Poverty: Theory and Practice*. New York: Oxford University Press.

Bailey, David. 1995a. "State Law Allows Adoptions by Same-Sex Couples: Appeals Court." *Chicago Daily Law Bulletin* July 18: 1.

———. 1995b. "Two Lesbian Couples Appeal Judge's Denial of Their Adoption Petitions." *Chicago Daily Law Bulletin* January 6: 1.

Bailey, Robert W. 1999. *Gay Politics, Urban Politics: Identity and Economics in the Urban Setting*. New York: Columbia University Press.

Baker, Wayne. 2005. *America's Crisis of Values: Reality and Perception*. Princeton, NJ: Princeton University Press.

Ball, Carlos A. 2003. *The Morality of Gay Rights: An Explanation in Political Philosophy*. New York: Routledge.

Banaszak, Lee Ann. 1996. *Why Movements Succeed or Fail: Opportunity, Culture, and the Struggle for Woman Suffrage*. Princeton, NJ: Princeton University Press.

———. 1998. "Use of the Initiative Process by Women Suffrage Movements." In *Social Movements and American Political Institutions*, ed. Anne N. Costain and Andrew S. McFarland, 99–116. Lanham, MD: Rowman and Littlefield.

Barclay, Scott, and Shauna Fisher. 2003. "The States and the Differing Impetus for Divergent Paths on Same Sex Marriage, 1990–2001." *Policy Studies Journal* 31 (3): 331–52.

———. 2004. "Give and Take: The Elimination of State Sodomy Laws and the Introduction of Anti-Same Sex Marriage Laws." Paper presented at the annual meeting of the American Political Science Association, Chicago, September 2.

Barkham, Patrick. 2005. "Navy's New Message: Your Country Needs You, Especially if You Are Gay." *The Guardian*, February 21, 3.

Barnett, Walter. 1973. *Sexual Freedom and the Constitution: An Inquiry into the Constitutionality of Repressive Sex Laws*. Albuquerque: University of New Mexico Press.

Barnum, David G. 1985. "The Supreme Court and Public Opinion: Judicial Decision Making in the Post–New Deal Period." *Journal of Politics* 47:652–66.

Bartels, Larry. M. 1991. "Constituency Opinion and Congressional Policy Making: The Reagan Defense Buildup." *American Political Science Review* 85:429–56.

Baumgartner, Frank R., and Bryan D. Jones. 1993. *Agendas and Instability in American Politics*. Chicago: University of Chicago Press.

Bawer, Bruce. 1993. *A Place at the Table: The Gay Individual in American Society*. New York: Poseidon Press.

Belkin, Aaron, and Melissa Levit. 2000. " Effects of Lifting of Restrictions on Gay and Lesbian Service in the Israeli Forces: Appraising the Evidence." Report prepared for the Michael D. Palm Center, University of California at Santa Barbara. www.palmcenter.org.

Belkin, Aaron, and Jason McNichol. 2000a. "Effects of Including Gay and Lesbian Soldiers in the Australian Forces: Appraising the Evidence." Report prepared for the Michael D. Palm Center, University of California at Santa Barbara. www.palmcenter.org.

———. 2000b. "Effects of 1992 Lifting of Restrictions on Gay and Lesbian Service in the Canadian Forces: Appraising the Evidence." Report prepared for the Michael D. Palm Center, University of California at Santa Barbara. http://www.palmcenter.org.

Bell, Casey. 2007a. "Legislation to Repeal Gay Military Ban Introduced." *Philadelphia Gay News,* March 9–15, 1.

———. 2007b. "U.S. House Passes Hate-Crimes Bill." *Philadelphia Gay News,* May 11–17, 1.

Benecke, Michelle M., and Kirsten S. Dodge. 1996. "Military Women: Casualties of the Armed Forces' War on Lesbians and Gay Men." In *Gay Rights, Military Wrongs: Political Perspectives on Lesbians and Gays in the Military,* ed. Craig A. Rimmerman, 71–108. New York: Garland.

Bergin, Mary. 2003. "A Child's Best Interest: Family Law Now Emphasizes Kids More." *Capital Times* (Madison, WI), January 16, 1F.

Bergren, Dennis. 2003. "Backing Sodomy Laws for Gays Is Indeed Bigotry." *Capital Times* (Madison, WI), July 10, 17A.

Berrill, Kevin T. 1992. "Anti-Gay Violence and Victimization in the United States: An Overview." In *Hate Crimes: Confronting Violence against Lesbians and Gay Men,* ed. Gregory M. Herek and Kevin T. Berrill, 19–45. Newbury Park, CA: Sage.

Berry, William D., and Frances Stokes Berry. 1999. "Innovation and Diffusion Models in Policy Research." In *Theories of the Policy Process (Theoretical Lenses on Public Policy),* ed. Paul A. Sabatier, 169–200. Boulder, CO: Westview.

Berry, William D., Evan J. Ringquist, Richard C. Fording, and Russell L. Hanson. 1998. "Measuring Citizen and Government Ideology in the American States." *American Journal of Political Science* 42 (January): 327–48.

Berube, Allan. 1990. *Coming Out under Fire: The History of Gay Men and Women in World War Two.* New York: Plume.

Beyondmarriage.org. 2006. "Beyond Same-Sex Marriage: A New Strategic Vision of All Our Families and Relationships." http://beyondmarriage.org.

Bianco, David Ari. 1996. "Echoes of Prejudice: The Debates over Race and Sexuality in the Armed Forces." In *Gay Rights, Military Wrongs: Political Perspectives on Lesbians and Gays in the Military,* ed. Craig A. Rimmerman, 47–70. New York: Garland.

Bickel, Alexander. 1962. *The Least Dangerous Branch.* Indianapolis: Bobbs-Merrill.

Bigner, Jerrry J., and R. Brooke Jacobsen. 1992. "Adult Responses to Child Behavior and Attitudes toward Fathering: Gay and Non-Gay Fathers." *Journal of Homosexuality* 23 (3): 99–112.

Bindman, Stephen. 1990. "Air Force Lesbian Wins Back Her Job." *Toronto Star,* August 16, A3.

————. 1992a. "Military Refuses to Reinstate Lesbian." *Toronto Star*, May 11, A4.

————. 1992b. "Military Says No to Gay Lieutenant." *Calgary Herald*, May 11, A1.

————. 1992c. "Military Survey Probes Sexual Preferences." *The Record*, June 1, C12.

————. 1992d. "Anti-Gay Policy Goes on Trial." *Vancouver Sun*, October 26, A3.

Birmingham News. 2003. "Readers' Opinions." *Birmingham* (AL) *News*, July 10.

Bleemer, Russ. 1995. "Appeals Panel Authorizes Same-Sex Partner's Adoption Rights." *New Jersey Law Journal*, November 6.

Bobo, Laurence, and Frederick C. Licari. 1989. "Education and Political Tolerance: Testing the Effects of Cognitive Sophistication and Target Group Affect." *Public Opinion Quarterly* 53:285–308.

Booth, Jenny. 1999. "Top Brass Out of Step and on the Defensive." *The Scotsman*, September 28, 4.

Boswell, John. 1980. *Christianity, Social Tolerance and Homosexuality*. Chicago: University of Chicago Press.

Bozett, Frederick W. 1989. "Gay Fathers: A Review of the Literature." *Journal of Homosexuality* 18 (1–2): 137–62.

Brace, Paul, and Melinda Gann Hall. 1997. "The Interplay of Preferences, Case Facts, Context and Rule in the Political of Judicial Choice." *Journal of Politics* 59 (4): 1206–31.

Branswell, Helen. 1999. "U.K.'s Ban on Gays in Army Discriminatory: Court." *Toronto Star*, September 28.

Brantner, Paula A. 1992. "Removing Bricks from a Wall of Discrimination: State Constitutional Challenges to Sodomy Laws." *Hastings Constitutional Law Quarterly* 19 (Winter): 495–533.

Brennan, William J., Jr. 1986. "The Bill of Rights and the States: The Revival of State Constitutions as Guardians of Individual Rights." *New York University Law Review* 61:535–53.

Brewer, Mark D., and Jeffrey M. Stonecash. 2007. *Split: Class and Cultural Divides in American Politics*. Washington, DC: CQ Press.

Brewer, Paul R. 2002. Framing, Value Words, and Citizens' Explanations of Their Issue Opinions. *Political Communication* 19 (3): 303–16.

————. 2003. "Values, Political Knowledge and Public Opinion about Gay Rights: A Framing-Based Account." *Public Opinion Quarterly* 67:173–201.

Brewer, Paul R., and Clyde Wilcox. 2005. "Trends: Same-Sex Marriage and Civil Unions." *Public Opinion Quarterly* 69:599–616.

Brewer, Sarah E., David Kaib, and Karen O'Connor. 2000. "Sex and the Supreme Court: Gays, Lesbians and Justice." In *The Politics of Gay Rights*, ed. Craig

A. Rimmerman, Kenneth D. Wald, and Clyde Wilcox, 377–408. Chicago: University of Chicago Press.

Brodzinsky, David M., Charlotte J. Patterson, and Mahnoush Vaziri. 2002. "Adoption Agency Perspectives on Lesbian and Gay Prospective Parents: A National Study." *Adoption Quarterly* 5:5–23.

Brooke, James. 1998. "Gay Man Dies rrom Attack, Fanning Outrage and Debate." *New York Times*, October 13, A1.

Brown, Kate. 2007. Interview on *Newshour with Jim Lehrer*, May 9.

Brown, William. 2002. "Not All Agree on Stance on Homosexual Adoption." *Rocky Mountain News* (Denver), February 23, 2W.

Bruni, Frank. 1995. "For Gay Couples, Ruling to Cheer on Adoption." *New York Times*, November 5, 41.

Bulkeley, Deborah. 2005. "Crime Bill's Failure Puzzles Advocates." *Deseret Morning News* (Salt Lake City, UT), March 3.

Bull, John M. R. 2001. "Long-Awaited Adoption Reform Criticized Before Senate Panel." *Pittsburgh Post-Gazette*, October 16, B8.

Bundy, Jennifer. 2001. "Troopers Seek Repeal of Hate-Crimes Law." *Charleston* (WV) *Gazette*, March 20, 2C.

Burelli, David F. 1994. "An Overview of the Debate on Homosexuals in the U.S. Military." In *Gays and Lesbians in the Military: Issues Concerns and Contrasts*, ed. Wilbur J. Scott and Sandra Carson Stanley, 17–32. New York: Aldine De Gruyter.

Burelli, David F., and Charles Dale. 2005. *Homosexuals and U.S. Military Policy: Current Issues.* CRS Report for Congress, RL30113. Washington, DC: Congressional Research Service.

Burstein, Paul. 1985. *Discrimination, Jobs and Politics: The Struggle for Equal Employment Opportunity in the U.S. since the New Deal.* Chicago: University of Chicago Press.

———. 1998. "Interest Organizations, Political Parties and the Study of Democratic Politics." In *Social Movements and American Political Institutions*, ed. Anne N. Costain and Andrew S. McFarland, 39–58. Lanham, MD: Rowman and Littlefield.

Burstein, Paul, and William Freudenburg 1978. "Changing Public Policy: The Impact of Public Opinion, Antiwar Demonstrations, and War Costs on Senate Voting on Vietnam Motions." *American Journal of Sociology* 84 (1): 99–122.

Button, James W., Barbara A. Rienzo, and Kenneth D. Wald. 1997. *Private Lives, Public Conflicts: Battles over Gay Rights in American Communities.* Washington, DC: CQ Press.

Cahill, Sean. 2005. "The Symbolic Centrality of Gay Marriage in the 2004 Presidential Election." In *The Future of Gay Rights in America*, ed. H. N. Hirsch, 47–80. New York: Routledge.

Cahill, Sean, Mitra Ellen, and Sarah Tobias. 2002. *Family Policy: Issues Affecting Gay, Lesbian, Bisexual and Transgender Families.* Washington, DC: Policy Institute of the National Gay and Lesbian Task Force.

Cahn, Naomi. 1997. "The Moral Complexities of Family Law." *Stanford Law Review* 50:225–71.

Cain, Patricia. 2000. *Rainbow Rights: The Role of Lawyers and Courts in the Lesbian and Gay Civil Rights Movement.* Boulder, CO: Westview.

Campbell, Colton C., and Roger H. Davidson. 2000. "Gay and Lesbian Issues in the Congressional Arena." In *The Politics of Gay Rights,* ed. Craig Rimmerman, Kenneth D. Wald, and Clyde Wilcox, 347–76. Chicago: University of Chicago Press.

Carmines, Edward G., and James A. Stimson. 1980. "The Two Faces of Issue Voting." *American Political Science Review* 74:78–91.

Carpenter, Dale. 2004. " The Unknown Past of *Lawrence v. Texas." Michigan Law Review* 102 (June): 1464–1527.

Carpenter, Mackenzie. 2002. "Ruling Benefits Gays' Children." *Pittsburgh Post-Gazette,* August 22, B1.

Casper, Jonathan. 1976. "The Supreme Court and National Policymaking." *American Political Science Review* 70:50–73.

Chandler, Kim. 2002. "Sexual Orientation-Hate Crime Bill Narrowly Clears Committee." *Birmingham* (AL) *News,* February 22.

Charlton, Peter. 1992a. "Army Mates, Yes—But Lovers Pose Problems." *Courier Mail* (Brisbane, Australia), February 23.

———. 1992b. "Kiss Them Goodnight, Sergeant-Major." *Courier-Mail* (Brisbane, Australia), September 22.

Chasin, Alexandra. 2000. *Selling Out: The Gay and Lesbian Movement Goes to Market.* New York: St. Martin's.

Chauncey, George, Jr. 1994. *Gay New York: Gender, Urban Culture and the Making of the Gay Male World, 1890–1940.* New York: Basic.

———. 1999. "Christian Brotherhood or Sexual Perversion? Homosexual Identities and the Construction of Sexual Boundaries in the World War I Era." In *Same Sex: Debating the Ethics, Science and Culture of Homosexuality,* ed. John Corvino, 235–57. New York: Rowman and Littlefield.

———. 2004a. "What Gay Studies Taught the Court: The Historians' Amicus Brief in *Lawrence v. Texas." GLQ: A Journal of Lesbian and Gay Studies* 10:509–38.

———. 2004b. *Why Marriage? The History Shaping Today's Debate over Gay Equality.* New York: Basic.

Cheevers, Jack. 1999. "Holy Homophobia!" *New Times Los Angeles,* August 19.

Chemerinsky, Erwin. 1991. "Ending the Parity Debate." *Boston University Law Review* 71:593–608.

Chicago Daily Herald. 2003. "Court Ruling Upholds Privacy Rights." *Chicago Daily Herald,* June 30, 8.

Choper, Jesse. 1980. *Judicial Review and the National Political Process.* Chicago: University of Chicago Press.

Cicchino, Peter M., Bruce R. Deming, and Katherine M. Nicholson 1991. "Sex, Lies and Civil Rights: A Critical History of the Massachusetts Gay Civil Rights Bill." *Harvard Civil Rights–Civil Liberties Law Review* 26:549–632.

Clark, James. 1998. "RAF Chief: Let Gays In." *Daily Mail* (Glasgow, Scotland), June 17, 26.

Clark, Karen, Minnesota state representative, personal communication, July 9, 2001.

Cohen, Jean L. 1985. "Strategy or Identity: New Theoretical Paradigms and Contemporary Social Movements." *Social Research* 52:663–716.

Cohen, Karen J. 1993. "Hate-Crime Bill Copies Wisconsin Law." *Wisconsin State Journal,* March 3, 1A.

Conger, John J. 1977. "Proceedings of the American Psychological Association." *American Psychologist* 32 (6): 408–38.

———. 1979. "Proceedings of the American Psychological Association." *American Psychologist* 35 (6): 501–36.

Connecticut General Assembly. 2000a. Debate before the Senate on HB5830, "An Act Concerning the Best Interests of Children in Adoption Matters," May 3. http://search.cga.state.ct.us/ (accessed 2003; hard copy in possession of the author).

———. 2000b. Debate before the House of Representatives on HB5830, "An Act Concerning the Best Interests of Children in Adoption Matters," April 28. http://search.cga.state.ct.us/ (accessed November 11, 2003; hard copy in possession of the author).

———. 2000c. Hearings before the Committee on the Judiciary on HB5830, "An Act Concerning the Best Interests of Children in Adoption Matters," March 13, http://search.cga.state.ct.us/ (accessed September 17, 2003; hard copy in possession of the author).

———. 2001. Hearings before the Committee on the Judiciary on the Legal Status of Same Gender Couples, March 16. http://search.cga.state.ct.us/ (accessed October 4, 2003; hard copy in possession of the author).

———. 2002. Hearings before the Committee on the Judiciary Concerning the Applicability of Certain Statutes to Same Sex Partners and HB5001, "An Act Concerning Same Sex Marriage." February 11. http://search.cga.state.ct.us/ (accessed October 6, 2003; hard copy in possession of the author).

———. 2003. Hearings before the Committee on the Judiciary Concerning Three Bills Concerning Gay Marriage, Civil Unions and Defense of Marriage, February 24. http://search.cga.state.ct.us/ (accessed October 6, 2003; hard copy in possession of the author).

Connecticut Post. 2003. "Study Finds Gay Adoption a Little Easier." *Connecticut Post* (Bridgeport, CT), December 18.

Connell, R. W. 1992. "A Very Straight Gay: Masculinity, Homosexual Experience, and the Dynamics of Gender." *American Sociological Review* 57 (December): 735–51.

Connolly, Adam. 1992a. "Military Chiefs Deadlocked on Gays Issue." *Courier-Mail* (Brisbane, Australia), March 24.

———. 1992b. "Chiefs Fail to Decide on Homosexuals in Military." *The Advertiser* (South Australia), March 24.

———. 1992c. "A Government Brawl on Gays in Army." *Courier-Mail* (Brisbane, Australia), March 25.

———. 1992d. "Government Ready for Battle on Gay Ban." *The Advertiser* (South Australia), June 19.

———. 1992e. "Cabinet Split Over Gays in Military." *The Advertiser* (South Australia), June 27.

Cooke, Sarah. 2005. "Lawmakers Consider Expanding Hate Crimes Law." *Associated Press State and Local Wire,* January 14.

Cosby, Carolyn, and Jonathan Malmude. 1994. "Gay Lobby Filled with 'Hate Crimes' Apologists." *Bangor* (ME) *Daily News,* October 20.

Costain, Anne N. 1992. *Inviting Women's Rebellion: A Political Process Interpretation of the Women's Movement.* Baltimore: Johns Hopkins University Press.

Costain, Anne, and Steven Majstorovic 1994. "Congress, Social Movements and Public Opinion: The Multiple Origins of Women's Rights Legislation." *Political Research Quarterly* 41:111–35.

Council for Public Interest Law (CPIL). 1976. *Balancing the Scales of Justice: Financing Public Interest Law in America.* San Diego: Council for Public Interest Law, University of San Diego School of Law.

Crary, David. 2003. "Nontraditional Families Gain Greater Legal Recognition and Rights." *Associated Press State and Local Wire,* August 4.

———. 2004. "Many Gay Couples Contemplating Marriage Are Experienced Parents." *Associated Press State and Local Wire*, March 22.

Crossley, Nick. 2002. *Making Sense of Social Movements*. Philadelphia: Open University Press.

Crowe, Robert. 2004. "Second-Parent Option Provides Equal Rights: Adoption Law Applies to Unmarried Couples." *Houston Chronicle*, June 25, A34.

Cullen, Kevin. 1999. "British Bristling at Reach of European Court of Human Rights." *Boston Globe*, October 13, A4.

Cunningham, Laurie. 2003. "Gay Adoption Ban Goes to Court." *Miami Daily Business Review*, March 4.

Currah, Paisley, and Shannon Minter. 2000. *Transgender Equality: A Handbook for Activists and Policymakers*, New York: National Gay and Lesbian Task Force.

Dahl, Robert A. 1957. "Decision-Making in a Democracy: The Supreme Court as a National Policymaker." *Journal of Public Law* 6:279–95.

Daily Mail. 1999. "Reformers Are Wrecking the Nation's Armed Forces." *Daily Mail* (Glasgow, Scotland), January 15.

Daily News. 2000. "Rudy's Record is Open Book." *Daily News* (New York), July 11, 32.

Daily News. 2003. "Sun Shines on Gay Parade." *Daily News* (New York), June 30, 9.

Daley, Yvonne. 1990. "Beating of Gay Man Raises Stakes for Vermont Hate Crimes Bill" *Boston Globe*, April 22, 73.

Dalfiume, Richard M. 1969. *Desegregation of the U.S. Armed Forces: Fighting on Two Fronts, 1939–1953*. Columbia: University of Missouri Press.

D'Amico, Francine 1996. "Race-ing and Gendering the Military Closet." In *Gay Rights, Military Wrongs: Political Perspectives on Lesbians and Gays in the Military*, ed. Craig A. Rimmerman, 3–46. New York: Garland.

D'Anjou, L. 1996. *Social Movements and Cultural Change: The First Abolition Campaign Revisited*. New York: Aldine De Gruyter.

Dao, James. 1995. "New York's Highest Court Rules Unmarried Couples Can Adopt." *New York Times*, November 3, A1.

Darnovsky, Marcy, Barbara Epstein, and Richard Flacks. 1995. "Introduction." In *Cultural Politics and Social Movements*, ed. Marcy Darnovsky, Barbara Epstein, and Richard Flacks, vii–xxiii. Philadelphia: Temple University Press.

Davenport, Paul. 2004. "Supreme Court Lets Stand Ruling Upholding Gay Marriage Ban." *Associated Press State and Local Wire*, May 25.

Davidson, Keay. 2001. "Sexual Orientation Found Irrelevant to Child-Rearing." *San Francisco Chronicle*, September 2, A5.

Delon, Michel. 1985. "The Priest, the Philosopher, and Homosexuality in Enlightenment France." *Eighteenth Century Life* 9:122–31.

D'Emilio, John. 1983. *Sexual Politics, Sexual Communities*. Chicago: University of Chicago Press.

———. 2000. "Cycles of Change, Questions of Strategy: The Gay and Lesbian Movement after Fifty Years." In *The Politics of Gay Rights*, ed. Craig A. Rimmerman, Kenneth D. Wald, and Clyde Wilcox, 31–53. Chicago: University of Chicago Press.

———. 2005. "Some Lessons from *Lawrence*." In *The Future of Gay Rights in America*, ed. H. N. Hirsch, 3–14. New York: Routledge.

———. 2007. "Will the Courts Set Us Free?" In *The Politics of Same-Sex Marriage*, ed. Craig A. Rimmerman and Clyde Wilcox, 39–64. Chicago: University of Chicago Press.

DeAgostino, Martin. 2005. "Panel Acts to Toughen Ban on Gay Marriage." *South Bend* (IN) *Tribune*, February 9, A1.

Demo, D. H., and M. J. Cox. 2000. "Families and Young Children: A Review of Research in the 1990s." *Journal of Marriage and the Family* 62:876–96.

Denver Post 2003. "Protecting All Children." *Denver Post*, February 18, B6.

Desch, Michael C. 2001. "Explaining the Gap: Vietnam, the Republicanization of the South, and the End of the Mass Army." In *Soldiers and Civilians: The Civil-Military Gap and American National Security*, ed. Peter D. Feaver and Richard H. Kohn, 289–324. Cambridge, MA: Belfer Center for Science and International Affairs.

Dewar, Helen. 2000. "GOP Shelves Expansion of Law on Hate Crimes." *Washington Post*, October 6, A14.

———. 2004a. "Congress Leaves Some Priority Bill Unfinished." *Washington Post*, October 14, A29.

———. 2004b. "Senate Backs Tougher Hate-Crimes Law." *Washington Post*, June 16, A4.

Dobbin, Ben. 2004. "Court Allows Joint Petition by Lesbian Couple in Adoption Case." *Associated Press State and Local Wire*, March 25.

Dobner, Jennifer. 2003. "Hate-Crime Bill Gains in House." *Deseret News* (Salt Lake City, UT), February 19, A9.

———. 2004. "New Push for Hate-Crimes Bill." *Deseret Morning News* (Salt Lake City, UT), November 3.

Domrzalski, Dennis. 1996. "Finance Committee Advances Hate-Crime Bill." *Albuquerque Tribune*, October 29, A7.

Donaldson, Gary. 1991. *The History of African-Americans in the Military.* Malabar, FL: Krieger.

Donovan, Todd, and Shaun Bowler. 1998. "Direct Democracy and Minority Rights: An Extension." *American Journal of Political Science* 42 (3): 1020–24.

Dorris, John B. 1999. "Antidiscrimination Laws in Local Government." In *Gays and Lesbians in the Democratic Process,* ed. Ellen D. B. Riggle and Barry L. Tadlock, 39–61. New York: Columbia University Press.

Dover, K. J. 1978. *Greek Homosexuality.* New York: Vintage.

Druckman, James N. 2001. "On the Limits of Framing Effects: Who Can Frame?" *Journal of Politics* 63 (November): 1042–44.

Dufour, Claude. 1998. "Mobilizing Gay Activists." In *Social Movements and American Political Institutions,* ed. Anne N. Costain and Andrew S. McFarland, 59–72. Lanham, MD: Rowman and Littlefield.

Dullea, Georgia. 1988. "Gay Couples' Wish to Adopt Grows, along with Increasing Resistance." *New York Times,* February 7, sec. 1, pt. 1, p. 26.

Duncan, Laura. 1994. "Lesbians' Right to Adopt Subject to Appeal." *Chicago Daily Law Bulletin,* March 15, 1.

Dunford, Bruce. 2001. "Cayetano Weighs Possible Veto of Hate Crimes Bill." *Associated Press State and Local Wire,* May 23.

Dunnewind, Stephanie. 1992. "Sides Clash on Effort to Protect Gays from Harassment." *Seattle Post-Intelligencer,* February 27, B1.

Earl, Jennifer. 2000. "Methods, Movements and Outcomes: Methodological Difficulties in the Study of Extra-Movement Outcomes." In *Research in Social Movements, Conflicts and Change,* vol. 22, ed. Patrick G. Coy, 3–25. Stampford, CT: JAI Press.

Economist. 1999. "Secret Relief." *Economist,* October 2, 61.

Egan, Patrick J., and Kenneth Sherrill. 2005a. "Marriage and the Shifting Priorities of a New Generation of Lesbians and Gays." *PS: Political Science and Politics* April: 229–32.

———. 2005b. "Neither an In-Law Nor an Outlaw Be: Trends in Americans' Attitudes Toward Gay People." www.publicopinonpros.com/features/2005/feb/sherrill_egan.asp.

Egan, Patrick, Nathaniel Persily, and Kevin Wallsten. 2006. "Gay Rights, Public Opinion and the Courts." Unpublished manuscript.

Egan, Timothy. 1993. "Voters in Oregon Back Local Anti-gay Rules." *New York Times,* July 1, A10.

Ehrenreich, Barbara. 1997. *Blood Rites: Origins and History of the Passions of War.* New York: Metropolitan.

Eichstaedt, Peter. 1997. "Hate Crime Bill Would OK Stiff Sentences." *Albuquerque Journal*, February 23, B4.

Eisinger, Peter K. 1973. "The Conditions of Protest Behavior in American Cities." *American Political Science Review* 57:11–28.

Ellis, Alan L., and R. Brent Vasseur. 1993. "Prior Interpersonal Contact with and Attitudes Towards Gays and Lesbians in an Interviewing Context." *Journal of Homosexuality* 25:31–45.

Ellison, Christoperh G., and Marc A. Musick. 1993. "Southern Intolerance: A Fundamentalist Effect?" *Social Forces* 72:379–98.

Elovitz, Marc E. 1995. "Adoption by Lesbian and Gay People: The Use and Mis-use of Social Science Research." *Duke Journal of Gender Law and Policy* 2:207–25.

Elshtain, Jean Bethke. 1987. *Women and War*. New York: Basic.

Ely, John Hart. 1980. *Democracy and Distrust*. Cambridge, MA: Harvard University Press.

Enloe, Cynthia. 1988. "United States." In Eva Isaksson, ed., *Women and the Military System*, 71–93. New York: St Martin's.

———. 1994. "The Politics of Constructing the American Woman Soldier." In *Women Soldiers: Images and Realities*, ed. Elisabetta Addis and Valeria E. Russo, 81–110. New York: St. Martin's.

Epstein, Lee, Jeffrey A. Segal, Harold Spaeth, and Thomas G. Walker. 2003. *The Supreme Court Compendium: Data, Decisions and Developments*, 3rd ed. Washington, DC: CQ Press.

Equality Utah. 2005. "Briefing Paper: Facts Regarding Utah's Hate Crimes Legislation, House Bill 90." Salt Lake City: Equality Utah.

Erikson, Robert S., Gerald C. Wright, and John P. McIver. 1993. *Statehouse Democracy: Public Opinion and Policy in the American States*. New York: Cambridge University Press.

Erskine, Hazel. 1967. "The Polls: Negro Housing." *Public Opinion Quarterly* 31 (Autumn): 482–98.

Eskridge, Willaim N., Jr. 1996. *The Case for Same-Sex Marriage: From Sexual Liberty to Civilized Commitment*. New York: Free Press.

———. 1997. "Law and the Construction of the Closet: American Regulation of Same-Sex Intimacy, 1880–1946." *Iowa Law Review* 82:1007–1136.

———. 2002. *Gaylaw: Challenging the Apartheid of the Closet*. Cambridge, MA: Harvard University Press.

———. 2004. "*Lawrence*'s Jurisprudence of Tolerance: Judicial Review to Lower the Stakes of Identity Politics." *Minnesota Law Review* 88:1021–1102.

Espenshade, Linda. 2002a. "Couple Fights for Equal Parental Rights." *Intelligencer Journal*, March 5, B4.

———. 2002b. "They Win Fight to Become Family: Lesbian Couple from Lancaster County Speaks about Long Adoption Battle." *Intelligencer Journal*, August 23, A1.

———. 2002c. "Homosexuals Have Been Adopting for Years in Lancaster County." *Intelligencer Journal*, March 5, B4.

———. 2002d. "Wanting In: Gays Seeking Right to Adopt Children of Their Partners." *Intelligencer Journal*, March 5, A1.

Estrada, Armando X., and David J. Weiss. 1999. "Attitudes of Military Personnel toward Homosexuals." *Journal of Homosexuality* 37 (4): 83–97.

Eule, Julian N. 1990. "Judicial Review of Direct Democracy." *Yale Law Journal* 99:1503–89.

Evening Sun. 2003. "Gay Paraders Rave about Sodomy Ruling." *Evening Sun* (Hanover, PA), June 30.

Fajer, Marc A. 1992. "Can Two Real Men Eat Quiche Together? Storytelling, Gender-Role Stereotypes, and Legal Protection for Lesbians and Gay Men." *University of Miami Law Review* 46 (January): 512–650.

Family Research Council (FRC). 2006. Home page. www.frc.org.

Farrington, Brendan. 2001a. "Florida's Ban on Homosexual Adoptions Found Valid." *Legal Intelligencer*, August 31, 4.

———. 2001b. "Federal Judge Upholds Florida Ban on Adoptions by Gays." *Associated Press State and Local Wire*, August 30.

Feaver, Peter D., and Richard H. Kohn, eds. 2001. *Soldiers and Civilians: The Civil-Military Gap and American National Security*. Cambridge, MA: Belfer Center for Science and International Affairs.

Feeney, Sheila Anne. 1997. "Two Men and a Baby: More Gay Male Couples Are Adopting—And Changing the System in the Process." *New York Daily News*, November 16, 52.

Feldblum, Chai. 1998. "A Progressive Moral Case for Same-Sex Marriage." *Temple Political and Civil Rights Law Review* 7:485–93.

Finn, Scott. 2001. "Hate Crimes Protection for Gays at Issue in Measure." *Charleston* (WV) *Gazette*, March 21, 1A.

Finnegan, Michael. 1997. "Gov's Push vs. Bias Crimes." *Daily News* (NY), February 14, 34.

Fiorina, Morris, with Samuel J. Abrams and Jeremy C. Pope. 2005. *Culture War? The Myth of a Polarized America*. New York: Pearson/Longman.

Fischer, Karin. 2000. "Hate Bill May Not See Vote; Decision on Divisive Issue to Await Wise's Successor." *Charleston* (SC) *Daily Mail,* August 3, P1C.

Flaks, David K., I. Ficher, F. Masterpasqua, and G. Joseph. 1995. "Lesbians Choosing Motherhood: A Comparative Study of Lesbian and Heterosexual Parents and Their Children." *Developmental Psychology* 31:105–14.

Flemming, Roy, John Bohte, and B. Dan Wood. 1997. "One Voice among Many: The Supreme Court's Influence on Attentiveness to Issues in the U.S., 1947–1992." *American Journal of Political Science* 41:1224–50.

Fletcher, Harrison. 1997. "Why Won't Governor Sign Bills on Hate Crimes?" *Albuquerque Tribune,* February 6, B1.

Florescue, Leonard G. 1995. "An Expanded Definition: Who Can Adopt?" *New York Law Journal* November 13.

Florio, Gwen. 1998. "Bias-Law Debate Heats Up." *Pittsburgh Post-Gazette,* October 13, A9.

Foucault, Michel. 1979. *The History of Sexuality: An Introduction,* vol. I. London: Allen Lane.

———. 1985. *The Use of Pleasure: Volume Two of the History of Sexuality,* trans. R. Hurley. New York: Vintage.

Fradella, Henry F. 2002. "Legal, Moral, and Social Reasons for Decriminalizing Sodomy." *Journal of Contemporary Criminal Justice* 18:279–301.

Francis, Delma J. 2004. "Lesbian Couple Off Adoption List." *Minneapolis Star Tribune,* February 20, 7B.

Francke, Linda Bird. 1997. *Ground Zero: The Gender Wars in the Military.* New York: Simon and Schuster.

Frank, John P. 1998. *The American Law Institute, 1923–1998.* Washington, DC: American Law Institute.

Frank, Nathaniel. 2002. "'Don't Ask, Don't Tell' v. the War on Terrorism." *New Republic,* November 18, 18.

Frank, Thomas. 2004. *What's the Matter with Kansas? How Conservatives Won the Heart of America.* New York: Metropolitan.

Freedman, Mark. 1971. *Homosexuality and Psychological Functioning.* Belmont, CA: Brooks/Cole.

Freeman, Jo. 1975. *The Politics of Women's Liberation.* New York: McKay.

Friedelbaum, Stanley H. 1991–92. "Judicial Federalism: Current Trends and Long-Term Prospects." *Florida State University Law Review* 19:1053–88.

Frisman, Paul. 2000. "Gay and Lesbian Adoptions Again Before Judiciary." *Connecticut Law Tribune,* March 20.

Funston, Richard. 1975. "The Supreme Court and Critical Elections." *American Political Science Review* 69:795–811.

Fusco, Chris. 2003. "Catholic Charities Reviewing Foster Care Policies." *Chicago Sun-Times,* August 6, 18.

Gade, Paul, David R. Segal, and Edgar Johnson. 1996. "The Experience of Foreign Militaries." In *Out in Force: Sexual Orientation and the Military,* ed. Gregory M. Herek, Jared B. Jobe, and Ralph M. Carney, 106–30. Chicago: University of Chicago Press.

Gal, Reuven. 1994. "Gays in the Military: Policy and Practice in the Israeli Self-Defence Forces." In *Gays and Lesbians in the Military: Issues, Concerns and Contrasts,* ed. Wilbur J. Scott and Sandra Carson Stanley, 181–90. New York: Aldine De Gruyter.

Gallup Organization. 1999. "Americans Support Hate Crimes Legislation that Protects Gays." http://www.gallup.com/poll/content/login.aspx?ci=3943 (accessed July 1, 2005; hard copy in possession of the author).

———. 2000. "Abortion, General." Furnished by the Roper Center for Public Opinion Research, Storrs, CT, April 10.

———. 2004. "Abortion, General." Furnished by the Roper Center for Public Opinion Research, Storrs, CT, January 20.

Gamble, Barbara. 1997. "Putting Civil Rights to a Popular Vote." *American Journal of Political Science* 41:245–69.

Gamson, Joshua. 1995. "Must Identity Movements Self-Destruct? A Queer Dilemma." *Social Problems* 42:390–407.

———. 1998. *Freaks Talk Back: Tabloid Talk Shows and Sexual Nonconformity.* Chicago: University of Chicago Press.

Gamson, William. 1968. *Power and Discontent.* Homewood, IL: Dorsey Press.

———. 1975. *The Strategy of Social Protest.* Homewood, IL: Dorsey.

Garvin, Charles D., and John E. Tropman. 1998. *Social Work in Contemporary Society,* 2nd ed., Boston: Allyn and Bacon.

Gates, Gary, M. V. Lee Badgtett, Jennifer Ehrle Macomber, and Kate Chambers. 2007. "Adoption and Foster Care by Gay and Lesbian Parents in the United States." Report. Los Angeles and Washington, DC: The Williams Institute, UCLA School of Law, and The Urban Institute.

Gehrke, Robert. 2000. Gay Adoption: Legislature Sets Sights on Banning Gay Adoption. *Associated Press State and Local Wire,* February 25.

Gentry, Cynthia S. 1987. "Social Distance Regarding Male and Female Homosexuals." *Journal of Social Psychology* 127:199–208.

Gerstmann, Evan. 1999. *The Constitutional Underclass: Gays, Lesbians, and the Failure of Class-Based Equal Protection* Chicago: University of Chicago Press.

———. 2004. *Same-Sex Marriage and the Constitution*. Cambridge, U.K.: Cambridge University Press.

Gillette, Clayton P. 1988. "Plebiscites, Participation, and Collective Action in Local Government Law." *Michigan Law Review* 86:930–88.

Gitlin, H. Joseph. 1995. "Adoption by Lesbians May Lead to High Court Action, Legislation." *Chicago Daily Law Bulletin,* September 1, 6.

Giugni, Marco. 1999. "How Social Movements Matter: Past Research, Present Problems, Future Developments." In *How Social Movements Matter,* ed. Marco Giugni, Doug McAdam, and Charles Tilly, xiii–xxxiii. Minnesota: University of Minnesota Press.

Glendon, Mary Ann. 1986. "Fixed Rules and Discretion in Contemporary Family Law and Succession Law." *Tulane Law Review* 60:1165–97.

———. 1989. *The Transformation of Family Law*. Chicago: University of Chicago Press.

Gluckman, Amy, and Betsy Reed. 1997. "The Gay Marketing Moment." In *Homo Economics: Capitalism, Community, and Lesbian and Gay Life,* ed. Amy Gluckman and Betsy Reed, 3–10. New York: Routledge.

Goldfield, Michael. 1997. *The Color of Politics: Race and the Mainsprings of American Politics*. New York: New Press.

Goldstein, Anne B. 1988. "History, Homosexuality, and Political Values: Searching for the Hidden Determinants of *Bowers v. Hardwick*." *Yale Law Journal* 97:1073–1103.

Goldwater, Barry. 1993. "The Gay Ban: Just Plain Un-American." *Washington Post,* June 10, A23.

Goleman, Daniel. 1992. "Studies Find No Disadvantages in Growing Up in a Gay Home." *New York Times,* December 2, C14.

Golombok, Susan, Ann Spencer, and Michael Rutter. 1983. "Children in Lesbian and Single-Parent Households: Psychosexual and Psychiatric Appraisal." *Journal of Child Psychology and Psychiatry* 24:551–72.

Goode, Erica. 2002. "Group Wants Gays to Have Right to Adopt a Partner's Child." *New York Times,* February 4, A17.

Goodrich, Herbert F., and Paul A. Wolkin. 1961. *The Story of the American Law Institute, 1923–1961*. St. Paul, MN: American Law Institute Publishers.

Gordon. Robert W. 1984. "Critical Legal Histories." *Stanford Law Review* 36 (1–2): 57–125.

Gorlick, Adam. 2000. "Bill Passes to Allow Gay and Unmarried People to Adopt Partners' Children." *Associated Press State and Local Wire*, March 17.

Gottman, Julie S. 1990. "Children of Gay and Lesbian Parents." In *Homosexuality and Family Relations*, ed. Frederick W. Bozett and Marvin B. Sussman, 177–96. New York: Harrington Park.

Grattet, Ryken. 2005. "The Policy Nexus: Professional Networks and the Formulation and Adoption of Workers' Compensation Reforms." In *Routing the Opposition: Social Movements, Public Policy and Democracy*, ed. David S. Meyer, Valerie Jenness, and Helen Ingram, 177–206. Minneapolis: University of Minnesota Press.

Guidos, Rhina. 2004. "Hate-Crimes Panel Discusses Legislation." *Salt Lake Tribune*, October 7, C2.

Gray, Steven. 2001. "New Families, New Questions: Same-Sex Couples Turn to Parenthood in Growing Numbers." *Washington Post*, April 12, T10.

Gray, Virginia. 1973. "Innovation in the States: A Diffusion Study." *American Political Science Review* (67): 1174–85.

Gray, Virginia, and Bruce Williams. 1980. *The Organizational Politics of Criminal Justice*. Lexington, VA: Lexington Books.

Green, Jamison. 2000a. "Introduction." In *Transgender Equality: A Handbook for Activists and Policymakers*, ed. Paisley Currah and Shannon Minter, 1–12. New York: National Gay and Lesbian Task Force.

Green, John C. 2000b. "Varieties of Opposition to Gay Rights." In *The Politics of Gay Rights*, ed. Craig A. Rimmerman, Kenneth D. Wald, and Clyde Wilcox, 121–38. Chicago: University of Chicago Press.

Green, John C., James L. Guth, and Clyde Wilcox. 1998. "Less than Conquerors: The Christian Right in States Republican Parties." In *Social Movements and American Political Institutions*, ed. Anne N. Costain and Andrew S. McFarland, 117–35. Lanham, MD: Rowman and Littlefield.

Green, Richard. 1978. "Sexual Identity of 37 Children Raised by Homosexual or Transsexual Parents." *American Journal of Psychiatry* 135 (6): 692–97.

———. 1982. "The Best Interests of the Child with a Lesbian Mother." *Bulletin of the American Academy of Psychiatry and the Law* 10 (1).

Green, Richard, Jane Barclay Mandel, Mary E. Hotvedt, James Gray, and Laurel Smith. 1986. "Lesbian Mothers and Their Children: A Comparison with Solo Parent Heterosexual Mothers and Their Children." *Archives of Sexual Behavior* 15:167–84.

Grene, Andrew. 1993. "Wisconsin Case May Decide Fate of Most States' Hate Crime Laws." *Chicago Daily Law Bulletin*, February 2, 1.

Gropman, Alan L. 1998. *The Air Force Integrates, 1945–1964.* Washington, DC: Smithsonian Institution Press.

Groth, A. Nicholas. 1978. "Patterns of Sexual Assault against Children and Adolescents." In *Sexual Assault of Children and Adolescents,* ed. Ann W. Burgess, 3–24. Lexington, MA: Lexington Books.

Guevara, Damian. 2003. "Decision Hailed as Gay-Rights Victory." *Cleveland Plain Dealer,* June 27, A10.

Guidos, Rhina. 2004. "Hate Crimes Panel Discusses Legislation." *Salt Lake Tribune,* October 7, C2.

Gyan, Joe, Jr. 2005. "Court's Union Ruling Praised." *Advocate* (Baton Rouge, LA), January 20, 1A.

Haddock, Geoffrey, Mark P. Zanna, and Victoria M. Esses. 2003. "Assessing the Structure of Prejudicial Attitudes: The Case of Attitudes Toward Homosexuals." *Journal of Personality and Social Psychology* 65:1105–18.

Haeberle, Steven H. 1999. "Gay and Lesbian Rights: Emerging Trends in Public Opinion and Voting Behavior." In *Gays and Lesbians in the Democratic Process,* ed. Ellen D. B. Riggle and Barry L. Tadlock, 146–69. New York: Columbia University Press.

Haider-Markel, Donald P. 1997. "From Bullhorns to PACs: Lesbian and Gay Politics, Interest Groups, and Policy," Ph.D. diss., University of Wisconsin–Milwaukee.

———. 1998. "The Politics of Social Regulatory Policy: State and Federal Hate Crime Policy and Implementation Effort." *Political Research Quarterly* 51: 69–88.

———. 1999. "Creating Change—Holding the Line: Agenda Setting on Lesbian and Gay Issues at the National Level." In *Gays and Lesbians in the Democratic Process,* ed. Ellen D. B. Riggle and Barry L. Tadlock, 242–68. New York: Columbia University Press.

———. 2000. "Lesbian and Gay Politics in the States: Interest Groups, Electoral Politics, and Policy." In *The Politics of Gay Rights,* ed. Craig A. Rimmerman, Kenneth D. Wald, and Clyde Wilcox, 290–346. Chicago: University of Chicago Press.

———. 2001. "Morality in Congress? Legislative Voting on Gay Issues." In *The Public Clash of Private Values,* ed. Christopher Z. Mooney, 115–29. New York: Chatham House.

Haider-Markel, Donald P., and Kenneth J. Meier. 1996. "The Politics of Gay and Lesbian Rights: Expanding the Scope of the Conflict." *Journal of Politics* 58:332–49.

Halley, Janet E. 1996. "The Status/Conduct Distinction in the 1993 Revisions to Military Anti-Gay Policy: A Legal Archaeology." *GLQ: A Journal of Gay and Lesbian Studies* 3:159–252.

Hamilton Spectator. 1992. "Military Drops Ban on Gays." *Hamilton* (Ontario) *Spectator,* October 28, A3.

Handler, Joel F. 1978. *Social Movements and the Legal System: A Theory of Law Reform and Social Change.* New York: Academic.

Harcourt, Benard E. 2004. "Foreword: 'You are Entering a Gay and Lesbian Free Zone': On the Radical Dissents of Justice Scalia and Other Post-Queers." *Journal of Criminal Law and Criminology* 94 (3): 503–50.

Harmon, M. D. 2003. "Today, Class, We'll Study Tolerance—So Let's Silence That Guy." *Portland* (ME) *Press Herald,* May 5, 7A.

Harrell, Margaret C., and Laura L. Miller. 1997. *New Opportunities for Military Women: Effects on Readiness, Cohesion and Morale,* Santa Monica, CA: RAND.

Hart, H. L. A. 1963. *Liberty and Morality.* Stanford, CA: Stanford University Press.

Harvard Law Review. 1977. "Implementation Problems in Institutional Reform Litigation." *Harvard Law Review* 91:428–63.

———. 1982. "Developments in the Law: The Interpretation of State Constitutional Rights." *Harvard Law Review* 95:1324–1502.

———. 2005. "Unfixing *Lawrence.*" *Harvard Law Review* 118:2858–81.

Hastings, Warren. 1990. "Senate Panel OK's Extra Penalty for Hate-Based Crime." *Union Leader,* March 17, 5.

Hayes, Ron. 2002. "Florida Law Banning Gay Adoption Faces Challenge." *Cox News Service,* March 16.

Hays, Scott P., and Henry R. Glick. 1997. "The Role of Agenda Setting in Policy Innovation: An Event History Analysis of Living Will Laws." *American Politics Quarterly* 25 (4): 497–516.

Hazard, Geoffrey C., Jr. 1994. "The American Law Institute: What It Is and What It Does." Centro di studi e ricerch di diritto comparator e straniero. Saggi, Conferenze e Seminari, #14, April.

Healy, Melissa. 1993. "The Times Poll: 74% of Military Enlistees Oppose Lifting Gay Ban." *Los Angeles Times,* February 28, A1.

Henderson, Lynne N. 1987. "Legality and Empathy." *Michigan Law Review* 85:1574–1653.

Hennessy, Patrick, and Jonathan Annells. 1999. "Victory for Forces Gays: Robertson Halts All Expulsions after Euro Court Ruling." *Evening Standard,* September 27, 1.

Henry J. Kaiser Family Foundation. 2001. "Inside-OUT: A Report on the Experiences of Lesbians, Gays and Bisexuals in America and the Public's Views on Issues and Policies Related to Sexual Orientation." Menlo Park, CA: Henry J. Kaiser Family Foundation.

Herald, The. 1997. "Scrap Hate Crime Bill." *The Herald* (Rock Hill, SC), January 6, 9A.

Herald-Sun. 2003. "What They're Saying." *Herald-Sun* (Durham, NC), June 27, A3.

Herek, Gregory M. 1988. "Heterosexuals' Attitudes toward Lesbians and Gay Men: Correlates and Gender Differences." *Journal of Sex Research* 25:451–77.

———. 1991. "Myths about Sexual Orientation: A Lawyer's Guide to Social Science Research." *Law and Sexuality* 1:133–72.

———. 1996a. "Social Science, Sexual Orientation, and Military Personnel Policy." In *Out in Force: Sexual Orientation and the Military,* ed. Gregory M. Herek, Jared B. Jobe, and Ralph M. Carney, 3–14. Chicago: University of Chicago Press.

———. 1996b. "Why Tell If You're Not Asked? Self-Disclosure, Intergroup Contact, and Heterosexuals' Attitudes toward Lesbians and Gay Men." In *Out in Force: Sexual Orientation and the Military,* ed. Gregory M. Herek, Jared B. Jobe, and Ralph M. Carney, 197–225. Chicago: University of Chicago Press.

Herek, Gregory M., and John P. Capitanio. 1995. "Black Heterosexuals' Attitudes toward Lesbians and Gay Men in the United States." *Journal of Sex Research* 32:95–105.

———. 1996. "Some of My Best Friends: Intergroup Contact, Concealable Stigma and Heterosexuals' Attitudes toward Gay Men and Lesbians." *Personality and Social Psychology Bulletin* 22:412–24.

Herek, Gregory M., and Eric K. Glunt. 1993. "Interpersonal Contact and Heterosexuals' Attitudes Toward Gay Men: Results from a National Survey." *Journal of Sex Research* 30:239–44.

Herman, Didi. 2000. "The Gay Agenda Is the Devil's Agenda: The Christian Right's Vision and the Role of the State." In *The Politics of Gay Rights,* ed. Craig A. Rimmerman, Kenneth D. Wald, and Clyde Wilcox, 139–60. Chicago: University of Chicago Press.

Herscher, Elaine. 2000. "At Long Last, They Are Family: State Permits Adoptions by Unmarried Couples." *San Francisco Chronicle,* January 11, A15.

Herzog, Mark. 1996. *The Lavender Vote: Lesbians, Gay Men, and Bisexuals in American Electoral Politics.* New York: New York University Press.

Heyser, Holly A. 2000. "Senate Panel Rejects Crimes Bill Seeking to Protect Homosexuals." *Virginian-Pilot* (Norfolk, VA), December 2, B7.

Hill, John. 1996. "Council OKs Bill to Punish Hate Crime." *Albuquerque Tribune*, December 17, A1.

Hirsch, H. N. 2005. *The Future of Gay Rights in America*. New York: Routledge.

Hobart Mercury. 1992a. "Military's New Aim: No Gays in Our Ranks." *Hobart* (Tasmania) *Mercury*, June 19.

———. 1992b. "Gay Police Show Way for the Army." *Hobart* (Tasmania) *Mercury*, August 11.

Hochschild, Jennifer L. 1984. *The New American Dilemma*. New Haven, CT: Yale University Press.

Hockey, John. 2003. "No More Heroes: Masculinity in the Infantry." In *Military Masculinities: Identity and the State*, ed. Paul R. Higate, 15–25. Westport, CT: Praeger.

Hoeffer, Beverly. 1981. "Children's Acquisition of Sex-Role Behavior in Lesbian-Mother Families." *American Journal of Orthopsychiatry* 51:536–43.

Hoffman, Kevin. 2003. "The Gayby Predicament: When Two Moms Split, One May Never Get to See Her Child Again. It's the Law." *Cleveland Scene*, January 22.

Holland, Judy. 2002. "Senate Hate-Crimes Bill Would Protect Gays, Lesbians." *Seattle Post-Intelligencer*, May 18, A2.

Holsti, Ole R. 2001. "Of Chasms and Convergences: Attitudes and Beliefs of Civilians and Military Elites at the start of a New Millennium." In *Soldiers and Civilians: The Civil-Military Gap and American National Security*, ed. Peter D. Feaver and Richard H. Kohn, 15–99. Cambridge, MA: Belfer Center for Science and International Affairs.

Horowitz, Donald. 1977. *The Courts and Social Policy*. Washington, DC: Brookings Institution.

Huggins, Sharon. 1989. "A Comparative Study of Self-Esteem of Adolescent Children of Divorced Lesbian Mothers and Divorced Heterosexual Mothers." *Journal of Homosexuality* 18 (1–2): 123–35.

Hull, Kathleen. 2006. *Same-Sex Marriage: The Cultural Politics of Love and Law*. New York: Cambridge University Press.

Hull, N. E. H. 1998. "Back to the 'Future of the Institute': William Draper Lewis's Vision of the ALI's Mission During Its First Twenty-Five Years and the Implications for the Institute's Seventy-Fifth Anniversary." Philadelphia: American Law Institute.

Human Development Service. 1982. *National Study of the Incidence and Severity of Child Abuse and Neglect*.

Human Rights Campaign. 2000a. *In Perspective: HRC Scorecard of Members of the 106th Congress*. www.hrc.org.

———. 2004. *HRC Congressional Scorecard of Members of the 108th Congress.* www.hrc.org/documents/2004scorecard.pdf.

———. 2006a. *The State of the Workplace for Gay, Lesbian, Bisexual and Transgender Americans: 2005–2006.* http://www.hrc.org/documents/SOTW20052006.pdf.

———. 2006b. *Measuring Support for Equality in the 109th Congress, Congressional Scorecard.* http://www.hrc.org/documents/hrcscorecard2006.pdf.

———. 2008. *Statewide Marriage Prohibitions.* http://www.hrc.org/documents/marriage_prohibit_20080616.pdf.

Humphrey, Mary Ann. 1990. *My Country, My Right to Serve.* New York: Harper Collins.

Hunt, Stephen. 2000. "Utah's Hate-Crime Law Enjoys Short-Lived Revival." *Salt Lake Tribune,* December 10, B2.

Hunter, James Davison. 1991. *Culture Wars: The Struggle to Define America.* New York: Basic.

———. 1994. *Before the Shooting Begins: Searching for Democracy in America's Culture Wars.* New York: Free Press.

Hunter, Nan D. 2004. "Sexual Orientation and the Paradox of Heightened Scrutiny." *Michigan Law Review* 102 (June): 1528–54.

Huppke, Rex W. 2000. "Experts Say Adoptions by Gays Getting a Bit Easier." *Associated Press State and Local Wire,* April 2.

Ihejirka, Maudlyne 1995. "Two Lesbian Couples Get Approval for Adoptions." *Chicago Sun-Times,* August 25, 18.

Ingersoll, Brenda. 2002. "Despite Wisconsin Law, Gay Adoptions Happen: Some Lawyers and Couples Fear They Might Not Survive Legal Challenges." *Wisconsin State Journal,* February 10, A1.

Inglehart, Ronald. 1990. *Culture Shift in Advanced Industrial Societies.* Princeton, NJ: Princeton University Press.

Intelligencer Journal. 2002a. "Gay Parents Do Provide Secure Homes." *Intelligencer Journal* (Lancaster, PA), March 18, A7.

———. 2002b. "Partners as Parents." *Intelligencer Journal* (Lancaster, PA), March 6, A8.

———. 2003. "Nation Discriminates Against Gays." *Intelligencer Journal* (Lancaster, PA), August 7, A11.

Irwin, Patrick, and Norman L. Thompson. 1977. "Acceptance of the Rights of Homosexuals: A Social Profile." *Journal of Homosexuality* 3:107–21.

Ivins, Molly. 2003. "Justices Having Fits of Rulings." *Charleston* (WV) *Gazette,* July 7, P4A.

Jacobs, James B., and Kimberly Potter. 1998. *Hate Crimes: Criminal Law and Identity Politics*. New York: Oxford University Press.

Jacobs, Janet. 2001. "Marchers Rally in Support of Texas Hate Crimes Bill." *Austin American-Statesman*, March 19, B1.

Jacobs, Sally. 1992. "Canada to Let Gays Serve in Forces." *Boston Globe*, October 28, 1.

Jacobson, Peter D. 1996. "Sexual Orientation and the Military: Some Legal Considerations." In *Out in Force: Sexual Orientation and the Military*, ed. Gregory M. Herek, Jared B. Jobe, and Ralph M. Carney, 39–64. Chicago: University of Chicago Press.

Jacob, Lawrence R., and Robert Y. Shapiro 2001. *Politicians Don't Pander: Political Manipulation and the Loss of Democratic Responsiveness*. Chicago: University of Chicago Press.

Jacoby, Jeff. 2000. "Hate Crime Laws Imply that Some Victims are Special." *Milwaukee Journal Sentinel*, June 27, 17A.

Janis, Irving. 1982. *Groupthink*. Boston: Houghton Mifflin.

Jeffords, Susan. 1989. *The Remasculinization of America: Gender in the Vietnam War*. Bloomington: Indiana University Press.

Jenkins, J. Craig. 1983. "Resource Mobilization Theory and the Study of Social Movements." *Annual Review of Sociology* 9:527–53.

Jenkins, J. Craig, and Charles Perrow. 1977. "Insurgency of the Powerless: Farm Worker Movements, 1946–1972." *American Sociological Review* 42 (April): 249–68.

Jenness, Valerie. 1995. "Social Movement Growth, Domain Expansion and Framing Processes: The Gay/Lesbian Movement and Violence against Gays and Lesbians as a Social Problem." *Social Problems* 47:145–70.

———. 1999. "Managing Differences and Making Legislation: Social Movements and the Racialization, Sexualization and Gendering of Federal Hate Crime Law in the U.S., 1985–1998." *Social Problems* 46:548–71.

———. 2000. *Building the Hate Crime Policy Domain: From Social Movement Concept to Law Enforcement Practice*. New York: Russell Sage Foundation.

Jenness, Valerie, and Kendal Broad. 1997. *Hate Crimes: New Social Movements and the Politics of Violence*. Hawthorne, NY: Aldine De Gruyter.

Jenness, Valerie, and Ryken Grattet. 2001. *Making Hate a Crime: From Social Movement to Law Enforcement*. New York: Russell Sage Foundation.

Jenny, Carole, T. A. Roesler, and K. L. Poyer. 1994. "Are Children at Risk for Sexual Abuse by Homosexuals?" *Pediatrics* 94:41–44.

Jensen, Derek. 2001. "Hate-Crimes Bill Faces Uphill Battle." *Deseret News* (Salt Lake City, UT), October 10, B3.

Johnson, Maureen. 2000. "Britain Ends Ban on Gays in the Military." *Associated Press,* January 12.

Jung, Patricia Beattie, and Ralph F. Smith. 1993. *Heterosexism: An Ethical Challenge.* Albany: State University of New York Press.

Kadish, Sanford H. 1987. *Blame and Punishment: Essays in the Criminal Law.* New York: Macmillan.

Kaiser Family Foundation. 2000. "Hate crimes." Poll compiled by the Roper Center for Public Opinion Research. http://poll.orspub.com/poll/lpext.dll/ors/h/hatecrimes/.

Karst, Kenneth L. 1991. "The Pursuit of Manhood and the Desegregation of the Armed Forces." *UCLA Law Review* 38:499–581.

Katzenstein, Mary Fainsod. 1996. "The Spectacle of Life and Death: Feminist and Lesbian/Gay Politics in the Military." In *Gay Rights, Military Wrongs: Political Perspectives on Lesbians and Gays in the Military,* ed. Craig A. Rimmerman, 229–49. New York: Garland.

Kelley, Janet. 2000. "PA Court Rejects Adoptions by Local Same-Sex Couple." *Lancaster New Era,* November, E8.

Kelman, Mark. 2005. "The Interdependence of Irreconcilable Foundational Beliefs." Unpublished manuscript on file with the Harvard Law School Library, Boston.

Kennedy, Helen. 2003. "Supremes Lift Sodomy Ban: Gays Cheer, Conservatives Seethe." *New York Daily News,* June 27, 5.

Kidd, Matthew. 2003. "Lawrence v. Texas: What Was Overlooked." *Washington Post,* July 11, A20.

Killian, Mary Lou. 2006 "Got Marriage? State-Level Policymaking Regarding Marriage Rights for Gays and Lesbians." PhD diss., Temple University.

Kinder, Donald R., and L. M. Sanders. 1996. *Divided by Color: Racial Politics and Democratic Ideals.* Chicago: University of Chicago Press.

Kirkpatrick, M., C. Smith, and R. Roy. 1981. "Lesbian Mothers and Their Children: A Comparative Study." *American Journal of Orthopsychiatry* 51:541–51.

Kitschelt, Herbert P. 1986. "Political Opportunity Structures and Political Protest: Anti-Nuclear Movements in Four Democracies." *British Journal of Political Science* 16 (January): 57–85.

Klandermans, Bert. 1989. "Grievance Interpretations and Success Expectations." *Social Behaviour* 4:113–25.

———. 1991. "New Social Movements and Resource Mobilization: The European and American Approach Revisited." In *Research on Social Movements,* ed. Dieter Rucht, 17–44. Frankfurt am Main, Germany: Campus Verlag.

Klawitter, Marieka, and Brian Hammer. 1999. "Spatial and Temporal Diffusion of Local Antidiscrimination Policies for Sexual Orientation." In *Gays and Lesbians in the Democratic Process,* ed. Ellen D. B. Riggle and Barry L. Tadlock, 22–38. New York: Columbia University Press.

Klein, Ethel D. 2005. "The Anti-Gay Backlash?" In *The Future of Gay Rights in America* , ed. H. N. Hirsch, 81–94. New York: Routledge.

Koppelman, Andrew. 2002. *The Gay Rights Question in Contemporary American Law.* Chicago: University of Chicago Press.

———. 2006. *Same Sex, Different States.* New Haven, CT: Yale University Press.

Kovitz, Marcia. 2003. "The Roots of Military Masculinity." In *Military Masculinities: Identity and the State,* ed. Paul R. Higate, 1–14. Westport, CT: Praeger.

Krause, Harry D. 1993. " 'Family Values' and Family Law Reform." *Journal of Contemporary Health Law and Policy* 9:116–20.

Kreider, Rose M., and Tavia Simmons. 2003. "Marital Status: 2000." Census 2000 Brief, U.S. Census Bureau, October.

Kriesi, Hanspeter. 1995. "The Political Opportunity Structure of New Social Movements: Its Impact on Their Mobilization." In *The Politics of Social Protest: Comparative Perspectives of States and Social Movements,* ed. J. Craig Jenkins and Bert Klandermans, 167–98. Minneapolis: University of Minnesota Press.

Laidlaw, R. 1992a. "Awkward Squad." *Courier-Mail* (Brisbane, Australia), February 25.

———. 1992b. "Bad Move: Homosexual Ban Should Remain." *Courier-Mail* (Brisbane, Australia), November 25.

Lainhart, John. 2003. "The Supreme Court's Last Day, Sounding Board for Readers." *Houston Chronicle,* June 27, A14.

Lambda Legal Defense and Education Fund. 2006. "Summary of States, Cities, and Counties which Prohibit Discrimination Based on Sexual Orientation." http://www.lambdalegal.org/cgi-bin/iowa/news/resources.html?record=217 (accessed 2006; hard copy in possession of the author).

———. 2007. "Adoption and Parenting." http://www.lambdalegal.org/our-work/issues/marriage-relationships-family/parenting.

Lancaster, John. 1992. "Many Allies Allow Gays in the Military." *Washington Post,* November 30, A1.

———. 1993. "Why the Military Supports the Ban on Gays." *Washington Post,* January 28, A8.

Lance, Larry M. 1987. "The Effects of Interaction with Gay Persons on Attitudes toward Homosexuality in College Students." *Sex Roles* 40:329–36.

Lanford, Rosario Ceballo, Antonia Abbey, and Abigail J. Stewart. 2001. "Does Family Structure Matter? A Comparison of Adoptive, Two-Parent Biological, Single-Mother, Stepfather and Stepmother Households." *Journal of Marriage and Family* 63 (3): 840–51.

Lawson, Steven F. 1991. *Running for Freedom: Civil Rights and Black Politics in America since 1941.* Philadelphia: Temple University Press.

Layman, Geoffrey C., and John C. Green. 2006. "Wars and Rumours of Wars: The Contexts of Cultureal Conflict in American Political Behavior." *British Journal of Political Science* 36 (January): 61–89.

Leeman, Sue. 1999. "European Court Ruling Reopens British Debate on Gay in Forces." *Associated Press,* September 27.

Leff, Lisa. 2003. "Gays Overjoyed, Conservatives Despair over Sodomy Ruling." *Associated Press State and Local Wire,* June 27.

Lehring, Gary. 2003. *Officially Gay: The Political Construction of Sexuality by the U.S. Military.* Philadelphia: Temple University Press.

Leslie, C. R. 2000. "Creating Criminals: The Injuries Inflicted by 'Unenforced' Sodomy Laws." *Harvard Civil Rights and Civil Liberties Law Review* 35:103–81.

Leveno, Elizabeth A. 1993–94. "New Hope for the New Federalism: State Constitutional Challenges to Sodomy Statutes." *University of Cincinnati Law Review* 62:1029–54.

Lever, Janet, and David E. Kanouse. 1996. "Sexual Orientation and Proscribed Sexual Behaviors." In *Out in Force: Sexual Orientation and the Military,* ed. Gregory M. Herek, Jared B. Jobe, and Ralph M. Carney, 15–38. Chicago: University of Chicago Press.

Levitt, Eugene E., and Albert D. Klassen. 1974. "Public Attitudes toward Homosexuality. Part of the 1970 National Survey by the Institute for Sex Research." *Journal of Homosexuality* 1:29–43.

Lewis, Gregory B. 1999. "Public Opinion and State Sodomy Laws." Paper prepared for the American Political Science Association Annual Meeting, Atlanta, GA, September.

Lewis, Gregory B., and Marc A. Rogers. 1999. "Does the Public Support Equal Employment Rights for Gays?" In *Gays and Lesbians in the Democratic Process,* ed. Ellen D. B. Riggle and Barry L. Tadlock, 118–45. New York: Columbia University Press.

Lewis, Gregory B., and Seong Soo Oh. 2006. "Public Opposition and State Action on Same-Sex Marriage." Paper presented at the American Political Science Association Meetings, Philadelphia, August 28–September 3.

Lindblom, Charles. 1980. *Politics and Markets.* New York: Basic.

Lipsky, Michael. 1968. "Protest as a Political Resource." *American Political Science Review* 62 (December): 1144–58.

———. 1970. *Protest in City Politics.* Chicago: Rand McNally.

———. 1980. *Street Level Bureaucracies: Dilemmas of the Individual in Public Services.* New York: Russell Sage Foundation.

Litchman, Lori. 2002. "PA High Court OKs Second-Parent Adoption." *Legal Intelligencer* 226 (96): 1.

Longcope, Kay. 1989. "Gay Rights Bill a Victory of Endurance." *Boston Globe,* November 19, 33.

Lotozo, Eils. 2003. "Gay Parenting Booming." *Pittsburgh Post-Gazette,* June 29, A16.

Love, Norma. 1999. "Shaheen Signs Law Ending Ban on Gay Adoption, Foster Care." *Associated Press State and Local Wire,* May 4.

Lowi, Theodore. 1972. "Four Systems of Policy, Politics and Choice." *Public Administration Review* 33:298–310.

Lowy, Joan. 1999. "Movement to Halt Gay Adoptions Gathers Steam." *Chattanooga Times Free Press,* February 28, A8.

Lyall, Sarah. 1999. "European Court Tells British to Let Gay Soldiers Serve." *New York Times,* September 28, A8.

———. 2005. "Open Minds on Open Seas: British Royal Navy Woos Gays and Lesbians." *International Herald Tribune* (Neuilly Cedex, France), February 2, 1.

MacCoun, Robert. 1993. "What Is Known about Unit Cohesion and Military Performance." In *Sexual Orientation and U.S. Military Personnel Policy: Options and Assessment,* 238–331. Santa Monica, CA: RAND, National Defense Research Institute.

MacGregor, Morris J. 1981. *Integration of the Armed Forces, 1940–1965.* Washington, DC: Center of Military History.

MacMillan, Susannah. 1999. "How Might of the Military Must Cope with Defeat on Gay Front." *Western Daily Press* (Bristol, UK), September 28, 6.

Malmgren, Jeanne. 2002. "Gay Adoption in Florida: It's Out of the Question." *St. Petersburg Times,* March 14, 1D.

Malone, Bernadette. 2003. "How to Derail Gay Marriage: Put Polygamy on Fast Track." *Union Leader,* July 6, B2.

Manegold, Catherine S. 1993. "The Odd Place of Homosexuality in the Military." *New York Times,* April 18, 4, 1.

Mansbridge, Jane J. 1986. *Why We Lost the ERA,* Chicago: University of Chicago Press.

———. 1999. "Everyday Talk in the Deliberative System." In *Deliberative Politics: Essays on Democracy and Disagreement,* ed. Stephen Macedo, 211–42. New York: Oxford University Press.

Manson, Patricia. 2003. "Painting a New Face on Today's Family." *Chicago Daily Law Bulletin,* August 11, 3.

Manzanares, Tamera. 2003. "Colorado Activists See Gay Rights on Rise." *Denver Post,* June 27, A4.

Mar, Jeannie. 1992. "Speakers in Olympia Debate Revisions in Hate Crimes Bill." *The Oregonian,* February 27, D3.

Maroney, Terry A. 1998. "The Struggle against Hate Crime: Movement at a Crossroad." *New York University Law Review* 73:564–620.

Marshall, Thomas. 1989. *Public Opinion and the Supreme Court.* New York: Longman.

Martin, Andrew D., and Kevin M. Quinn. 2002. "Dynamic Ideal Point Estimation via Markov Chain Monte Carlo for the U.S. Supreme Court, 1953–1999." *Political Analysis* 10:134–53. Datasets are found at http://adm.wustl.edu/supct.php.

Martinis, Cheryl. 1994. "Gay Rights Ballot Showdown Unfolds in Three Valley Cities." *The Oregonian,* March 9, B2.

Maryland Senate. 2001. Transcription of audiotaped debate on Senate Bill 205, "The Anti-Discrimination Act of 2001." March 26.

Massachusetts House of Representatives. 1989. Transcription of videotaped debate on H4071, "A Bill Making it Unlawful to Discriminate on the Basis of Sexual Orientation." March 27–28.

Mayer, William G. 1992. *The Changing American Mind: How and Why American Pubic Opinion Changed between 1960 and 1988.* Ann Arbor, MI: University of Michigan Press.

McAdam, Doug. 1982. *Political Process and the Development of Black Insurgency, 1930–1970.* Chicago: University of Chicago Press.

———. 1988. *Freedom Summer.* New York: Oxford University Press.

———. 1994. "Culture and Social Movements." In *New Social Movements: From Ideology to Identity,* ed. Enrique Larana, Hank Johnston, and Joseph R. Gusfield, 36–57. Philadelphia: Temple University Press.

———. 1999. "The Biographical Impact of Activism." In *How Social Movements Matter,* ed. Marco Giugni, Doug McAdam, and Charles Tilly, 119–48. Minneapolis: University of Minnesota Press.

McAdam, Doug, John McCarthy, and Mayer N. Zald. 1988. "Social Movements." In *Handbook of Sociology,* ed. Neil J. Smelser, 695–737. Newberry Park, CA: Sage.

McCahey, J. P., M. Kaufman, C. Kraut, and J. Zett. 1996. *Child Custody and Visitation Law and Practice*. New York: M. Bender.

McCandlish, Barbara M. 1987. "Against All Odds: Lesbian Mother Family Dynamics." In *Gay and Lesbian Parents*, ed. Frederick W. Bozett, 23–38. New York: Praeger.

McCann, Michael. 1986. *Taking Reform Seriously: Perspectives on Public Interest Liberalism*. Ithaca, NY: Cornell University Press.

McCarthy, J., and Mayer N. Zald. 1973. *The Trend of Social Movements*. Morristown, NJ: General Learning.

———. 1977. "Resource Mobilization and Social Movements." *American Journal of Sociology* 82:1212–41.

McCormick, Gavin. 2002. "Hate Crime Expansion Proposal Draws Passion." *Associated Press State and Local Wire*, February 6.

McCoy, Donald R., and Richard T. Ruetten. 1973. *Quest and Response: Minority Rights and the Truman Administration*. Lawrence: University Press of Kansas.

McDonough, Molly. 1999. "Justices OK Adoptions, Rap 'Biased' Judge." *Chicago Daily Law Bulletin*, July 2, 1.

McGann, Chris. 2006. "A Long-Awaited Win for Gay Rights, Senate Ok's State Anti-Bias Bill." *Seattle Post-Intelligencer*, January 28, A1.

McKee, Mike. 1995. "What Makes a Family? Wilson Cracks Down on Unmarried Adoptions, But It's Still Up to the Judge." *The Recorder*, American Lawyer Media, April 6.

Mead, Margaret. 1949 [1967]. *Male and Female: A Study of the Sexes in a Changing World*. New York: Morrow.

Meade, Geoff. 1999. "Everyone Has Right to Respect for Private Life, Say Judges." *Press Association*, September 27.

Megowan, Patrick. 1999. "New Armed Forces Code Forbids All Sex." *Evening Standard* (London), November 15, 4.

Meier, Kennth J. 1994. *The Politics of Sin*. Armonk, NY: M. E. Sharpe.

Melucci, Alberto. 1985. "The Symbolic Challenge of Contemporary Movements." *Social Research* 52:781–816.

———. 1996. *Challenging the Codes: Collective Action in the Information Age*. Cambridge, UK: Cambridge University Press.

Mershon, Sherie, and Steven Schlossman. 1998. *Foxholes and Color Lines: Desegregating the U.S. Armed Forces*. Baltimore: Johns Hopkins University Press.

Mill, John Stuart. 1859 [1982]. *On Liberty*. New York: Penguin.

Miller, Brian. 1979. "Gay Fathers and Their Children." *Family Coordinator* 28, 544–52.

Miller, Judith Ann, and Jerry J. Bigner. 1981. "The Child's Home Environment for Lesbian vs. Heterosexual Mothers: A Neglected Area of Research." *Journal of Homosexuality* 1:49–56.

Miller, Karen. 1999. "Bills Call for Stiffer Hate-Crime Sentences." *Commercial Appeal* (Memphis, TN), February 18, B5.

Miller, Laura L. 1994. "Fighting for a Just Cause: Soldiers' Views on Gays in the Military." In *Gays and Lesbians in the Military: Issues Concerns and Contrasts,* ed. Wilbur J. Scott and Sandra Carson Stanley, 69–86. New York: Aldine De Gruyter.

Miller, Laura L., and John Allen Williams. 2001. "Do Military Policies on Gender and Sexuality Undermine Combat Effectiveness?" In *Soldiers and Civilians: The Civil-Military Gap and American National Security,* ed. Peter D. Feaver and Richard H. Kohn, 361–402. Cambridge, MA: Belfer Center for Science and International Affairs.

Millham, Jim, Christopher L. San Miguel, and Richard Kellog. 1976. "A Factor Analytic Conceptualization of Attitudes toward Male and Female Homosexuality." *Journal of Homosexuality,* 2:3–10.

Minnesota House. 1997. Floor debate, Defense of Marriage Act HF925. May 15, 19.

Minnesota House, Judiciary Committee. 1997. Hearings on the Defense of Marriage Act HF925, A-25 Amendment. March 19, tape 1.

Minnesota Senate. 1993. Transcription of audiotaped debate on Senate Bill SF444, "An Amendment to the Minnesota Human Rights Act," March 18.

———. 1997. Transcription of audiotaped debate on Senate Bill SF830, Defense of Marriage Act as part of debate on SF1908, "Omnibus Health and Human Services Appropriations." May 16.

Mintrom, Michael. 2000. *Policy Entrepreneurs and School Choice.* Washington, DC: Georgetown University Press.

Mishler, William, and Reginald S. Sheehan. 1993. "The Supreme Court as a Countermajoritarian Institution? The Impact of Public Opinion on Supreme Court Decisions." *American Political Science Review* 87:87–101.

———. 1996. "Public Opinion, the Attitudinal Model, and Supreme Court Decision-Making: A Micro-Analytic Perspective." *Journal of Politics* 58 (February): 169–200.

Mitchell, Roger S. 1969. *The Homosexual and the Law.* New York: ARCO.

Mohr, R. 1988. *Gays Justice: A Study of Ethics, Society, and Law.* New York: Columbia University Press.

Monroe, Alan D. 1979. "Consistency between Public Preferences and Natonal Policy Decisions." *American Politics Quarterly* 7:3–19.

Montagu, Ashley. 1978. "A Kinsey Report on Homosexualities." *Psychology Today* 12.

Monti, Daniel J . 1980. "Administrative Foxes in Educational Chicken Coops." *Law and Policy Quarterly* 2 (April): 233–56.

Mooney, Christopher Z. 2001a. "The Public Clash of Private Values: The Politics of Morality Policy." In *The Public Clash of Private Values,* ed. Chrisopher Z. Mooney, 3–20. New York: Chatham House.

———. 2001b. "Modeling Regional Effects on State Policy Diffusion." *Political Research Quarterly* 54 (1): 103–24.

Mooney, Christopher Z., and Mei-Hsien Lee. 1995. "Legislating Morality in the American States: The Case of Pre-*Roe* Abortion Regulation Reform." *American Journal of Political Science* 39:599–627.

———. 2000. "The influence of Values on Consensus and Contentious Morality Policy: U.S. Death Penalty Reform, 1956–82." *Journal of Politics* 62 (1): 223–39.

Mooney, Christopher Z., and Richard G. Schuldt. 2006. "Does Morality Policy Exist? Testing a Basic Assumption." Paper presented at the Annual Meeting of the American Political Science Association, Philadelphia, August 31–September 3.

Morin, Monte, and Erika Hayasaki. 2003. "Court OKs Adoption by Unwed Pairs." *Los Angeles Times,* August 5, part 2, 1.

Morris, Aldon D. 1984. *The Origins of the Civil Rights Movement: Black Communities Organizing for Change.* New York: Free Press.

———. 1993. "Birmingham Confrontation Reconsidered: An Analysis of the Dynamics and Tactics of Mobilization." *American Sociological Review* 58:621–36.

Morris, Aldon D., and Carol McClurg Mueller, ed. 1992. *Frontiers in Social Movement Thoery.* New Haven, CT: Yale University Press.

Morris, Nigel. 2000. "Army Gays Ok. *The Mirror* (London), January 13, 2.

Morton, Desmond. 1992. "General Faces Off against the 'Family Caucus.'" *Ottawa Citizen,* July 9, A13.

Moskos, Charles, Jr. 1994. "From Citizens' Army to Social Laboratory." In *Gays and Lesbians in the Military: Issues, Concerns and Contrasts,* ed. Wilbur J. Scott and Sandra Carson Stanley, 53–68. New York: Aldine De Gruyter.

Motley, Wanda. 1992. "House Urged to Expand Bias Law to Protect Gays." *Philadelphia Inquirer,* April 23, B1.

Mucciaroni, Gary. 1995. *Reversals of Fortune: Private Interests and Public Policy.* Washington, DC: Brookings Institution.

Munday, Dave. 2003. "South Carolinians Clash on Gay Adoptions." *Post and Courier* (Charleston, SC), August 1, 5A.

Munro, Catherine. 1992. "Allowing Gays in Armed Forces Stirs Debate in Australia." *Japan Economic Newswire,* December 2.

Murakawa. 2005. "Electing to Punish: Congress, Race and the American Criminal Justice State." PhD diss., Yale Univ.

Murphy, Jane C. 1999. "Rules, Responsibility and Commitment to Children: The New Language of Morality in Family Law." *University of Pittsburgh Law Review* 60:1111–1205.

Murray, Frank J. 2003. "Texas' Gay-Sodomy Law Argued in Supreme Court." *Washington Times,* March 27, A3.

Murray, Shailagh. 2007. "Quandry over Gay Rights Bill: Is It Better to Protect Some or None?" *Washington Post,* October 19, A23.

National Association of Social Workers (NASW). 1988. "Lesbian and Gay Issues." In *Social Work Speaks: NASW Policy Statements.* Silver Spring, MD: National Association of Social Workers.

———. 2003a. *Government Relations/Political Action Unit Year End Report.* 104th Congress, 1st session, pp. 1–15.

———. 2003b. "Social Workers in State and Local Offices 2003." http://www.socialworkers.org/pace/state.asp.

———. 2004a. "Ask Your Senators to Vote No on the Federal Marriage Amendment." Government Relations Action Alert, July 9. http://www.socialworkers.org/advocacy/alerts/070904.asp (accessed February 12, 2005; hard copy in possession of the author).

———. 2004b. "Same Sex Marriage Position Statement." July 28. http://www.socialworkers.org/diversity/lgb/062804.asp.

National Conference of Commissioners on Uniform State Laws. 1995. *Handbook of the National Conference of Commissioners on Uniform State Laws.* Chicago: National Conference of Commissioners on Uniform State Laws.

National Gay and Lesbian Task Force (NGLTF). 2005. "States, Cities and Counties with Civil Rights Ordinances, Policies or Proclamations Prohibiting Discrimination on the Basis of Sexual Orientation." www.thetaskforce.org/ (hard copy in possession of the author).

———. 2006. "Policy Priorities for the LGBT Community: Pride Survey 2006." http://www.thetaskforce.org/downloads/reports/reports/2006pridesurvey.pdf (hard copy in possession of the author).

———. 2007a. "Anti-Gay Marriage Measures in the U.S." http://www.thetaskforce.org/downloads/reports/issue_maps/GayMarriage_09_25_07.pdf.

———. 2007b. "Hate Crime Laws in the U.S." http://www.thetaskforce.org/downloads/reports/issue_maps/hate_crimes_11_07_color.pdf.

———. 2007c. "State Nondiscrimination Laws in the U.S." http://www
.thetaskforce.org/downloads/reports/issue_maps/non_discrimination
_09_07_color.pdf (hard copy in possession of the author).

———. 2007d. "Adoption Laws in the U.S." http://www.thetaskforce.org/
downloads/reports/issue_maps/adoption_laws_09_07_color.pdf.

———. 2007e. "Second-Parent Adoption in the U.S." http://www.thetaskforce
.org/downloads/reports/issue_maps/2nd_parent_adoption_5_07_color.pdf.

———. 2007f. "Unprecedented Series of Gains Coast to Coast for Lesbian, Gay,
Bisexual and Transgendered People." Press release, May 9. http://www
.thetaskforce.org/press/releases/prstates_050907.

———. 2008. "Relationship Recognition for Same-Sex Couples in the U.S."
http://www.thetaskforce.org/downloads/reports/issue_maps/relationship_
recognition_1_08_color.pdf (hard copy in possession of the author).

Neely, Richard. 1981. *How Courts Govern America*. New Haven, CT: Yale
University Press.

Neier, Aryeh. 1982. *Only Judgment: The Limits of Litigation in Social Change*.
Middletown, CT: Wesleyan University Press.

Nelson, Thomas E., and Donald R. Kinder. 1996. "Issue Frames and Group-
Centrism in American Public Opinion." *Journal of Politics* 58 (4): 1055–78.

Nelson, Thomas E., Rosalee A. Clawson, and Zoe M. Oxley. 1997. "Media
Framing of a Civil Liberties Conflict and its Effect on Tolerance." *American
Political Science Review* 91 (3): 567–83.

Nethaway, Rowland. 2003. "Sodomy Ruling Clears Way to End Discrimination
Against Gays." *Cox News Service*, July 10.

Neuborne, Burt. 1977. "The Myth of Parity." *Harvard Law Review* 90:1105.

Neuman, Johanna. 2006. "Gay Rights Activists Hopeful about Agenda's New
Prospects." *Los Angeles Times*, December 3, A21.

———. 2007. "Bill to Expand Job Protections to Gay Workers Passes House."
Los Angeles Times, November 8, A12.

New York Law Journal. 1994. "Adoption by Lesbian Partner Is in Children's Best
Interest." *New York Law Journal*, January 25, 21.

———. 1995. "Domestic Relations Law: Adoption by Mother's Partner." *New York
Law Journal*, November 3, 25.

New York Times. 1970. "Homosexual Wins a Suit over Hiring." *New York Times*,
September 20, 56.

———. 1990. "Why Not Stronger on Race Crimes?" *New York Times*, May 22, A26.

———. 1993a. "Two Gay Adoption Cases Go to Appeals Courts." *New York Times*,
April 18, 25.

———. 1993b. "Court Grants Parental Rights to Mother and Lesbian Lover." *New York Times*, September 12, 42.

———. 1993c. "Lesbian Wins Appeal on Vermont Adoptions." *New York Times*, June 20, 20.

———. 2000a. "Gay Troops in Europe." *New York Times*, January 15, A16.

———. 2000b. "O.K. You're Gay. So? Where's My Grandchild." *New York Times*, December 21, F1.

———. 2003. "When Six Justices Changed the Law of the Land, They Turned to Its History." *New York Times*, July 20, sec. 4, p. 4.

Newton, D. 1978. "Homosexual Behavior and Child Molestation: A Review of the Evidence, Adolescence." *Adolescence* 13:29–43.

Nice, David C. 1988. "State Deregulation of Intimate Behavior." *Social Science Quarterly* 69 (March): 203–11.

Nolan, John. 2004. "Businesses Say Perception of Cincinnati as Intolerant Hurts Recruiting." *Associated Press State and Local Wire*, February 10.

Norrander, Barbara. 2000. "The Multi-Layered Impact of Public Opinion on Capital Punishment Implementation in the American States." *Political Research Quarterly* 53 (4): 771–93.

Norrander, Barbara, and Clyde Wilcox. 1999. "Public Opinion and Policymaking in the States: The Case of Post-*Roe* Abortion Policy." *Policy Studies Journal* 27 (4): 707–22.

North Atlantic Treaty Organization (NATO). 2002. "International Military Staff: United States." Committee on Women in NATO Forces. http: www.nato. int/ims/2001/win/us.htm.

Nyberg, Kenneth L., and Jon P. Alston. 1976. "Analysis of Public Attitudes toward Homosexual Behavior." *Journal of Homosexuality* 2:99–107.

Oberschall, A. 1973. *Social Conflict and Social Movements*. Englewood Cliffs, NJ: Prentice-Hall.

Oberstone, Andrea K., and Harriet Sukoneck. 1976. "Psychological Adjustment and Life Style of Single Lesbian and Single Heterosexual Women." *Psychological Women Quarterly* 1 (2): 172–88.

O'Connor, Karen. 1996. *No Neutral Ground? Abortion Politics in an Age of Absolutes*. Boulder, CO: Westview.

O'Connor, Robert E., and Michal E. Berkman. 1995. "Religious Determinants of State Abortion Policy." *Social Science Quarterly* 76:447–59.

O'Donnell, Maureen. 1994. "Lesbians to Fight Adoption Ruling." *Chicago Sun-Times*, December 6, 14.

Olmstead v. United States. 1928. 277 U.S. 438, 478.

Oregonian, The. 1991. "Bid to Add Special Groups Kills Hate-Crime Bill." *The Oregonian,* April 4, D6.

Orfield, Gary. 1978. *Must We Bus? Segregated Schools and National Policy,* Washington, DC: Brookings Institution.

Osher, Chris. 2001. "Support Up for Hate-Crime Bill, Pryor Says." *Arkansas Democrat-Gazette,* February 20, B8.

O'Toole, Roger. 1999. "House Votes to Repeal NH's Gay Adoption Ban." *Union Leader,* March 19, 1.

Pacelle, Richard L., Jr. 1996. "Seeking Another Forum: The Courts and Lesbian and Gay Rights." In *Gay Rights, Military Wrongs: Political Perspectives on Lesbians and Gays in the Military,* ed. Craig A. Rimmerman, 195–216. New York: Garland.

———. 2002. *The Role of the Supreme Court in American Politics: The Least Dangerous Branch?* Boulder, CO: Westview.

Padawer, Ruth. 1997. "Gay Couples Can Adopt in N.J.: Landmark Case Sets U.S. Precedent." *The Record* (Bergen Co., NJ), December 18, A1.

———. 2002. "Adoption by Gay Couples Backed: Pediatrics Group Urges Recognition." *The Record* (Bergen Co., NJ), February 4, A1.

Page, Benjamin I., and Robert Y. Shapiro. 1983. "Effects of Public Opinion on Policy." *American Political Science Review* 77:175–90.

Palmer, Louise D. 1997. "Groups Working Quietly to Expand Hate Crimes Law." *Times-Picayune* (New Orleans), November 9, A23.

Pandolfi, Anne. 1999. "Civil Rights Leaders Push for Expanded Hate Crime Legislation." *Associated Press State and Local Wire,* July 12.

Paquette, Carole. 1996. "Couples Wary on Same Sex Adoptions." *New York Times,* November 17, 1.

Park, Rosemary E. 1994. "Opening the Canadian Forces to Gays and Lesbians: An Inevitable Decision but Improbable Reconfiguration." In *Gays and Lesbians in the Military: Issues, Concerns and Contrasts,* ed. Wilbur J. Scott and Sandra Carson Stanley, 165–80. New York: Aldine De Gruyter.

Parshall, Lisa K. 2005. "Redefining Due Process Analysis: Justice Anthony M. Kennedy and the Concept of Emergent Rights." *Albany Law Review* 69:237–98.

Partlow, Joshua. 2003. "Wal-Mart Forbids Bias Against Gays: New Policy, Hailed by Rights Groups, Follows Corporate Trend." *Washington Post,* July 3, E2.

Patterson, Charlotte J. 1992. "Children of Lesbian and Gay Parents." *Child Development* 63:1025–42.

———. 1994. "Children of the Lesbian Baby Boom: Behavioral Adjustment Self-Concepts and Sex-Role Identity." In *Lesbian and Gay Psychology: Theory,*

Research and Clinical Applications, ed. Beverly Greene and Gregory M. Herek, 156–75. Thousand Oaks, CA: Sage.

———. 2000. "Family Relationships of Lesbians and Gay Men." *Journal of Marriage and Family* 62 (4): 1052–69.

Paulson, Steven K. 2005. "Gay Rights Groups Hope New Law Will Help Track Hate Crimes." *Associated Press State and Local Wire*, June 29.

Peltason, Jack W. 1971. *Fifty-Eight Lonely Men: Southern Federal Judges and School Desegregation.* Champaign: University of Illinois Press.

Pennsylvania Law Weekly. 2002. "Supreme Court OKs Second-Parent Adoption." *Pennsylvania Law Weekly*, August 26, 1.

Perlstein, Rick. 2003. "What Gay Studies Taught the Court." *Washington Post*, July 13, B3.

Pertman, Adam. 2000. *Adoption Nation: How the Adoption Revolution Is Transforming America.* New York: Basic.

Peterson, C. J. 1996. "Lesbian and Gay Families with Children: Implications of Social Science Research for Policy." *Journal of Social Issues* 52:29–50.

Peterson, Kavan. 2004. "50 State Rundown on Gay Marriage Laws." http://www .stateline.org/live/ViewPage.action?siteNodeId=136&languageId=1&contentId =15576.

Pinello, Daniel R. 2003. *Gay Rights and American Law.* New York: Cambridge University Press.

Pittsburgh Post-Gazette. 2002a. "The Capacity to Love." *Pittsburgh Post-Gazette*, September 8, B2.

———. 2002b. "For Some Groups, Religious Views Transcend Concern for Kids." *Pittsburgh Post-Gazette*, August 29, A18.

———. 2003. "Shutting the Bedroom Door a Victory for Privacy Nevertheless Brings up the Issue of Gay Marriage." *Pittsburgh Post-Gazette*, July 1, A15.

Piven, Frances Fox, and Richard Cloward. 1977. *Poor People's Movements: Why They Succeed, Howe They Fail.* New York: Pantheon.

Plohetski, Tony. 2002. "For Texas Gays, Adopting Kids Is Difficult but Not Impossible." *Austin American-Statesman*, April 1, A1.

Polikoff, Nancy. 1989–90. "This Child Does Have Two Mothers: Redefining Parenthood to Meet the Needs of Children in Lesbian-Mother and Other Non-traditional Families." *Georgetown Law Review* 78:459–575.

Post Standard. 1995. "Hate Crimes Laws Can't Enforce Love, but Offenses Motivated by Prejudice Should Be Named, and Outlawed." *Post Standard* (Syracuse, NY), July 17.

————. 2000. "Hate Crimes Still Time to Pass Federal Measure to Punish Offenses against Gays." *Post Standard* (Syracuse, NY), October 10.

Pratte, Trish. 1993. "A Comparative Study of Attitudes toward Homosexuality: 1986 and 1991." *Journal of Homosexuality* 26 (1): 77–83.

Price, Joyce. 1992. "Gay Ban Backed in Ranks." *Washington Times*, November 18, A1.

Pritchard, Amy L. 2003. "A Brief History of Gay Rights Related Initiatives and Referendum." In *Initiative and Referendum Almanac*, ed. M. Dane Waters, 494–96. Durham, NC: Carolina Academic Press.

Providence Journal-Bulletin. 2003. "Adoption Agencies Weigh Gay Applications. *Providence Journal-Bulletin*, October 29, A4.

Pugliese, David. 1992. "Gay Ruling Has No Effect on Forces." *Ottowa Citizen*, August 8, A4.

Purnell, Sonia. 1999. "Gay Rights Revolution: European Court Will Order Change in the Laws Limiting Homosexuality." *Daily Mail* (Glasgow, Scotland), September 25, 39.

Quinn, Justin. 2003. "Constitution Party Leader Denounces Gay-Sex Ruling." *Intelligencer Journal*, July 3, A1.

Quirk, Paul J., and Sarah Binder. 2005. *Institutions of American Democracy: The Legislative Branch*. London: Oxford University Press.

RAND Corporation. 1993. "Sexual Orientation and U.S. Military Personnel Policy: Options and Assessment." Santa Monica, CA: RAND, National Defense Research Institute.

Rasky, Susan F. 1990. "Bush is Sent Bill Requiring Data on Bias Crimes." *New York Times*, April 4, A1.

Raspberry, William. 2000. "Hate-Crime Laws Punish Thought." *Times Union* (Albany, NY), September 12, A13.

Raum, Tom. 2000. "Senate Passes Hate Crimes Measure, 57–42." *Associated Press State and Local Wire*, June 20.

Rayside, David M. 1996. "The Perils of Congressional Politics." In *Gay Rights, Military Wrongs: Political Perspectives on Lesbians and Gays in the Military*, ed. Craig A. Rimmerman, 147–84. New York: Garland.

Record, The. 1999. "Editorials from Other Newspapers." *The Record* (Bergen County, NJ), October 12, L14.

Reed, Jack. 2000. "Aye for Hate-Crime Laws." *Providence* (RI) *Journal-Bulletin*, August 25, 6B.

Reinert, Patty, and Armando Villafranca. 2003. "Court's Decision Viewed as Step toward Equal Treatment for Gays." *Houston Chronicle*, June 28, 3.

Rhode Island General Assembly, House of Representatives. 1990. Transcription of videotaped debate on Senate Bill 2227, June 28.

Rhode Island General Assembly, Senate. 1995. "An Act Relating to Civil Rights." House Bill 6678. Transcription of videotaped debate, May 19.

Ricketts, Wendell, and Roberta Achtenberg. 1987. "The Adoptive and Foster Gay and Lesbian Parent." In *Gay and Lesbian Parents*, ed. Frederick W. Bozett, 89–111. New York: Praeger.

Riding, Alan. 1992. "In NATO, Only U.S. and British Ban Gay Soldiers." *New York Times*, November 13, A12.

Riggle, Ellen D. B., and Sharon S. Rostosky. 2007. "The Consequences of Marriage Policy for Same-Sex Couples' Well-Being." In *The Politics of Same-Sex Marriage*, ed. Craig A. Rimmerman and Clyde Wilcox, 65–84. Chicago: University of Chicago Press.

Rimmerman, Craig A. 1996a. "Introduction." In *Gay Rights, Military Wrongs: Political Perspectives on Lesbians and Gays in the Military*, ed. Craig A. Rimmerman, xix–xxvii. New York: Garland.

———. 1996b. "Promise Unfulfilled: Clinton's Failure to Overturn the Military Ban on Lesbians and Gays." In *Gay Rights, Military Wrongs: Political Perspectives on Lesbians and Gays in the Military*, ed. Craig A. Rimmerman, 111–26. New York: Garland.

———. 2002. *From Identity to Politics: The Lesbian and Gay Movements in the United States*. Philadelphia: Temple University Press.

Rivera, Rhonda R. 1986. "Queer Law: Sexual Orientation Law in the Mid-Eighties." *University of Dayton Law Review* 11:275–329.

Rizzo, Kate. 2000. Testimony before the Judiciary Committee of the Connecticut General Assembly, March 13, p. 129. http://prdbasis.cga.state.ct.us/ (accessed September 17, 2003; hard copy in possession of the author).

Roanoke Times. 2005. "Repeal of Sodomy Law Overdue in Virginia." *Roanoke Times*, September 19, B6.

Robinson, Herb. 1991a. "A Matter of Protecting Human Dignity." *Seattle Times*, March 18, A8.

———. 1991b. "Growing Problem of Hate Crimes Here." *Seattle Times*, February 8, A10.

Robinson, Paul H., and Markus Dirk Dubber. 1999. "An Introduction to the Model Penal Code." http://papers.ssrn.com.

Rochefort, David, and Roger Cobb, eds. 1994. *The Politics of Problem Definition: Shaping the Policy Agenda*, Lawrence: University Press of Kansas.

Rochon, T. 1998. *Culture Moves: Ideas, Activism and Changing Values.* Princeton, NJ: Princeton University Press.

Rolison, Garry L., and Thomas K. Nakayama. 1994. "Defensive Discourse: Blacks and Gays in the U.S. Military." In Wilbur J. Scott and Sandra Carson Stanley, ed., *Gays and Lesbians in the Military: Issues, Concerns and Contrasts,* 121–34. New York: Aldine De Gruyter.

Rom, Mark Carl. 2007. "Introduction." In *The Politics of Same-Sex Marriage,* ed. Craig A. Rimmerman and Clyde Wilcox, 1–38. Chicago: University of Chicago Press.

Roper Center for Public Opinion Research. 2008a. General social survey question of March 2006. iPoll databank. http://www.ropercenter.uconn.edu/data_access/ipoll/ipoll.html (accessed February 19, 2008; hard copy in possession of the author).

———. 2008b. CBS/*New York Times* poll of October 2006. iPoll databank. http://www.ropercenter.uconn.edu/data_access/ipoll/ipoll.html (accessed February 11, 2008; hard copy in possession of the author).

———. 2008c. General social survey question of May 2007. http://www.ropercenter.uconn.edu/data_access/ipoll/ipoll.html (accessed February 19, 2008; hard copy in possession of the author).

———. 2008d. CNN/Opinion Research Corporation poll, May 2007. iPoll databank. http://www.ropercenter.uconn.edu/data_access/ipoll/ipoll.html (accessed February 11, 2008; hard copy in possession of the author).

———. 2008e. Gallup/*USA Today* poll, July 2007. iPoll databank. http://www.ropercenter.uconn.edu/data_access/ipoll/ipoll.html (accessed February 11, 2008; hard copy in possession of the author).

———. 2008f. Gallup poll, May 2007. iPoll databank. http://www.ropercenter.uconn.edu/data_access/ipoll/ipoll.html (accessed February 11, 2008; hard copy in possession of the author).

———. 2008g. Pew Forum on Religion and Public Life survey, August 2007. iPoll databank. http://www.ropercenter.uconn.edu/data_access/ipoll/ipoll.html (accessed February 11, 2008; hard copy in possession of the author).

———. 2008h. Fox News/Opinion Dynamics poll, November 2006. iPoll databank. http://www.ropercenter.uconn.edu/data_access/ipoll/ipoll.html (accessed February 11, 2008; hard copy in possession of the author).

Rosenberg, Gerald N. 1991. *The Hollow Hope: Can Courts Bring about Social Change?* Chicago: University of Chicago Press.

Rosenblum, Darren. 1996. "Geographically Sexual? Advancing Lesbian and Gay Interests through Proportional Represenation." *Harvard Civil Rights–Civil Liberties Law Review* 31:119–54.

Rostow, Eugene V. 1952. "The Democratic Character of Judicial Review." *Harvard Law Review* 66: 193.

Rotundo, Anthony. 1993. *American Manhood: Transformations in Masculinity from the Revolution to the Modern Era.* New York: Basic.

Rowett, Michael. 2003. "Senate Committee Endorses Measure about Hate Crimes." *Arkansas Democrat-Gazette,* March 18, 8.

Rubenfeld, Abby R. 1986. "Lessons Learned: A Reflection upon *Bowers v. Hardwick.*" *Nova Law Review* 3:59–60.

Rubenstein, William B. 1999. "The Myth of Superiority." *Constitutional Commentary* 16:599–625.

Safire, William. 2003. "The Bedroom Door." *New York Times,* June 30, 21.

Salokar, Rebecca Mae. 2001. "Beyond Gay Rights Litigation: Using a Systemic Strategy to Effect Political Change in the United States." In *Sexual Identities, Queer Politics,* ed. Mark Blasius, 256–85. Princeton, NJ: Princeton University Press.

Salter, Stephanie. 1994. "Statistics Support Gay Adoptions." *South Bend* (IN) *Tribune,* August 5, A9.

Sam Houston State University Criminal Justice Center. 1980. *Responding to Child Sexual Abuse: A Report to the 67th Session of the Texas Legislature.* Huntsville, TX: Sam Houston State University.

Sandalow, Marc. 2000. "House Backs Expanded Hate-Crime Legislation." *San Francisco Chronicle,* September 14, A1.

Sanko, John. 2002. "Two Lawmakers to Offer Bias Bill Again; Hate-Crime Law Would Be Extended to Gays." *Rocky Mountain News,* January 7, 14A.

Sarbin, Theodore R. 1996. "The Deconstrictuon of Stereotypes: Homosexuals and Military Policy." In *Out in Force: Sexual Orientation and the Military,* ed. Gregory M. Herek, Jared B. Jobe, and Ralph M. Carney, 177–96. Chicago: University of Chicago Press.

Sarche, Jon. 2001. "House Panel Kills Bill to Expand Hate-Crimes Law." *Associated Press State and Local Wire,* April 24.

Savage, Dan. 2001. "Is No Adoption Really Better than a Gay Adoption?" *New York Times,* September 8, A13.

Sax, Joseph L. 1971. *Defending the Environment: A Strategy for Citizen Action.* New York: Knopf.

Scanlon, Bill. 2005. "1 Veto, 1 Victory: Setback for Gay Workers; Gain on Hate-Crimes Law." *Rocky Mountain News*, May 28, 4A.

Schattschneider, E. E. 1960. *The Semi-Sovereign People*. New York: Rinehart and Winston.

Scheingold, Stuart A. 1974. *The Politics of Rights: Lawyers, Public Policy, and Political Change*. New Haven, CT: Yale University Press.

Schmalz, Jeffrey. 1993. "Homosexuals Wake to See a Referendum: It's on Them." *New York Times*, January 31, 4, 1.

Schmitt, Eric. 1993a. "Joint Chiefs Fighting Clinton Plan to Allow Homosexuals in Military." *New York Times*, January 23, A1.

———. 1993b. "Compromise on Military Gay Ban Gaining Support among Senators." *New York Times*, May 12, A1.

———. 1993c. "Pentagon Chief Warns Clinton on Gay Policy." *New York Times*, January 25, A1.

———. 1993d. "Start of a Consensus: Lawmakers Focusing on Drawing Up Rules for Behavior by Homosexuals in Military." *New York Times*, May 20, B10.

———. 1993e. "Joint Chiefs to Get 2 Options on Homosexuals." *New York Times*, May 22, 1, 8.

———. 1993f. "A Military Town Makes Its Anti-Gay Feelings Clear." *New York Times*, March 25, A16.

———. 1993g. "Military Cites Wide Range of Reasons for Its Gay Ban." *New York Times*, January 27, A1.

———. 1993h. "Months after Order on Gay Ban, Military Is Still Resisting Clinton." *New York Times*, March 23, A1.

Schneider, Anne, and Helen Ingram. 1993. "Social Construction of Target Populations: Implications for Politics and Policy." *American Political Science Review* 87 (2): 334–47.

Schroedel, Jean Reith. 1999. "Elite Attitudes toward Homosexuality." In *Gays and Lesbians in the Democratic Process*, ed. Ellen D. B. Riggle and Barry L. Tadlock, 89–117. New York: Columbia University Press.

Schumaker, Paul D. 1975. "Policy Responsiveness to Protest-Group Demands." *Journal of Politics* 37:488–521.

Schuman, Howard, Charlotte Steeh, and Lawrence Bobo. 1985. *Racial Attitudes in America: Trends and Interpretations*, Cambridge, MA: Harvard University Press.

Schwartz, Fred K. 2002. "Letter to the Editor." *Pasadena Star-News*, February 22.

Schwartz, Louis B. 1963. "Morals Offenses and the Model Penal Code." *Columbia Law Review* 63:669–86.

Scott, Wilbur J., and Sandra Carson Stanley. 1994. "Introduction: Sexual Orientation and Military Service." In *Gays and Lesbians in the Military: Issues, Concerns and Contrasts,* ed. Wilbur J. Scott and Sandra Carson Stanley, xi–xx. New York: Aldine De Gruyter.

Seemann, Luke. 1997. "Push Is On for Governor to Approve Hate-Crimes Law for N.M." *Albuquerque Tribune,* November 11, A3.

Segal, David R., Paul A. Gade, and Edgar M. Johnson. 1994. "Social Science Research on Homosexuals in the Military." In *Gays and Lesbians in the Military: Issues, Concerns and Contrasts,* ed. Wilbur J. Scott and Sandra Carson Stanley, 33–52. New York: Aldine De Gruyter.

Segal, Jeffrey A., and Harold J. Spaeth. 1993. *The Supreme Court and the Attitudinal Model.* New York: Cambridge University Press.

———. 2005. *The Supreme Court in the American Legal System.* Cambridge, U.K.: Cambridge University Press.

Segall, Cary. 1994. "Lesbian Partner Can't Adopt Child, Court Says." *Wisconsin State Journal,* June 9, A1.

Segura, Gary M. 1999. "Institutions Matter: Local Electoral Laws, Gay and Lesbian Representation, and Coalition Building across Minority Communities." In *Gays and Lesbians in the Democratic Process,* ed. Ellen D. B. Riggle and Barry L. Tadlock, 220–41. New York: Columbia University Press.

Seidman, Steven. 2002. *Beyond the Closet: The Transformation of Gay and Lesbian Life.* New York: Routledge.

Seiler, Fanny. 2001. "Rights Advocate Seeks Expanded Hate-Crime Bill." *Charleston* (WV) *Gazette,* March 9, P8A.

Seltzer, Richard. 1993. "AIDS, Homosexuality, Public Opinion and Changing Correlates over Time." *Journal of Homosexuality* 26:85–97.

Settle, Michael. 2000. "Plan to Ban Gays from Front Line Action." *The Herald,* October 4, 6.

Shaiko, Ronald G. 2007. "Same-Sex Marriage, GLBT Organizations, and the Lack of Spirited Political Engagement," In *The Politics of Same-Sex Marriage,* ed. Craig A. Rimmerman and Clyde Wilcox, 85–103. Chicago: University of Chicago Press.

Shalikashvili, John M. 2007. "Second Thoughts on Gays in the Military." *New York Times,* January 2, 17.

Shanker, Thom. 2007. "Top General Explains Remarks on Gays." *New York Times,* March 14, A15.

Shapiro, Julie. 1995–96. "Custody and Conduct: How the Law Fails Lesbian and Gay Parents and Their Children." *Indiana Law Journal* 71:623–71.

Sharp, Elaine B. 1999. "Introduction." In *Culture Wars and Local Politics,* ed. Elaine B. Sharp, 1–20. Lawrence: University Press of Kansas.

Shen, Fern. 1991. "Hate Crime Bill Rejected in Maryland House." *Washington Post,* March 22, C1.

Shepard, Scott. 2002. "GOP Senators Block Vote to Expand Hate Crime." *Palm Beach Post,* June 12, 5A.

Shepsle, Kenneth A., and Barry R. Weingast. 1987. "Why Are Congressional Committees Powerful?" *American Political Science Review* 81:937–45.

Sherrill, Kenneth. 1993. "On Gay People as a Politically Powerless Group." In *Gays and the Military: Joseph Steffan versus the United States,* ed. Mark Wolinsky and Kenneth Sherrill, 84–120. Princeton, NJ: Princeton University Press.

———. 1996. "The Political Power of Lesbians, Gays and Bisexuals." *PS: Political Science and Politics* 29 (3): 469–73.

———. 2005. "Same-Sex Marriage, Civil Unions, and the 2004 Presidential Vote." In *The Future of Gay Rights in America,* ed. H. N. Hirsch, 37–45. New York: Routledge.

Shilts, Randy. 1993. *Conduct Unbecoming: Lesbians and Gays in the U.S. Military, Vietnam to the Persian Gulf.* New York: St. Martin's.

Silbey, Joel H, ed. 1991. *Encyclopedia of the American Legislative System,* vol. 1. New York: Charles Scribner's Sons.

Silverstein, Charles. 1976–77. "Even Psychiatry Can Profit from Its Past Mistakes." *Journal of Homosexuality* 2 (2): 153–58.

Silverstein, L. B., and C. F. Auerbach. 1997. "Deconstructing the Essential Father." *American Psychologist* 54:397–407.

Silvestrini, Elaine. 2003. "Court's Sodomy Ruling Barely Affects Florida." *Tampa Tribune,* June 27, 10.

Simon, Jim. 1991. "Surprise Vote Kills Hate-Crimes Bill." *Seattle Times,* April 4, C1.

Simon, Richard. 2007. "Senate Adds Hate-Crime Measure to War Bill." *Los Angeles Times,* September 28, A11.

Skocpol, Theda, Peter B. Evans, and Dietrich Rueschemeyer, eds. 1985. *Bringing the State Back In.* Cambridge, U.K.: Cambridge University Press.

Sloat, Bill. 2004. "Cincinnati Rewrites Ballot Issue in Effort to Save Gay-Rights Vote." *Cleveland Plain Dealer,* August 31, B3.

Smith, Christopher E. 1993. *Courts and Public Policy.* Chicago: Nelson-Hall.

———. 1997. *Courts, Politics and the Judicial Process,* 2nd ed. Chicago: Nelson- Hall.

Smith, David M., and Gary J. Gates. 2001. *Gay and Lesbian Families in the United States: Same-Sex Unmarried Partner Households, A Preliminary Analysis of the*

2000 United States Census Data, August 22. Washington, DC: Human Rights Campaign and the Urban Institute.

Smith-Rosenberg, Carroll. 1985. *Disorderly Conduct: Visions of Gender in Victorian America.* Oxford: Oxford University Press.

Sniderman, Paul M., and Thomas Piazza. 1993. *The Scar of Race.* Cambridge, MA: Belknap Press.

Snow, David A. 1992. "Master Frames and Cycles of Protest." In *Frontiers of Social Movement Theory,* ed. Aldon Morris and Carol McClug Mueller, 133–55. New Haven, CT: Yale University Press.

Snow, David, E. Rochford, S. Worden, and R. Benford. 1986. "Frame Alignment Processes, Micro-Mobilization and Movement Participation." *American Sociological Review* 51:464–81.

Song, Jaymes. 2001. "Hate Crimes Bill Signed into Law." *Associated Press State and Local Wire,* June 13.

Songer, Donald R. 1995. "Integrated Models of State Supreme Court Decision Making." Paper presented at the Annual Meting of the American Political Science Association, Chicago, August 31–September 3.

South Bend Tribune. 1998. "Voice of the People: Don't Allow Gay Adoption." *South Bend* (IN) *Tribune,* December 22, A10.

———. 2000. "Hate Crimes Law the Wrong Way to Go." *South Bend* (IN) *Tribune,* July 6, A10.

Spaeth, Harold J. 1995. "The Attitudinal Model." In *Contemplating Courts,* ed. Lee Epstein, 296–314. Washington, DC: CQ Press.

Spann, Girardeau A. 1993. *Race against the Court: The Supreme Court and Minorities in Contemporary America.* New York: New York University Press.

Spencer, Gary. 1995. "Lesbian Partner Permitted to Adopt: 4–3 Decision on Unmarried Couples." *New York Law Journal,* November 3.

Spencer, Geoff. 1992. "Lifting of Gay Ban Softens Australia's Tough Man Image." *Associated Press,* December 9.

Spidaliere, John M. 2003. "Reaction Strong Here to Demise of Gay Sex Ban." *Lancaster New Era,* June 27, A1.

Spiegel, Peter. 2007. "Tune is Changing on Gays in Military." *Los Angeles Times,* August 9, A1.

St. Petersburg Times. 1992. "Vatican Supports Bias against Gays in Some Cases." *St. Petersburg Times,* July 18, 1A.

Stacey, Judith. 2001. "Family Values Forever: In the Marriage Movement, Conservatives and Centrists Find a Home Together." *The Nation,* July 9. http://www.thenation.com/docprem.mhtml?i=20010709&s=stacey.

Stacey, J., and T. Biblarz. 2001. "How Does the Sexual Orientation of the Parents Matter?" *American Sociological Review* 66:159–83.

Stachelberg, Winnie. 2002. "Should Congress Expand Federal Protections of Gays in the Workplace?" *Insight on the News*, April 1, 40.

Staggenborg, Suzanne. 1995. "Can Feminist Organizations Be Effective?" In *Feminist Organizations: Harvest of the New Women's Movement*, ed. Myra Marx Ferree and Patricia Yancey Martin, 339–55. Philadelphia: Temple University Press.

Stashenko, Joel. 2000. "Court Could Make Landmark Public Policy Statement." *Associated Press State and Local Wire*, July 27.

Steves, David. 2005. "Court Annuls Gay Marriages." *Register Guard* (Salem, OR), April 16.

Stiehm, Judith Hicks. 1989. *Arms and the Enlisted Woman*. Philadelphia: Temple University Press.

———. 1994. "The Military Ban on Homosexuals and the Cyclops Effect." In *Gays and Lesbians in the Military: Issues, Concerns and Contrasts*, ed. Wilbur J. Scott and Sandra Carson Stanley, 149–64. New York: Aldine De Gruyter.

Stimson, James A., Michael B. Mackuen, and Robert S. Erikson. 1995. "Dynamic Representation." *American Political Science Review* 89 (3): 543–65.

Stockwell, Jamie. 1999. "Panel Approves Bill Clarifying Hate Crime." *Houston Chronicle*, March 12, 25.

Stoller, Robert J. 1985. *Presentations of Gender*. New Haven, CT: Yale University Press.

Stone, Deborah. 1988. *Policy Paradox and Political Reason*. Glenview, IL; Scott, Foresman.

Studlar, Donley. 2001. "What Constitutes Morality Policy? A Cross-National Analysis." In *The Public Clash of Private Values*, ed. Christopher Z. Mooney, 37–54. New York: Chatham House.

Sullivan, Andrew. 1993. "Gay Values, Truly Conservative." *New York Times*, February 9, A21.

———. 1996. *Virtually Normal: An Argument about Homosexuality*. New York: Vintage.

Sullivan, Joseph F. 1993. "Court Backs Lesbian's Right to Adopt a Partner's Child." *New York Times*, August 11, B5.

Sullivan, Julie. 2002. "Oregon Family at Vortex of Ban on Gay Adoption." *The Oregonian*, March 14, A1.

Sullivan, Ronald. 1992. "Judge Lets Gay Partner Adopt Child." *New York Times*, January 31, B1.

Summerskill, Ben. 2000. "It's Official: Gays Do NOT Harm Forces." *The Observer,* November 19, 5.

Sunday Herald Sun. 1992. "Gays 'Make Good Soldiers.'" April 19.

Sunstein, Cass. 1999. *One Case at a Time: Judicial Minimalism and the Supreme Court.* Cambridge, MA: Harvard University Press.

Susoeff, Steve. 1985. "Assessing Children's Best Interests when a Parent Is Gay or Lesbian: Toward a Rational Custody Standard." *UCLA Law Review* 32:852–903.

Tadlock, Barry L., C. Ann Gordon, and Elizabeth Popp. 2007. "Framing the Issue of Same-Sex Marriage." In *The Politics of Same-Sex Marriage,* ed. Craig R. Rimmerman and Clyde Wilcox, 193–214. Chicago: University of Chicago Press.

Tarrow, Sydney. 1992. "Mentalities, Political Cultures and Collective Action Frames: Constructing Meanings through Action." In *Frontiers in Social Movement Theory,* ed. Aldon D. Morris and Carol McClurg Mueller, 174–202. New Haven, CT: Yale University Press.

———. 1994. *Power in Movement: Social Movements, Collective Action and Politics.* Cambridge, U.K.: Cambridge University Press.

———. 1998a. *Power in Movement: Social Movements and Contentious Politics.* Cambridge, U.K.: Cambridge University Press.

———. 1998b. "'The Very Excess of Democracy': State Building and Contentious Politics in America." In *Social Movements and American Political Institutions,* ed. Anne N. Costain and Andrew S. McFarland, 20–38. Lanham, MD: Rowman and Littlefield.

Tasker, Fiona L., and Susan Golombok. 1991. "Children Raised by Lesbian Mothers." *Family Law* 21:184–87.

Tate, C. Neal. 1981. "Personal Attribute Models of the Voting Behavior of U.S. Supreme Court Justices' Liberalism in Civil Liberties and Economic Decisions, 1946–78." *American Political Science Review* 75:355–67.

Taylor, Verta, and Nicole C. Raeburn. 1995. "Identity Politics as High-Risk Activism: Career Consequences for Lesbian, Gay and Bisexual Sociologists." *Social Problems* 42:252–73.

Taylor, Verta, and Nancy Whittier. 1992. "Collective Identity in Social Movement Communities: Lesbian Feminist Mobilization." In *Frontiers in Social Movement Theory,* ed. Aldon Morris and Carol Mueller, 104–29. New Haven, CT: Yale University Press.

Teepen, Tom. 1991. "Religious Right Helps Bigotry Win in House." *Atlanta Journal and Constitution,* February 14, A17.

Tharpes, Yvonne L. 1987. "Comment: *Bowers v. Hardwick* and the Legitimization of Homophobia in America." *Howard Law Journal,* 30:537–49.

Thomas, Alice. 1998. "Legal, Social Obstacles Made Adoption Difficult for Gays." *Columbus* (OH) *Dispatch,* September 3, D10.

Thomas, Evan. 2003. "The War over Gay Marriage." *Newsweek,* July 7, 38.

Thomas, Patricia J., and Marie D. Thomas. 1996. "Integration of Women in the Military: Parallels to the Progress of Homosexuals?" In *Out in Force: Sexual Orientation and the Military,* ed. Gregory M. Herek, Jared B. Jobe, and Ralph M. Carney, 65–85. Chicago: University of Chicago Press.

Thomma, Steven. 2006. "Election Changes Hue of Red States." *News and Observer* (Raleigh, NC), November 22, A8.

Tilly, Charles. 1978. *From Mobilization to Revolution.* Reading, MA: Addison-Wesley.

Time, CNN, and Yankelovich Partners. January 1993 and June 1994. Poll data, collected by the Roper Center at University of Connecticut. Public Opinion Online through LexisNexis.

Times-Picayune. 1994. "Pass Hate Crimes Bill." *Times-Picayune* (New Orleans), June 19, B10.

———. 1998. "Hate Crimes Law Just, Popular." *Times-Picayune* (New Orleans), October 20, B4.

Tipton, Virgil. 1991. "Hate-Crime Bill Lacks Council Support." *St. Louis Post-Dispatch,* June 21, 3A.

Tolbert, Caroline J., and Rodney E. Hero, 1996. "Race/Ethnicity and Direct Democracy: An Analysis of California's Illegal Immigration Initiative." *Journal of Politics* 58:806–18.

Toner, Robin. 1990. "Senate, 92 to 4, Wants U.S. Data on Crimes that Spring from Hate." *New York Times,* February 9, A17.

———. 2007. "In This Turn at the Top, Democrats Seek the Middle on Social Issues." *New York Times,* January 16, A1.

Toronto Star. 1992a. "Violating Gay Rights." *Toronto Star,* February 12, A20.

———. 1992b. "Allow Gays in Military, Most Canadians Tell Survey." *Toronto Star,* December 10, A21.

Touraine, Alain. 1985. "An Introduction to the Study of Social Movements." *Social Research* 52:749–87.

Tribe, Lawrence H. 2004. *"Lawrence v. Texas:* The "Fundamental Right" that Dare Not Speak Its Name." *Harvard Law Review* 117:1894–1955.

Tsong, Nicole. 1998. "Civic Groups Urge Congress to Pass Bill Barring Hate Crimes." *San Antonio Express-News,* July 9, 4A.

Tuhus, Melinda. 2000. "Easing the Fears of a Parent, Gay or Not." *New York Times,* July 30, 14CN, 3.

Tulsa World. 2003. "Bad Bills." *Tulsa* (OK) *World*, A20.

Tysver, Robynn. 2001. "Court to Tackle Gay Adoption Question." *Omaha World Herald*, October 3, B2.

———. 2002. "Ruling Leaves Gay Adoption Question Open: Narrow Scope of Court Decision Rejects It in One Case but Not All." *Omaha World Herald*, March 9, B1.

United Press International. 1992. "Australia Lifts Defense Force Ban on Homosexuals." November 23.

USA Today. 2007. "Old Prejudice Dishonors New Military Generation." *USA Today*, March 15, 9A.

U.S. Census Bureau. 2006a. "United States by State and Puerto Rico—CGT-T1 Population Estimates." Population Estimates Program. http://factfinder .census.gov/ (accessed June 25, 2006).

———. 2006b. "2006 American Community Survey." American Community Survey Selected Population Profile. http://factfinder.census.gov/.

———. 2006c. "Resident Population—States: 1980 to 2005." *Statistical Abstract of the United States.* http://www.census.gov/statab/www/ (accessed November 6, 2006; now found at http://www.census.gov/compendia/statab/).

———. 2006d. "Population of the 100 Largest Urban Places, 1980, 1990." *Statistical Abstract of the United States.* http://www.census.gov/statab/www/ (accessed November 5, 2006; now found at http://www.census.gov/ compendia/statab/).

———. 2006e. "Persons 25 Years Old and Over with a Bachelor's Degree or More, 2004." *Statistical Abstract of the United States*, State Rankings. http:// www.census.gov/statab/ranks/rank19.html.

U.S. Congress, House of Representatives. 1993. "The National Defense Authorization Act for Fiscal Year 1994." *Congressional Record*, H.R. 2401, 103rd Congress, 1st session, February 3–4, August 4, September 28.

———. 1996. "The Defense of Marriage Act." *Congressional Record*, H.R. 3396, July 11–12.

———. 2000. "Motion to Instruct Conferees on HR4205, Floyd D. Spence National Defense Authorization Act for Fiscal Year 2001." *Congressional Record*, 106th Congress, 2nd Session, September 13.

———. 2003. "Hate Crimes Legislation." *Congressional Record*, 108th Congress, 1st session, May 7.

———. 2004a. "Republicans Strip Hate Crime Prevention Provisions from Defense Authorization Bill."*Congressional Record*, 108th Congress, 2nd session, October 9.

———. 2004b. "Reintroduction of Local Law Enforcement Hate Crimes Prevention Act." *Congressional Record*, 108th Congress, 2nd session, April 22.

———. 2004c. "Appointment of Conferees on H.R. 4200, National Defense Authorization Act for Fiscal Year 2005." *Congressional Record*, 108th Congress, 2nd session, September 28.

U.S. Congress, Senate. 1993. "The National Defense Authorization Act for Fiscal Year 1994." *Congressional Record*, S. 1298, 103rd Congress, 1st session, September 7, 9.

———. 1996a. "Employment Non-Discrimination Act." *Congressional Record*, S. 2056, 104th Congress, 2nd session, September 6, 9.

———. 1996b. "The Defense of Marriage Act." *Congressional Record*, S. 1749, 104th Congress, 2nd session, May 8–9, June 6, September 9–10.

———. 1999. "Hate Crimes." *Congressional Record*, 106th Congress, 1st session, October 18.

———. 2000a. "National Defense Authorization Act for Fiscal Year 2001." *Congressional Record*, 106th Congress, 2nd session, June 19, 20.

———. 2000b. "Hate Crimes Prevention Act Amendment." *Congressional Record*, 106th Congress, 2nd session, June 16, 21, 22, September 26.

———. 2000c. "Shootings in Pittsburgh, Pennsylvania." *Congressional Record*, 106th Congress, 2nd session, May 8.

———. 2003a. "National Defense Authorization Act for Fiscal Year 2005." *Congressional Record*, 108th Congress, 1st session, June 14, 15, 16.

———. 2003b. "Local Law Enforcement Act of 2001." *Congressional Record*, 108th Congress, 1st session, January 9.

———. 2003c. "Statements on Introduced Bills and Joint Resolutions." *Congressional Record*, 108th Congress, 1st session, May 1.

———. 2003d. "Hate Crimes Legislation." *Congressional Record*, 108th Congress, 1st session, July 11.

———. 2003e. "Rally against Hate." *Congressional Record*, 108th Congress, 1st session, June 17.

———. 2004a. "Dr. Martin Luther King, Jr. Day, 2004." *Congressional Record*, 108th Congress, 2nd session, January 20.

———. 2004b. "Conference Reports on the Ronald W. Reagan National Defense Authorization Act for 2005." *Congressional Record*, 108th Congress, 2nd session, October 9.

———. 2004c. "Local Law Enforcement Act of 2003." *Congressional Record*, 108th Congress, 2nd session, October 8.

U.S. Department of Defense. 1982. "Enlisted Administrative Separations." Directive No. 1332, 14, 1-9–1-13. Washington, DC: U.S. Department of Defense.

U.S. Department of Justice, Bureau of Justice Statistics. 1998. *State Court Organization, 1998.* http://www.ojp.usdoj.gov/bjs/pub/pdf/sco9801.pdf.

U.S. Department of Public Health, Administration for Children and Families, National Center on Child Abuse and Neglect. 1996. *The Third National Incidence Study of Child Abuse and Neglect.* Washington, DC: Government Printing Office.

U.S. Government Accountability Office. 1992. *Defense Force Management: DOD's Policy on Homosexuality,* June. Washington, DC: Government Accountability Office.

Vaid, Urvashi. 1995. *Virtual Equality: The Mainstreaming of Gay and Lesbian Liberation.* New York: Anchor.

Van der Meide, Wayne. 2000. *Legislating Equality: A Review of Laws Affecting Gays, Lesbians, Bisexuals and Transgendered People in the U.S.* Washington, DC: National Gay and Lesbian Task Force.

Vander Wielen, Ryan. 2006. "U.S. Congressional Conference Committees and Policy Outcomes." Ph.D. diss., Washington University, St. Louis.

Veiga, Alex. 2002. "ACLU Launches Campaign against Florida's Gay Adoption Ban." *Associated Press State and Local Wire,* March 14.

Vienneau, David, and Jack Lakey. 1992. "Ruling Seen as Precedent in Job Bias against Gays." *Toronto Star,* October 28, A1.

Waaldijk, K. 2001. "Small Change: How the Road to Same-Sex Marriage Got Paved in the Netherlands." In *Legal Recognition of Same-Sex Partnerships: A Study of National, European and International Law,* ed. R. Wintemute and M. Andenaes, 437–64. Oxford, UK: Hart.

Wald, Kenneth D. 2000. "The Context of Gay Politics." In *The Politics of Gay Rights,* ed. Craig A. Rimmerman, Kenneth D. Wald, and Clyde Wilcox, 1–30. Chicago: University of Chicago Press.

Wald, Kenneth D., James W. Button, and Barbara A. Rienzo. 1996. "The Politics of Gay Rights in American Communities: Explaining Antidiscrimination Ordinances and Policies." *American Journal of Political Science* 40 (November): 1152–78.

Walker, Jack. 1969. "The Diffusion of Innovation among the American States." *American Political Science Review* 63:880–99.

Wallace, Jim. 2002. "Hate Crime Bill Opponents Low-Key." *Charleston* (SC) *Daily Mail,* February 21, 1C.

Walsh, Mary Williams. 1992. "Canada Far Ahead of U.S. in Recognizing Gay Rights Justice." *Los Angeles Times,* December 29, A1.

Walters, Suzanna Danuta. 2001. *All the Rage: The Story of Gay Visibility in America.* Chicago: University of Chicago Press.

Warbis, Mark. 1999. "Lawmakers Reject Adding Anti-Gay Bias to Hate Crimes Law." *Associated Press State and Local Wire,* January 20.

Warner, Michael. 1999. *The Trouble with Normal: Sex, Politics, and the Ethics of Queer Life.* New York: Free Press.

Warren, Carol. 1980. "Homosexuality and Stigma." In *Homosexual Behavior: A Modern Reappraisal,* ed. Judd Marmor, 123–41. New York: Basic.

Warren, Samuel D., and Lewis D. Brandeis. 1890. "The Right to Privacy." *Harvard Law Review* 4 (5): 193–220.

Washingtonpost.com. 2006. "Gay-Marriage Ban Upheld by Calif. Court." Washingtonpost.com. http://pqasb.pqarchiver.com/washingtonpost/access/1141361751.html?dids=1141361751:1141361751&FMT=ABS&FMTS=ABS:FT&date=Oct+6%2C+2006&author=&pub=The+Washington+Post&edition=&startpage=A.11&desc=Gay-Marriage+Ban+Upheld+Calif.+Court (accessed March 4, 2008).

Waugh, Paul. 1999. "Services Plan to Replace Bar on Gays with Ban on All Sex." *The Independent.* November 15, 9.

Weeks, Jeffrey, B. Heaphy, and C. Donovan. 2001. *Same Sex Intimacies: Families of Choice and Other Life Experiments.* London: Routledge.

Weston, K. 1991. *Families We Choose: Lesbians, Gays, Kinship.* New York: Columbia University Press.

Whereatt, Robert. 1993. "Gay Rights and Other New Laws Take Effect." *Star Tribune* (Minneapolis), August 1, 1B.

Whittig, Erin. 1999. "Sexual Orientation Not Added to Law." *Spokane* (WA) *Review,* January 21, B1.

Wilcox, Clyde, and Robin M. Wolpert. 1996. "President Clinton, Public Opinion and Gays in the Military." In *Gay Rights, Military Wrongs: Political Perspectives on Lesbians and Gays in the Military,* ed. Craig A. Rimmerman, 127–45. New York: Garland.

———. 2000. "Gay Rights in the Public Sphere: Public Opinion on Gay and Lesbian Equality." In *The Politics of Gay Rights,* ed. Craig A. Rimmerman, Kenneth D. Wald, and Clyde Wilcox, 409–32. Chicago: University of Chicago Press.

Wilcox, Clyde, Paul R. Brewer, Shauna Shames, and Celinda Lake. 2007. "If I Bend This Far I Will Break? Public Opinion about Same-sex Marriage." In

The Politics of Same-Sex Marriage, ed. Craig A. Rimmerman and Clyde Wilcox, 215–42. Chicago: University of Chicago Press.

Wilson, Thomas C. 1995. "Urbanism and Unconventionality: The Case of Sexual Behavior." *Social Science Quarterly* 76 (June): 346–63.

Wise, Jon. 2004. "RAF Target Gays in Recruitment Drive." *Daily Star* (London), August 27, 35.

Witt, Stephanie L., and Suzanne McCorkle. 1997. *Anti-Gay Rights: Assessing Voter Initiatives,* Westport, CT: Praeger.

Women's Law Project. 1995. *Lesbian and Gay Parenting: A Guide to Legal Rights in Pennsylvania,* 2nd ed. Philadelphia: Women's Legal Project.

Woodward, Samuel K. 1995. "Adoption Not Intended to Help Homosexuals' Self-Esteem." *The Columbian* (Vancouver, WA), July 5, A11.

Wright, Gloria. 1997. "Lesbian Couple Adopts Boy: The Child is the First Adopted by Unmarried Partners in Onodaga County since the State's Highest Court Said in 1995 the Adoptions Are Legal." *Post-Standard* (Syracuse, NY), December 8, B1.

Yackle, Larry W. 1994. *Reclaiming the Federal Courts.* Cambridge, MA: Harvard University Press.

Yang, Alan S. 1997. "Attitudes toward Homosexuality." *Public Opinion Quarterly* 61:477–507.

———. 2003. "Mass Opinion Change and Social Activism: The Politics of Knowledge and the Modern Lesbian and Gay Movement." Ph.D. diss., Columbia University.

Yarbrough, Jeff. 1993. "The Life and Times of Randy Shilts." *The Advocate,* June 15, 36.

Young, Graham. 1998. "Gay Heroes of the Armed Forces." *Birmingham* (UK) *Evening Mail,* September 29, 27.

Young, Sheryl. 2005. "Watch Your Words—They May Be 'Hate Speech.'" *Tampa* (FL) *Tribune,* November 21, 17.

Young, Thomas J. 1991. "Regional Differences in Sodomy Laws." *Psychological Reports* 68 (February): 228–30.

Zellman, Gail L. 1996. "Implementing Policy Changes in Large Organizations: The Case of Gays and Lesbians in the Military." In *Out in Force: Sexual Orientation and the Military,* ed. Gregory M. Herek, Jared B. Jobe, and Ralph M. Carney, 266–89. Chicago: University of Chicago Press.

Zimmerman, Janet. 2003. "The Changing Face of Families: Adoptions Increasing by Same-Sex Couples: Gay Partners Finding Less Resistance, More Acceptance." *Press Enterprise Riverside* (CA), August 11, A1.

Index